WATCHING WILDLIFE

EAST AFRICA

David Andrew
Susan Rhind

Lonely Planet Publications
Melbourne Oakland London Paris

INDIAN OCEAN

200 km
100 mi
100
50
1:8,000,000
0

MOMBASA

Kilifi
Kwale
Shimoni
Wete
Chake Chake
Pemba Island
Tanga
Lunga Lunga
Shimba Hills NR
Mkomazi Game Reserve
Lushoto
Mombo
Korogwe
Muheza
Same
Handeni
Makata
Saadani GR
Zanzibar
Zanzibar (Unguja) Island
Bagamoyo
Ngerengere
DAR ES SALAAM

Mafia Island
Kilindoni

Mkomazi NP
Lake Manyara
Makuyuni
Mbulu
Babati
Tarangire National Park
Lake Eyasi
Bereko
Kondoa
Mwometo
Msata
Morogoro
Mvometo

Masai Steppe

Kibiti
Mohoro

Kilwa Kivinje
Kilwa Masoko
Nangurukura
Lindi
Mingoyo
Mtwara
Mikindani
Namiranga
Quionga
Palma
Mocimboa da Praia
Mucojo

Mtwara Plateau
Masasi
Newala
Mueda
Ruvuma River

MOZAMBIQUE

Makindi
Dodoma
Kongwa
Mpwapwa
Kilosa
Chipogolo
Mikumi
Kidatu
Ifakara
Lupiro
Mahenge
Ilonga

Mikumi National Park
Selous Game Reserve
Rufiji River
Kilombero River

Meia Meia
Kisigo Game Reserve
Martyoni
Singida
Sekenke
L. Kitangiri

Shinyanga
Nzega
Kahama
Bukombe
Kigosi GR
Moyowosi GR
Kigosi River
Moyowosi River
Igombo River

TANZANIA
Tabora
Sikonge
Kitunda
Ugalla River
Ugalla River Game Reserve
Ligoila River
Rungwa Game Reserve
Rungwa
Kipembawe
Kitunda
Uwanda Game Reserve
Lake Rukwa
Rungwa River

Mwyombe
Iringa
Taveta
Njombe
Makambako
Malinyi
Udzungwa Mountains NP
Mafinga

Songea
Mbinga
Mbamba Bay
Lujachi
Likoma Island
Mchimbe

Lake Malawi
Nkhata Bay
Nyika NP
Vwaza GR
Nkhotakota
MALAWI
Kasungu NP
Nkhunga GR
Lundazi

Lake Malawi

Mbeya
Tunduma
Tunduru

Mpanda
Namanyere
Sumbawanga
Sumbawanga
Lake Tanganyika

Katavi National Park
Mahale Mountains NP
Uvinza
Kigoma
Ujiji
Kalemie
Niemba
Kapona
Mcba

BURUNDI
BUJUMBURA
Rumonge
Fizi
Lulimba
Cibofi
Wakamba
Nyanza-Lac
Kasulu
Kibondo

DEMOCRATIC REPUBLIC OF CONGO (ZAÏRE)
Pweto
Chiengi
Lake Mweru
Mweru Wantipa NP
Kawambwa
Kasenga
Lake Bangweulu

Mbala
Sumbu NP
Sumbu
Mporokoso
Kasama
Isangano NP

ZAMBIA
North Luangwa NP
Mpika
South Luangwa NP
Luambe NP
Lukusuzi NP
Lavushi NP
Kasanka NP

Mbeya
Lunenga Plain NP

ELEVATION
3000m
2000m
1000m
500m
250m
0

Watching Wildlife East Africa
1st edition – May 2001

Published by
Lonely Planet Publications Pty Ltd ABN 36 005 607 983
90 Maribyrnong St, Footscray, Victoria 3011, Australia

Lonely Planet Offices
Australia Locked Bag 1, Footscray, Victoria 3011
USA 150 Linden St, Oakland, CA 94607
UK 10a Spring Place, London NW5 3BH
France 1 rue du Dahomey, 75011 Paris

Photographs
Many of the images in this guide are available for licensing from
Lonely Planet Images.
lpi@lonelyplanet.com.au

Front cover photograph
Cheetahs (Alex Dissanayake)

Back cover photographs (from left to right)
Yellow-billed hornbill (Dennis Jones)
Impala (Dennis Jones)
Chameleon (David Andrew)

ISBN 1 86450 033 6

Printed by The Bookmaker International Ltd
Printed in China

CONTENTS

6 Contents

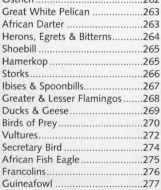

AUTHORS

David Andrew

After his father was mauled by a gorilla at Howletts Zoo, David and his family fled the wilds of England to live somewhere safer – Australia! There David revolutionised the face of birdwatching by creating *Wingspan* and *Australian Birding* magazines; edited *Wildlife Australia* magazine; and among other jobs has been a research assistant in Kakadu NP, a birding guide for English comedian Bill Oddie and an editor of Lonely Planet guides. He is coordinating author for *Watching Wildlife East Africa* and contributed to *Watching Wildlife Australia*. David is amassing a bird list to bequeath to the nation.

Susan Rhind

Susan was raised on a farm in Western Australia and has always been besotted by animals. After working as a nurse and science teacher she became a wildlife biologist, and after completing a PhD went to work in Africa for a rest. Susan spent nearly two years in Africa – until work for Lonely Planet interrupted the good time she was having in Namibia – traversing seven countries and exploring about 45 national parks. She has scientifically studied dolphins, monkeys and Australian marsupials, and is now back in Western Australia publishing her research. Susan's next ambition is to find a job within cycling distance of home.

FROM THE AUTHORS

David Andrew

Grateful thanks to all who helped with logistics, sound advice and local knowledge, but in particular to Steve Turner (EAOS), Anthony Hyde, Kirsty Sutherland, Claire Anampio and Patrick Shah (A&K), Gail Paul (UTC), Jane and Paul Goldring (G&C Tours), Pamela and Jonathan Wright (Semliki Safaris), Andrew Mukooza (Volcanoes), Chris Chan-Piu (Sheraton Hotels), Mary Lewis (JGI), and Nigel Arensen and Shane Kennedy (Bike Treks). All the drivers and guides who assisted my relentless quest to find creatures from gorilla to zorilla, and aardvark to flappet lark, but particularly Willis Oketch and Edwin Selempo (EAOS), Alfred Twinomujuni (Bwindi) and Simon (Lake Baringo Country Club). The many researchers who let me stick my nose into their business: Dedee Woodside, Julia Lloyd, Malcolm Wilson, Jason Gilchrist, Jonathan Rossouw, Mike Clifton, Stuart Williams, Michel Masozera and Richard Wrangham. The staff of Game-trackers, Mara Intrepids, Little Governor's Camp, Siana Springs, Mara Safari Club, Lake Baringo Country Club and the Terminal Hotel. Bernadette Hince and Nick Drayson for good food and company, and for finding me a root-rat; Matt Fletcher and Clare Irvine for a great trip to Meru NP; and Bianka Martens and Knut Kaepler for hospitality at Elsa's Kopje. Thanks also to everyone at LP's Outdoor Activities Unit for ideas and encouragement. And special thanks to Robyn Coventry for snapping away with our cameras and for putting up with a man obsessed.

Susan Rhind

Thanks in Tanzania to: Nahid Patwa (Coastal Travels), Ian Williamson (Silver Sands), Buck Tilley (Thomson Safaris); Liz and Neil Baker, David Moyer (WCS), Rod East; Abercrombie & Kent, Rolf Baldus (GTZ), Chumbe Island Coral Park, Dive Africa (Zanzibar), Gibb's Farm, Guy Norton (ABRU Mikumi), Flycatcher Safaris (Rubondo), Anthony Collins (Gombe), Saleh Mohamed (Marlin Tours, Zanzibar), Mikumi Wildlife Camp, Mbuyu Camp, Mountain Village Lodge, Migration Camp, Momela Lodge (Lion Safaris), Chris Fox (Mwagusi Safari Camp), Paul Oliver (Oliver's Camp), Ras Kutani, Roland Purcell (Mahale/Katavi), Rufiji River Camp, Selous Safari Camp, Tarangire Safari Lodge, Tent with a View, Serengeti Balloon Safaris, Serena Lodge and Seronera Lodge. In Kenya: John Watkin (Nairobi), Gametrackers, Melinda Rees (eco-resorts.com), Graeme Backhurst (Tsavo and other parks), Tansy Bliss (Arabuko–Sokoke) and Lallie Didham (Malindi).

THIS BOOK

DAVID Andrew researched and wrote the introductory chapters (Nature in East Africa, Wildlife-Watching and Habitats), the Wildlife Gallery plus the Uganda, Rwanda, DRC and Kenya (co-writer) sections for the Parks and Places chapter. Susan Rhind researched and wrote the Tanzania section and co-wrote the Kenya section for the Parks and Places chapter.

The Photography section was written by Luke Hunter; Luke and Andrew van Smeerdijk contributed to several sections; and Dudley Iles advised on the Zanzibar & Pemba section.

FROM THE PUBLISHER

THE idea for this series came from David Andrew and was supported by Chris Klep, Nick Tapp and Sue Galley. The concept was developed further by Sean Pywell and Jane Bennett; Sean became the first series editor and Mathew Burfoot designed the layout for the series.

Maps for *Watching Wildlife East Africa* were drawn by Simon Tillema and Chris Klep. Editing and proofing were done by Miranda Wills, Sean Pywell, David Andrew and Andrew van Smeerdijk. Layout was by Mathew Burfoot, Vicki Beale and Wendy Wright. Most of the photos were sourced and supplied by LPI – and special thanks to Annie Horner, Phil Weymouth, Brett Pascoe and all at LPI who put in much extra effort for this title. Indra Kilfoyle and Andrew Weatherill designed the cover. Mapping was checked by Teresa Donnellan; layout was checked by Teresa, Lindsay Brown, Glenn van der Knijff, Jane Hart and Michael Blore. The index was created by Janet Brunckhorst and Glenn van der Knijff. Thanks also to Fiona Kinniburgh, Darren Elder and Sean Pywell for ideas and advice.

PREFACE

WHEN I started my studies of chimpanzees more than 40 years ago in what is now Gombe Stream National Park (Tanzania), travel in many parts of Africa was truly an adventure: roads and infrastructure were almost nonexistent in many places, and to journey overland or by aeroplane during the wet season was to sometimes put oneself at the mercy of the elements. Travel literature then often consisted of lengthy tomes compiled by explorers and adventurers after years on the 'road'; popular (and portable) travel guides were simply not available for destinations far from western Europe or North America. Likewise, the appreciation of wildlife as a pastime – that is, watching and enjoying live animals for their own sake and in their own environment – was a privilege afforded to few.

All that has changed, of course, in this era of instant communications and fast transport: previously inaccessible and virtually unknown creatures and places appear almost daily in the mass media; travel guidebooks are now available to nearly every place on earth; and a massive growth in ecotourism has encouraged the proliferation of wildlife identification guides.

Watching Wildlife East Africa is a new type of guide. Not only does it help the reader to identify what they're seeing – with beautiful photos and graphics – it tells them where to look for it in East Africa's many superb wildlife reserves. But this handy guide goes even further: in language that anyone can understand, it explains what wildlife is doing – what it is eating, how it interacts with others of its own kind and other species, and how it copes with environmental factors such as climate and terrain. This is the first title in the Watching Wildlife series to deal with Africa's great wildlife spectacles, and ranges from the traditional safari circuits of Kenya, Uganda and Tanzania to the once inaccessible rainforest strongholds of the great apes.

For the first time in history virtually all of the world's natural wonders are accessible to those with a yen to seek them out. Yet watching wildlife is still a great privilege, albeit one that involves patience and dedication (like many great human endeavours). By using this guide you will certainly get more out of your safari, gorilla or chimp tracking and birdwatching. Lest we become too complacent, consider you belong to one of the last generations who will be able to enjoy wildlife in its pristine state.

Jane Goodall PhD CBE
Dr Jane Goodall's study of wild chimpanzees in Gombe Forest (now Gombe Stream NP) began in 1960 and continues today. In 1977 she founded the Jane Goodall Institute (www.jane goodall.org), which aims to empower individuals to take informed and compassionate action to improve the environment for all living things. Her passion has taken her to almost every corner of the globe as an advocate for conservation – for human and nonhuman primates, and for all living things. The Institute's philosophy is 'Every individual makes a difference.'

INTRODUCTION

FROM the coral reefs off Kenya and Tanzania to the summits of Africa's highest mountains, nowhere else on earth within a similar geographical area is so great an assemblage of large animals supported by such a range of environmental and climatic variation – elements which continue to shape animal distribution and behaviour today.

But too often watching wildlife in East Africa involves being shuttled from one herd or pride to the next, a two-dimensional experience not unlike watching a TV documentary. A more expansive experience can be had by understanding the elements of an ecosystem and their inextricable linkage. For example, the abundance of tiny insects at the bottom of a food chain can affect the behaviour of predators at the top; and entire habitats can appear or disappear according to the behaviour of animals – and people.

The stimulation of the sheer variety and endless activity of forest and savanna should be justification in itself to find out why, how and when it all started, and what makes the cogs turn. And if the emotions stirred by the experience prompt you to take further action for the conservation of what you have seen, then a greater understanding will make that action more effective.

Few visitors come away unmoved from tracking mountain gorillas or our closest living relatives, chimpanzees; for many the experience challenges preconceptions about human nature and evolution. Yet habitat favoured by early humans – mosaics of riverine forest, savanna and lake shore – remain today much as they did a million years ago. Extensive fossil beds in Kenya and Tanzania show that large numbers of existing animal species shared the savannas of East Africa when our ancestors first began to walk upright. If not for the evolutionary pressures that caused their extinction, those early hominids could still be living and reproducing alongside modern lions, antelopes, giraffes… and human beings.

So in a sense the East African wildlife-watching experience is also a direct and profound link with the origins of every human being on the planet. As Karen Blixen wrote in her famous book, *Out of Africa*: 'In Africa…you woke up in the morning and thought: Here I am, where I ought to be.'

HOW TO USE THIS BOOK

YOU'RE here to see the animals and we'll help you: Watching Wildlife East Africa shows you how to recognise the major players and advises you where to find them. But this book is also packed with background information on wildlife habitats, advice on getting started, when to go and how to prepare. There are also watching tips (eg, which trail or lake to go to), and clues on the best time to look. Read on to help plan your wildlife-watching adventure and to get the best out of this treasure-trove.

Nature

Wildlife-Watching

Habitats

Parks and Places

Wildlife Gallery

Each chapter is colour coded to help you navigate through the book – look for the thumb tabs.

Getting Started There are two main ways to go about watching wildlife: pick your animals and then find out where to go; or choose where you want to go and then find out what's there. In East Africa you'll see a lot of the same wildlife in a lot of places (eg, giraffes and zebras); but for other animals you'll need to go to certain places (eg, flamingos are best sought at Rift Valley lakes). The key chapters cover both approaches: Parks and Places describes where to go and what's there; and the Wildlife Gallery tells you about the animals. Flipping between these chapters will tell you almost everything you need to know.

Index The quickest way to find out about an animal or reserve is to look it up in the Index. Animals are arranged into groups according to their common names (Grevy's zebra comes under zebras) – page numbers in bold indicate a photo of that animal. Reserves are listed alphabetically by name.

Table of Contents This gives you a quick overview of the book. We've colour-coded each chapter to help you find your way around until you're more familiar with the layout.

Wildlife Gallery A run down on all the key species and groups: what they look like (and how to tell them apart) and the kinds of things you can see them doing. This chapter is divided into three sections: Mammals, Birds, and Other Creatures Great and Small (eg, reptiles).

Key animals are presented as feature pages which describe unusual and interesting aspects of their ecology. A sidebar next to the main text summarises some of their main characteristics (eg, behaviour, breeding and preferred habitat); Swahili names are included for most species; and a Hotspots box lists some places where they might be

Group page   *Animal's range*   *Highlight page*

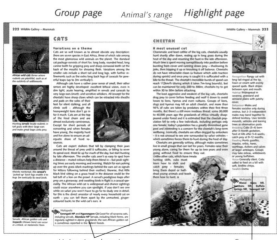

Hotspots: where to find animals

Summary information

found (use this as a link to the Parks and Places chapter). A small map indicates each species' range.

Other animals appear in family (or closely related) groups – these pages are packed with photos to help you work out what's what.

Parks and Places Organised country by country and starting with an introduction to the overall region, this chapter describes the best national parks, reserves and other places in which to see wildlife. Each country section begins with an overview (including itineraries) and includes an urban section if wildlife can be seen there, eg, in Nairobi. Specific destinations, eg, national parks and other reserves, are ordered alphabetically according to their importance for wildlife-watching. Thus, major attractions, such as Serengeti NP, are given detailed treatment and less-frequented reserves may be covered in only one page. Wildlife highlights, watching tips and facts for travellers are summarised for each; and a colour map points out major features and good wildlife-viewing areas.

Wildlife-Watching Essential background reading. This chapter tells you when to go and what time of day to look, and explains the ins and outs of safaris, guides, equipment and field guides. Special features cover game drives, gorilla and chimp tracking, birdwatching and some safari alternatives, such as walking.

Nature in East Africa We explain the reasons behind East Africa's great biodiversity and introduce some of the conservation issues.

Habitats Explains East African ecosystems in simple terms.

Resource Guide This lists recommended field guides and other books, reliable tour operators and wildlife-related websites.

Glossary Explains any confusing words in the text.

Wildlife highlights   **Parks and Places**   *Park map*

General park information   *Watching tips*

Wildlife-Watching

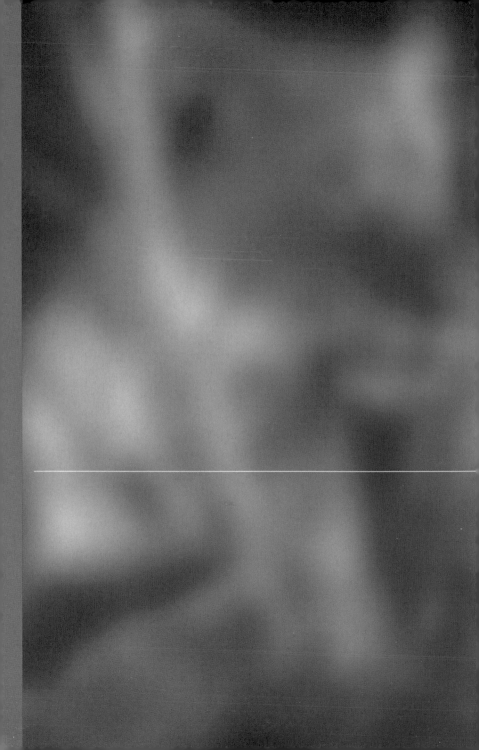

NATURE IN EAST AFRICA

*An introduction to East Africa's
natural history*

THE EAST AFRICAN ENVIRONMENT

Complex habitats supporting astonishing diversity

East Africa's incredible biodiversity reflects many ages of change in an ancient continent, and a climate which fosters a complex variety of habitats (although no major habitat is restricted to the region) – a vast mosaic of savanna, grasslands, forests and woodlands. From north to south, the modern landscape climbs from the semiarid scrubland of northern Kenya to high savanna-covered plateaus rolling south across Tanzania. On the east coast, mangroves fringe a narrow coastal plain from where savanna stretches west around Lake Victoria. Inland, where the East African region abuts the Zaïre River basin, high rainfall and rich volcanic soils encourage the growth of extensive rain-forests. Lake Victoria, Africa's largest, is flanked by two great rift valleys that formed where bulging areas of geological uplift fractured. The Eastern Rift Valley runs north-south and forms a chain of shallow lakes, some with hot springs and geysers; the course of the Albertine Rift Valley is marked by Lakes Albert, Edward, Kivu and Tanganyika, which separate the great savannas from the Zaïre basin. Large rivers include the Tana, Galana and Ewaso Nyiro in Kenya; Ruvuma and Rufiji in Tanzania; Kagera in Rwanda; and the Nile in Uganda. The great lakes support many unique species; and other habitats that further contribute to East Africa's biodiversity are high forested mountains (including massive extinct volcanoes such as Mt Kilimanjaro; and the Rwenzoris, Africa's highest chain), coral reefs in the Indian Ocean and islands such as Zanzibar.

A dynamic landscape

Africa was once joined to other parts of the southern hemisphere, including South America and Australia, as part of the supercontinent Gondwana, which broke up between 270 and 200 million years ago. For another 30 million years Africa and Eurasia were periodically linked by land bridges, which enabled the spread of mammals between the two continents. Extensive volcanic activity in East Africa 12 million years ago uplifted the land by some 1300m, and formed the great mountain peaks; at the same time, much of the present Congo rainforest was submerged under a vast lake which eventually drained into the Zaïre River 10 to 11 million years ago. The last million years have been marked by violent tectonic activity and further development of the rift valleys.

Climatic changes caused by ice ages in the northern hemisphere caused the expansion and contraction of habitats in Africa. The icy peaks of Mt Kenya, Mt Kilimanjaro and the Rwenzoris are remnants of once extensive glaciations, which during the ice ages would have linked these great mountains. During glacial periods the climate at lower altitudes was drier than at present, enabling savannas to expand and restricting forests to isolated pockets. Between ice ages wetter conditions prevailed and forests spread while drier habitats retreated. Some evidence for this is provided by the fact that those animals reaching their greatest diversity in West African forests, such as duikers, are also found in isolated patches as far east as Zanzibar. The repeated isolation of areas of habitat is another reason for East Africa's high biodiversity, with isolated populations of a single species evolving along separate paths. For example, expanding forests cut off populations of savanna-dwelling ground hornbills that eventually became two separate species that today live within 50km of each other but don't interbreed.

Rain – the vital ingredient

The most important immediate influences on the distribution of East Africa's vegetation and wildlife are rainfall and elevation. These elements vary greatly and it is largely this range of conditions that is responsible for the diversity of today's habitats. Between April and October the south-east trade winds blow in from the Indian Ocean, and a north-east monsoon blows from November to March. Climatic cycles are characterised by wet and dry seasons: most of Kenya experiences two wet seasons annually, from late March to mid-June, and late October to mid-December. Northern Kenya and Uganda have one long wet season from April to October, while most of Tanzania experiences rain from December until May. Where rainfall exceeds 1200mm, such as in western Uganda and the Democratic Republic of the Congo (DRC – formerly Zaïre), seasons tend to merge and forest vegetation dominates. Cold 'wintry' weather is experienced only at high altitudes, and mountain ranges create 'islands' of low temperature with endemic plants and animals.

The amount of rain that falls varies greatly from year to year, and has a direct influence on vegetation growth, and the breeding, dispersal and migration of animals (especially those that must drink regularly). Changes to animal populations are most obvious in areas of great seasonal contrasts; where water is only seasonally available; and where fire destroys cover or preferred food. Mammals with low moisture requirements, such as gazelles, can remain on open plains during dry seasons, but in general the habits of most animals change with the seasons: great movements can occur in response to rainfall and the availability of green growth, eg, the wildebeest migration; wet seasons prompt courtship and breeding in forest birds; and food preferences change according to availability, eg, young lions in Tanzania may switch to eating people during wet seasons when grazing herds disperse. Daily temperature fluctuations also greatly influence activity: many species are most active at night and seek shelter to avoid high daytime temperatures.

The East African environment is far from stable. It is constantly reshaped by complex elements. For example, fire has long swept through coarse grasslands during the dry season, promoting new growth. In the absence of fire and grazing animals, woody growth dominates until elephants open it up and it reverts to grasslands. Now, however, it is humans that are the main shaper of the landscape: elephants are often forced into unnaturally high densities by diminishing habitats, where they destroy woodlands at unsustainable rates.

WILDLIFE

Still-evolving centre of mammal diversity

Large mammals are more abundant and diverse in East Africa than in virtually any other region on earth, yet fossil beds show that diversity was even higher as recently as one million years ago. The fossil record also shows Africa to be the centre of evolution for groups such as apes and monkeys, elephants, hyraxes, bats and the aardvark, which closely resembles *Phenacodus* – a 60 million-year-old fossil proto-ungulate from which rhinoceroses and hippos also evolved. Evolutionary forces are still at work: the kongoni has appeared only in the last million years and already several races are distinguishable by the shape of their horns; in time each variety may become genetically isolated and develop into a distinct species. Of great biological interest are the families whose nearest living relatives are found only in South-East Asia, such as pangolins and the water chevrotain – their presence shows how closely connected these ancient continents once were.

Whatever their origins, the mammals of East Africa have reached an extraordinary diversity, particularly in the savannas and at the eastern edge of the rainforests of the Zaïre River basin. The total number of species depends on which classification system is accepted; and varies because some species become locally extinct, others are discovered or rediscovered, and still others are reclassified in light of new research (sometimes a single species is split into different species; sometimes previously recognised separate species are deemed to be one and the same, and so lumped together). To a tally of about 30 primates (ie, monkeys, apes etc) can be added 41 carnivores (mongooses, otters and mustelids – weasels and their kin – as well as cats and dogs) and 59 more peaceable large mammals such as antelopes, elephants and rhinos; other groups include hyraxes, elephant shrews, pangolins and hares, and hundreds of species of rodent, shrew and bat. Uniquely African groups, such as otter shrews, elephant shrews and the aardvark, are all found in East Africa.

It is not really useful to talk of animal distribution in terms of political boundaries since, in East Africa at least, these are bio-

A snapshot in geological time

The Usambara Mountains region in north-east Tanzania provide a snapshot of the cooler, wetter conditions that prevailed millions of years ago when dense forests originating in the Zaïre River basin stretched east across the continent. When climatic change forced the surrounding plains to revert to savanna, forest species were 'stranded' in the Usambaras and some evolved into new species (evolution can often happen rapidly, relatively speaking, in small populations). The Usumbaras' forests are too small to support large mammals (although Abbott's and Aders' duikers are found only here and in a few other restricted localities), but are particularly rich in endemic invertebrates and their predators. Insectivorous mammals are represented by 10 species of shrew and four of elephant shrew, and there are more species of robin and thrush – birds that feed on small animals in leaf litter – than in any other part of Africa. Frogs and lizards also show a high degree of endemicity in the Usambaras, and the area's diversity has reached millions of households through one of its best known relicts – the African violet.

logically arbitrary. Some mammal groups have reached a high diversity (eg, 46 species of antelope), but many species are wide-ranging and few are unique to East Africa. Endemic mammals tend to be biologically and physically isolated in 'islands' of habitat, eg, a species of root-rat found only on Mt Kenya. Others, such as the hirola (Hunter's hartebeest) have become isolated by habitat destruction and other human influences. Conversely, several species are more abundant in East Africa than in any other part of the world, eg wildebeests.

Showcase of birds

East Africa's hugely varied and abundant birdlife has inspired many a passive observer to take up birdwatching. Approximately 15% of the world's bird species have been recorded in the region; well over 1000 have been recorded in Kenya, Uganda and Tanzania; and BirdLife International has identified in the region several Endemic Bird Areas as priorities for the conservation of bird biodiversity. Several bird families are unique to Africa, including turacos, mousebirds and four monospecific families (ie, containing only one species): the ostrich, secretary bird, hamerkop and shoebill. Representatives of all these families are found in East Africa; some such as the hamerkop, mousebirds and even the showy turacos are common, while others such as the shoebill live only in specialised habitats.

While the distribution of no bird family is restricted to East Africa, several groups are particularly well represented, such as the birds of prey (80 species), larks (24), cisticolas (31), sunbirds (53), weavers (74) and starlings (32). Other conspicuous groups include long-legged wading birds, pigeons and doves, hornbills and swallows. Some families are not so diverse but include common and conspicuous species, such as crows and bulbuls.

Although many species are wide ranging, exact distribution closely follows the preferred habitat of each group or species, eg, the distribution of herons or ducks is wide but generally associated with water, whereas the scarlet-tufted malachite sunbird is restricted to high altitudes on mountain ranges throughout the region. Most abundant and diverse are the hundreds of resident breeding birds, some of which undergo spectacular plumage changes during the courtship season. But East Africa is also both a staging post and an overwintering site for migrating shorebirds, waterfowl, swallows and warblers en route to and from their breeding grounds in Eurasia. Arriving from as far away as the Arctic tundra, they sit out the colder months in Africa before leaving in March and April. Many resident species undertake regular local migrations: a number of species (eg, Abdim's stork) migrate north-south without leaving Africa; and montane birds escape to lower altitudes during wet seasons.

Below the tip of the ecological iceberg

Of course mammals and birds are just 'peak' groups in a complex web of codependent plants and animals numbering thousands of species. Other groups that reach particular abundance or diversity are butterflies, unique alpine vegetation and the incredibly varied life forms of coral reefs. Lake Tanganyika, the second deepest in the world, supports 300 fish species, 90% of which are endemic, and molluscs similar to those known from marine fossils dating back to the Jurassic era. East Africa's reptiles and amphibians reach their peak of diversity in coastal woodlands and 'islands' of endemicity such as the Usambaras in Tanzania.

HUMANS AND WILDLIFE

In the beginning

Evidence from extensive fossil beds in Tanzania, Kenya, Uganda and other parts of Africa now leave little doubt that Africa, if not East Africa, is where ancestral apes evolved into hominids and hence modern human beings. From its early beginnings as just one of many predators in the savanna, obliged to fortify itself against a hostile environment, the adaptable, increasingly populous and aggressively inventive human species now dominates the planet.

The early traces are scanty, but from assemblages of bones at famous digs such as Olduvai Gorge and Sibiloi a picture is gradually building up to show that humans evolved in Africa an estimated three million years ago among rich plant and animal communities. Carl Linnaeus, the father of modern taxonomy, correctly classified human beings as apes, although it can only have been the genteel behaviour he observed in the bourgeois drawing rooms of 17th-century Europe that led him to name his fellow species *Homo sapiens* – 'wise man'. Yet the environmental pressures affecting the evolution of every other species also applied to the rise of *Homo sapiens*, and its continued survival depended on the same factors – the availability of water and food, the ability to avoid predation, and the survival of disease.

The nearest living apes to humans are the two species of chimpanzees and recent research has provided biological, behavioural and ecological evidence of early humans' metaphorical walk out of the forest. But things didn't get off to a good start, and for many highly specialised large mammal species, contact with early human hunters proved to be fatal at a time when climate change was causing their habitats to contract.

The great wildebeest migration

There are probably more wildebeests in Kenya and Tanzania now than ever before. European explorers found the Maasai tribes tending their cattle in apparent harmony with grazing plains mammals, which they did not as a rule hunt for food. But in 1891 an outbreak of rinderpest decimated the Maasai's herds and wiped out nearly 90% of the region's buffaloes and wildebeests. Famine struck and the tribes abandoned the area for several decades. The resulting proliferation of woodlands in the absence of wild and domestic grazing animals made ideal habitat for tsetse flies, which carry trypanosomiasis (sleeping sickness), and the area was shunned by people and their livestock. The wildebeest population recovered for several decades, but until 1920 numbered only 120,000 to 130,000. However, after WWII fires set by hunters and honey gatherers destroyed much of the woodland, once again opening the region up to grazing animals, and during the 1960s and 70s the wildebeest population exploded from about 250,000 to 1.3 million. The famous 'migration' between the Serengeti and Mara on its current scale is only a recent phenomenon. Before 1960, most of the Mara wildebeests came from a separate population in the Loita Plains and reached the Mara from the Serengeti only in very dry years. With the massive population increase, the Mara is now a dry season refuge for some 500,000 wildebeests which give birth during the wettest part of the year in the Serengeti, moving north into the Mara as their food supply diminishes.

Three species of African elephant alone are known to have died out during the rise of *Homo sapiens*, and other species known to have become extinct include giant species of pig and buffalo, and several giraffes, hippos, horses and hyenas.

Pastoralism and life in the forests

Apart from hunting, the first great change wrought on the landscape was fire, which until about 350,000 years ago was lit either accidentally or deliberately, to smoke out beehives and aid progress through grasslands. Within the last 5000 to 6000 years pastoralists dependent on livestock, and cultivators dependent on crops, have further modified vegetation over large areas.

East Africa's pastoral peoples have always lived alongside wildlife, and their cultures and traditions reflect the plants and animals with which they came in daily contact. Some tribes, such as the Maasai of southern Kenya and northern Tanzania, are famously indifferent to wildlife, respect turning to malice only when crops, livestock or human life are at stake. The Maasai consider the hunting of wild animals for food beneath them and would rather starve than eat birds or reptiles; thus large numbers of large mammals remain in former or current pastoral areas. The Waliangulu on the other hand were master bushmen of the arid plains and active hunters of elephants, hunting them with poisoned arrows fired from great bows.

Few people today in the region live as their ancestors did, and of the few who still do, the best known are probably the tribes of Central Africa, DRC and western Uganda. Collectively known as pygmies, many still rely on the forests for their livelihood. Pygmies, who are mainly hunter-gatherers, have ancient associations with other forest dwellers who practice shifting cultivation. Forests were and continue to be a great source of traditional materials for building, food such as honey and bush medicine, as well as meat for protein.

Exploitation and population explosion

The 20th century saw a complete reversal in the roles of people and nature in East Africa, occasional deaths from lions and other animals notwithstanding. Within the last 100 years and especially within the last 50, environmental change has accelerated: owing to livestock and overgrazing, the clearance of natural systems for agriculture and an exploding human population. The arrival of Europeans and the advent of firearms ushered in the most enduring mass slaughter of wildlife – or 'game'. Their legacy is the modern tourists' pursuit of the 'big five' – lion, leopard, rhino, elephant and buffalo, so-called because they were reputedly the most dangerous to hunt. These safaris spawned numerous legends about both the game and its adversaries, among them famous miscreants such as Theodore Roosevelt and Ernest Hemingway. But 100 years ago large animals were abundant and people few; nobody saw where it was all leading and the hunting safaris took an immense toll of four-legged animals.

Fortunately, many hunters eventually reformed to become active conservationists and many great conservation initiatives have been driven by individuals – native African and European. Some are almost household names worldwide, and an incomplete list includes Bernhard Grzimek, Dian Fossey, Jane Goodall, Daphne Sheldrick, Iain Douglas-Hamilton and Richard Leakey.

If most of the hazards to human life in East Africa have been conquered, then one natural adversary still holds the trump card – disease. Malaria and trypanosomiasis (sleeping sickness) have affected the spread of people in East Africa: sleeping sickness afflicts people and livestock, and limited the spread of both until the 20th century; and malaria continues to pose a threat, albeit mitigated by preventative medicine. But Africa is an evolutionary hothouse, and in the great forests of the Zaïre River basin microorganisms continue to evolve alongside larger plants and animals. Another killer, AIDS, is now rampant.

CONSERVATION

Changing issues and priorities

At the millennium the traditional role of conservation bodies, such as reserve management, protection of wildlife and fulfilling the obligations of international conservation treaties, must be achieved in a climate of unprecedented population growth and the manifold demands it creates. Wildlife management must involve politically and socially acceptable solutions that are ecologically sustainable and economically viable, against a backdrop of regional poverty, endemic corruption, powerful market forces and, in some countries, political instability. A high percentage of wildlife lives outside the reserve system (an estimated 70% in Kenya alone) and conservation priorities are increasingly dictated by the people who come into daily conflict with large animals – which may involve problems as immediate as crop damage from migrating elephants, and the deaths of people and livestock.

Problems old and new

The main conservation issues are poaching, deforestation and encroaching human settlement. These are exacerbated by overpopulation and its corollaries, demands for land and food; and by environmental factors such as drought, overgrazing and erosion.

The battle against well-armed gangs poaching ivory and rhino horns was ultimately won through a combination of adverse international publicity, political pressure and a violent struggle. Elephants are again on the increase, but far less publicised and now more pressing is the slaughter of forest animals for bushmeat, and the side effects caused by accidental snaring. Demand for bushmeat has escalated with a rapidly rising population, and refugee camps are putting massive pressure on national parks in the DRC.

An expanding, impoverished population leads to the illegal settlement of reserves and consequent deforestation, poaching and grazing pressures. Livestock causes widespread erosion by destroying root systems and contributes to desertification. Ironically, fires lit to encourage fresh shoots for livestock also attract antelope; and woody plants are smothering grazing grounds where elephants and rhinos, which once kept the areas open, have been eliminated.

'Eponymous, my dear Forbes-Watson ...'

Dozens of birds and mammals bear common and scientific names that are often the sole commemoration of the quest to catalogue East Africa's rich natural history by long-dead explorers, naturalists and zoologists. Some are such a part of safari vocabulary (eg Thomson, Grant and Grevy) they hardly stand out; and like some that have remained internationally famous (such as Speke and Livingstone), many of these men traipsed the length and breadth of Africa in search of new and unusual wildlife. Others were rich enthusiasts who paid for new additions to their collections (eg the Lords Rothschild and Derby). And among them were some remarkable and colourful personalities, such as Colonel Meinertzhagen (after whom the giant forest hog *Hylochoerus meinertzhageni* was named), a British bird enthusiast and crack soldier who posed as a birdwatcher while operating behind Turkish lines during WWI. The diversity enabled some to have more than one species named after them (or their spouses – the wife of an eminent ornithologist is commemorated by Mrs Moreau's sunbird). However, one name stands out – Klaas, after whom a cuckoo was named; neither adventurer or pioneer, Klaas was a manservant to the great French explorer François Levaillant and the only black African after whom an animal has been named.

Human conflicts can have mixed effects on wildlife. Large animals in several Ugandan reserves were decimated by starving troops during various conflicts; national park staff were killed during recent fighting in the DRC; and poaching and deforestation have begun apace near encampments of Rwandan refugees that now encroach on reserves. However, politically unstable areas (such as north-west Uganda) can create human population vacuums where wildlife enjoys a respite from both poaching and encroachment.

Diseases from domestic animals is another threat. Epidemics of rinderpest during the 20th century nearly wiped out buffaloes and wildebeests, and reservoirs of contagion in domestic herds pose a threat of further outbreaks. Canine distemper originating from domestic dogs has severely affected populations of hunting dogs.

Outside and local helpers

High-profile international bodies active in East African conservation, include UNESCO (United Nations Educational, Scientific and Cultural Organisation); IUCN (International Union for the Conservation of Nature), which publishes a Red Data Book for many endangered groups; and WWF (Worldwide Fund for Nature), which cooperates with other bodies in rainforest conservation projects. Other big players include FFPS (Flora and Fauna Preservation Society), the New York and Frankfurt Zoological Societies, African Wildlife Foundation and Wildlife Conservation International. BirdLife International has nominated numerous areas in East Africa as centres of biodiversity; and education at a local level is provided by Wildlife Clubs in Uganda, Kenya and Tanzania. Earthwatch runs participatory programs for paying customers who help with scientific projects in Kenya and Tanzania.

The International Gorilla Conservation Project (IGCP) was launched by the African Wildlife Foundation and WWF to aid gorillas in DRC, Uganda and Rwanda. High-profile mammals such as gorillas, elephants and rhinos all benefit from intensive study, international aid and funding from tourism. Yet Kenya's black rhinos were nearly wiped out in the space of 20 years: from an estimated 40,000 in 1980, about 450 were left at the millennium. Less 'glamorous' species, such as the hirola, Africa's rarest antelope, receive comparatively little attention; and the imminent extinction of dugongs in East African waters will probably go uncontested.

Governments and nongovernment organisations (NGOs) are now aware that policies shaped without local participation inevitably lead to local opposition. Community conservation projects encourage local involvement, leading to a strong sense of ownership and benefits such as crop protection, and health and education funding. For example, Bwindi Impenetrable NP has a multi-use forest program; income from tourism is shared among local communities; and several international groups cooperate on aspects of gorilla tourism training and management. Such projects have shown sometimes sceptical locals that wildlife can benefit all, not just overseas tourists and government.

The future?

Reserves are now effectively islands awash in cultivation, ranches and humanity, and many priority areas for conservation still lie outside the reserve system. East Africa includes some of the poorest nations in Africa; the population has doubled in the last 20 years and is predicted to multiply another three times in the next 20 years. In times of crisis, such as famine and political instability, conservation can fall off the agenda altogether: Rwanda, one of the most densely populated countries on the continent, recently downsized PN de l'Akagera by 70% to accommodate refugees. A substantial amount of foreign revenue is earned from wildlife tourism in all East African countries (Bwindi Impenetrable NP earns US$1 million per year alone); and a tourist presence in an area helps conserve wildlife there. If the beleaguered reserves disappear wildlife tourism will quickly lose its focus and a much-needed source of hard currency will dry up.

PARKS AND RESERVES

National parks and other reserves

The cornerstone of wildlife conservation in East Africa has historically been national parks (in this book, abbreviated in the

Victoria's last gasps?

Lake Victoria once supported the world's most diverse community of freshwater fishes, with some 500 species – and most were endemic. Today, Nile perch and tilapia introduced as food fish have wiped out half the native species, and even the commercial fisheries are threatened. Fertiliser run off from agriculture and effluent from the 30 million people who live around the lake, both increasing, have raised the level of nutrients entering Lake Victoria. This results in decreased oxygen levels and encourages algal blooms that choke the surface. However, the most pressing problem is the dense, floating mats of water hyacinth, introduced to East Africa as an ornamental plant. The weed is now so thick and spreading so rapidly that it surrounds entire islands and blocks the passage of cargo boats. Without the collective presence of native fishes, which once thrived on decaying plant and animal matter, mosquitoes and snails proliferate among hyacinths rotting in shallow water – spreading malaria and bilharzia. Attempts at controlling hyacinth include hauling it out by hand, spraying with herbicides and the introduction of a weevil that feeds exclusively on the weed. Scientists warned against upsetting Victoria's ecological balance three decades ago; now even its partial restoration will be prohibitively expensive and require the long-term commitment of three nations.

names of parks as NP) and other reserves declared under colonial governments. Management problems notwithstanding, these continue to provide the highest level of official protection to wildlife and ecosystems across the region, and the focus for most wildlife tourism, although many were created with no regard for preserving biodiversity. Tanzania, Kenya and Uganda all have an established infrastructure and a substantial tourist presence, but in Rwanda and the DRC, refugee and military crises threaten the integrity of existing reserves.

On paper at least, national parks protect all wildlife from exploitation such as hunting and fishing, and prohibit cultivation, settlement and all other disturbances. Kenya's marine national parks provide similar protection, but also allow the use of waters for recreation. Other categories of reserve allow limited exploitation in recognition of traditional usage by pastoralists or fishermen, eg, Kenya's national reserves (NR) and national marine reserves (NMR); other recreational pursuits, eg, controlled trophy hunting in Tanzania's game reserves (GR); and the traditional harvesting of food and medicinal plants from forest reserves (FR).

International and local initiatives

The establishment and maintenance of protected areas in each country is handled by a national body, but in practice law enforcement and reserve management are hampered by lack of funding and other chronic problems. Conservation is a low priority in several countries and resources are thinly spread. In recognition of the region's biodiversity, NGOs such as IUCN and WWF have a permanent presence in some countries under the United Nations Environment Program (UNEP). Social and political collapse in Rwanda forced the suspension of all conservation projects in the late 1990s and similar threats affect eastern DRC.

A growing number of privately-owned reserves in Kenya protect wildlife from bureaucratic corruption and poaching; others are set up so local communities have a say in conservation matters and benefit financially from wildlife tourism (see the Other Sites sections in Kenya and Tanzania). Controlled trophy hunting can give a dollar value to wildlife in marginal areas outside the reserve system, but is subject to abuse from poor controls and corruption.

All East African countries are signatories to the World Heritage Convention, although only two have nominated sites: DRC (PNs des Virunga and Kahuzi–Biéga) and Tanzania (Kilimanjaro and Serengeti NPs, Selous GR and Ngorongoro Conservation Area). Reserves nominated under UNESCO's Man and the Biosphere Program are designated for a range of reasons, including research and conservation. Kenya has nominated Amboseli, Mt Kenya, Mt Kulal, and Malindi–Watamu and Kiunga MNRs; Rwanda the PN des Volcans; Tanzania Lake Manyara NP and the Serengeti–Ngorongoro system; and Uganda Queen Elizabeth NP.

Kenya and Uganda have nominated Lakes Nakuru and George, respectively, as wetlands of international significance under the Ramsar Convention, which protects wetlands and wetland wildlife of outstanding conservation significance. ■

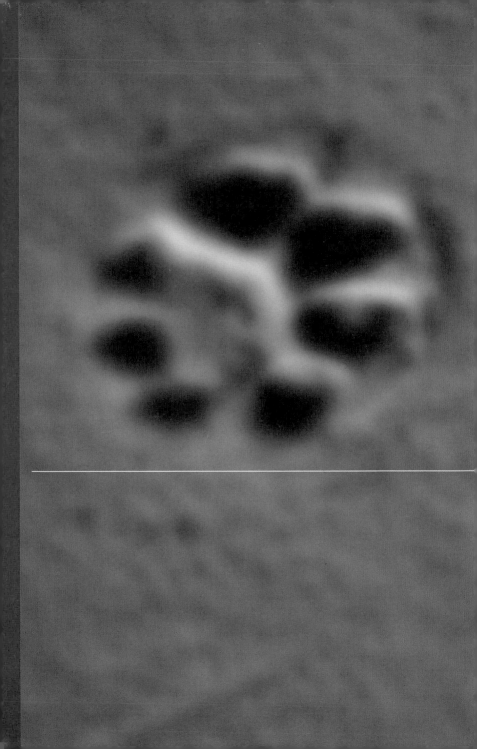

WILDLIFE-WATCHING

*Tips and hints on the art
of watching wildlife*

UP at first light, a quick gulp of coffee and into the vehicle for an early game drive – few experiences compare with sunrise over the savanna. There's no way of knowing what each day will bring, but be assured that each day will bring something. Whether you want to see as much variety as possible or get better acquainted with an old favourite, it is essential that you plan your trip to get the most out of every day and location. The following pages offer tips to help you maximise your wildlife-watching experiences, but it is invaluable to read as much as possible before you go (see the Resource Guide for a list of useful references) and talk to people who've been – watching documentaries and attending public lectures is also a good way of keeping up to date with new discoveries on the wildlife scene.

WHEN TO GO

Possibly the single most important influence on the behaviour of wildlife – and therefore your chances of seeing it – is rain (see the Nature in East Africa chapter for more on rainfall patterns). Rain affects plant growth, the seasonal availability of fruits and drinking water, and the number, distribution, breeding and/or migration of prey animals and their predators. Of course, it also affects the personal comfort of the observer and the condition of roads.

Savannas During the dry seasons (which coincide with the peak tourist seasons) animals can usually be found reasonably close to permanent water – elephants in particular remain nearby – and burnt or trampled grasses make viewing easier. Rain on the savannas brings on spurts of green growth and triggers the breeding or migration of many herbivores and predators, the courting and breeding of birds, and the appearance of wild-flowers. By late in the wet seasons visibility is greatly reduced by high grass, and wildlife has dispersed as water and food is more widely available – but tourists are then fewer in number. Getting around is usually no problem in dry seasons, but can become difficult, and in places impossible, during wet seasons.

Forests Rainforests can be very wet places at any time of year, but don't let the wet put you off – carry a light umbrella so observation can continue during showers. Dry seasons will mean easier but hotter tracking of the forest-dwelling great apes, but they are active year-round (their movement is dictated mainly by the availability of food). Bird courtship – and therefore peak activity – tends to coincide with wet seasons.

Mountains Rain, falling as snow on the high peaks, forces antelopes, elephants and birds to lower altitudes during wet seasons. Cold and wet conditions on the great mountains can pose a physical challenge to visitors at any time of year (although dry seasons are usually fine) and every care should be exercised – see Lonely Planet's *Trekking in East Africa* for more information.

There's no way of knowing what each day will bring, but be assured that each day will bring something.

HOW TO LOOK

Looking at the right time and place

Animals are free to roam and may not be where you want them to be, but the better informed you are, the more likely you are to see what you are after. If you are on a tour, your knowledge will complement that of the guide and will often be in demand by other members of the party.

Time of Day Arguably the most important factor in successful wildlife-watching. Learn what time of day your quarry is most active, how it spends other times and how these might vary according to season and weather conditions – and plan your days to make the most of these factors. An early start may catch nocturnal predators still on the move; birds are most active in the early morning, although raptors ride thermals as the day warms up; and nocturnal animals may be active in overcast conditions. Activity dies off during the heat of the day, especially during the dry season (large mammals shelter under trees or shrubs, and birds rest in shade), picking up again in the late afternoon and peaking near sundown.

Weather Daily, as well as seasonal, temperature and rainfall patterns also make a difference. For example, puff adders are often on the move after rain; lizards like to bask in early sunshine; and monkeys are more active when the day warms up. A storm can bring on a flurry of activity – swifts moving through on the front, termites swarming, and, in the aftermath, predators snapping up wind-blown insects and rodents swept about. And predators generally hunt into the wind – this helps guides predict where they'll be the next day.

Food Sources Food availability can change with season, and knowing your quarry's food preferences can help. Note what's about, eg, trees in flower attract birds, butterflies and bats; termite swarms are snapped up by many animals, from jackals to rollers; and some lions follow the wildebeest migration.

Water For many animals daily access to water is essential and during dry seasons they will stay close to a ready source; naturally the concentration of prey will attract predators. The daily ebbing and flowing of tides affects marine life, and the roosting and feeding of shorebirds on mudflats.

Know Your Habitat Some knowledge of where an animal lives will be of great value in finding it, eg, don't expect gorillas on the savanna (see the Habitats chapter for more details). Learn what to expect in each major habitat and by patiently waiting – sooner or later something will show. For example, a cliff face may harbour klipspringers, a leopard's den or an owl's nest. Once you make the link between species and habitat, your 'search pattern' will change and new things will reveal themselves. The area where one habitat merges into another is usually especially productive, eg, woodland abutting grassland provides food and shelter to both grazers and browsers; and in the sunny woodland edge grow flowering plants that attract birds and butterflies. Check likely shelters, such as tree hollows, cliff overhangs or termite mounds, and dead trees and overhanging branches that are often used as lookouts or perches. Remember, habitats and their species composition also vary with altitude.

Put in the Hours Don't rely on beginner's luck – the longer you spend observing, waiting and watching in the field, the more you will see. As a famous sportsman once said, 'The more I practise the luckier I get'.

Identification

The identification of animals is usually the first step towards finding out more about them. Most people categorise what they see without realising it, eg, a jackal is automatically recognised as a member of the dog family. But the finer points of identifying East Africa's 400 or so mammal and 1000-plus bird species usually requires more than a cursory examination.

The first step, usually made with no conscious effort, separates things by shape, eg, an elephant, a cat, some kind of antelope. Other basic indicators are pattern or colour, eg, leopards and lions have a similar shape, but different coloration; and size – both servals and leopards are spotted, but servals are much smaller. Looking for the basic differences will come naturally after a short time, and with practice the subtle differences attributable to sex, age and geographical variation will also become familiar. Bird identification is a science in itself (and for birdwatchers an abiding passion) with its own techniques and terminology.

For birds or mammals nothing beats practice in the field, backed up by reading (field guides are a good place to start – see the Resource Guide for recommended titles), taking field notes and, if you have the talent or inclination, sketches or photos.

Searching for wildlife

Prime your senses (especially sight and hearing), keep quiet and look for clues. Watch for silhouettes against the sky in the forest canopy; body parts (eg, a leg dangling from a branch or twitching ears above long grass) and shadows; movement and moving vegetation; and shapes that don't fit. Look in both foreground and background; look at the ground and into the trees, and both upstream and downstream when crossing a river. Use your peripheral vision (especially at night) and watch where other creatures are looking, eg, Tommies staring at a cheetah.

Listen for alarm calls (which themselves indicate that predators are nearby), rustling bushes, snorting breath, splashing water and changes in the activity of other creatures, eg, monkeys screaming at a crowned eagle. Cupping your hands behind your ears helps to funnel sounds and to detect faint calls (rotate your head to judge the direction of sounds). Many large animals give off a distinctive odour or attract insects. Relax – animals can detect tension; keep quiet and heed your own instincts, such as the feeling you're being watched, or the hair standing up on the back of your neck.

If on foot, learn to use the environment to your advantage: walk slowly, using cover such as bushes and trees; stay downwind of animals (ie, keep the wind in your face); and avoid wearing strong artificial scents in the field which will help to give you away. Don't stare at an animal as you approach – this can be seen as a threat. Avoid making sudden movements and loud noises which startle mammals (birds are less concerned with noise than movement); and don't point at great apes – they may feel threatened and retaliate. Don't sneak up on animals – they may think you're stalking them and react accordingly. Sit still awhile against a tree or termite mound (animals look for movement and if you don't move, probably won't pay much attention). Stake out a burrow or den that appears to be in use – fresh droppings nearby are a promising sign.

Learn from the professional guides – listen to their stories, learn their techniques and ask questions.

Hides, observation towers and boardwalks

A hide (also called a blind) is any artificial structure that allows the watcher to remain hidden while wildlife behaves more or less as normal. Your safari vehicle is an effective hide, simply because most animals don't make the connection between vehicles and their occupants. Stationary hides are usually covered wooden shelters with horizontal openings through which wildlife can be observed or photographed; some are just fences, others more elaborate, eg, game lodges that overlook waterholes. Bird hides are sometimes erected next to waterholes and can be great places for wildlife photography.

Wooden observation towers allow you to scan across vegetation from a height, and look at birds or monkeys at eyelevel (a great luxury). Boardwalks over water can also act as observation platforms by getting the observer deep into otherwise inaccessible habitat.

Using calls

Calls (vocalisations) are particularly important for locating birds and amphibians, but many mammals also make loud or

Spotlighting – look then move on

A host of wildlife takes advantage of darkness to move about and feed, and the best way to see it is by spotlighting. Unfortunately it's not allowed in many reserves, but where it is possible you should take the opportunity to get out after dark. Safari companies should supply powerful spotlights that plug into your vehicle's cigarette lighter and run off the battery; the bigger torches (flashlights), such as those manufactured by Maglite are also quite useful. The idea is to drive (or walk) along slowly, scanning the bush on either side of the vehicle for eyeshine (the telltale reflection from an animal's tapetum – a layer of reflective cells in the eye of a nocturnal animal). There's a knack to doing it effectively and you must look directly along the light beam to see the eyeshine. Identification can be more difficult at night, with even the most familiar animal appearing quite different (although different coloured eyeshine gives a clue, eg, antelope eyeshine is green-blue while bushbaby eyeshine is red). It's amazing what previously hidden wildlife and activity can be seen after dark: predators on the move, animals that hide in burrows during the day, eg, aardvarks; birds such as owls and nightjars; and even large spiders and scorpions. Beware that extended exposure to bright lights can damage an animal's eyes and disturb its behaviour, so look then move on.

dramatic calls, eg, elephants, hippos and lions. Homing in on vocalisations is an important part of tracking primates; and an imitation of a bleating wildebeest can rouse a lion from slumber. Birdwatchers know that even a poor imitation of some calls can bring birds in for a closer look – a favourite trick is 'pishing', ie, making a high-pitched kissing sound with the mouth to attract small birds (kissing the back of your hand can have the same effect). Similar sounds can be made with a 'squeaker' (available from birdwatchers supply shops), and by rubbing polystyrene foam against glass (eg, a windscreen).

High-quality cassette or CD players are available with microphones for recording a call and playing it back to attract the animal in question. Most birds respond well to playback, and it is often the best way to locate and identify some species, such as flufftails, owls or nightjars. However, always use discretion and restraint with any of these techniques. Animals attracted to your calls are having their normal routine disrupted, which can potentially have seriously adverse effects – a lion checking out your wildebeest calf call may be missing a real opportunity to hunt. And a bird responding to what it perceives as a territorial challenge may be distracted from a real intruder; it may be deprived of valuable feeding time; or it may fail to notice the presence of a predator. If overused, the playback technique can also make individual mammals and birds so inured that they don't respond at all.

Tracks and signs

Animal tracks (spoor) and droppings (scats) are a great way of finding out what's around, especially those hard-to-see nocturnal species, even if you don't see the beast in question. Some signs, such as those of elephants, are immediately recognisable (especially the droppings), but most others are also distinct and a few can be learned quite quickly.

Experienced trackers can read a great deal from spoor and scats (eg, where an animal has rested, whether it was hunting, etc). Spoor and scats change and disintegrate over time (eg, owl pellets break down quickly in wet forests), and years of practice are needed to pick up the subtleties of the tracker's art. Excellent 'field guides' are available for the beginner – see the Resource Guide.

Examples of signs to look for include fur on fences or acacia thorns; nests of squirrels (called dreys) or birds; burrows, eg, those used by warthogs in abandoned termite mounds; flattened grass where an antelope has been lying-out; a smooth tree trunk where an elephant has been rubbing; animal trails leading to a waterhole, food source or shelter; 'whitewash' left by birds – especially raptors – on cliffs, rocks and termite mounds; and pellets of undigested material regurgitated by owls and hyenas. Carcasses can also be telltale signs of predators, eg, a dead impala dragged into a tree by a leopard. Tracking gorillas and chimps offers an opportunity to get to grips with tracks and signs while on foot, where broken or flattened vegetation, discarded fruit, droppings and disused nests make an interesting detective story (see the gorilla and chimp tracking section).

Beyond looking

For many people the simple pleasure of looking at wildlife evolves into photography, writing, art or learning more about animal behaviour (plant behaviour happens much more slowly, but is no less fascinating). The realisation that a vast, milling mob of wildebeests is actually a structured, complex community of interacting animals opens up a whole new world of watching wildlife to complement the thrill of the chase. How does one bull react to another? Why are most females in the middle of the group? Follow one animal – what does it do? To which individuals is it submissive or dominant? Each observation can answer one question but pose several more.

But if you want to keep chasing new species, 'ticking', 'twitching' or 'listing' (ie, keeping a list of what you have seen and pursuing those species that you haven't yet seen), can become a lifelong hobby. Listing is a reflection of the natural desire to collect and catalogue objects, and a harmless fulfilment of the hunting instinct. Should it need any justification, listing takes people to places they wouldn't otherwise visit, as they pursue the rare or unusual, or a new bird to complete the set; it hones the senses, powers of observation and skills of identification; and it leads to an appreciation of the diversity of life. Birds and, to a lesser extent, mammals are the usual targets of twitchers, but such is the stimulation of watching East African wildlife that it is easy to start ticking other diverse, conspicuous and colourful groups, such as butterflies and tropical fish.

Equipment

Binoculars and Spotting Scopes A good pair of binoculars is probably the most important piece of equipment on safari and the best investment a wildlife-watcher can make. Any working pair is better than none at all: a rustle in the bushes can become a brilliant sunbird, and a cheetah at full pelt after an antelope can be brought close-to. Take your own (don't expect someone else to share), but if you are serious about watching wildlife it is worth investing in quality optics; prices range from $100 to thousands of dollars. There's any number of brands on the market and a few things are worth knowing before you buy.

Factors to consider are size (to suit your hands), weight (they could be hanging from your neck for hours at a time) and whether you wear glasses (special eyecups are available for spectacle wearers). Decent models also have a dial (diopter), which allows you to compensate for any focussing difference between left and right eyes. Good binoculars are hinged, allowing adjustment for the distance between your eyes.

Like cameras, with binoculars you get what you pay for. Top-end brands such as Zeiss, Leica, Bausch & Lomb and Swarovski offer superb optics, last for years, and are waterproof and dustproof. More affordable brands, such as Bushnell, and midrange to upper models from respected camera manufacturers (eg, Pentax, Canon and Nikon) are perfectly good for most wildlife-watching. Good quality compact models are worth considering, but don't be tempted by supercheap compacts or by binoculars with 'zoom' optics (they usually have poor light-gathering ability).

The realisation that a vast, milling mob of wildebeests is actually a structured, complex community of interacting animals opens up a whole new world of watching wildlife.

Numbers are usually stamped on every pair of binoculars, eg, 10x50, 7x32. The first number refers to the number of times the image is magnified when you look through the eyepieces: at 10x, an object 100m away will appear as if only 10m away; at 7x, it will appear as if 14m away etc. The most useful magnifications for wildlife-watching are 7x, 8x or 10x. The second number, most commonly between 20 and 50, refers to the diameter in millimetres of the objective lens (ie, the lens farthest from the eye); the wider the lens (ie, the higher the number) the more light enters and therefore the brighter the image.

Larger objective lenses increase light-gathering ability and hence image brightness. Higher magnification reduces brightness. Not only is a brighter image clearer, it is also more colour accurate – a sometimes crucial point for identification. Light gathering ability can be estimated (it's not a perfect guide) by dividing the objective diameter by the magnification – the higher the result, the more light enters the binoculars. Thus, 10x50s and 8x40s perform similarly, but 7x42s often give a brighter image. Special interior coatings can also increase image brightness. Having extra light gathering ability may not be all that useful during the middle of the day (your eye can take only so much light before your irises start to close), but in dim conditions, such as at dusk or in a rainforest, you'll want all you can get. As your irises can only open so far (and this decreases with age), opting for greater light gathering power may be a waste. To check, test out different binoculars in dim light before you buy a pair.

Larger objective lenses also mean a larger field of view, ie, the 'width' of the area (usually indicated in degrees) that fits into the image you see. Field of view is also a trade-off against magnification, ie, higher magnifications reduce the field of view. The narrower the field of view, the harder it is to locate your target, especially if it is moving.

Internal lenses can also affect quality. Most binoculars have porro prism lenses, which are offset from each other to give the familiar 'crooked' barrels. Roof prism lenses are aligned directly behind each other and allow compact, straight barrels: cost is their only drawback. Good compromises of all factors are configurations such as 7x35, 7x40 and 8x40. Birders tend to favour 8x40 or 10x50 for the sometimes critical extra magnification.

Spotting scopes are essentially refracting telescopes designed for field use. Birders use 'scopes' most often in open habitats, eg, when watching waterbirds and waders. Scopes offer higher magnifications than binoculars (usually starting at 20x or 25x), but must be mounted on a tripod or monopod to reduce shaking (not usually feasible in a vehicle). Disadvantages include weight and bulk; and a narrow field of view makes scopes difficult to use effectively in rainforests. Again, a quality scope will be expensive; Kowa, Leica, Celestron, Nikon and Bushnell are all excellent brands.

Clothing Suitable clothing maximises comfort to the wearer and minimises disturbance to wildlife. Subdued colours, eg, greens or browns make your presence in the landscape less obtrusive, but avoid camouflage clothing – in Africa it's for military use.

Predawn departures can be chilly, especially in open vehicles with the wind whipping past, and be prepared for sudden storms during the wet; dress in layers and peel off or add clothes as conditions dictate.

Cotton or cotton-synthetic blends are cooler in hot weather; wear synthetics that breathe and are waterproof in cool conditions. Sleeveless photographers jackets have many pockets, which are very useful for carrying the paraphernalia necessary for wildlife-watching (like field guides and notebooks). A hat is important: light cotton protects your head against the sun, but opt for wool or synthetics in cold conditions; and a wide brim cuts down glare and helps hide your eyes (looking directly at an animal can be taken as a threat).

Gorilla and chimp tracking is usually hot, and sometimes wet, work – carry a light waterproof jacket with a hood in your day pack. Trekking in high mountains requires specialised equipment and clothing – see Lonely Planet's *Trekking in East Africa*.

Field Guides Field guides are (usually) pocket-sized books that depict the mammals, birds, flowers etc, of a specific area with photos or colour illustrations. Important identification pointers and a distribution map are usually provided for each species; sometimes there are also brief natural histories, summarising breeding, behaviour, diet and the like. Guides to animals are usually organised in taxonomic order, a system that shows evolutionary relationships between species and is generally consistent between guides. Plant guides often follow other systems, eg, wildflowers may be ranked by colour.

Ideally you should combine your own observations, notes and sketches with what you read in field guides, but on safari the excitement and overwhelming variety often make this impractical. Don't assume that because the field guide says species X is found here, it must be species X. If you find something unusual – birds in particular often wander outside their usual range – take notes and refer to other books when you get a chance. Depending on how much you value the book's appearance, consider colour-coding the outside margin of the pages so you can flip to a section easily.

Field guides are a handy tool that have made an incalculable contribution to the popularity of wildlife-watching. But rarely are they the last word on a subject and further reading of weightier texts can provide valuable detail not covered in your field guide – refer to the Resource Guide for suggested reading.

What's good for the goose is good for a gander

Your final choice of binoculars will depend on budget, likely amount of use, and desire for quality and comfort. But before you spend a lot of money, talk to people and test their binoculars in the field. Read manufacturers' brochures and product reviews in birdwatchers' magazines. Birdwatchers carry weight in the marketplace and conduct exhaustive tests in the field; if a particular brand and/or configuration passes their (usually stringent) requirements it'll be good enough for use in East Africa. Recommendations usually come in different price categories.

A useful Web site that tests new releases and has a host of background information, plus lists of retailers and manufacturers, can be found at ⌨ www.betterviewdesired.com

GETTING IN & AROUND

Doing it yourself

In East Africa's competitive safari market virtually anything is possible, but much depends on your comfort requirements and budget. A vehicle is essential in most reserves (for safety) so even if you could get there by public transport you won't be allowed in without a lift. Hire cars are readily available but expensive unless you share the costs among several people; most of the time you're as well to hire a driver (who may or may not be your safari guide – see the 'Guides and tours' section) so you are free to watch animals instead of the road. Road conditions vary from good to abysmal; dry season travel generally presents few problems, but in wet seasons a 4WD is advisable and sometimes essential. You are allowed into reserves in your own vehicle as long as you pay the requisite entrance fees. If you want to be independent of an operator, you could hire a vehicle – ask around for an accredited (in Kenya) or competent guide (elsewhere) and go for it. Some safari operators may rent out camping equipment.

Safaris are a big leisure pursuit among expats and if you have the time, getting to know a local enthusiast is one of the best ways to see some wildlife. Various clubs and societies offer regular talks, outings and campouts – see the Resource Guide.

Certain organisations take volunteers to help with projects, although in many cases appropriate qualifications and/or experience are required. Glamorous though it sounds, field work is usually rough, demanding and dirty work; most hopefuls are weeded out to ensure a high level of dedication. There's no harm in trying, of course, and if you do join a project you will be party to a privileged view of wildlife. Earthwatch and other organisations such as Taita Discovery Centre (see boxed text) are a way to get involved as a paying 'volunteer'.

Do-it-yourself travellers can camp in designated sites or hire cheap bandas in many parks: Uganda with its community-based ecotourism projects is best-serviced in this regard, Kenya less so and Tanzania in its scramble for foreign revenue is trying to push tourists upmarket. Other forms of accommodation, such as tented camps and safari lodges, are both popular and well run in nearly all reserves. These offer a high standard of service and comfort, and although the sky's the limit for prices, they are part of the safari tradition and definitely worth trying at least once.

Guides and tours

Wildlife is the mainstay of East African tourism, and there is no shortage of operators willing to take you and your money – shop around. With any tour company you will see some animals and many travellers will be content with that. But if your main interest is wildlife you will get far more out of a specialist company, particularly one that uses accredited guides. Beware of exhortations to 'support local companies' – many of the more expensive operators are locally owned, and more professionally run than the tempting, cheap tours aimed at backpackers.

Specialised wildlife tours are also organised from countries outside East Africa; these tours generally stay in comfortable accommodation where it is available – with a corresponding price tag – but welcome beginners and virtually guarantee results (see the Resource Guide).

Touts are hyperactive on the streets of Nairobi and Arusha; they are essentially harmless but can be persistent – don't be pressured into taking a tour you don't want, and use only operators that belong to tourist associations, such as KATO (Kenya Association of Tour Operators) and AUTO (Association of Uganda Tour Operators) – see the Resource Guide.

Your safari guide is usually also your driver. Kenya has recently introduced an accreditation system for safari guides, but the majority still aren't accredited and it shows. Guide accreditation ensures a minimum standard of knowledge: those guides who take the trouble to sit the accreditation exam at least show self-motivation and many have a specialised interest (eg, medicinal plants). Importantly, accredited guides can command a higher fee, and demand for their services will benefit themselves as well as the industry in general. Don't hesitate to ask whether an operator uses accredited guides – if they aren't on staff they can usually be hired for an additional cost. Ask around for personal recommendations.

To date, Uganda and Tanzania have no accreditation system, although official park guards can sometimes be hired as guides (some are helpful, others not – again, ask around for a recommendation); specialist guides for gorilla and chimp tracking are usually very good value; and expert locals can be sought out at places where a high demand exists, eg, Uganda's Kibale Forest and Queen Elizabeth and Bwindi Impenetrable NPs.

Parks and reserves
National parks and other reserves are the cornerstone of wildlife-watching in East Africa. Most safari companies include one or more on their itineraries, but some are serviced only by upmarket companies and are difficult to get to. Dry seasons and school holidays are the busiest times.

Wildlife tourism and reserves are an important source of revenue and entrance fees apply to most. These vary according to country and park, and range from US$250 to track gorillas at Bwindi to a few dollars for some lesser-visited national parks. Further information can be obtained from the relevant wildlife authorities in each country – see the Resource Guide. There is some form of accommodation in most parks – see the 'Doing it yourself' section earlier in this chapter for more details.

Taita Discovery Centre
Situated in a wilderness of arid shrubland with abundant wildlife, Taita Discovery Centre (www.sav annahcamps.com/taita.html) is an environmental education centre on Rukinga Ranch south of Tsavo West NP in Kenya. For a modest nightly fee, TDC offers travellers an opportunity to participate in projects designed to help and educate local communities on environmental issues, such as tree planting and manufacturing elephant-dung paper for souvenirs. Visitors can also monitor the elephants that migrate through Rukinga or help local communities directly with building programs.

LIVING WITH WILDLIFE

Close encounters

Accidental encounters with large and potentially dangerous animals are a distinct possibility, but with common sense and care you will come to no grief. Most big animals move away as you approach and little else can harm you. Wildlife-viewing from a vehicle is very safe, but more intimate encounters could be expected on a walking safari – it's part of the excitement, but remember to exercise extreme caution even when accompanied by an armed guide. Monkeys can become a pest around camping grounds – assert your dominance early on before they get too cocky.

Biting tsetse flies are bothersome in some areas. Wear light-coloured clothes in affected zones – tsetse flies are attracted to dark colours, especially blue. Mosquitoes can be a serious pest in rainforest, coastal lowlands and near swamps. Take adequate precautions against getting bitten – malaria is rife in East Africa, and yellow fever and black water fever are endemic to central Africa.

Ticks are usually only picked up by walking through long grass – inspect for ticks each night and remove with tweezers or by applying a lighted match. Scorpions are most common in hot, dry areas and are best avoided; don't walk around barefoot at night.

All snakes should be treated with extreme caution – a few are dangerous and on no account should you try to pick one up (injured snakes can be especially dangerous). African bees have a reputation for being dangerous in swarms – if you are unlucky enough to encounter a swarm, take whatever cover you can find.

Driving

There's a strict curfew on driving at night in most reserves; outside the reserves it's not a good idea to be on the roads after dark because of the danger of hitting animals or of running into bandits. During the day most of your wildlife-watching will be inside reserves, where a speed limit of around 40km/h is usually enforced and animals have right of way (if no speed limit is indicated, use 40km/h as a guide). The chances of getting bowled over by an elephant are pretty slim; however, if an elephant, buffalo or rhino charges you it's a very good idea to get out of its way – drivers don't usually need to be told and will start the engine as soon as a large animal starts to look stroppy.

Feeding wildlife

Some lodges have feeding stations that attract birds and monkeys by day, and galagos and genets at night. However, for you there's one simple rule – don't feed wild animals. Artificial feeding can foster a dependence on handouts, change natural behaviour and in the long term even cause malnutrition (visitors' bags usually contain sugary foods, rather than beetle grubs). Monkeys and baboons are intelligent, opportunistic animals that quickly learn how to get a free feed; if one is suddenly denied a coveted morsel, it can turn ugly very fast: at best this will mean a tantrum that will convince you to deliver the goods, at worst physical aggression that you don't want to be involved with.

Animal welfare

Most travellers are aware of the debate over buying souvenirs made from animal products such as ivory. It might be difficult to relate that innocent-looking souvenir to a real animal, but don't fool yourself, your purchases can be one more nail in the coffin of a species. And don't assume that a product openly on sale is legal – even if it is, it does not mean that it meets any standards for wildlife sustainability or the humane treatment of animals. Many countries have strict laws about quarantine and the importation of prohibited animal or plant products – check your own country's regulations before wasting money on a potentially prohibited import – the penalties are sometimes severe.

Disturbing wildlife

In popular reserves animals become used to vehicles and often behave more or less naturally a few metres from camera-snapping tourists. This has had unfortunate side-effects, such as the spectacle of lions or cheetahs being literally surrounded by safari vehicles; cheetahs being so harassed that they cannot hunt effectively; the destruction of vegetation; and drivers churning up the countryside by cutting new tracks in their pursuit of animals. Even more serious, gorillas habituated to people on foot have become targets for poachers.

Remember, watching wildlife under natural conditions at such close range is a privilege. With that privilege comes the responsibility to ensure wildlife continues to live unhindered, both for its own survival and so that other people can enjoy the same experience. Strict ethical codes exist for game-viewing, and for gorilla and chimp tracking; visitors are usually briefed before setting out. Of course you'll want quick results for all the money you've forked out, but it is important for everyone to stick to the rules; should a serious breach occur don't hesitate to report your (or someone else's) driver – it's in their interests to keep their comparatively well-paid jobs. Immense benefits – personal, aesthetic, recreational, conservation and financial – stem from the wildlife-watching 'industry', and it is important for all concerned – especially the animals – to ensure that wildlife tourism is carried out responsibly. ■

Dos and don'ts on safari

- Large animals can be dangerous; don't drive too close to animals and don't drive between a female and her young.
- Don't make loud noises, such as tooting the horn or banging the side of your vehicle, to attract an animal's attention.
- Stay well clear of a predator on the hunt – it or its young may starve if the hunt is unsuccessful.
- Leave things better than you find them. Do not drive off designated tracks because it destroys vegetation and encourages erosion. Pick up other people's rubbish and keep your own rubbish until you can dispose of it properly. Do not throw matches or cigarettes out and put all fires out completely. Do not collect souvenirs such as bones, horns, feathers, shells etc – they also play a role in the natural environment.
- Move in towards an animal gradually or in stages; that way you'll eventually get closer without disturbing it.
- Respect your own life. Do not get out of the vehicle except at designated areas, and don't stand or sit on a roof or hang out a window – predators and primates can move very quickly.

ON SAFARI

GAME drives are the backbone of most safaris and the idea is to spend as many hours as possible in the bush searching for animals. A game drive can be done at any time of day, but certain times are better than others, as explained below. see also the Alternative Safaris section later in this chapter.

Game drives

On organised safaris the usual plan is an early wake-up call with a hot drink, then a game drive before breakfast. The same wisdom applies if you are doing it yourself: the importance of an early start cannot be stressed too highly. You will see large animals at virtually any time of day, but the earlier you set out the better your chances of seeing nocturnal species still on the prowl or predators gathered at a kill; and there's a greater chance of interesting interactions in the early hours. Besides, it's usually cooler.

Young animals are often curious of onlookers and sometimes behave boldly – this young spotted hyena is tasting a tyre.

Savanna is an excellent environment in which to spot large animals and you don't normally go far without seeing something. The basic technique is to drive along slowly, stopping for photos as you like. After an hour or two driving around, it's back to camp or lodge for breakfast, time to freshen up and then a midmorning game drive. Again, this is a good time of day: large raptors such as eagles and vultures are starting to take to the thermals as the land warms up, many grazers are still moving about and primates have shaken off the night's chill. Activity wanes noticeably as noon approaches and animals seek shade and rest; primates also head for the shade – where they may remain active all day.

By late afternoon things are on the move again and afternoon game drives typically last from about 3 pm until the park's closing time. Unfortunately, things tend to get most interesting just as the sun sets and it's time to leave.

Night drives

As the sun sets wildlife action cranks up a notch – night drives are an activity not to be missed wherever they are available.

Darkness covers much wildlife activity normally hidden from people – night drives are usually a highlight of any safari and offer all the thrills of a game drive with a whole new suite of players. An essential prerequisite for a night drive is a spotlight (preferably one that plugs into the vehicle's cigarette lighter – your safari operator should be able to supply this or a powerful torch – see the boxed text in the preceding When, Where and How section). Drive along slowly and look for eyeshine reflected in the light; even small animals can be detected using this technique.

Night drives are conducted regularly on Kenya's private reserves and conservancies; they are forbidden in most national parks and reserves, although high-tech night vision equipment has been installed in some vehicles in Masai Mara NR and Meru NP. In Uganda park wardens sometimes grant permission for a night drive – you'll probably be obliged to take a park ranger along with you (be prepared to negotiate a fee).

Vehicles

Safari vehicles come in many permutations. You'll be spending quite a bit of time in a vehicle and as a rule the more money you shell out – whether going along on a tour or renting your own vehicle – the more comfortable the ride. Most are Land Rovers or Land Cruisers seating anything up to nine people, but most comfortably only four, with open sides, side windows or roll-back canvas flaps; the roof can be pop-top, flip-top, roll-back etc. A 4WD vehicle is the most desirable way to travel in the wet season and essential in some areas, eg, parts of the Masai Mara NR.

Minivans – the target of much derision by 'serious' safari operators – are not usually 4WD but are often driven as if they were. Again, they come in varying degrees of comfort, usually with a pop-top: those with a single, long pop-top provide the best viewing for all occupants; those with two or three smaller pop-tops offer less viewing flexibility and comfort. Those with a central aisle rather than bench seats give greater room for everyone to move around or take pictures. Minivans have the advantage of normally being cheaper than 4WDs (and most budget companies use them), but their use can be limited during wet seasons.

Drivers

Your driver normally doubles as your guide, and is there to help you see wildlife and to get you back to camp safely. Most will do their utmost to make sure you enjoy your safari – after all, their livelihood depends on it. Establish a dialogue early on: if you want to stop, tell them, and make it clear if you want to take photos – they may have to be reminded to switch off the engine.

You are entitled to an early start if you want one and to be at the reserve gates by opening time if necessary – arrange this the night before your game drive.

Unless you direct otherwise, drivers tend to follow each other to a kill, pride of lions or whatever. If you don't want to be part of the 'minivan circus', let your driver know; likewise, if you are happy to spend hours watching a herd of something less glamorous, eg, antelopes, just say so – you're the boss. ∎

Large animals, such as this elephant in Ngorongoro Crater, are a big draw and often attract a circle of safari vehicles.

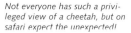

Not everyone has such a privileged view of a cheetah, but on safari expect the unexpected!

BIRDWATCHING

EAST Africa is one of the 'killer' birdwatching destinations of the world. If it is your first birding trip outside Europe, America or Australia you'll probably double your life list (for the uninitiated, a life list is the tally a birder keeps of all the bird species he or she has seen around the world). A tally of 500 species is easily achievable in an average visit and some hardcore birders clock up 700 'ticks' in a month-long trip to Kenya or Uganda. Birds are incredibly diverse and abundant, and groups familiar in other parts of the world take on a new significance – starlings occur in dazzling variety and iridescent colour; and the sparrow family is represented by dozens of species of weaver living in noisy colonies. Uniquely African groups such as the hamerkop, turacos and mousebirds are common, and those in search of a challenge can wrestle with the identification of dozens of species of cisticolas, larks and pipits.

Bee-eaters (this is a white-fronted bee-eater) are one of East Africa's many bird highlights – 16 species have been recorded and most are easy to see.

How it's done

Read as much as possible before arriving: familiarise yourself with new bird families and prioritise sites according to the species you most want to see. Most birders try to see as many of the country endemics and unique African groups as possible, such as turacos or the shoebill, and concentrate less on cosmopolitan groups like migrant shorebirds. Prime birding locations are described in trip reports available through mail-order natural history booksellers and in websites devoted to birding (see the Resource Guide). Coverage will depend on time, money and competing interests, but if your trip is restricted to one country, thoroughly work as many habitats as possible; if you are going to two or more, remember that rarities in one might be common elsewhere and plan accordingly. Consider hiring an expert bird guide for an area that might prove challenging, such as Bwindi Impenetrable NP; some of these guides have superb eyesight and an ear for the calls (you'll also encourage local interest in birdwatching). Inquire through one of the specialised bird tour companies listed in the Resource Guide for a recommendation.

Expert bird guides can be hired at Kakamega and Arabuko–Sokoke forests. By hiring local talent you will help promote interest in birdwatching and conservation.

What to take

Make sure your binoculars are waterproof and dustproof, since a typical itinerary ranges from rainforest to dry plains; good configurations for picking the subtleties of identification include 8x40 and 10x40; 10x50 is useful for looking into rainforest canopy (see the preceding section on Binoculars and Spotting Scopes for more on selecting the right equipment). Spotting scopes are probably only necessary if you're doing a lot of wader watching, eg, at Lake Nakuru NP; most birders find a scope useful for only a small percentage of sightings and too cumbersome for rainforest work. A tape recorder and directional mike are extremely useful for calling in forest birds, especially skulkers, such as flufftails, and nocturnal goodies. Avoid stressing birds with the overuse of playback.

Top spots to go

Endemic Bird Areas listed by BirdLife International are good places to start planning your East African birding trip; many high-profile reserves fall into these areas, although a few (eg, Pemba Island) are off the usual tourist circuit.

For a good swipe at Kenya's 1100 species, try to cover coastal lowland forests (Arabuko-Sokoke FR), high grasslands (Nairobi NP or Masai Mara NR), alpine habitat (eg, Mt Kenya NP), rainforests (Kakamega Forest) and semidesert (Samburu NR, Meru NP or Lake Baringo). And don't miss the flamingo spectacle at Lake Bogoria NR.

Tanzania has the highest number of endemics (23) among its 1040 recorded species. As well as the grasslands of the Serengeti or Ngorongoro Crater and the alpine habitat on Mt Meru, time should be spent exploring Udzungwa NP (and/or the Usambara Mountains) and Pemba Island, where many of the unique species are found.

The presence of only one endemic among 1017 species shows Uganda's high overlap with neighbouring Kenya and the DRC, but it offers the advantage of being a comparatively compact area. Savanna species are best sought in Lake Mburo and Queen Elizabeth NPs; explore Kidepo Valley and Murchison Falls NPs for semiarid specialities, and Mt Elgon NP for high-altitude birds. But the main event is where the rainforests of the Zaire River basin spill into Bwindi Impenetrable and Semliki NPs and sensational birding includes 23 species endemic to the Albertine Rift Valley.

Rwanda's tally of 670 species includes the shoebill and red-fronted barbet at PN de l'Akagera, and RF de Nyungwe features many Albertine Rift endemics and birds common to the Zaire River basin. Over the border in the DRC the possibilities are endless for the intrepid birder with time to spare and who's willing to rough it; incredibly, some birds of the Zaire River basin have a South-East Asian spin: Grauer's rush warbler, Congo peacock, Congo bay-owl and African green broadbill.

And don't fret about missing out on other wildlife – most good birding reserves are also good for mammals, and you'll see plenty because birders spend so much time in the field.

Wide ranging and easily seen birds include abundant large wading birds, such as storks – this is a Eurasian white stork.

Field guides

Identification is well-documented for Uganda, Kenya and Tanzania. Don't leave home without the *Field Guide to Birds of Kenya and Northern Tanzania* by Zimmerman, Turner and Pearson; it's a superb book and the last word on the area it covers (the soft cover version is recommended for ease of use in the field). For the rest of Tanzania plus Uganda, the *Illustrated Checklist to Birds of Eastern Africa* by van Perlo is the most useful book. As yet there is no guide covering the birds of the Zaire River basin, although those species that reach western Uganda are covered in van Perlo. Flipping through guides in search of the right section among the sheer dazzling variety can be time-consuming in the field – consider colour-coding the pages for quick reference. See the Resource Guide for other recommended bird books. ∎

GORILLA & CHIMPANZEE TRACKING

TRACKING gorillas and chimpanzees through the forests of East Africa are among the world's great wildlife experiences and should not be missed. National parks in Uganda, Rwanda and DRC (Zaïre) protect important populations of both species, and several of the parks run well-established tracking programs. International conservation bodies work closely with communities surrounding many of the parks; in these areas tangible benefits flow on from tourism to the local people because of their involvement in tracking, infrastructure and support.

Adult gorillas often show indifference to your presence, and may continue to eat and doze as if you weren't there.

What to take

Don't be fazed by the possible hardships – but be prepared. Wear walking shoes with adequate grip for muddy slopes (don't even think about trying it in thongs – among other things you might run into safari ants). You can expect rain at any time of year, so carry a light waterproof in your day pack (make sure it's large enough to fit over your day pack as well). While gorilla tracking you may need both hands for the scramble up steep hillsides and through brakes of dense cane – carry gardening gloves in case you have to push your way through stinging nettles or thorny vines. In some parks, eg, Mgahinga Gorilla NP and PN des Volcans, it can also get quite cold, so take a warm top. Rain or no, tracking can be hot work: carry plenty of water (preferably a couple of litres). If you get too hot or tired, your guide will probably carry your pack for you, and cut you a walking stick if there's a steep descent; if you have lots of gear porters can usually be hired at park HQs.

Don't forget camera and film, but flash photography is not permitted so you'll need at least 400 ISO, and preferably 800 or 1600 ISO, to cope with the often gloomy light conditions among undergrowth (these film speeds are rarely available in East Africa so bring an adequate supply from home). At a pinch, you could also 'push' slower film by exposing it at a higher ISO setting than its actual film speed, and processing it accordingly when you get back home (see Lonely Planet's *Travel Photography*).

Some individuals offer only tantalising glimpses through the undergrowth; rest assured though, they're aware of your presence.

How it's done

Gorilla tracking Gorilla tracking can involve negotiating steep hills and gullies (a reasonable level of fitness will help you to enjoy the day), but the effort is amply repaid by your allotted hour spent in the company of these largest of all primates. Check into the park office as close to opening time as possible – only a specified number of tracking permits are issued daily: 12 at Bwindi and Mgahinga Gorilla NPs (Uganda), and 18 at PN des Volcans (Rwanda). Tour companies often block-book a proportion of permits and it's first come, first served for those left over.

You will be allocated to a group with a guide; starting from where trackers watched them bed down the night before, you will follow the gorilla's trail – usually obvious as crushed vegetation, temporary nests and broken food plants. Trackers will clear a path for you where necessary, but gorillas can cover ground quickly: some groups of tourists are lucky enough to come across them within a few minutes, but most can expect an hour or two of hard slog. You're expected to tip guides, trackers and porters after a successful tracking.

Chimpanzee tracking Chimp tracking attracts far less publicity (and tourists) than gorilla tracking, but offers an exciting alternative: in your allotted hour of viewing with habituated chimps you can expect lots of noise and a good chance of seeing some boisterous action. And all for a fraction of the cost. Organised 'primate walks' are run regularly from some reserves with a high density of primate species, and usually offer a good chance of encountering chimps. However, wild chimps are generally shy of humans and even where parties have been habituated contact is never guaranteed. Even when you do meet up, chimps can move very quickly through forest: if a party is on the go, you'll have to leg it to keep up – and that can be very hot work.

Top spots to go
Gorilla tracking Uganda Bwindi Impenetrable NP is currently Africa's number one destination for gorilla tracking and sightings are almost 100% guaranteed. A high success rate is also experienced at Mgahinga Gorilla NP although it can be wet and cold, and gorillas are usually present only from March to May and September to December. Tracking permits cost US$250 per person plus a US$15 park entrance fee.
Rwanda Tourist security and gorilla sightings are now guaranteed in PN des Volcans; tracking permits cost US$250 per person.
DRC At the time of writing, national parks in the DRC were closed owing to political unrest; however, this situation could change – check with a reliable tour operator.

Chimpanzee tracking Uganda Part of a large, well-studied chimp population has been habituated at Kibale Forest NP, where primate walks operate daily and chimps are encountered on about 80% of walks. Primate walks at Kibale cost US$10 per person, plus US$7 park entrance fee. Two locations in Budongo FR (Kaniyo Pabidi and Busingiro) also offer a high encounter rate; walks are US$6 plus US$4 park fee (US$15 at Kaniyo Pabidi). Chimps may also be seen on walks at Kyambura Gorge in Queen Elizabeth NP (US$30 per person plus US$15 park fee); and at Semliki Valley WR (US$7). Orphaned chimps have been released on Ngamba Island in Lake Victoria (accessible from Entebbe), and at the time of writing chimp communities were being habituated at various other locations – check with the Uganda Tourist Board (UTB) or Uganda Wildlife Authority (UWA).
Tanzania Gombe Stream NP, famous as the site of Jane Goodall's long-running chimp research project, supports some 150 well-habituated chimps. Park fees are US$100 per day; guides cost US$20 per group. Chimps can also be found at Mahale Mountains NP, where park fees are US$50 per day and a guide costs US$20 per group.
Rwanda Chimps in Rwanda's RF de Nyungwe are in the process of being habituated to tourists. ■

The most habituated chimp community is at Tanzania's Gombe Stream NP, but sites in Uganda, such as Kibale Forest NP, are easier to get to.

SNORKELLING

CORAL reefs the world over are among the great natural spectacles, and the coasts of Kenya and Tanzania offer some fine examples where snorkelling can be enjoyed in safety and comfort at a relatively low cost. Some basic equipment is all that is required to enjoy a constantly moving parade of fish in every imaginable shape and colour; crabs, shrimps and shells with intricate and outlandish camouflage; and the great reefs of coral that form the basis for this fascinating ecosystem.

An amazing underwater world opens up with a few simple techniques and a little effort.

What you'll need

The minimum requirements are a mask, snorkel and fins (only beginners call them 'flippers'); those who don't carry these as part of their normal travel gear can hire them at various coastal resorts, although check their condition before forking out any money. If you wear spectacles and do a lot of snorkelling, consider getting a mask made up with glass to your eyes' prescription; these are not available in East Africa so you'll have to get it done at home. If you have contact lenses (again, bring them from home) then you should definitely wear these when under the water!

The sun's strength can be deceptive when you're wet so wear a T-shirt to cover your back against sunburn; lightweight diving suits perform the same task. If you really want to feel the sun on your back (especially if you're escaping a northern winter!) make sure you apply liberal amounts of sunblock. And if you're heading out in a boat for a few hours remember to take adequate drinking water – and drink it!

Scuba diving is a skill requiring equipment and training outside the scope of this book – see Lonely Planet's *Pisces* series of diving books and *Dive Sites of Kenya and Tanzania* by A Koornhof for details.

Snorkellers commonly encounter schools of soldierfish among coral or in open water between reefs.

How it's done

Wade out until there's enough water in which to float, then lay your arms along the side of your body, point face and mask downwards and kick gently along with the fins. A little effort goes a long way and the stiffer fins the better the propulsion. The snorkel fits into the mouth and is gripped with the teeth; breathe through your mouth when floating on the surface, and hold your breath for forays underwater. With practice it is possible to dive a few metres underwater: take a deep breath and duck dive (vertically) from the surface; fins work just fine beneath the surface, and a surprising distance can be covered with little effort. When you surface, blow sharp and hard to eject the water from the snorkel. Mastering the basics takes a few minutes, but that's it – only stamina and curiosity will limit your exploration. Some reefs in East Africa can be reached only by boat – there are plenty available to take you out (see the Parks and Places chapter for details on where to go).

Snorkelling can give hours of pleasure for very little effort, but there are few hazards you should know about. Sunburn, fatigue and cramp from cold water can affect anyone – check local conditions and currents before venturing out. Be aware that some marine life is dangerous; coral cuts and scrapes are the commonest cause of discomfort, but don't touch anything alive underwater – certain fish and cone shells can deliver a lethal sting.

During wet seasons, underwater visibility can be reduced by silted rivers emptying into the sea, and heavy weather might make access to reefs by boat difficult.

Top spots to go

All reefs in Kenya's marine national parks and reserves are reached by boat and snorkelling gear can generally be hired at resorts or hotels. Day trips to Kisite MNP can be arranged from Diani and diving trips to the Pemba Channel can be arranged from Shimoni Reef Lodge (HQ for Kisite MNP). Clear water and reefs at Watamu MNP are 1 to 2km offshore and reached by glass-bottomed boat; giant rock cod and underwater caves at Mida Creek can also be visited. Snorkelling and diving can be arranged in Malindi for trips to Malindi MNP; and islands near Lamu, such as Manda Toto and Kiwayu, offer what is reputed to be some of the best underwater viewing on the coast. Migrating whale sharks are a big attraction at Watamu in January and February.

Tanzania's best underwater spots fringe the islands of Pemba (wall and drift diving, manta rays and schools of hammerhead sharks); Unguja (Zanzibar – especially the east coast, but also at Chumbe Island Coral Park near Zanzibar town); and Mafia, where guesthouses on Chole Bay organise snorkelling and diving in nearby Mafia Island MNP. Several islands close to Dar es Salaam have snorkelling and diving, and trips can be arranged from Dar or the northern beaches.

Viewing the mighty – but harmless – whale shark is an attraction at Kenya's Watamu Marine NP.

Field guides

Various field guides will help you identify marine organisms, especially reef fish. *The Guide to the Seashores of Eastern Africa and the Western Indian Ocean Islands* edited by M Richmond is an excellent book covering many types of marine life – see the Resource Guide for more information. Unfortunately, books can't be read underwater, although you could laminate colour photocopies of fish ID sheets before leaving home. A waterproof drawing crayon and sketching board are handy for jotting down details of colours and shapes to help identify what you've seen once you're back on shore or on the boat. The coral reef is a dazzling ecosystem which can be enjoyed just for its own sake, but learning how to identify its many inhabitants helps to piece together the ecological jigsaw and enhances your appreciation of what you see.

Refer to Lonely Planet's guides to *Kenya* and *Tanzania, Zanzibar & Pemba* for full listings of accommodation, and snorkelling or diving operators at the various marine national parks and marine national reserves along East Africa's coast. ■

ALTERNATIVE SAFARIS

ALTERNATIVES to the usual safari in a vehicle can give a different – and even enhanced – wildlife experience. Camel, horse and bike safaris are not usually organised by companies that specialise in wildlife-watching, although you will undoubtedly see some animals on these trips. See the Resource Guide at the back of this book, and Lonely Planet's *East Africa*; *Kenya*; and *Tanzania, Zanzibar & Pemba* guides for operators.

Walking in reserves

Many guides and old safari hands swear that walking is the only way to see Africa. If you are fortunate enough to try a game walk, you will experience the great pleasures of small things like flowers, tortoises and birdsong. Walking trims the senses as well as the waist – you'll smell the bush, and hearing an elephant rumble nearby could be a matter of life or death. Good trackers should be able to read the bush and avoid confrontations. However, accidents occasionally happen and for this reason an armed guard usually accompanies walking parties. Maasai guides usually don't carry guns, only a spear and *rungu* (wooden club), and are great companions on a walk. The only big disadvantage of walking is that most mammals are wary of people on foot and it is generally hard to approach to within less than 100m or so – binoculars are essential.

Unaccompanied walking is possible in Kenya at Hell's Gate, Saiwa Swamp and Mt Kenya NPs, plus Kakamega and Arabuko-Sokoke Forests; accompanied walks are possible at Shimba Hills NR, and just outside the Masai Mara NR in the Sekenani Valley and Siria Escarpment – inquire at the various lodges and camps. There are no official restrictions on accompanied walks in private reserves and conservancies (see Other Sites in the Kenya chapter).

Apart from organised gorilla and chimp tracking (see separate section), in Uganda accompanied walks are possible in Semliki Valley WR, and by arrangement at Lake Mburo NP.

Lodges and camps in Tanzania's Selous GR offer accompanied walks; trekking is possible on Mts Kilimanjaro and Meru; and walks are possible in Udzungwa NP and Saadani GR.

Night walks

Sunset on the savannas is magic, but all too often heralds the end of a day's activity – for the viewer at least. Walking about with a torch at night is simply not on in most national parks and national reserves, but in Kenya nocturnal walks can be organised in Kakamega and Arabuko-Sokoke Forests, and at private reserves and conservancies; and organised night walks are a regular feature at Kibale Forest NP in Uganda. Night walks are

Cruises along major waterways are an excellent way to get close to hippos, crocs and waterbirds.

Horse riding is a great alternative to a vehicle-based safari, although it is only possible outside official reserves.

a great way to see a different suite of mammals and birds: you may get quite close to owls, galagos, genets and nocturnal mongooses, or find sleeping monkeys or birds, and see lots of smaller animals, such as insects and amphibians.

Hot-air balloons

For an unforgettable vulture's-eye view of the wildebeest migration (in season) try an early-morning hot-air balloon trip in Masai Mara NR or over Serengeti NP. Balloon safaris leave at sunrise, weather permitting (optimum viewing time is July to October), and usually last an hour or so. Vehicles following behind set up a swanky breakfast for your arrival then provide a leisurely game drive back to your accommodation. Highly recommended if you've got the cash.

Camel safaris

Although camel riding is not rated highly for comfort, it is a great way to get right off the beaten track in the semiarid parts of Kenya. Safaris usually travel 15 to 18km a day in morning and afternoon stints. Camels offer a good vantage point and if you're reasonably fit you can walk alongside your beast.

Horse riding

This is an excellent way to get close to large animals – although at times skittish, herbivores generally don't make the connection between people and horses, and are generally very approachable; lions, of course, love horses – an armed guide will help dissuade them though. Horse riding is available in a few private reserves (eg, Lewa Downs WC in Kenya); longer treks involving camping are also available. Zebroids (horse zebra hybrids) are used as pack animals on some safaris.

Many people regard walking as the best way to experience Africa – be prepared for some intimate encounters with animals large and small.

Boats

The best way to get close to large water animals such as hippo and crocs, boat trips also afford a chance to approach waterbirds closely enough to photograph them. Excellent boat trips are run in Uganda along the Kazinga Channel in Queen Elizabeth NP and the Victoria Nile in Murchison Falls NP; and in Tanzania on the Rufiji River in Selous GR and the Wami River in Saadani GR. Do-it-yourself buffs can hire canoes at Lake Mburo NP and on crater lakes in the Maramagambo Forest (QENP) – this is a good way to get into vegetation at the water's edge, where you might winkle out an African finfoot or get close to otters (watch out for hippos).

Mountain bikes

Fit people looking for a change of locomotion can try mountain biking in the Sekenani Valley outside Masai Mara NR or at Hell's Gate NP (both in Kenya). ■

PHOTOGRAPHY

WILDLIFE photography is a highly specialised field but the quality of today's equipment – even modestly priced, nonprofessional gear – means that excellent results are possible for anyone. In many destinations, wild animals are so used to visitors that exceptional chances for photography often arise.

What to take

If you're buying your first camera the selection is mind boggling. Canon or Nikon are the choice of most professional wildlife photographers, largely because they offer formidable lens quality, but all established brands are good. Cameras essentially all do the same thing, though with varying degrees of complexity and technological assistance. Most modern cameras have a full range of automatic functions, but you should select a model that also allows full manual operation. Once you've mastered the basic techniques, you'll probably find it limiting if you're unable to begin experimenting with your photography.

It's tempting to snap away as soon as you see an animal, but with antelopes this often results in a rear-end shot as they walk away. Switch off the engine and wait awhile for best results.

More important than camera bodies are the lenses you attach to them – and for wildlife, think long. A 300mm lens is a good starting point, though bird portraits require something longer. Lenses of 400 to 600mm focal length are probably out of the price range of most people, though 'slower' lenses (lenses with a relatively small maximum aperture), such as a 400mm f5.6, are reasonably priced and very useful when a 300mm doesn't quite reach. Dedicated (ie, 'brand name') lenses have superb optical quality and are more expensive than generic brands (eg, Tamron), but unless you're a pro you'll probably notice only a slight difference.

Zooms are generally not as sharp as fixed focal length lenses (ie, lenses which do not zoom), but the difference is only important if you're thinking about publishing your pictures. Many brands offer zooms around the 100 to 300mm range which, when paired with a short zoom like a 35 to 70mm, covers most situations for recreational photographers. Recently released 'superzooms' provide a comprehensive range of focal lengths in one lens. Canon's 35 to 350mm and 100 to 400mm, and Sigma's 170 to 500mm are worth investigating. None is cheap, but they yield publication-quality results in one versatile package.

Open-top safari vehicles come in many styles and allow all-round viewing for photographers.

Hundreds of accessories can be used to enhance shots, but one that's vital is the tripod. Many shots are spoiled by 'camera shake', particularly when using longer lenses. Tripods can be cumbersome to include in your luggage, but sturdy, compact models such as Manfrotto's 190 ('Bogen' brand in the USA) fit into a sausage bag. Collapsible monopods are light and easy to carry, but do not offer nearly as much stability as a tripod.

Most wildlife photographers in East Africa are restricted to a vehicle, where it is impractical to use a tripod. An excellent alternative for vehicle-based photography is a beanbag. A small cloth bag with a zip opening takes up almost no room and can be filled with dried rice when you arrive at your destination.

Simply roll down your window, lay the beanbag on the top of the door and rest the camera lens on it (or, if you're a passenger in a minivan, lay the beanbag on the roof if it opens).

In the field

Before you go anywhere, know how your camera works. Visit the local zoo or park and shoot a few rolls to familiarise yourself with its controls and functions. Many good wildlife moments happen unexpectedly and pass in seconds; you'll miss them if you're still fiddling with dials and settings. For the same reason, when in reserves, leave your camera turned on (and pack plenty of batteries).

Most cameras have shutter- and aperture-priority functions. In shutter-priority mode, you set the shutter speed and the camera selects the appropriate aperture for a correct exposure; the reverse applies for aperture-priority. These two functions are probably the most valuable for wildlife photographers – but you need to know when to use them. Shutter priority is excellent for shooting action. If you want to freeze motion, select the highest shutter speed permitted with the available light and the camera takes care of the aperture setting. On the other hand, if you're trying to emphasise depth of field in your shot, opt for aperture priority. Large apertures (low 'f-stops') reduce the depth of field – a useful trick for enhancing a portrait shot by throwing the background out of focus. However, if you're shooting a scene where you want everything in focus, such as a thousands of wildebeests on a vast plain, select a small aperture (high f-stops).

Leopards pose a challenge to find, let alone photograph!

Composition is a major challenge with wildlife as you can't move your subject around; try different vantage points and experiment with a variety of focal lengths. If you're too far away to take a good portrait, try to show the animal in its habitat. A 400mm lens might give you a close up of a seabird's face while a 28mm will show the entire colony receding into the background – all from the same position. Try to tell a story about the animal or illustrate some behaviour. Jackal pups transfixed by grazing gazelles might be too shy for a decent close-up, but could make a lovely subject if you include the antelopes and surroundings.

Unless you're packing a very powerful flash, wildlife photography relies on the vagaries of natural light and the best shots are invariably those taken in the 'golden hour' – just after dawn and just before dusk. Where possible, get into position early, whether it's a bird hide, waterhole or scenic lookout you noted the day before. Don't always assume front-on light is the best. Side lighting can give more depth to a subject; back lighting, particularly when the sun is near the horizon, can be very atmospheric.

Above all else, when photographing wildlife, be patient. You never know what will appear at the waterhole next or when a snoozing predator will suddenly spot a chance for a kill. You cannot always anticipate when an opportunity will arise, but if you're willing to wait you'll almost certainly see something worth shooting. ∎

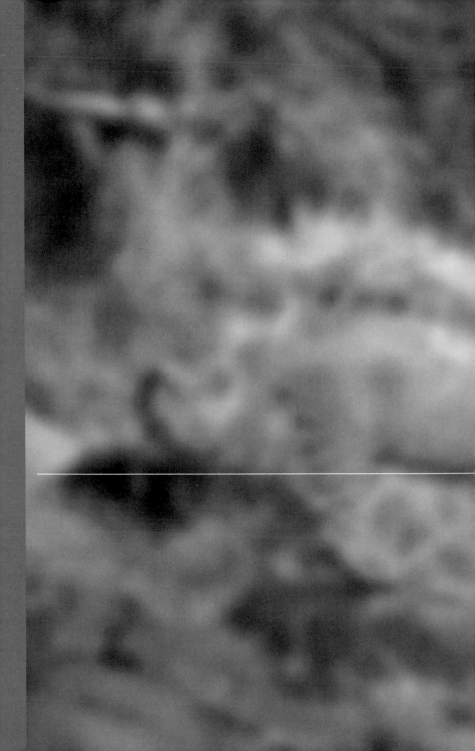

HABITATS

*The East African environment
and its wildlife*

SAVANNAS

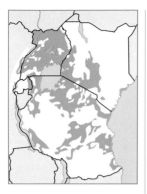

Colonies of biting ants that live in the galls on whistling thorn trees provide an extra deterrent to browsers. Wind blowing across holes in the galls causes the thorn trees to whistle.

THE popular image (thanks to documentaries, films and books) of East Africa as a land of rolling plains of grass dotted with acacias, perhaps with a dramatic montane backdrop, pretty closely matches the reality. This habitat, generally called savanna, covers vast areas and straddles all the countries of the region, reaching its greatest extent in Kenya and Uganda, but merely poking into the Democratic Republic of the Congo (DRC – formerly Zaïre) via river valleys across the Albertine Rift Valley.

Under a multitude of definitions and conditions, East African savanna is a dynamic ecosystem that supports more herds of large mammals and their predators than any other habitat on earth. Broadly speaking, savanna develops where annual rainfall falls in one long wet season followed by a long dry. Usually it is characterised by an understorey of grassland and taller vegetation such as various species of *Acacia* (pictured, inset) many of which have distinctive shapes and can withstand the grass-fires that sweep through during dry seasons. Think of it as a vast mosaic: over long periods of time, savanna advances into adjoining woodlands destroyed by fire and elephants; but if fire and elephant damage become too concentrated savanna may be reclaimed by grassland.

Sprouting dung piles

The relationship between some savanna plants and animals is subtle and complex, and reflects cyclical patterns that may take decades to complete. For example, the seed pods of the flat-topped umbrella acacia, *Acacia tortillis*, are shed in the dry season and covered in nutritious pulp that attracts browsers, such as antelopes and giraffes, when other food is scarce. Animals that eat the pods transport and distribute the seeds in their dung, and germination and resistance to insect predation appears to be higher in seeds that have passed through an animal's digestive tract than those that haven't.

The mutual advantage extends still further: since the seeds are typically dropped at rest sites the saplings germinate away from competing plants, and the grown trees provide shade for

Opposite page: East Africa's vast savannas quickly take on a green flush after the long rains.

Opposite inset: The famous flame tree grows wild in Kenya's savannas.

large animals. Similarly, the spread of *Borassus* palms has been attributed to elephants, which relish the palm nuts and spread them in their droppings. The palms germinate more readily in elephant dung than otherwise and *Borassus* dominates some patches of savanna, in turn making nest sites and lookouts for various birds.

In drier areas candelabra euphorbias may dominate, and in coastal Kenya and Tanzania baobabs are a distinctive savanna tree that attract the attention of birds such as hornbills.

Lurking among the boulders

Rocky outcrops that rise, sometimes dramatically, from the plains as jumbled piles of massive boulders provide islands of shelter in the savanna. Known as kopjes, the natural crevices and overhangs are dens for predators such as leopards and spotted hyenas; pythons hunt between the boulders; and small carnivores such as mongooses and genets chivy out prey – a favourite of which are hyraxes, the quintessential kopje dwellers. Take care when walking around kopjes: they are a favourite shade spot for lions.

Thickets are dense growths of woody shrubs, often starting on an old termite mound, that provide refuge from floods and grassfires. Once the first plants have taken hold, seeds deposited in the droppings of birds and bats germinate in the mound and add to the growth: within a few years a miniature forest develops. Birds nest in the dense foliage, small animals live in the undergrowth, and bushbucks and buffaloes in particular like to shelter in thickets. Dense bush dominated by *Commiphora*, a favourite haunt of kudus, rhinos and elephants, is also called thicket: the boundary between savanna and the semiarid zone is indistinct over huge areas of Kenya and Tanzania.

Making the most of it

Much of your time in savanna will be spent in a vehicle, but you'll still get a feel for this important habitat and start to ap-

Kopjes are rocky outcrops that dot the savanna, providing shelter for predators – such as lions and leopards – and small animals such as hyraxes.

The march out of the forest

Although the golden age of elephants has passed, the African elephant remains the largest and arguably most charismatic animal on the savanna. But it is probably only a recent arrival, descended from much smaller forest elephants that live in the Zaïre River basin. Several species of elephant once roamed the plains, and their extinction at the hands of humans opened up a niche into which forest elephants expanded, perhaps as recently as 10,000 to 20,000 years ago. Apart from their small size, forest elephants differs from African elephants in having straight and sometimes greatly reduced or vestigial tusks. Despite their differences, the forest elephant is generally considered to be a subspecies of the African elephant, and interbreeding occurs among some populations. That African elephants evolved from forest elephants and not vice versa is supported by the formers' large daily water requirement, both for drinking and cooling off; and because they seek moist refuges during dry seasons, in keeping with their forest kin. Given enough time and a corresponding freedom from disturbance, both elephants will probably become separate species.

Different tree species dominate the savanna according to rainfall and aspect, but the genus Acacia is usually well represented.

preciate its fragrant smell. The great and famous parks of the region – Serengeti, Masai Mara, Amboseli, Tsavo and Queen Elizabeth – all have huge areas of savanna in which you are going to see large animals. There's no real knack to it, other than putting in the hours and getting in the field early.

Look down from a ridge with the vehicle as a vantage point to spot large mammals; elephants, giraffes and buffaloes stand out because of their sheer size, although even they can get lost at a distance. Watercourses are marked by lines of tall trees and denser bush – these are productive areas to seek animals during the dry season and during the heat of the day; leopards in particular like this habitat. Birds are abundant; expect several species of raptor at any time and a constant parade of weavers, hornbills, barbets, woodpeckers and others throughout the day. Finding some animals takes patience, but watch for the signs – vultures volplaning down to a kill, birds mobbing a mongoose or antelopes fleeing a predator. ∎

GRASSLANDS AND WOODLANDS

Grassland
Woodland

The black-bellied bustard (this is a male) is one of dozens of bird species, ranging in size from ostriches to cisticolas, that are specialised grassland inhabitants.

MOST of East Africa's woodlands grow in Tanzania, although patches grow elsewhere, such as north-western Uganda – the only location where the giant eland occurred in East Africa (whether it still does is a moot point). In a long succession from east to west, woodlands probably represent a transition from savanna to the rainforest of the Zaïre River basin, and thrive where 800 to 1200mm of rainfall is concentrated between November and May.

Normally woodland has a more or less continuous canopy, but during dry months the combined effects of fires (lit naturally or by nomadic hunters and honey gatherers) and elephant activity break the woodlands into a 'mosaic' of vegetation at different stages of growth. Grazing animals often concentrate around areas of regrowth after these periodic disturbances, but where too much interference occurs woodlands can eventually revert to grasslands – for example, the once extensive forests of Murchison Falls NP have been virtually destroyed by elephants. Where fire-resistant trees such as *Brachystegia* dominate, such associations are known as brachystegia woodlands or miombo. Few mammals are specialised to life in woodlands – the mosaics are the key to miombo diversity, allowing a variety of animals to graze on adjoining grasslands and take cover among the trees. In certain places grassy areas known as mbugas form, especially on seasonally flooded black cotton soil, that make important dry season pasture for woodland animals.

Fingers of woodland

Miombo particularly favours the proliferation of tsetse flies – the biting flies that can spread sleeping sickness – and therefore discourages the activities of humans and livestock. Of the larger animals, only plains zebras are abundant in miombo, although hartebeests and sable antelopes also have their strongholds here. Smaller inhabitants include many that feed on insects, such as aardvarks, ground pangolins and elephant shrews; miombo is excellent for birds, and one small mammal that is

Opposite page: The annual migration of the great grazing herds across the Serengeti Plains has shaped the grasslands through generations of grazing, trampling and fertilisation.

Opposite inset: Black-eyed Susans are native to East Africa's grasslands.

particularly successful is the ratel, or honey badger, that thrives in the presence of the many beehives.

Fingers of woodland extend into adjoining savanna where a tall, spreading acacia, the yellow fever tree (inset, page 58), grows along permanent and semipermanent waterways. Again, this is not a habitat with specialised inhabitants, but leopards in particular like to lounge on the sometimes huge boughs of fever trees, and a dense understorey can shelter antelopes and ground birds such as francolins; primates such as vervet monkeys and black-and-white colobus; and birds such as woodpeckers, barbets and wood-hoopoes.

It's a jungle down there

Large tracts of Serengeti NP and Masai Mara NR are covered in grass, at times virtually empty – just endless ripples in the wind – but at others crowded with herbivores. Although they look simple, grasslands are complex communities that vary dramatically according to rainfall, aspect, drainage and soil chemistry; and the further effects of fire, elephants and other grazers. Look at a head of grass – the shape of the seeds and flowers is distinct for each species, forming a canopy over which you and other large animals tower – a bonus for the observer, of course, because the wide vistas make for easy watching.

Low down lives a host of insects and ground nesting birds, such as larks, pipits and bustards, and a few reptiles. But out there in the fields most larger animals are vulnerable, and camouflage or mobility are the secrets to success. Small mammals, like mongooses and bat-eared foxes, shelter in thickets or termite mounds, or dig their own burrows; apart from the prospect of death from above, there is the very real danger of being trampled by millions of hooves. Which of course are what most people come to see in the grasslands – the great herds of herbivores and the well-organised gangs of predators that hunt them.

An endless cycle

Cycles of wet and dry, flood and fire dictate which grasses dominate and consequently which animals graze. Each species

Candelabra euphorbias are succulents that can grow to a great size. Euphorbias growing in abandoned termite mounds can create islands of dense vegetation in a sea of grass.

A fine balance

During the rains in Tanzania's Rukwa Valley, topis move to higher ground and a tall marsh grass growing in the valley floor, *Vossia*, sprouts as high as 3m. At the end of the rains the heavyweight grazers – elephants, hippos and buffaloes – feed on *Vossia*; their combined presence tramples, chews and recycles the grass until the floodwaters recede and they move on to other pastures. After their departure the flattened grass shoots anew, attracting zebras, elands, hartebeests and topis. Grazing by these more selective herbivores keeps the grass short and a flush of green at the end of the dry season coincides with the birth of topi calves. But when the floods are exceptional the cycle is thrown out of balance: elephants, hippos and buffaloes disperse and don't smash down the *Vossia*. The topis descend from the hills as usual, but must feed in swampy ground on unsuitable pasture; many die under these conditions until they learn to break down the *Vossia* themselves.

has a different preference for type and age of grass, and the
actions of each shape the grasslands to the benefit or detriment
of others. Thus, zebras crop the coarsest species, seed heads
and all, followed by the more selective wildebeests; topis, hartebeests and gazelles are even more specialised. The huge herds
recycle nutrients in a vast cycle of mowing, trampling and fer-
tilising, paving the way for the next wave and carried on over
vast areas.

Least selective are the elephants, whose actions help shape
grasslands by destroying woody growth and even tree cover;
fires become more frequent as the habitat reverts to grassland,
further encouraging grass and grazers. Once the grazing herds
moved over empty plains in a great cycle that took centuries or
even millennia to complete, and allowed grasslands to recover
in their wake. But fires are also encouraged by modern pastoralists, who graze their livestock in competition with native
herbivores. Ironically, because they overstock the land their
herds of cattle and goats kill off the grasslands and encourage
woody growth again – only now there are far fewer elephants
left to repeat the cycle. In northern Uganda the destruction of
elephants 100 years ago has favoured the spread of lesser
kudus into the modified woody growth. ■

*Walk with care in grasslands:
prides of lions use tall grass as
cover when stalking the many
species of grazer on the plains.*

RAINFORESTS

Uganda's Bwindi Impenetrable NP protects one of the few remaining areas in East Africa where lowland rainforest is contiguous with highland rainforest.

Opposite page: The slopes of high mountains, such as Mt Kenya, can receive enough rainfall to sustain dense montane forest. Animal and plant communities in such forests can differ dramatically from those of lowland rainforests.

Opposite inset: The Gloriosa lily, native to Kenya's Kakamega Forest, grows at the rainforest edge.

INCREDIBLY rich in biodiversity and much studied yet little understood, rainforests support more animal species than any other terrestrial ecosystem. In past ages, vast rainforests formed an evolutionary hothouse in the Zaire River basin and stretched east across the rift valleys, before retracting with climatic change to leave far-flung relicts such as Kenya's Kakamega Forest. Today the largest tracts creep over the Albertine Rift Valley into western Uganda, particularly at Bwindi Impenetrable NP and the Semliki Forest, and into Rwanda's RF de Nyungwe. Some of these forests are still extensive enough to support large mammals such as gorillas, chimpanzees, okapis and forest elephants; and most are heaving with hundreds of bird species, and uncountable insects and other small animals.

Light and dark, silence and chaos

To enter the rainforest is to walk into a luxuriant world of growth and decay, the humid air full of the rich smell of dampness. Deep leaf litter makes a spongy carpet through which grow 3m-wide buttressed trees with trunks that barrel straight up to the canopy 30m or more above your head. Massive interlocked branches sprout bracket fungi, deep cushions of moss, and miniature gardens of epiphytic orchids and ferns. Shafts of light piercing the gloom form pools on the ground that explode in a cloud of butterflies as you approach. At times bustling with activity, at others silent, the rule in rainforests is much variety but small numbers. Thus, mammals (apart from primates) are usually few and far between. Birds tend to move in feeding parties sometimes comprised of two dozen or more species, but only one or two individuals of each kind. But when you hit a wave all hell breaks loose in the scramble to see the hornbills, barbets, flycatchers, woodpeckers, warblers and cuckoos moving through; squirrels also may join the fray, and monkeys ahead of the pack disturb insects that are snapped up by the bird party.

From the wildlife-watcher's point of view, the most productive part of the forest is where it adjoins another habitat, such as savanna or cultivated land. Here sunlight reaches all levels, allowing a great diversity of plants to grow, often in a tangle of competing creepers, herbage and saplings; monkeys sun themselves, and birds and butterflies are at their most active, feeding on insects, fruits and blossom. It's also worthwhile to stake out a fruiting fig tree and watch for the birds and primates that visit.

Jungle gym

Rainforests present a three-dimensional habitat for animals and observers alike. The forest floor, with its cover of fallen vegetation, is a thoroughfare for large mammals. Insects, snails (such as the 15cm African giant snail shown on page 62) and spiders thrive in the rich layer of rotting vegetation, and in turn become prey for amphibians, reptiles, birds and mammals. Trunks, branches and hollows are utilised as shelter, nesting and resting places, and as highways to the bounty of fruits and blossom in the canopy. Birds, bats and primates in turn disperse seeds around the forest in their droppings. Trees fruiting at different times ensure a year-round supply, and vegetation dislodged from the canopy helps sustain ground-dwelling animals such as antelopes, pigs and rodents. Birds, anomalures (flying squirrels) and bats take advantage of the comparatively open forest interior to move about.

Fungi – including mushrooms and toadstools – flourish in rainforests, and play a vital role in breaking down rotting plant matter and returning it to the soil.

Lowland rainforest is richer in mammal and bird species than any other. It is thought to be ancient and has acted as a refuge for early rainforest species as surrounding habitats became increasingly arid. Evidence for this is provided by the presence of birds and mammals in the Zaïre River basin whose only close relatives live in the rainforests of South-East Asia (Africa and South-East Asia were connected millions of years ago): the water chevrotain, the sole representative of these small deerlike animals in Africa; and birds such as the African green broadbill, Congo peafowl and Congo bay-owl. Highland rainforest grows on mountain ranges as high as 2700m where rainfall is sufficient, but

---

Ruthless rainforest predators

The most important predators in the rainforest are common, abundant and put the big cats to shame. They measure less than an inch long, but driver ants form predatory swarms that march through the forest, sweeping all before them – catching and killing anything too slow to escape, and sending large animals packing. Studies in Uganda's Kibale Forest NP have shown the combined weight of driver ants in a given area of rainforest is more than that of all the large predators combined in an equal area of Serengeti savanna – and devours more weight of prey. Several members of the thrush family – akalats, ant-thrushes and alethes (collectively known as 'ant-birds') – follow ant columns and snap up insects disturbed by their progress. So specialised is this relationship that there is even a pecking order – in Rwanda's RF de Nyungwe red-throated alethes dominate, chasing off white-starred robins and equatorial akalats when they try to join the feast. At least one alethe species is known to breed only if a driver ant colony lives in its territory.

lowland rainforest usually supports different species – birds in particular show remarkable variation between the two habitats. In only a few surviving patches, such as Bwindi Impenetrable NP, have lowland and highland forest survived contiguously (ie, growing adjacently and running together).

Rustling through the leaves

Watching wildlife in rainforest can be frustratingly difficult. Undergrowth hides skulking birds; monkeys crash through the trees then give only tantalising glimpses as they silently scamper away; and looking up into the canopy can be neck-breaking work to see something that may be only a silhouette high up in the leafy ceiling. Vegetation can rustle only a couple of metres from your nose yet an animal can remain completely hidden, or worse, cross the path behind you and start to rustle about on the other side. A day in productive rainforest is by turns tiring – be prepared to sweat – challenging and exhilarating. But be warned: rainforests can be addictive – few environments on earth house such bizarre, colourful and spectacular creatures. ■

The edge – known as the ecotone – is the most productive part of the rainforest (or indeed of any habitat) for seeing wildlife: sunlight allows the proliferation of flowering plants, which attract birds and butterflies, and monkeys sun themselves in glades.

THE HIGH MOUNTAINS

Two of East Africa's extinct volcanoes – Mts Kilimanjaro and Meru – are so vast they poke through the clouds.

THE isolated peaks of massive extinct volcanoes – Mts Kilimanjaro, Kenya and Elgon – and high ranges such as the Rwenzoris (pictured below), represent 'islands' of distinctive vegetation rising from the surrounding savanna. Forest covers the lower slopes (if it hasn't been cleared for agriculture) and above it vegetation grows in distinctive bands dominated by one or more species according to altitude and aspect. Broadly speaking, dense forests grow as high as 2700m; thickets of bamboo straddle the slopes between 2500 and 3000m; an ericaceous zone – so-called because it is dominated by giant heathers of the genus *Erica* – grows above the bamboo usually between 3000 and 3500m (rosewood forests straddle the zone between the giant heather and bamboo where both occur); and above 3500m vast swathes of tussock grass, dotted by giant herbs, stretch to the snowline.

Land of the giants

The high peaks are a barren world of rocky crags, snow and permanent ice where few animals venture and none survive permanently. Swifts and large raptors (particularly lammergeiers) patrol the greatest heights, the former ranging far for insects, the latter for carcasses of animals that have perished.

Swathes of soft, blonde and waist-high tussock grassland, also known as alpine moorland, reach down from the snowline to the giant heather zone, punctuated by the so-called 'big game' plants – giant examples of common herbs like groundsels and lobelias. This unique Afro-alpine vegetation grows at its densest above 4000m; various species of giant lobelia and groundsel grow on all the great peaks, some towering 4m high with tall flowering spikes that attract sunbirds.

The only permanent residents in alpine moorland are birds and hyraxes, and rodents that burrow to escape the cold, although many large mammals ascend the great peaks during dry seasons. Thus elephants, plains zebras, common elands, duikers

Opposite page: Few plants and no animals live permanently on Mt Kenya's rocky crags, but even at these heights swifts and lammergeiers are seen occasionally.

Opposite inset: Giant lobelias – closely related to the common herb – grow in the alpine moorlands of all East Africa's great mountains.

and hartebeests might all be encountered along walking trails, and predators such as lions, spotted hyenas and leopards are seen occasionally. Verreaux's eagles feed on the abundant rock hyraxes and mountain buzzards hunt rodents; and several bird species are found only at these altitudes – such as scarlet-tufted malachite sunbirds, alpine chats and Jackson's francolins.

Vertical bogs and mossy parklands
The ericaceous, or giant heather zone, is dominated by *Erica* heaths that in wet conditions, such as those in the Rwenzoris, can grow as high as 15m. Other distinctive trees scattered among the giant heathers can include scattered hagenias, a giant form of St John's wort (*Hypericum*) and lobelias, with an often sodden understorey of deep moss, tall spikes of orchids and sticky bogs. Where they occur in sufficient numbers, duikers and tree hyraxes attract leopards and African golden cats; and birds include sunbirds (some endemic to these heights), seedeaters and wood-hoopoes.

Interlacing the lower edge of the giant heather zone are more giants – rosewood trees (*Hagenia*) – their branches thick with moss cushions and hanging with epiphytes; and St John's wort, a herb in northern climates that attains tree size on East African mountainsides. The most extensive stands of *Hagenia* on the Virunga volcanoes grow as an open, parklike zone rich in wildflowers, ground herbs and epiphytes, and are particularly favoured by mountain gorillas. Hollows in the gnarled trunks shelter small mammals such as genets and rodents; and birds are also abundant in the foliage.

From giant grass to giant trees
The bamboo zone can be a pure stand of these woody grasses, or mixed with *Hagenia*, *Hypericum* and the ground-covering *Mimulopsis*. On drier aspects bamboo may grow only in sheltered locations such as in valleys and ravines. Bamboo and *Mimulopsis* flower and die en masse at intervals; the latter is toxic at some stages of growth and causes the deaths of animals such as giant forest hogs and bongos that eat it at these times. Bamboo shoots are a favourite food of primates, such as gorillas and golden monkeys (a subspecies of blue monkey), and of

Swathes of blonde tussock grass carpet the great peaks above the ericaceous zone. Alpine chats, scarlet-tufted malachite sunbirds and rodents are commonly encountered in this zone.

Rules for conquering the giant peaks
The great peaks are comparatively recent in origin and few mammals have yet evolved to specifically exploit the niches they have presented. For example, the hyraxes of alpine outcrops are only races of widespread and adaptable lowland species that have conquered the heights. But the process of speciation (the evolution of new species) seems to be taking place. Under certain conditions mammals conform to biological 'rules' that formulate the characteristics enabling their survival. Thus, Bergman's Rule states that in cold environments an animal's body size becomes larger, and its fur longer and thicker: the hyraxes on Mt Kenya and the Rwenzoris are indeed heavier, larger and furrier than their lowland counterparts. Another rule, Allen's, states that short limbs, ears and tail are helpful traits in low temperatures: again, alpine-dwelling hyraxes fit the bill perfectly.

elephants. Buffaloes and elephants make trails through the thickets (their droppings litter the ground) which are easily navigable by people, although there's always the prospect of a chance encounter along the way. Numerous birds live in this zone, particularly warblers and various skulking members of the thrush family. The change from forest to bamboo occurs quite dramatically in some places (such as along the Naro Moru Route on Mt Kenya, where a rustling wall of cane suddenly frames the road).

Forest grows thickly below the bamboo; the bark of tall olives and junipers is encrusted with lichen and their branches are festooned with beard moss. Biologically, this is the most diverse part of the montane habitat, although there are few specialists and many of the inhabitants are also found in lowland forests. For example, elephants and buffaloes, numerous antelopes (particularly dwarf antelopes and duikers) and even black rhinos ascend the forests of the great mountains. Birdlife is profuse and again many species are found only in these high forests. And while bamboo usually marks the upper limit of primates, the forests lower down can support several species, of which black-and-white colobus and blue monkeys are conspicuous. ■

Although Mts Kilimanjaro, Kenya and Elgon were all once mighty volcanoes, Oldoinyo Lengai (part of Tanzania's Crater Highlands) is one of the few remaining active volcanoes in East Africa.

THE SEMIARID ZONE

Bat-eared foxes are most common in semiarid country, where their main prey, termites and other insects, is easily excavated from sandy soil.

A T the northern extremity of East Africa rainfall declines considerably and occurs irregularly. The driest and harshest areas – such as the Chalbi Desert of northern Kenya – support little plant life and a low diversity of animals, although the popular conception of drifting sand dunes doesn't apply until still further north in the Sahara. Kenya's deserts are mainly stony – the remains of ancient lava flows through which grows sparse vegetation able to withstand high daytime temperatures and scouring winds.

Among the few permanent animal inhabitants, those that burrow or have low moisture requirements are the most successful – rodents, lizards and scorpions are often abundant. Dry, sandy river beds cut across the landscape, their course marked by denser stands of thorny vegetation which support browsers such as gerenuks, kudus and dik-diks. When rain does fall, these dry watercourses fill quickly and plant life puts on a spurt of growth before the precious water drains away or evaporates. Oryxes (pictured, inset), Grant's gazelles and Grevy's zebras move in from adjoining habitat to graze on the sudden bounty; and birds such as larks, sandgrouse and bustards eke out a living, the strongest flying species following showers to arrive in the wake of seeding plants.

Braving the heat

Adjoining true desert is a much larger area of semidesert, where rainfall is slightly higher (and more regular) and the vegetation thicker. Kenya's Tsavo NP, and Samburu and Buffalo Springs NRs, protect fine examples of semiarid habitat. Between 250mm and 500mm of rain falls annually in semidesert, usually from April to May and in November, but up to six months may pass without any at all. Shrubs, rather than trees, dominate, with an understorey of hardy grasses.

As in true desert, those animals least dependent on water most successfully exploit the semiarid zone. Insects – grasshoppers, termites and beetles – are the staple of small mammals, such as hedgehogs, mongooses and elephant shrews. Larger mammals include herbivores that can live independently of

Opposite page: Succulent plants, such as aloes and sanseverias, store moisture in their fleshy stems that enables them to survive prolonged dry conditions. When the rains arrive, desert roses (shown here) and many other species burst into flower.

Opposite inset: Scorpions are abundant in dry country, where they obtain all their moisture requirements from their prey.

permanent drinking water, such as gerenuks and oryxes, and elephants, zebras and black rhinos move through when conditions are suitable. A nocturnal lifestyle is one strategy commonly employed to escape daytime temperatures; to this end many animals, such as the highly specialised bat-eared fox, spend the day below ground, emerging to feed after dark.

Conserving every drop

The semiarid zone's long dry season brings on a profound change in the landscape as many plants shed their leaves to conserve moisture. Some herbivores, such as elephants and black rhinos, can survive for a time on the many succulents (plants with fleshy, moisture-holding leaves, such as *Sanseveria* and *Aloe*) that grow in this climate. With the green flush of the wet season, browsers and grazers disperse, but during the dry season large, water-dependent mammals tend to congregate near watercourses. Thus buffaloes and zebras are common near rivers and springs, and giraffes too are more likely to be seen browsing on permanent greenery.

Small antelopes such as dik-diks are found among woody shrubs at any time of year, obtaining their moisture from dew on their fodder, and unstriped ground squirrels are one of the few small mammals that are commonly abroad during the day. Insects and their predators are abundant, and many species of bird are able to exploit this environment in times of plenty before moving on. Large predators, including bat-eared foxes, jackals and hyenas, and even lions and cheetahs, are able to obtain most of their moisture requirements from their prey. Birds of prey likewise live independently of water in the semiarid zone, and it is not unusual to see several species of raptor in the sky at once.

Waterhole processions

Few animals go completely without water if it is available, and waterholes become the focus of much activity as the dry season wears on in the semiarid zone. Some animals make a visit to the

Grevy's zebras are not dependent on permanent water, but ironically are threatened by the creation of artificial waterholes, which allow water-dependent cattle to colonise the zebras' former domain.

Naked desert rats

Several rodent species live almost permanently underground and one in particular, the naked mole-rat, is a remarkable mammal by any standards. This almost hairless burrower, also known as the 'sand-puppy', lives in colonies of up to 75 individuals that almost never visit the surface, and obtain all their nutritional and water requirements from underground bulbs, stems and tubers. Like social insects such as bees and termites, they have a distinct social order that includes a dominant female (the largest), 'drones' and workers. Only the dominant 'queen' breeds, mating with the few drones, who are usually her own sons or brothers. The rest of the colony are nonbreeding workers or soldiers (their reproduction suppressed by pheromones produced by the queen): the soldier caste protects the warren; the workers dig tunnels, forage, carry food to the others and tend the young. Piles of earth on sandy tracks show where naked mole-rats have been digging – sometimes workers can be seen in the early morning at their tunnel entrances, especially along tracks in Samburu NR and Meru NP.

waterhole a regular part of their daily routine and there's even a drinking hierarchy (if you have the time it's worth staking out a waterhole for a few hours to watch the procession). Mixed herds aggregate, zebras rubbing shoulders with antelopes and giving way to elephants and rhinos – predators take advantage of the situation to lay ambushes. Birds flock to waterholes, especially in the early morning, when a constant turnover includes sandgrouse lining up to drink, pigeons and doves, and weavers and other finches.

As the waterholes in an area dry up completely, most of the animals must move on. Some can linger a little longer: Grevy's zebras dig in dry stream beds for water and defend the resulting puddle; elephants, which suck up water with their trunks before squirting it into their mouths, can extract water from deep holes beyond the reach of other animals; and baboons also dig for water. But eventually the struggle of moving between feeding grounds and the increasingly scattered remaining water becomes too much, and mammals, especially those that must drink daily, such as elephants and buffaloes, move out of the semiarid areas until the next rains bring them back. Birds too may be fewer and further between, but their mobility enables many to remain and exploit the desiccated country in all but the driest of years – strong-flying nomads such as sandgrouse and bustards are among the most successful. ∎

Ancient lava flows created vast fields of rock near Lake Turkana, Kenya. Little grows in this habitat, yet small animals such as ground squirrels are common.

LAKES, RIVERS & SWAMPS

WATER appears in many forms and quantities across the region, from the great lakes to dew trapped in alpine plants, savanna waterholes to solid masses frozen in glaciers. Rain in the high watersheds of the Albertine Rift Valley feeds the mighty Nile River that flows 2000km to the Mediterranean Sea. And the greatest lake of all, Lake Victoria, creates its own weather patterns and is a major source for evaporation – which together water the rainforests of Uganda.

Water sustains all life: hundreds of species of fish and invertebrate equipped with gills draw oxygen from water and live all or part of their lives in it; it's a reservoir of prey for many air-breathing animals that wade, swim, fly or perch; a refuge for creatures that also spend much time on land; and essential for the daily drinking or bathing routine for many large animals.

Life support systems

Shallow water margins are packed with life, and water is a great medium for witnessing first-hand the often complex biological web. Sunlight filtering through the shallows promotes the growth of algae which is fed upon by huge numbers of tiny crustaceans and single-celled animals. These support fish (which exploded in diversity in Lakes Victoria and Tanganyika), tadpoles and the larvae of many insects, all of which in turn become prey for larger aquatic animals and land-based predators, such as otters and birds. Larger fish living in deeper water feed crocodiles, pelicans and African fish eagles; and the water itself supports and cools the largest aquatic animal of all, the hippo, between its nocturnal forays into adjoining grasslands.

A host of birds – herons, storks, ibises, spoonbills and egrets – feed in ways sufficiently different to allow mixed aggregations to feed side by side; ducks likewise feed by different strategies and great flotillas build up where pickings are rich. Floating mats

Dragonflies are the largest and fastest insect predators in wetlands. Even their larvae are voracious predators: they develop underwater and lie in wait for other small animals.

Opposite page: The hippopotamus is Africa's largest aquatic mammal, yet it can live in surprisingly small waterholes as long as there is ample grazing nearby.

Opposite inset: African jacanas spend almost their entire lives on floating vegetation: even their eggs are laid on lily pads.

of water lilies and Nile cabbage shelter aquatic invertebrates and fish, and provide feeding grounds and nesting platforms for jacanas and long-toed plovers. The margins of Lakes Baringo and Naivasha are particularly rich in floating vegetation, and partially floating islands on the Victoria Nile in Murchison Falls NP support crocodiles, waterbucks, hippos and many birds.

The water's edge

A succession of vegetation between the floating mats and the shore can, over time, alter the course of rivers by choking and silting up bends that eventually are claimed by land plants and animals. Where water levels remain more or less constant, dense ranks of tall bulrushes, reeds and grasslike sedges mark the transition to dry land. Snakes hunt amphibians and marsh mongooses hunt both; and bitterns, crakes and rails live almost exclusively in these grass forests. The tall stems are too slender for most predators to ascend, and many small birds build their nests, and sometimes thousands roost, in the security of reed beds. Where running water is slowed and trapped by vegetation, otters hunt for fish, crabs and shellfish; waterbucks graze, often belly-deep in water; and the semiaquatic sitatunga feeds, walking over submerged vegetation on splayed hooves.

The great papyrus stands of Lake Victoria, PN de l'Akagera and Murchison Falls NP choke swamps and support a number of birds specialised to this habitat, such as papyrus gonoleks, papyrus canaries and shoebills. Drowned trees and large, overhanging branches along rivers and lakeshores make secure nest platforms for colonies of herons, pelicans and cormorants, which sometimes form mixed colonies; sandbanks are basking sites for hippos and crocs, and roosts for gulls, terns and ducks; kingfishers and bee-eaters dig nest tunnels in steep banks; and de Brazza's monkeys live in the protection of flooded forests. Where banks are not too steep, a procession of animals large and small visits the water's margin to drink, wallow or bathe. At this point all but the largest are at their most vulnerable, and even lions and leopards occasionally fall prey to large crocs.

Floating mats of vegetation, such as waterlilies, water hyacinth and Nile cabbage (shown here), provide shade for animals beneath the surface and a platform for birds on top of the water.

Lifeline for a living fossil

When waterways contract during dry seasons, their inhabitants must either adapt to a lack of water or move to another source. Animals such as fish are usually forced to complete their life cycles before drought strikes, but the lungfish overcomes the problem with a remarkable adaptation. All fish have gills with which they filter oxygen from water, but adult lungfish also have a lung and can rise to the surface to gulp air in stagnant, oxygen-starved swamps. Best described as living fossils, lungfish are found only in Africa, South America and Australia, showing the ancient connection of these three continents where lungfish evolved 340 to 400 million years ago. As waterholes dry out, the lungfish digs a pit in the mud 50 to 80cm deep and rests in the bottom (protected against dehydration by a sac of mucus it secretes) – which is connected to the air above by a narrow opening. Lungfish have been recorded living thus for up to four years before rains soften the surrounding soil and they break out of their prison.

Saline lakes

The great lakes of the Eastern Rift Valley run in a string from Lake Natron in Tanzania to Lake Turkana in northern Kenya. Some, such as Lakes Nakuru, Bogoria, Natron and Magadi are normally high in minerals which favour the proliferation of algae and tiny crustaceans, but are not conducive to fish and most other aquatic life. These conditions favour a few specialised species, and what the saline (also called alkaline or 'soda') lakes lack in diversity of large animals they tend to make up for in numbers. For example, the masses of birds at Lake Bogoria in Kenya are composed of millions of one species (lesser flamingo), thousands of another (greater flamingo) and at most a few hundred other waterbirds. Apart from flamingos, other birds present may include assorted ducks and grebes, shorebirds and predators such as African fish eagles which, in the absence of fish, have taken to preying on the flamingos themselves. ∎

Shallow wetlands form in low-lying areas after the long rains – quickly attracting flocks of birds, such as flamingos, and large animals that must drink daily.

SEA & SHORES

Several species of dolphin, including bottlenose dolphins, live in oceanic waters off the East African coast.

F EW other habitats are as challenging to survival as the zone where land meets the sea. Its inhabitants must be adapted to a daily pattern of inundation with sea water (with its high salt concentration) and, often, a pounding by the waves, followed by exposure to fresh water if it rains or baking sun for hours at a stretch. But this is a classic edge habitat, a zone rich in re-sources exploited by human and animal predators alike.

From the soup of plankton, which originates in the warm surface waters and underlies most of the ocean's food chains, to rocky shelves supporting hardy molluscs and crustaceans, the shallow waters above the continental shelf support one of the most diverse faunas on earth. Where conditions are suitable, coral reefs put on a show rivalled only by the wildlife of tropi-cal rainforests and best appreciated underwater. A dazzling display awaits anyone who dons snorkel and mask: fishes in every shape and colour, from neon blue to fluorescent orange; crustaceans, many also in bright colours, but often camou-flaged with weed, pebbles or even living sponges; and the many coloured corals themselves, supported by solid lime skele-tons constructed over millennia by tiny organisms.

Underwater meadows

Where rivers empty into the sea, suspended silt deposited over millennia has formed expansive mudflats rich in nutrients and small animals, such as molluscs and crustaceans. In places the fine but fertile mud supports underwater meadows of seagrass, grazed by animals as large as the dugong (or 'sea cow') and sheltering a suite of fishes and crustaceans different to those of coral reefs. Some have adapted to spend short spells out of water at low tide (like mudskippers, which lie partly submerged in puddles or burrows and flip between pools across the mud); and fiddler crabs, which emerge to pick tiny food particles from the surface. Mudflats attract a host of birds, such as herons, kingfishers and the many thousands of shorebirds that pass through the region on migration twice each year. Mudflats are excellent places to watch wildlife at low tide but don't expect any large mammals (although jackals and baboons are known to exploit the rich pickings).

Opposite page: A hawksbill turtle swimming in a coral garden. Marine turtles live their entire lives at sea, females returning to land only to nest on sandy beaches.

Opposite inset: A red lace coral, one of hundreds of species of invertebrate that make up the complex coral reef ecosystem.

Away from the estuaries, sandy beaches are one of the most demanding of environments and consequently support the fewest life forms, although shorebirds pick over the incoming tide and hermit crabs scavenge from dead animals washed up on the sands. The largest users of the beaches visit only briefly, and then at night: female marine turtles haul themselves up the sand to dig nest chambers and lay their eggs.

Saltwater forests

Forming a buffer between sea and shore, mangroves are trees unique for their ability to withstand daily inundation in sea water. Some have distinctive 'prop' roots, which elevate them above normal tidal limits, as well as other roots (pneumatophores – they look like asparagus spears) which stick up through the suffocating mud and extract oxygen directly from the air at low tide.

Mangrove seeds are carried away by the tides and take root wherever conditions are suitable, but usually on sheltered points and in calm backwaters. Silt accumulates around the roots and eventually forms a deep ooze in which crustaceans and fishes burrow. Zones of different mangrove species develop – those less able to withstand salt grow closer to land, trapping more debris and eventually allowing land plants to grow. Their extensive root systems calm wave action and slow coastal erosion, and shelter hatchling fishes and crustaceans.

Exploring the channels between mangroves by boat is a rewarding experience: at high tide birds roost in branches and on aerial roots; bats roost and birds nest on branches overhanging the water; and at low tide many birds and reptiles feed among the mud. Good stands of mangroves grow at Mida Creek adjacent to Arabuko-Sokoke Forest in Kenya.

Mangroves are pioneer plants that can withstand both daily inundation by the tides and extended exposure to the sun.

The deep blue sea

Open ocean beyond the continental shelf is the realm of great hunting fishes, such as sharks, tuna and marlin; marine mammals such as whales and dolphins; sea turtles which return to land only to lay their eggs; and birds that wander far in search of fish, such as cormorants (inset, page 78) boobies, terns and frigatebirds.

Island relict of Malagasy wildlife

The island of Pemba, part of the Zanzibar Archipelago, is home to several endemic birds. Some show affinities with those of the nearby mainland (eg, the Pemba green pigeon is obviously a close relative of the African green pigeon), but others have origins on the island of Madagascar, some 1500km to the south. For example, the nearest relative of the Pemba scops owl is the Madagascar scops owl, and other relics of Malagasy wildlife that occur only on Pemba include a day gecko of the genus *Phelsuma* and the Pemba flying-fox (true flying-foxes are not found on the African mainland). Madagascar's wildlife was formerly more widespread, but successive waves of 'modern' animals – over many millions of years – pushed most to extinction on continental Africa. Today the closest relatives of these creatures exist only where they have been isolated by sea on islands that competing forms could not reach.

Cruising the channels between the islands and the mainland could yield sea mammals or pelagic birds.

Fauna on Pemba, Unguja (Zanzibar) and Mafia Islands have been isolated from the mainland for many thousands of years and some animals, such as the Zanzibar leopard, have developed unique forms. The ancient connection of these islands to continental Africa is demonstrated by the presence of mammals, such as duikers, that originated in the forests of the Zaire River basin and spread east, becoming relict when the forests eventually contracted. For example, Aders' duiker is found on Zanzibar, but elsewhere only in Kenya's Arabuko-Sokoke FR. In contrast, flying-foxes occur only on Pemba and Unguja, and not on the adjacent mainland, and probably spread from Asia to islands in the Indian Ocean. Pemba is rich in endemic bird species while Mafia hosts breeding colonies of seabirds. ■

The zone between the tides' lowest and highest reaches offers rich pickings for beachcombing predators – such as humans.

OTHER HABITATS

W HILE we tend to think of East African habitats as forests, savannas and grasslands (to name a few), there are many other, less obvious habitats that animals use – some of which overlap the boundaries of our own 'habitats'. And there are good reasons for animals to partake of human hospitality: our endeavours provide extra sources of food, shelter and breeding sites for creatures equipped to make the transition from natural to human-designed environments. But not all of these habitats are human-engineered and some are simply overlooked.

Villages, towns and cities

Although generally bereft of large animals, urban environments are utilised by some species opportunistically and in a few cases are the habitat of choice. Into the latter category fall various rodents, but birds fare better than mammals as a rule, because the latter are often sought for food and discouraged as competition or carriers of disease. What this means for the visitor is that large city parks can support at least some living things, such as squirrels, roosts of bats and even troops of monkeys.

Opportunistic birds such as pied crows and black kites swoop for scraps near markets; starlings and sparrows nest in buildings whose vertical faces are effectively cliffs; and marabou storks perch like sentinels overlooking savanna and city squares alike. Several species of weaver build large colonies of nests right in the middle of settlements and fruit-bats also may roost in towns, both probably because the risk of predation is less – although raptors hunt above city streets through the 'canyons' created by buildings.

Agriculture and cultivation

Where land is cleared for cultivation, the end result is comparatively poor in both plants and animals. Most large animals quickly desert these changes, or if unable to move far, die out – others are hunted to local extinction. And when elephants, absent for months in other parts of their range, return along traditional migration routes to find crops and dwellings in their way, conflict with people inevitably develops. Similarly, the fencing of fields across wildebeest migration routes causes the animals to change course.

Nonetheless some animals, particularly birds and small mammals such as mongooses and genets, readily adopt agricultural land as an extension of their natural habitat. While driving along highways you can expect to see various weavers and sparrows, doves, and blossom-feeding sunbirds; the ubiquitous common bulbul; and orchard-raiding hornbills, crows and starlings. Watch for secretary birds, bustards and storks picking over burnt fields; cattle egrets among livestock; and shrikes perched on overhead wires. Ironically, when agriculture does benefit a species, it can be to such a degree that animals such as rats, normally held in check by natural predators, become a major pest. Thus baboons are expanding their numbers and range at the interface between cultivation and

Uganda and Rwanda support a high rural human population: terraced cultivation extends up even the steepest slopes on fertile volcanic soils.

Opposite page: Termites recycle vast amounts of vegetation, but their mounds also provide scratching posts for elephants and rhinos, and lookouts for cheetahs on the hunt.

Opposite inset: Lions too use the natural vantage points provided by termite mounds.

savanna, and red-billed queleas can descend on crops in millions – causing widespread damage.

Termite mounds

Termite biology and behaviour is itself fascinating, but the earthen mounds of these silent armies play an important role in the life cycles of many other creatures. At various stages termitaria form important refuges for other animals; for example, monitor lizards lay their eggs and various birds dig nest tunnels in mounds; aardvarks and pangolins dig out shelters in abandoned mounds; and animals ranging from small bats and snakes to warthogs, ratels, porcupines and jackals use hollow mounds as shelters and nurseries. Topis and cheetahs use mounds as vantage points, and elephants and rhinos rub against them for a scratch.

Termite mounds also help to shape the environment by encouraging the growth of certain plants. For example, mounds on floodplains become islands during wet seasons that plants colonise – in turn sheltering more plants and animals, and encouraging the growth of thickets. It's pretty hard to miss termite mounds on the savanna, but look also for arboreal termitaria – in which kingfishers excavate nest tunnels – and the distinctive mushroom-shaped structures made by some termite species.

The air up there

Habitat is usually described in terms of objects, but for a vast number of animals the main event is actually the space above or between objects, and 'habitat' in the conventional sense is just a backdrop (albeit one to which all creatures ultimately must return at some time or other). Although generally transparent, air is not just empty space. It behaves like other matter except that it's much lighter than most and there's a lot more of it. It stands still and moves – sometimes very quickly or in circles. Air heats up and cools down, sometimes rapidly and in quick succession; bumps into things and fills voids such as

Wet seasons often feature spectacular storms and sudden downpours. Yet even at the storm front birds such as swifts gather to hawk for insects.

Miniature mushroom farmers

Termite mounds are a wonder of natural engineering. Alone, these insects are helpless, but somehow colonies (sometimes numbering millions) cooperate to build protective fortresses by cementing together grains of earth with saliva. Inside, the temperature and humidity remain more or less constant, regulated by ventilation shafts and chimneys; other passages serve as brood chambers. The hub of the colony is the queen, whose main task in life is to squeeze out millions of eggs. Most eggs hatch into workers, who tend the queen, forage for food, and build and repair the mound; others become soldiers that defend the nest. A mound's inhabitants can consume tonnes of vegetation annually; once chewed the vegetation is deposited in storage chambers in the mound where it sprouts a fungus that is consumed by the termites. Pretty impressive so far, but consider this: during the rains termites of several species spread the fungus on the ground outside, where it sprouts edible mushrooms that set spores, which the termites gather to renew their underground supply. Not bad for tiny, blind insects.

great caves. It also acts as an agent of dispersal, carrying the seeds of plants and the young of spiders and insects over many kilometres.

All these factors are exploited by a few mammals, a myriad of insects and by most birds. To them it is a dining room, highway, playground, courtship arena or observation post. Air can communicate the presence of food: thunderheads on the horizon stimulate termites to hatch – millions drift upward like plumes of smoke, attracting birds and mammals alike – and swifts move ahead of the storm front to feast on the bounty. Vultures take advantage of thermals as they look for a kill; their volplaning is a clear signal to predators to move onto a kill themselves. And smoke, often visible from kilometres away, signals a grassfire to which bustards, raptors and jackals are drawn in their search for a meal. ■

Vultures and eagles cruise at great heights (lammergeiers soaring to over 5000m) in their search for prey; tiny insects and spiders drift on the wind; and entire swarms of larger insects sometimes get swept away in an updraft.

PARKS AND PLACES

The best wildlife-watching destinations in East Africa

INTRODUCTION

FROM the open plains of Kenya and Tanzania with their immense herds of wildebeests, to coral reefs off Zanzibar and the densely forested slopes of Rwanda's Virunga volcanoes, East Africa presents a vast range of wild places in which to watch wildlife. Varied topography and climatic influences have created a host of natural environments in which animals and plants have developed an extraordinary diversity (see the Nature in East Africa chapter), making the region's national parks and reserves among the best in the world for experiencing wildlife.

Kenya's Masai Mara NR and Amboseli NP, and Tanzania's Serengeti NP and Ngorongoro CA are famous for their high concentrations of large mammals; in other reserves a single species is the drawcard (eg, mountain gorillas at Uganda's Bwindi Impenetrable NP); and a host of other special places are interesting in their own right. With such a choice, and road conditions making efficient travel a challenge, it helps to do some planning before you set out – and that's where this chapter comes in. The parks and other special places it points you towards have been chosen for their wildlife value and accessibility, to help you make the most of what East Africa has to offer.

The mainstay of this chapter is a profile of each destination renowned for wildlife-watching. These are arranged according to their importance for seeing wildlife (indicated by the number of pages each receives, thus six-page parks are followed by four-page parks and so on) and then by alphabetical order.

Each destination features a rundown on what is there, what's special and, importantly, where to find it. It is certainly not meant to be a complete listing of each area's fauna, and indeed the vast majority of species cannot be done justice in such a short space. But you will get a good feel for the mammals, birds and other large animals you can reasonably expect to see; and with the many inside tips you will often be able to go that step further and see or appreciate something that might otherwise remain hidden.

We also mention sites (including cities) worth visiting if you are passing through; and summarise many other sites, ranging from huge but seldom-visited reserves offering a good range of wildlife, to small hotspots renowned for particular specialities. The maps give you an idea of where things are located and highlights where some of the animals can be found, but are not intended for precise navigation. As in any voyage of discovery, local knowledge is always worth seeking out.

The destinations included here are great stages on which to view the dynamic habitats, plants and animals of East Africa. Animals move around, seasons change, weather varies. There is no guarantee that you'll see absolutely everything you're after, but with the right directions you should see something amazing in just about any part of East Africa. We wish you a rewarding journey.

Planning your trip

It may be stating the obvious, but the more time you have to go on safari the more you will see; and the richness of East Africa's wildlife diversity means that even after some weeks you will encounter new species and new behaviours. Do as much research and reading as possible before you go, and concentrate on the areas with the key wildlife that matches your interests, eg, a priority for many people is to see the Big Five, while bird-watchers may want to spend as much time as possible in rainforests or other specialised habitats. Unless your entire trip has been organised by a safari operator, you'll also need to allow time for organising each stage of your trip (Lonely Planet's travel guides – *Kenya*; *Tanzania, Zanzibar & Pemba*; and *East Africa* – will help with logistics). Following are some suggestions for prioritising your trip.

Two weeks Probably the minimum requirement for a worthwhile safari (unless money is no object), allowing you time to visit two or three reserves comfortably. If it's your first trip to East Africa, we advise you to spend two or three days in one of the major reserves in Kenya (eg, Masai Mara NR) and/or Tanzania (eg, Ngorongoro CA, Serengeti NP) to get a feel for the great herds of herbivores and their predators. As a complete contrast you could do no better than to seek out the great apes in Uganda's rainforests – most people opt for gorilla tracking at Bwindi Impenetrable or Mgahinga Gorilla NPs, but chimp tracking (at, for example, Kibale Forest NP) is definitely worthwhile. Depending on how hard you like to travel, you could also squeeze in a side trip to another reserve that grabs your attention, eg, one of the Rift Valley lakes for flamingos or one of the marine national parks for some snorkelling.

Four weeks Extra time will allow you to take in a few parks at a more relaxed pace. Once again, first-timers should go to one of the popular reserves in Kenya or Tanzania. Depending on where you start, follow this with a two or three day trip to one of the semiarid parks, eg, Tsavo NP, Meru NP or Samburu/Buffalo Springs NRs in Kenya, or Selous GR or Ruaha NP in Tanzania, and a couple of days in a smaller park (eg, a Rift Valley lake). Gorilla and/or chimp tracking should still be high on your agenda; allow a week to do both, but if you attempt only one then take a trip to either Queen Elizabeth or Murchison Falls NPs as well (Uganda's size makes getting about fairly straightforward). With a week in hand, consider exploring the coral reefs and coastal forests of either Kenya or Tanzania (ie, Zanzibar). Keen birdwatchers will also want to head to hotspots such as Arabuko–Sokoke Forest (Kenya) or Udzungwa Mountains NP (Tanzania) – see the Birdwatching special section in the Wildlife-Watching chapter. ■

KENYA

Highlights

- The sound and smell of half a million bleating wildebeests on the move – the great migration in the Masai Mara
- Saiwa Swamp, a tiny national park with de Brazza's monkeys, aquatic sitatungas and great birdwatching
- The great cats – lions, leopards and cheetahs – supreme savanna hunters
- Stalking 'big game plants' (giant groundsels and lobelias) that grow on Mt Kenya's high plains
- Millions of flamingos massed against a backdrop of hot springs and geysers at Lake Bogoria
- A young elephant's fumbling attempts to eat grass on the red, dusty plains of Samburu NR
- Listening for the call of the rare Sokoke scops owl at dusk in Arabuko–Sokoke Forest
- Sorting through a bird wave in the rainforest of Kakamega Forest.

A staggering diversity

FROM coral reefs to the icy peaks of Africa's second-highest mountain (Mt Kenya) and vast savannas stretching to northern deserts, Kenya has long been famous as one of the world's great wildlife watching destinations. A staggering biological diversity is generally easy to see in an excellent network of reserves: hundreds of mammal species include all of Africa's 'big five' (elephants, rhinos, buffaloes, lions and leopards); birds are abundant, common and diverse, with 1114 species – several of which are endemic; and other highlights include succulent plants and 871 species of butterfly.

Although Kenya is wholly tropical, its climate (and therefore its habitats and wildlife) varies greatly with rainfall and elevation. At one extreme, high rainfall affects Aberdare, Mt Kenya and Mt Elgon NPs – where montane forests and giant herbs are best appreciated in the dry seasons. And biologically rich rainforests in the west – now restricted to patches such as Kakamega Forest – abound with birdlife, and many animals and plants of West African origin. Vast areas of semiarid scrub in the north and east, drained by the Tana and Ewaso Nyiro rivers, support a high diversity of wildlife protected in Samburu NR, and Tsavo and Meru NPs. Little rain falls in the arid far north, where ancient fossil beds, specialised animals and lava flows border Lake Turkana.

Rainfall and elevation rise in the south and west, where rolling savannas support the biggest numbers of large animals – attracting tourists who flock to the famous Amboseli NP and Masai Mara NR (scene of the annual migration of half a million wildebeests from the Serengeti plains – the greatest concentration of large animals on earth). East of the Rift Valley most rain falls in two distinct periods: the so-called 'long rains' (March to May) and the 'short rains' (November to December). Dry seasons make access and wildlife viewing easier; but rains bring fewer tourists and a flush of green to the savannas, and trigger the breeding of many species.

The eastern arm of the Great Rift Valley extends through Kenya forming sheer 1000m cliffs and a chain of shallow freshwater and alkaline ('soda') lakes, which attract concentrations of flamingos and other waterbirds. Lake Bogoria NR and Lake Nakuru NP support masses of flamingos; and Lake Baringo offers a suite of other waterbirds in a semiarid setting.

Arabuko-Sokoke Forest is East Africa's most important coastal forest and the last refuge for many endemic species; birdwatchers and butterfly enthusiasts in particular make an effort to pick through its riches. Nearby, Malindi and Watamu Marine NPs protect the great biodiversity of Kenya's inshore coral reefs; migrating whale sharks are an added attraction. And Kenya's numerous wildlife conservancies and private ranches boast successes in breeding rare species such as rhinos. ∎

KAKAMEGA FOREST
Relict of West African rainforests; excellent birdwatching plus monkeys and butterflies

SAMBURU & BUFFALO SPRINGS NRs
Semiarid wilderness; lions, elephants, cheetahs, reticulated giraffes, gerenuks, bat-eared foxes and dry country birds

MALINDI & WATAMU MNPs
Superb snorkelling, first-class diving and a chance to see migrating whale sharks in season

MASAI MARA NR
Abundant lions and elephants; grazing herds of antelopes and the great wildebeest migration

ARABUKO–SOKOKE FR
Home of several endemic bird species, golden-rumped elephant shrews, plus Kenya's greatest variety of frogs and butterflies

Suggested itineraries

One week Spend two nights in the famous Masai Mara then head north to Lake Nakuru NP; call into Lake Bogoria NR then finish at Lake Baringo for hippos and some stylish birding.

Alternatively, overnight at Amboseli NP then head for the coast via Tsavo West NP for a taste of semiarid wildlife. Snorkel at Malindi or Watamu and finish off in Arabuko–Sokoke FR.

Two weeks Sweep west after the Masai Mara (2–3 nights) to take in Kenya's best rainforest wildlife at Kakamega Forest and sitatungas at Saiwa Swamp NP. Return to Nairobi via Lakes Baringo (overnight), Bogoria (flamingos) and Nakuru (rhinos).

Or do the Masai Mara and the three Rift Valley lakes before heading to Tsavo, Meru or Samburu for semiarid wildlife.

One month Follow the two-week itinerary but take time to winkle out the specialities at each park, eg, cheetahs in the Mara, leopards at Lake Nakuru and rhinos in Tsavo. Fly to Lake Turkana for desert and prehistoric remains, or trek up Mt Kenya. Finish off on the coast with a day or two at Arabuko–Sokoke FR, then snorkel at Malindi or Watamu MNPs.

MASAI MARA NATIONAL RESERVE

Plains games

Wildlife highlights

One of the great wildernesses of the world. Large mammals are varied, abundant and easy to see. Vast grasslands stretch south to Tanzania's Serengeti NP, from where some 500,000 wildebeests migrate annually into the Mara, accompanied by herds of plains zebras and many lions. Resident among the park's mammals are Masai giraffes, buffaloes, elephants, topis, kongonis (Coke's hartebeests), elands, defassa waterbucks, impalas, Thomson's and Grant's gazelles; hippos live in the Mara and Talek rivers; and a few black rhinos remain in the east and centre, but can be difficult to track down. Leopards and spotted hyenas are commonly encountered, cheetahs less so, and striped hyenas and hunting dogs rarely. Smaller attractions include black-backed jackals, servals, caracals and four species of mongoose. The Mara boasts 540 bird species including 57 raptors; sought-after specialities include Denham's bustards, rock cisticolas and Jackson's widowbirds. Birds of prey range from the snappy little grey kestrel and other species hovering above the grasslands, to large eagles and six species of vulture wheeling in the thermals.

ALL wildlife viewing in this popular reserve must be done from a vehicle and the Mara has developed a reputation as a minivan circus during busy times (such as the wildebeest migration and school holidays); but at other times, especially during the long rains, it can be virtually deserted. To get the most out of your visit use a reputable company with accredited guides and preferably a 4WD vehicle. Since the Mara isn't fenced, don't ignore the surrounding areas – the Loita Plains north of the Sekenani Gate, the Sekenani Valley and the dispersal area north of the Musiara Gate are all productive.

Browsers in sheltering thickets

The Sekenani Gate in the east leads into the rolling Ngama Hills, dominated by stands of dense *Croton* bushes, soft silvery leleshwa – used by the Maasai as a deodorant – candelabra euphorbias and thorny acacias. Plenty of animals can be seen along tracks leading off the main access road: **warthogs**, **lions**, **elephants** and **buffaloes** are generally about, and this habitat is favoured by **antelopes** such as **Grant's gazelles**, **impalas** and the **common eland**, as well the park's 40-odd **black rhinos**, which disperse across the central Olmisigiyoi region and south-

The wildebeest migration is peak activity time in the Mara for predators and tourists. The route changes each year, but early in the migration expect to see wildebeests crossing rivers en masse.

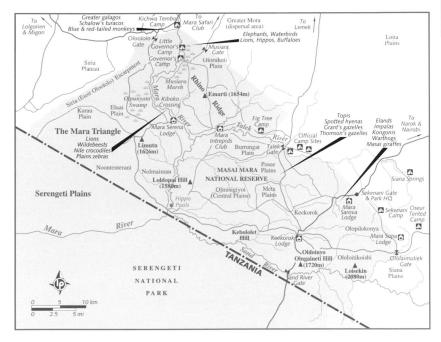

eastern corner of the reserve. **Kirk's dik-diks** (which live only in the thickets) and **steinbucks** are also common in this habitat. Birdwatching is excellent and features several species not seen in other parts of the Mara, such as **Denham's bustard**, **magpie shrikes** (especially near Siana Springs) and **African penduline tits**. **Kestrels** – **grey**, **common** and **lesser** – hunt rodents over the grasslands; **white-bellied go-away-birds** mock from the top of trees; and **yellow-mantled widowbirds**, **purple grenadiers** and **cinnamon-breasted rock buntings** all feed along the tracks. A night drive in the Sekenani Valley will almost certainly clock up **spotted hyenas**, **black-backed jackals**, **Kirk's dik-diks** and **springhares**; **pearl-spotted owlets** and **African scops owls** are also common.

Elephant topiary

The Talek Gate opens onto the undulating grasslands of the Posee, Meta, Central and Burrungat Plains that stretch between the Ngama Hills and the Mara River. Lone euphorbias, *Balanites* and flat-topped acacias – browsed by the distinctively marked **Masai giraffes** – dot a landscape once covered in woody shrubs. Herds of **elephants** slowly destroyed the thickets, allowing grasses to proliferate, and now the central and western Mara is one of the best areas to see grazing animals and their predators. **Kongonis** (Coke's hartebeests), **topis**, and **Thomson's** and **Grant's gazelles** are present all year round, although they may be absent from great swathes of grasslands and concentrated in others; several species can sometimes be seen milling together, especially at the top of

Hippos are best seen in large rivers such as the Mara and Talek, but early risers may catch one out in the open, especially near Musiara Marsh.

ridges as night approaches. Troops of **vervet monkeys** and **olive baboons** fan out to forage, and the dry season brings the great herds of **wildebeests** and **plains zebras**. **Lions, cheetahs, servals** and **caracals** could all be encountered; large grassland birds include **common ostriches, secretary birds, southern ground hornbills** and three species of **bustard**; and **dark chanting goshawks, vultures** and **eagles** nest in the surviving trees. These grasslands are incredibly beautiful during the rains, when the sound and smell of **buffaloes** and **elephants** ripping the grass is punctuated by the plaintive whistling of **rufous-naped larks**; and cloud shadows move across the softly riffling swards littered with wastepaper flowers.

Miniature protein factories
Millions of termites ceaselessly chew through the grasslands digesting cellulose, and in turn become a valuable source of

Grass widows
During the long rains (beginning in March) the normally drab male Jackson's widowbird moults into glossy black breeding plumage and grows a long flowing tail. But his courtship display is even more dramatic: he tramples an arena of grass in which he sways sideways and jumps forward while vibrating his wings and calling, then jumps up to 1m high, as if trying to see over the grass heads, with wings outstretched, head arched back and feet thrashing the air. Several males perform in loose colonies and the display is repeated until a watching female either loses interest or decides to mate with him. It is thought the famous jumping of Maasai warriors is partly based on this display; and when a lion in long grass flicks up its tail, from a distance the tuft looks uncannily like a little black bird jumping in the grass...

protein for other animals – nocturnal **aardvarks** and **aardwolves** feed almost exclusively on them. Large earthen termite mounds dot the plains and during the rains active colonies build funnels, out of which fly vast numbers of adults relished by **jackals** and **mongooses**; and birds such as **lilac-breasted rollers**, which gather to hawk them on the wing, and **capped wheatears**. Derelict termite mounds serve as shelter for **mongooses**, nest chambers for **jackals** and **hyenas**, and lookouts for **cheetahs** and sleek tan-and-gunmetal **topis**. The grasslands also support a rich community of small birds, including 12 species of **cisticola** (whose identification poses a birdwatcher's headache); **quail**, **francolins** and **red-necked** and **yellow-necked spurfowl**; drably-coloured **larks** and **pipits**, **yellow-throated** and almost neon-bright **rosy-breasted longclaws**; and many **finches**, **weavers** and **widowbirds**.

The greatest game show of all

The vast, bleating herds of **wildebeests** usually enter the Mara from the adjoining Serengeti in June or July, although the timing

Location 270km south of Nairobi. Good roads as far as Narok and Ngorengore can become atrocious further south – 4WD is recommended in wet seasons.

Facilities Rangers can be hired at park HQ (Sekenani Gate). Most lodges have resident naturalists. Game walks are possible in the Sekenani Valley and Siria Escarpment. Night drives outside the reserve are run by various operators.

Accommodation Large range of lodges and tented camps in the reserve; camping grounds and lodges outside.

Wildlife rhythms Wildebeests and zebras present during dry season (mid-June to mid-October). Buffaloes calve March to May and many carnivores are born early in the wet. Great flocks of Abdim's and white storks feed on termites and frogs in October to November rains; long rains trigger breeding displays of widowbirds.

Contact Masai Mara National Reserve (☎ 0305-2178/2337), PO Box 60, Narok.

Ecotours Bike Treks (☎ 02-44 63 71) has a tented camp in the Sekenani Valley and offers night drives; LAOS (☎ 02-33 11 91) has a tented camp on the Mara River and expert naturalist guides; Abercrombie & Kent (☎ 02-22 87 00) has accommodation in the reserve and can organise bird guides.

Herds of elephants are a common sight on the Mara, and can be reliably seen near the Musiara Marsh.

and exact route changes from year to year. Waves of **plains zebras** arrive first, mowing through the tall, coarse grass stems that shot up during the rains, and exposing the green leafy grasses preferred by the wildebeests following behind them. At several points the herds cross the Mara and Talek rivers, trotting down in single file then charging across in an attempt to avoid waiting **Nile crocodiles**. Thousands are eaten, crushed or drowned in the crossings; **lions** (and minivans) wait in ambush at the other side; and **vultures** and other scavengers enjoy good pickings. Large numbers of lions follow the herds, although some stay to slug it out for dominance of an established territory. A smaller population of about 100,000 wildebeests heads west from the Loita Plains to mingle with the Serengeti herds in the Mara dispersal area north of the reserve. As the grasslands dry out in late October or early November the wildebeests and zebras move back to the Serengeti and Loita Plains.

Killseekers

For much of the day **lions** and **spotted hyenas** laze around, panting off the night's meal and twitching flies. But as the afternoon draws on ears prick and noses dip into the breeze, and the prides and packs stalk **zebras, wildebeests, antelopes** and even dangerous prey such as **buffaloes**. Most of the action takes place at night (infra-red spotting gear is used on night drives by Mara Intrepids Club), but in the morning there is usually plenty of activity around a kill: **vultures** circling overhead attract hyenas and **jackals** that wait for the lions to finish; if the hyenas outnumber the lions they may drive off a pride. Jackals wait in line – **black-backed jackals** are most common – and vultures and **marabou storks** pick over the bones when the mammals have departed. Kills are most frequently seen during the wildebeest migration. Of the Mara's three spotted cats the most glamorous and eagerly sought is the **cheetah**, though they are more abundant in the short grass plains to the north. **Leopards** are probably best seen along wooded rivers such as the Talek and Mara, and in dense vegetation at the foot of the Siria Escarpment. Seeing smaller cats such as **servals**, **African wild cats** and **caracals** is a matter of luck, and **hunting dogs** are the scarcest predator of all, although a pack is thought to live in the Aitong area north of the Mara. **Striped hyenas** are occasionally encountered on night drives.

The dik-dik and the elephant

The Mara's smallest antelope, Kirk's dik-dik, stands only 40cm high, and marks territories in patches of dense woody vegetation such as *Croton, Acacia* or *Commiphora* with scent glands and by depositing middens of little dung pellets.

'One day a careless elephant crapped on a baby dik-dik and buried it; its parents looked everywhere but couldn't find their missing fawn. When the parents realised what had happened, grief turned to anger and, to seek revenge, from that day on all dik-diks started to pile up their droppings high enough to bury a baby elephant'.

David, Maasai guide.

Sadly, a dik-dik midden takes months to pile up a few centimetres – only to be washed away in the next rains.

Western wetlands and rivers

The steep Siria Escarpment overlooking the reserve's western reaches is inhabited by **Chanler's mountain reedbucks, klipspringers** (both also found in the Sekenani Valley), **steinbucks** and **Kirk's dik-diks**. The Musiara Marsh, a permanent wetland drained by the Mara River, supports **defassa waterbucks, impalas** and large herds of **elephants** and **buffaloes**. **Lions** are common in this area, and several well-established – and fiercely defended – territories take advantage of the abundant **antelopes**, and seasonal **zebras** and **wildebeests**. The rivers support some 2000 **hippos**, which wallow in pools during the day and emerge to graze the adjacent grasslands at night; early risers often see them far from water, but they can always be seen at well established hippo pools along the rivers. **Nile crocodiles** bask on sandbars and **Nile monitors** are common; and the riverine forest is home to **olive baboons, vervet monkeys, bushbucks, Harvey's duikers,** and nocturnal **tree hyraxes** and **greater galagos** (which visit feeding stations at lodges). This area and a small patch of forest at Kichwa Tembo offer some of the Mara's best birdwatching: **African fish eagles** hunt along the rivers; Musiara itself attracts seasonal, resident and migrant **waterbirds**; and fruiting fig trees attract **Schalow's turacos, African green pigeons,** laughing parties of **green wood-hoopoe** and **black-and-white-casqued hornbills**. ∎

The Mara is one of the best places in Kenya to see lions: prides are resident throughout the park and during the migration you may even see a kill.

Watching tips

Arrange with Kenya Wildlife Service (KWS) to accompany the Rhino Patrol, which leaves from the Sekenani Gate. Patas monkeys are most often seen in grasslands near the Tanzanian border and red-tailed monkeys live in the small patch of forest at Kichwa Tembo. Rock cisticolas inhabit the Siria Escarpment and hills behind Mara Safari Club.

TSAVO EAST & WEST NATIONAL PARKS

Kenya's elephant and rhino capital

> ### Wildlife highlights
> Kenya's largest reserve supports the 'big five', and features the country's largest elephant population (which includes released orphans) and lions in good numbers. Two rhino sanctuaries make it Kenya's most important rhino conservation location, and other large mammals include buffaloes, hartebeests, lesser kudus, elands, waterbucks, Grant's gazelles, impalas and giraffes. Steinbucks, Kirk's dik-diks and klipspringers are common. The park has over 600 bird species; highlights include birds of the semiarid zone, such as Somali (Tsavo East) and common ostriches (Tsavo West), golden pipits and golden-breasted starlings. Bird banding at Ngulia Lodge is an annual major event.

AT around the size of Wales, Tsavo NP is the largest reserve in Kenya and one of the largest in the world. Split into East and West sections by the main Nairobi–Mombasa highway, it contains the biggest **elephant** population in Kenya (in excess of 6000) and is famous for its **lions**. Tsavo is also home to many mammals able to tolerate drought conditions, such as **gerenuks**, **fringe-eared oryxes** and **black rhinos**. But for all its diversity Tsavo is not a park where you will see animals constantly: it is a huge, semiarid wilderness straddling the Taru Desert and much of its appeal lies in its dramatic scenery and sense of space. If possible, go to Tsavo with some time to spare – it is not a place to dash about and tick off animals; it's a place to soak up atmosphere – and if you get off the beaten track (the roads are good) you could have it to yourself.

Views from below and on high

Tsavo West is smaller, better watered and more often visited than Tsavo East. Mzima Springs is the highlight and 220,000,000L of water gush out of the ground every day to form a river some 70m wide – home to **Nile crocodiles** and **hippos**. **Elephants**, **plains zebras**, **gazelles** and other animals drink at the river; **blue** and **vervet monkeys** frequent the surrounding fever trees and *Acacia tortillis*; and fringing reeds, vines, figs and palms are prime spots for birds.

Tsavo's bird beacon

Each November and December Eurasian birds migrating south at night along the eastern flyway become disorientated in the rainy season mists. Both birds and birders descend on Ngulia Lodge, in Tsavo West, where bright game-viewing lights become Tsavo's bird beacon. Graeme Backhurst and David Pearson run the Ngulia Bird Ringing Project – Africa's foremost Eurasian migratory bird-banding project. Since 1969 around 274,000 birds have been banded and individuals have been re-located in 38 different countries as far flung as Kazakhstan, Finland, Russia and Zimbabwe. In all 57 Palaearctic species and 197 Afrotropical species have been banded. Graeme describes the whole experience as magic. 'As we are at the mist nets at night...migrating birds are constantly flitting past us and often alight on our heads, shoulders or even hands. All this takes place in misty conditions which tend to deaden sound, although we do hear the occasional hyena and lion roaring. In the early days of Ngulia, elephants and rhinos were frequent visitors to the lodge's salt licks and proved to be major hazards!'

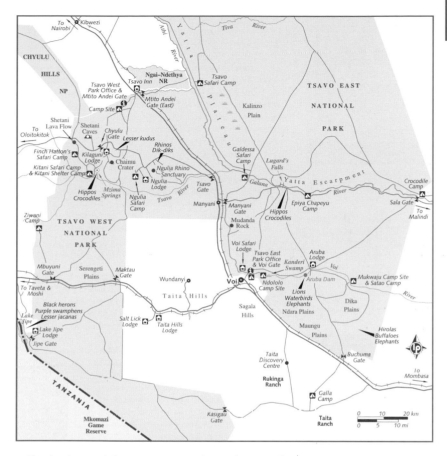

The river is crystal clear at its source and an underwater observation chamber has been built. The **hippos** stay out of range of the chamber, but you will see various freshwater fishes, such as **barbels** and **suckers**, close up. The best place to watch hippos is from the lower pool lookout; the stream here is also a favourite with small **crocodiles** and the huge fig around which the viewing platform is built attracts fruit-eating animals.

Not far north from Mzima is Kilaguni Lodge, where you can indulge in some wildlife watching at a waterhole. Roaring Rocks observation point is well worth a visit: **eagles** cruise at eye level and the westerly vista takes in the Chaimu Hills, Chyulu Hills and – on a clear day – Mt Kilimanjaro. The easterly view looks down on the winding watercourse of Ngulia Spring in Rhino Valley: you're likely to see **elephants**, **hippos** and **gazelles** from up here. Drive down into the valley and follow the watercourse to get closer, and search among the trees for animals seeking shade. Looking up, the face of the rocky scarp is the place to locate raptors such as **bateleurs**. A road here leads to Chaimu Crater (Lava Flow) and winds through rocky terrain that is ideal

Tsavo NP is Kenya's most important reserve for black rhino conservation.

Common genets are often so bold at lodges that they'll get within arm's length and help themselves to food.

habitat for **klipspringers**. Although they are shy and frequent dense thickets, **lesser kudus** are readily seen here.

Tsavo West is dotted with features of recent volcanic activity: the Chyulu Hills are composed of cinders resulting from volcanic activity less than 500 years ago and are one of the world's newest mountain ranges. Water percolates straight down through the porous soil before hitting solid rock and flowing underground to emerge at Mzima and other springs. Eastwards, at the base of the Ngulia Hills, Ngulia Rhino Sanctuary protects between 30 and 40 **black rhinos** plus a suite of other animals, including **giraffes**, **zebras**, **lesser kudus** and **leopards** (the surrounding fence is quite low so many animals are not confined). The sanctuary's five waterholes are the obvious places to look for rhinos, otherwise rhino-spotting is mighty difficult because of the thick vegetation. **Kirk's dik-diks** thrive in this habitat and you are sure to see many pairs. Keep an eye out for the **golden pipit**, which in flight and coloration resembles a giant golden butterfly – it and the gorgeous **golden-breasted starling** are quite abundant.

Water in the desert

Tsavo East is less visited than the park's western section and only the southern part, below the Galana River, is open to the public. This permanent river is a feature of the park, and its greenery contrasts with the endless grasses and occasional saltbush thicket or thorn tree that characterise much of Tsavo East. Except during the rains (May to June, and November) when large animals disperse, sightings of **elephants** are virtually guarantee by following the river route from Sala Gate to Manyani Gate – especially around Sala Gate itself and the Sobo Camp area. Herds of **waterbucks**, **plains zebras** and **impalas** are common, and **hippos** and **crocodiles** are found at Crocodile Point below Lugard's Falls. A pride of **lions** is frequently seen near Sala Gate, and another small family of lions lives near the Sobo area. **Giraffes** are regulars along the river route as are numerous **dik-diks**, a few **gerenuks**, **Somali ostriches**, **kori bustards**, **bateleurs**, **carmine bee-eaters**, **waterbirds** and an East African speciality – the **vulturine guineafowl**. A highlight in this area is a family of melanistic (black) **servals**.

Near Lugard's Falls is the Black Rhino Sanctuary, which now has over 50 **rhinos**. This can be visited and explored on foot (escorted by an armed ranger) with prior permission of KWS or if

---

Poaching and pestilence

Tsavo has had a chequered history and the effects linger. Poaching for rhino horn in the 1970s nearly took the black rhino to extinction, and poaching for ivory in the 1980s reduced the park's elephant population from around 17,000 to about 8000. The Kenyan Wildlife Service's war on poachers started in 1989 and was won and mostly fought in north-east Tsavo, which remains largely closed to the public. But drought (1993–94) followed by an outbreak of rinderpest in eastern Kenya in 1994–95 decimated Tsavo's hoofed animals: buffalo numbers in the region crashed from an estimated 34,600 in 1991 to 5500 by 1997; kongonis (Coke's hartebeests) from 16,000 to 4100, and elands from 10,000 to 760. Most hoofed species declined over the 1990s, including greater kudus, waterbucks, Grant's gazelles, gerenuks, impalas, Masai giraffes and fringe-eared oryxes. But herds of up to 200 buffaloes are now being seen so a recovery could be on the horizon.

you are staying at Galdessa Camp. Numerous **black-backed jackals** and **bat-eared foxes** inhabit this area but, being nocturnal they are seen most often in the early morning or late afternoon.

Yatta Escarpment forms a backdrop to the Galana River for most of its length through Tsavo. This ancient lava flow is the largest in the world and runs along the north bank of the river almost all the way to Nairobi, 200km away. By driving along the Galana you should see a good selection of Tsavo's wildlife. Away from the river towards Manyani Gate the vegetation becomes thicker and visibility decreases, but this area is worth searching for **lesser kudus** and **black rhinos**. Between Manyani Gate and Voi is Mudanda Rock, a favourite spot for taking panoramic photos and a great vantage point for looking down on a dam which attracts many **elephants**. This area is a known **leopard** haunt, but daytime sightings are rare. As you approach Voi the bush thins out to grasslands, which can be covered in herds of **impalas, buffaloes, plains zebras** and **elephants**.

Voi is well known for **elephants**. Several orphans raised by the Daphne Sheldrick Trust roam the area, the older released elephants acting as guides for the younger orphans (the KWS rangers at Voi Gate generally know their whereabouts). The savanna around Voi is punctuated by isolated rocky hills that are worth exploring for **lions**; and the waterhole at Voi Safari Lodge is normally visited in the mornings by herds of **buffaloes, zebras** and **elephants**. There are also plenty of bold **yellow baboons** in this area so keep your vehicle windows closed if you don't want your lunch to disappear up a tree.

Near Voi Gate is Kanderi Swamp, which in the drier months provides one of only two drinking areas this side of the park: **buffaloes, impalas** and other **antelopes, yellow baboons** and **lions** are quite often found here. Further on is Aruba Dam, which usually holds water throughout the year and is frequented by huge numbers of **ibises**, and many **grey herons** and other **waterbirds**. The tall trees in the camping ground and deserted lodge are home to **woodpeckers, sunbirds, starlings** and **pigeons**. Aruba Dam is part of the territory of a large pride of **lions**, which can usually be seen in the dam's vicinity. ■

Location 300km south-east of Nairobi, 200km north-east of Mombasa – accessible all year to 2WD vehicles.
Facilities Various observation and picnic points, nature trail and underwater viewing tank, rhino sanctuaries (open from 4 to 6 pm daily), waterholes at lodges and camping grounds.
Accommodation Several lodges, permanent tented camps, self-service bandas and camping grounds.
Wildlife rhythms Large animal concentration is highest during the dry seasons, ie, September to October and January to March.
Contact Kenyan Wildlife Service, Tsavo West HQ (☎ 302-22480/22483), PO Box 71, Mtito Andei; KWS, Tsavo East HQ (☎ 147-30049), PO Box 14, Voi.
Ecotours All major operators in Nairobi and Mombasa visit Tsavo, with Mombasa operators specialising in the East. Walking safaris are conducted by Sobo, Galdessa and Kulalu camps (organise in advance). Experienced bird banders can participate in Ngulia Bird Ringing Project: contact Graeme Backhurst (e) graeme@wananchi.com or Ngulia Safari Lodge (fax 147-30006), PO Box 42, Mtito Andei, Kenya.

Watching tips

A succession of animals comes to drink in the mornings at Voi Lodge waterhole. Aruba Dam is a busy spot for animals and if lions are your thing, camp here – their roaring will probably keep you awake at night. A leopard is seen at bait at Ngulia Lodge just about every night. Hirolas (Hunter's hartebeests) translocated from Arawale NR in northern Kenya can sometimes be seen between Aruba Dam and Buchuma Gate in Tsavo East.

ARABUKO–SOKOKE FOREST RESERVE

A haven for the small and rare

Wildlife highlights

A bird list in excess of 230 includes six globally threatened species, and coastal specialities such as Fischer's turaco and the Kenyan race of the crested guineafowl. Rare mammals include the golden-rumped elephant shrew and Aders' duikers. Sokoke is renowned for butterflies (263 species have been recorded), and frogs make it a rainy season delight. Nearby Mida Creek offers superb birdwatching: it is a significant area for migratory waders and crab plovers are a highlight.

ARABUKO–SOKOKE ('Sokoke') Forest is the largest and most important patch of coastal forest remaining in East Africa. Its uniqueness is apparent from the number of species that bear the forest's name, such as the **Sokoke scops owl**, **Sokoke pipit** and **Sokoke bushy-tailed mongoose**. An abundance of interesting small creatures makes up for a dearth of big animals, and birders will find several coastal endemics in Sokoke – species otherwise found only in the nearby Shimba Hills and in Tanzania's Usambara Mountains. This is the last stronghold of the **golden-rumped elephant shrew** and one of only two places where **Aders' duiker** survives; Sokoke also features an amazing variety of **butterflies** and has one of the richest diversities of **frogs** in Kenya. You are free to drive and walk about unescorted as long as you stick to designated tracks (**elephants** and **buffaloes** occur in low numbers, but you're unlikely to bump into them).

Birding with and without a guide

Arabuko–Sokoke is recognised by BirdLife International as an internationally Important Bird Area (IBA) because of the number of near-endemic species present. Three distinctive habitats dominate Sokoke and it's worth spending time in each as they all support different animals. The wetter parts of the reserve support a rich mixed closed-canopy forest formerly dominated by *Afzelia* trees

A species in crisis

Aders' duiker is a small forest antelope that survives only in two places: Arabuko–Sokoke FR (where it lives in pairs among *Cynometra* thickets) and on Zanzibar. The IUCN states that the Sokoke population is in 'danger of immediate extinction' unless it can be effectively protected. Numbers are not known for Sokoke, but the Zanzibar population is under serious threat: in 1995 there were estimated to be only 1400 remaining. On Zanzibar they are still hunted for meat and the population continues to dwindle because of habitat destruction. The Friends of Arabuko–Sokoke Forest, established in 1996, helps protect Sokoke and its rare and restricted species. Support by local and international visitors aids the cause; information on providing support is available at the reserve's Visitors Centre. Friends of Arabuko–Sokoke Forest (e) FoASF@Bigfoot.com, www.watamu.net/foasf.htm) can be contacted at PO Box 383, Watamu, Kenya.

(most have long since been felled for timber). Interspersed with the mixed forest are more open *Brachystegia* woodlands. These woodlands (pictured inset, opposite page) offer ideal birding, especially when, as often happens, a feeding flock composed of several species moves through. Two specialities are found only in this habitat: **Clarke's weaver**, which often moves through the canopy in large flocks (try the Lower Mida Track), and the **Amani sunbird**, which is relatively common and can be seen rapidly gleaning insects among the upper leaves. The woodlands are also important for the **Sokoke pipit** – it can be seen in virtually any patch, but the Kararacha Track is a good bet. A scarce summer visitor that you won't see in Kenya outside the Sokoke area's forests is the **spotted ground thrush**, but even here finding it will be hard work.

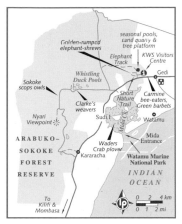

Forest dominated by *Cynometra* trees, punctuated by candelabra euphorbias, covers almost half of the reserve, and is home to Sokoke's real birding prize – the **Sokoke scops owl**. Although this diminutive owl is quite common, it is virtually impossible to see without assistance: to see it, you'd best hire a specialised guide and be prepared to squeeze though the bushes bent double and for long waits in the darkness.

Birders without transport should try the track between the Visitors Centre and the Nature Trail car park. In addition to the resident birds commonly seen – **white-browed coucal**, **green barbet**, **scaly babbler** and **collared sunbird** – watch for migratory **Eurasian** and **white-throated bee-eaters** between October and April. The northern race of the large and spectacular **carmine bee-eater** is generally abundant from September to January. This open scrubby area backing onto forest is also excellent for spying **Fischer's turaco**, a coastal speciality (its loud call makes it easy to detect early in the morning).

Among the mixed forest along the Nature Trail, you'll have to rely more on hearing to find birds and it's probably best to hire a guide. The **Sokoke pipit** can also be found here, but it takes an expert ear to locate it by call. **Blue monkeys** and **yellow baboons** are the most commonly seen animals on this circuit – a troop of about 70 inquisitive baboons frequents the area. There is also a good chance you'll find the **golden-rumped elephant shrew**. About the size of a rabbit, this diurnal insectivore has a gold-coloured rump and is largely restricted to Sokoke (90% of its population survives here). It can often be heard scuffling about pursuing insects in leaf litter, and when alarmed taps a foot or thumps its tail. Elephant shrew territories often span both sides of the trail, so you may see one scamper across the path as it does its rounds of boundary reinforcement.

Seasonal frog pools

Seasonal pools occur on both the Nature Trail and the track leading to the sand quarry. These are the places to look for **frogs** in the rainy season (April to May). Of the 25 frog species in the area there's the wonderfully named **Bunty's dwarf toad** (which mates belly-to-belly), the **marbled shovel-snout**, the **common squeaker** (the young skip the tadpole stage and develop

Location 1.4km from the Gedi junction on the Malindi–Mombasa road. Accessible all year (high clearance vehicles advised).
Facilities Well-equipped Visitors Centre with comprehensive information. Marked nature trails; treetop platform.
Accommodation A wide range in nearby Malindi and Watamu; camping in the reserve (fee applies).
Wildlife rhythms Good any time; waders present October to April, frogs best April and May; Clarke's weavers return in March.
Contact KWS Tourism Ranger (**e** Sokoke@africaonline.co.ke), PO Box 1, Gedi.
Ecotours Arabuko–Sokoke Forest guides can be hired at Sokoke; tours are organised by Mrs Simpson's (☎ 0122–32023) or the Community and Conservation Centre at Turtle Bay Beach Resort (☎ 0122–32003/32226).

The Sokoke scops owl is restricted to only a few sites in remnant coastal woodland. Trained guides at Arabuko-Sokoke Forest can help you find this elusive bird.

straight into froglets), various **leaf-folding frogs** and the **red-legged pan frog**; white masses dangling from branches overhanging water are the nests of the communally-breeding **foam-nest tree frog** (pictured inset, opposite page). A platform 10m up in a tree overlooking the quarry gives great views over a revegetated area: in the wet season there is a good chance of seeing **waterbirds** in the pools and **raptors** are often overhead during mornings and evenings.

Butterflies are abundant and many common species have names that double as descriptions, such as **large striped** and **narrow green-banded swallowtails**, **banded gold tips** and **dark blue pansies**. Whenever near water in Sokoke, check the damp edges for butterflies mud puddling. The **gold-banded forester** is often encountered gliding close over forest tracks in front of you as you walk, and is recognisable by purple and gold bands on its wing tips. The **white flip-flop butterfly** is another common species – it flies in a jerky motion around knee height.

Ancient plants and a quartet of duikers

For the energetic there is a long distance walking track (the 14km Elephant Track) and those with transport can explore 50km of tracks. Although you won't see much wildlife from a car, the main driving track gives a perspective of the three different vegetation zones: it begins in mixed forest before passing through a large area of *Brachystegia*; on higher ground, you'll encounter dense thickets of *Cynometra*. The denser vegetation is favoured habitat of duikers. While you are unlikely to encounter the rare **Aders' duiker** (see boxed text page 102), keep a look out for other **duikers** – **blue**, **red** and **common duikers** all inhabit the forests. The main drive is topped off by Nyari Viewpoint, which is best visited in the afternoon or at sunset. On the way there take an amble around the Whistling Duck Pools: apart from any **waterbirds** that might be here, there is a fine specimen of *Encephalartos hildebrandtii* – one of Sokoke's **cycads** – on the trail (this plant is ancient both in evolutionary terms and because some live for centuries).

The Mida touch

It is essential that birders visit Mida Creek adjacent to the reserve: the extensive mangrove fringed mudflats are Kenya's

---

Natural treasures benefit local communities

The Kipepeo Butterfly Farm, adjacent to Gedi Ruins, was established in 1993 to provide a small income for local farmers, and partly compensate those whose shambas had been damaged by elephants and baboons living in Arabuko–Sokoke Forest. Live pupae collected from the forest by the farmers are taken to Kipepeo, from where many are shipped to live butterfly displays around the world. But many pupae are also hatched under controlled conditions into adult butterflies and displayed in a large flight cage at Kipepeo (which means 'butterfly' in Swahili). Guides can show you the various stages of butterfly development; and in the flight cage you'll get close enough to photograph a few of the hundreds of species in the region (depending on what's hatching at the time of your visit). Arabuko–Sokoke Forest is constantly under threat from the demands of local people for land and firewood. More than 500 farmers are now involved with the Kipepeo butterfly project, which has shown how local people can benefit economically from the preservation of this important woodland remnant. Kipepeo Butterfly Farm (☎ 0122-32380, e kipepeo@africaonline.co.ke, 🖵 www.watamu.net/Kipepeo.html) is open daily between 8 am and 5 pm.

most important site for overwintering **waders**. From November to April large numbers can be seen feeding on the mudflats; the wader line-up includes a host of long distance migrants, such as sandpipers, godwits, whimbrels, curlews and plovers; and larger birds such as **greater flamingos, yellow-billed storks, egrets** and **black herons**. Birds to look out for in the mangroves include **Retz's** and **chestnut-fronted helmet-shrikes, mangrove kingfishers** and, overhead, **northern carmine bee-eaters**. But the prize sighting here is the rare **crab plover** – this large wader is endemic to the Red Sea area and hundreds are occasionally recorded at Mida Creek. Some crab plovers are present all year, but your chances are greater between August and April, when numbers swell with the arrival of migrants from their breeding grounds. Getting to Mida Creek is a little tricky – ask one of the guides at Arabuko–Sokoke to show you the best access tracks.

Low tide at Mida Creek exposes sheets of mud crawling with mudskippers and crabs, which in turn attract birds such as egrets and waders.

Life among the ruins

Mature forest growing on the coral rag around and among the historic Gedi Ruins has a different species composition to nearby Arabuko–Sokoke Forest. There's an impressive diversity of tree species, including baobabs, and the area is well worth exploring for wildlife. Keep an eye out for semitame **blue monkeys**, which are common among the ruins, and at dusk for **bats** emerging from between tumbled and broken boulders. **Lizards** rustling through the leaf litter also find plenty of cover among the coral rag; and the area is famous for **butterflies** (see boxed text). Birders in particular will find good pickings at Gedi: although thick, the forest is not extensive and skulkers can be relatively easy to see here. Gedi is known as a reliable location for **great sparrowhawks, Fischer's turacos** and **bearded scrub robins**; and tantalising possibilities include the **African pitta** (although sightings are few and far between these days) and **bat hawks** (keep an eye out around dusk for these crepuscular raptors). ∎

Watching tips

To see Kenyan crested guineafowl, drive about just after rain – the guineafowl then come out of the forested areas and should appear on the open tracks. Bird the *Brachystegia* woodland in the early morning then concentrate on the cooler mixed and *Cynometra* forest after 9 am, when bird activity starts to slow down. Carry the butterfly identification chart (available from the Visitors Centre) while wandering about. The best birding at Mida Creek is one to two hours before high tide.

AMBOSELI NATIONAL PARK

Famous animals with a famous backdrop

Wildlife highlights

Famous for large herds of elephants – and big tuskers at that. Open plains allow fabulous wildlife viewing and photography, and mammals are very relaxed after years of tourism. Wildebeests, buffaloes, plains zebras, gazelles, spotted hyenas and elephants are abundant; lions occur in small numbers and cheetahs are sometimes seen. Permanent marshes are frequented by hippos, elephants and buffaloes. Prolific birdlife – 425 species have been recorded – includes waterbirds, plains and woodland species; Amboseli is particularly good for grey crowned cranes.

LAKE Amboseli takes up a large part of this relatively small park (which is also an International Biosphere Reserve) and Mt Kilimanjaro provides it with an extremely picturesque backdrop. The lake is typically dry and the park's few patches of trees are mostly in the east, but run-off from surrounding mountains feeds Amboseli's permanent swamps and creates a marshy green belt across the middle of the park. The swamps are a centre of activity for **elephants**, **hippos**, **buffaloes** and abundant **waterbirds**, and the surrounding flat grasslands are home to grazing **antelopes**. **Spotted hyenas** are plentiful, and **jackals**, **warthogs**, **olive baboons** and **vervet monkeys** all occur. **Lions** can still be found in Amboseli, although the famous black-maned lions are no longer here and black rhinos are also now extinct in the park.

Marshy centres of activity

Normatior, also known as Observation Hill, provides an ideal lookout from which to orientate yourself to the plains, swamps and roads below. From the top you can spot hundreds of dots on the plains (typically **plains zebras, Grant's** and **Thomson's gazelles** and **wildebeests**), with larger masses near the swamp edges and in the swamps themselves (**hippos, buffaloes** and **elephants**). Amboseli is well known for its 700 resident elephants,

Trunk calls

Amboseli's elephants are probably the best known of all: Cynthia Moss and her team have studied them since 1972. And Moss knows *all* of the park's elephants by sight – 53 families and 900 individuals. How? Like a lion's whisker spots, a cheetah's tail bands or a zebra's stripes, each elephant has unique identifiers: the profile of the ear and its filigree of veins are the equivalent of fingerprints. Yet elephants probably don't rely on sight to recognise each other. Research shows that they can identify at least 100 individuals by their calls. They even remember the voice of dead companions: when researchers played the calls of an elephant that had died two years earlier, her family responded with the 'I know you' call.

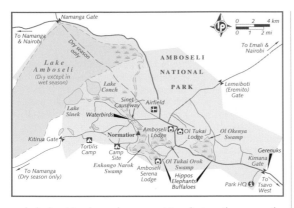

Location 265km south-east of Nairobi; road access limited in wet seasons; all-season airstrip.
Facilities Lodges run game drives, some have nature walks. Guides can be hired from park HQ.
Accommodation Two camping grounds and four lodges.
Wildlife rhythms Mammals easier to see near water during dry seasons; migratory birds peak November to March.
Contact Senior Warden (☎ 0302-22251, fax 22250), Amboseli NP, PO Box 18, Namanga.
Ecotours Numerous operators visit Amboseli from Nairobi and Arusha (Tanzania) – but shop around. Amboseli Lodge runs guided bird walks.

and elephant herds can be seen raising dust as they cross the plains to drink and feed at the swamps.

From Observation Hill the northern route runs across the Sinet Causeway, which makes an excellent place from which to start birdwatching over the swamp. In and near the marshes **African jacanas** are abundant and you'll typically find several species of **heron**, such as **squacco**, **grey**, **goliath** and **black-headed**, plus **great white egrets**, **glossy ibises**, **Egyptian geese**, and **blacksmith** and **spur-winged plovers**. There's also great birding along the causeway between the airstrip and Ol Tukai if you travel slowly: the list is long, but includes **saddle-billed storks**, **white-faced whistling-ducks**, **African fish eagles**, **little egrets**, **red-billed teal** and the migratory **purple heron** (which overwinters at Amboseli). Large numbers of **flamingos** may be present in season.

Amboseli is also home to less-commonly seen species including **common redshanks**, **purple swamphens** and **Eurasian thick-knees**. Among the various weavers that you should encounter in the wooded areas are **white-headed buffalo-weavers** and **grey-capped social weavers**. **Superb starlings** will help themselves to leftovers, and **drongos**, **red-billed hornbills** and **grey-headed sparrows** are also common. Anywhere they can find a vantage point, **lilac-breasted rollers** – a hot favourite with photographers – are likely to be seen perching and scanning for ground insects and lizards. Look for **grey crowned cranes** out on the plains.

During dry seasons Amboseli's herds kick up clouds of dust as they file down to waterholes.

Birds migrating from the north begin to arrive in October (departing again in March), so a visit after the short rains begin in November could give you a good shot at Amboseli's full complement of birds. Depending on the rains, Lake Amboseli may hold water and other small lakes may appear; by meandering around these temporary wetlands (as the roads allow) you can get away from the congested main wildlife viewing circuit.

If you leave Amboseli by the Kimana Gate on the way to Tsavo West NP, you'll probably find **Masai giraffes** in the acacia woodland. Better still, this is the place to spot **gerenuks**, particularly just outside the park on the road leading away from Kimana. These unusual gazelles browse by standing on their hind legs and stretching their neck – this behaviour is fairly easy to observe. ■

> **Watching tips**
> Amboseli is one of only two places where you can see the Taveta golden weaver, but it is common around lodges and camps.

KAKAMEGA FOREST
The best of the monkeys

> **Wildlife highlights**
> Largest surviving stand of rainforest in Kenya, now marking the easternmost distribution of many West African species. Blue and red-tailed monkeys plus black-and-white colobus easily seen among seven primate species, and red-legged sun and giant forest squirrels frequent the canopy. First-rate rainforest birding includes turacos, bee-eaters and hornbills among a list of 330 species; others include a selection of greenbuls, finches, barbets and starlings. Butterflies are also profuse – 400 species recorded – and reptiles with a West African spin include the Gaboon viper.

MONKEY activity is at its best firstly once the day warms up and again a few hours before sunset. **Black-and-white colobus** are abundant and sometimes keep company with **blue monkeys**; both, plus **red-tailed monkeys**, can usually be seen near Isecheno Forest Centre. Red-tailed monkeys also associate with blues and both visit fruiting trees at Rondo Retreat to feast on brightly coloured fruit – **African crowned eagles** overhead send them into a screaming panic. **Olive baboons** loiter near camping grounds at Isecheno and Buyangu, and raid shambas around Kisere Forest. Kisere Forest is also a good place to look for **de Brazza's monkeys**.

Red-legged sun squirrels, easily identified by their rich red thighs, and **giant forest squirrels** are both regular canopy visitors at Rondo Retreat. **Bushbucks** are becoming rare, but **blue** or **Harvey's duikers** might be startled on forest trails – they normally freeze to avoid detection. **Servals** have been seen occasionally in glades south of Buyangu Hill. **Rhinoceros** and **Gaboon vipers**, two superbly camouflaged snakes, are rarely seen, but **Nile monitors** may be seen wandering throughout the forest, especially around Isiukhu Falls. Forest edges and grasslands are favoured habitat for **skinks**, and **dwarf chameleons** – a mere 10cm in length – are a Kakamega speciality. **Butterflies** are most active by late morning; large charaxes and swallowtails congregate around animal dung along trails.

Peerless forest birdwatching

Kakamega is the largest remaining stronghold in Kenya for 84 bird species whose main distribution lies further west. Rondo Retreat is an excellent place to start looking: **Mackinnon's fiscals** are common in the grounds; **starlings**, **barbets** and **weavers** sun on top of great trees; **snowy-headed robin-chats** inhabit the gully behind the gardens; and **grey parrots** sometimes roost nearby. **Cinnamon-chested bee-eaters** pursue passing insects from prominent perches; **blue-headed bee-eaters** are another speciality better sought on the Ikuywa Trail; and **little bee-eaters** nest in banks near Buyangu Hill. **Great blue** and **Ross' turacos** are commonly seen at Rondo and Isecheno; and another noisy canopy dweller, the **black-and-white-casqued hornbill**, lives throughout Kakamega Forest.

A natural medicine chest

Local people have long used Kakamega Forest as a source of natural products: wood for building, cooking fires and charcoal; grass for thatches, lianas for rope and bark for making blankets; and the *Raffia* palms growing along forest rivers for weaving baskets. But with the rapidly increasing human population the supply will soon be exhausted, and perhaps more serious is the potential loss of an estimated 50 medicinal plant species that grow here. For example, the bark of *Croton megalocarpus* and *Olea* trees is soaked, pounded and used as a remedy for intestinal worms; *Fagaropsis* roots are boiled and used to treat chest pains; and *Diospyros* roots are burnt and licked as a cure for tonsillitis. Animal products also have remedial uses – antelope droppings are soaked and used as a remedy for stomach ache – but species that are eaten, such as antelopes and porcupines, are becoming scarce.

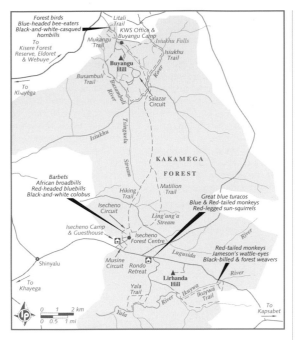

Trails near the Ikuywa River also support abundant **rainforest birds** (plus **monkeys** and **butterflies**) such as **barbets, greenbuls, starlings, cuckoo-shrikes, wattle-eyes** and **cuckoos**; unsociable forest weavers such as **brown-capped** and **black-billed weavers**; and the **yellowbill**, a forest cuckoo. The dazzling **red-headed bluebill** is common along roads and trails. Forest glades – especially along the Hiking Trail – harbour **harlequin quails** and **button-quails**, the **white stork** (a seasonal visitor) and **grey crowned cranes**. **African black ducks** and **giant kingfishers** frequent the river along the Isiukhu Trail and **crested guineafowl** is most common in the northern Buyangu area.

Creatures of the night

After sundown the noise of insects and **frogs** is drowned out only by the frequent thunderstorms. **African giant snails**, **goliath beetles** and **fireflies** become active, and spotlighting along roads and trails could reveal some of Kakamega's nocturnal gems: **bushpigs** are quite common; **aardvarks** are recorded occasionally; and you might pick out the huge eyes of a **potto**. **Lord Derby's anomalure** glides across clearings, and mammals that truly fly include the **hammer-headed fruit-bat** – Africa's largest – and smaller **insect-eating bats**, which emerge en masse at dusk from old mine shafts in Lirhanda Hill. **Marsh mongooses** live near waterways throughout the forest, which are also patrolled by **African clawless otters**; **brush-tailed porcupines** favour valley bottoms; and **tree pangolins** are most common in habitat mosaics. Forest owls that might be encountered are the **African wood owl** and **red-chested owlet**. ■

Location 45km north of Kisumu; 418km west of Nairobi. 4WD recommended on forest roads after rain.
Facilities Marked walking trails. Guides can be hired at Buyangu KWS office and at Isecheno Forest Station. Night walks by permission.
Accommodation Camping ground and guesthouse at Isecheno, camping ground and bandas at Udo's; guesthouse at Rondo Retreat; hotels in Kakamega.
Wildlife rhythms The end of heavy rains triggers breeding of forest birds (June to August) and the emergence of many butterflies (best August to September). Up to 30 species of migrant bird arrive in October.
Contacts Kenya Wildlife Service (☎ 0331-20425), PO Box 879, Kakamega.
Kakamega Forest Station, PO Box 88, Kakamega.
Ecotours Expert bird guides can be arranged through EAOS (☎ 02-33 11 91) and Sirikwa Safaris (☎ 0325-20061 c/o Soy Trading), PO Box 332, Kitale.

Watching tips

The Pumphouse Trail near Isecheno Forest Centre is good for monkeys and birds – African broadbills and white-spotted flufftails are seen along here. Spotlighting is probably the best chance of seeing a hippo on the Yala River (rare), and a Kakamega speciality, the giant otter shrew. A night walk in Kisere Forest might turn up a genet or African civet. African grass owls and African white-tailed nightjars have been recorded on the Falls Trail.

MOUNT KENYA NATIONAL PARK

Rare mammals on lofty peak

> **Wildlife highlights**
> Colourful wildflowers, and giant groundsels and lobelias are among at least 10 endemic plants of alpine meadows. Dense forests and bamboo shelter elephants, buffaloes and black rhinos; larger herbivores such as plains zebras and common elands graze as high as alpine meadows; bushbucks and defassa waterbucks are common in forests; and leopards reach the lofty passes. Sykes' monkeys (a local race of blue monkey), black-and-white colobus and tree hyraxes live in forests, where common birds include Hartlaub's turacos, white-headed wood-hoopoes and red-fronted parrots; high altitude birds are an attraction.

DISTINCT vegetation zones form horizontal bands across the slopes and valleys that radiate from Mt Kenya's peaks. Tall forests of camphors, cedars and African olive cloak the lower slopes, their trunks fluted like Greek columns or twisted like giant sticks of barley sugar. Beard moss swaying in the breeze looks like the dangling tail tufts of **black-and-white colobus**, which leap into the overgrown ravines when spotted; **Sykes' monkeys** also feed along the roadsides. **Elephants** and **buffaloes** generally keep out of sight, but **bushbucks** and **defassa waterbucks** are common, and **black-fronted duikers**, **sunis** and **giant forest hogs** all live in the understorey.

Pairs of **Hunter's cisticolas** 'duet' on top of bushes; **Hartlaub's turacos** glide across the road with crimson wing flashes; **silvery-cheeked hornbills** and **red-fronted parrots** sun themselves on the topmost branches (especially near the Naro Moru park entrance); parties of **white-headed wood-hoopoes** probe cracks; and **cinnamon-chested bee-eaters** snap up prey from exposed branches. **Tree hyraxes** start screeching after sunset, and **white-tailed mongooses** might be spotlighted along roads. Once a stronghold of **black rhinos**, about half a dozen are thought to remain in Mt Kenya's forests; other rarities include **golden cats**, and melanistic (black) **servals** and **leopards**.

At about 2400m, dense thickets of 12m-high bamboo appear, broken by the trails of **elephants** and **buffaloes** whose

Coping with summer every day and winter every night

Giant groundsels and lobelias have various adaptations to Mt Kenya's extreme daily temperature fluctuations. Rosettes of densely-packed leaves close at night around a central bud, like an artichoke, protecting them from bitter winds and subzero temperatures. Dead leaves hanging off groundsels insulate sap in the stem and hold heat absorbed during the day; and a fluffy white tuft (called a tomentum) on the underside of the cabbage groundsel (*Senecio brassica*) helps trap warm air.

Lobelia keniensis (pictured) secretes a fluid into its rosettes – it looks like rainwater – that freezes over to insulate the plant at night. Only a thin layer of ice has time to form overnight; the rising sun causes rosettes to reopen within minutes and the ice to melt. Each rosette grows about 2.5cm per year for several decades, produces one flowering spike then dies; ostrich plume (*L. telekii*) flowers once every 40 to 70 years.

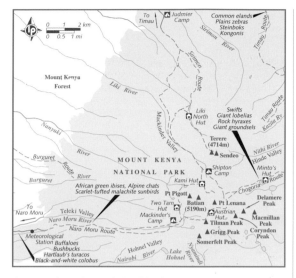

Location 193km north-east of Nairobi. 4WD essential to reach trailheads when wet.
Facilities Various walking trails to summits.
Accommodation Basic huts on main climbing routes; huts at Meteorological Station; bandas and lodges outside park; hotels in Nanyuki.
Wildlife rhythms Large mammals move to higher altitudes during dry seasons (January to March and July to October). High altitude birds may move to lower elevations during rains (March to June and October to December).
Contact Mt Kenya NP (☎ 0171-2575), PO Box 69, Naro Moru.
Ecotours Bike Treks (☎ 02-44 63 71), Savage Wilderness Safaris (☎/fax 02-52 15 90) and Mountain Club of Kenya (☎ 02-50 17 47) can organise walks, plus equipment, porters and guides.

droppings litter the roads; **bushbucks** are still common on grassy verges at this height, **black-fronted duikers** and **bongos** are far more secretive. Above 2600m spreading East African rosewood (*Hagenia*) trees grow in open glades, becoming stunted at the treeline; the mossy ground is pierced by wildflowers, bracken and tall forest lobelias. Beyond 2900m head-high giant heather shelters herds of **buffaloes**, **common elands** and **plains zebras** (although large animals are sighted only occasionally by walkers); **lions** are also sometimes encountered. **Sunbirds** probe aromatic proteas, and other wildflowers include everlastings, gladioli and the brilliant blue *Delphinium*. **Alpine chats** perch fearlessly at arm's length if you stop long enough and **scarlet-tufted malachite sunbirds** sip from red-hot pokers (this popular garden flower is native to East Africa's highlands).

Above 3300m vast swathes of tussock grass stretch to the snowline. Gladioli add a scarlet slash to the scene and at about 3500m fleshy lobelias and groundsels – the so-called 'big game plants' – reach gargantuan proportions: two species of giant groundsel grow as high as 6m. **Rock hyraxes** live among the outcrops, watchful of **Verreaux's eagles** and **mountain buzzards** patrolling overhead. **Elephants** and **buffaloes** have been seen as high as 4000m in the Teleki Valley; and the northern slopes support resident grazers such as **kongonis**, **steinbucks** and herds of **plains zebras** (there's a chance of seeing all of these along the Timau Route). Herds of **elands** are also resident – the Sirimon roadhead is a good place to see them. Rodents abound up here: **groove-toothed rats** scuttle across the trails and chattering **African common dormice** keep hikers awake at night in the huts. Birds include **African snipe** in the grasslands, **African black ducks** on tarns and **white-naped ravens** scavenging around huts. The mighty **lammergeier** cruises the greatest heights – try Sendeo or Terere Peaks on the Sirimon Route; **mottled** and **scarce swifts** are common, and **alpine swifts** can be seen near Two Tarn Hut. ■

Watching tips Earth mounds produced by Rüppell's root-rat (*Tachyoryctes splendens*), endemic to Mt Kenya, can be seen in the Hinde Valley. Mackinder's eagle-owl (a race of Cape eagle-owl) is common in the Teleki Valley – a park ranger may know of a roost. Leopards are the most common predator and have been seen even near the summit of Point Lenana. Spotted hyenas travel far up the Teleki Valley, cheetahs are occasionally seen on the Timau and Sirimon Trails, and lions hunt high on the Naro Moru Route.

NAIROBI NATIONAL PARK

Plains drama next to international airport

Wildlife highlights
Plains mammals such as black and white rhinos, Masai giraffes, plains zebras, buffaloes, kongonis (also known as Coke's hartebeests) and wildebeests (in season). A good chance of lions and cheetahs, and leopards and spotted hyenas also resident; also olive baboons, vervet and blue monkeys, hippos and Nile crocodiles. Grassland birds a speciality among 550 recorded bird species.

FIRST wildlife impressions of Nairobi city will probably consist of a few birds: opportunistic **pied crows** and **black kites** wheeling over the market; **red-winged starlings** clinging to walls as if they were cliff faces; platoons of **marabou storks** and **cattle egrets** on playing fields; and chittering flocks of **little swifts** near Nairobi University. It's not the most prepossessing city on earth, but this is Kenya so something living can usually be seen in even the smallest patch of greenery: **variable sunbirds** – one of the most common city birds – a **common bulbul** or two, iridescent **greater blue-eared starlings**, and a few **rufous sparrows** or **speckled mousebirds**. **Butterflies**, such as swallowtails, flit about in parks and hotel gardens; **silvery-cheeked hornbills** and showy **Hartlaub's turacos** are common in leafy suburbs; and even in the middle of town the comical honking of **hadada ibises** will be heard most days. The musical 'tink' of tree frogs at night is actually **epauletted bats**, a type of fruit-bat (some roost under eaves at Nairobi Museum); other nocturnal garden visitors include **African wood owls** and **montane nightjars**.

Fortunately, only half an hour's drive south from the city centre there is excellent – and safe – wildlife viewing at Nairobi NP. Most of the popular characters play out the drama of the plains right next to Jomo Kenyatta international airport: there are no elephants, but **plains zebra**, **Masai giraffes**, **buffaloes**,

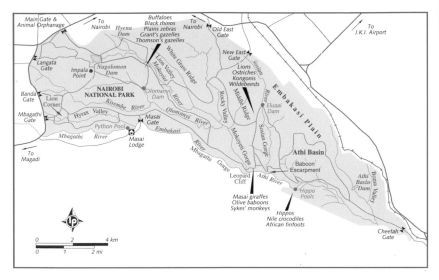

antelopes and gazelles complement a cat list headed by **lions** and **cheetahs**. Nairobi NP has Kenya's highest density of **black rhinos** (about 50) and there's a good chance of seeing **white rhinos** (which were introduced to the park). **Spotted hyenas** and **leopards** also occur – the latter a possibility along rivers in tall trees. Small antelopes – **oribis, steinbucks, Kirk's dik-diks** and **bushbucks** – live among the whistling thorn and *Cordia* bushes on high ground in the park's west.

Impala Point is a good place from which to scan the grasslands for **rhinos, Masai giraffes, buffaloes**, and **antelopes** such as **common elands** and **kongonis** (Coke's hartebeests). **Grant's** and **Thomson's gazelles**, **impalas** and **warthogs** can be encountered virtually anywhere on the plains. **Wildebeests** cross the park's southern boundary to disperse across the Kitengala Plains during the rains, but a few are normally present year-round – try the Embakasi Plain. **Plains zebras** join the dispersal, but can usually be seen year-round in the park. **Marabou storks, vultures** and **hawk-eagles** sit in tall acacias, and grassland birds such as **secretary birds, ostriches, bustards** and **Jackson's widowbirds** are park specialities.

Baboon cliffs and hippo pools

Hippos wallow in the Athi River, emerging to graze on the banks at night, and **terrapins** and **Nile crocodiles** bask on exposed mud. A ranger guide should be available for the Nature Trail at the Hippo Pools, where **vervet monkeys, pigeons, barbets** and **starlings** feed in African fig trees along the banks. **Defassa waterbucks** are common along the Athi, and **rock hyraxes, klipspringers** and **Chanler's mountain reedbucks** frequent the steep slopes of Mbagathi Gorge. **Olive baboons**, and **vervet** and **blue monkeys** loiter at the top of the Baboon Escarpment, where **rock hyraxes** also wait for handouts and red-headed **agama lizards** nod to prospective mates. ∎

Location 9km south of Nairobi.
Facilities Animal Orphanage just inside the main entrance.
Accommodation None in park. Hotels, hostels and backpacker accommodation in Nairobi.
Wildlife rhythms Wildebeests disperse November to May, returning July to October and also in March. Fields of wildflowers appear after rains. Male Jackson's widowbirds display March to May.
Contact Kenya Wildlife Service (☎ 02-50 06 22, fax 50 17 52), PO Box 40241, Nairobi.
Ecotours Good park roads can easily be negotiated by hire car, although 4WD may be necessary during rains. EAOS (☎ 02-33 11 91) and UTC (☎ 02-33 19 60) can organise tours from Nairobi.

> **Watching tips**
> White rhinos often graze near the main entrance. Ask rangers at the main entrance for directions to see cheetahs and lions. African finfoots live along the Mbagathi River.

SAMBURU, BUFFALO SPRINGS & SHABA NATIONAL RESERVES

Diverse predators on semiarid plains

Wildlife highlights

Healthy numbers of predators, with lions, leopards and cheetahs frequently seen; also spotted and striped hyenas, bat-eared foxes and hunting dogs (rare). Elephants, buffaloes, hippos, plains zebras, reticulated giraffes, lesser and greater kudus complemented by herbivores typical of semiarid plains: Grevy's zebras, beisa oryxes, gerenuks, Kirk's and Günther's dik-diks, and the northern race of Grant's gazelle. Good pickings among 395 bird species, includes 47 birds of prey, Somali ostriches, vulturine guineafowl, Verreaux's eagle-owls, sandgrouse and hornbills.

LARGE, domed termite mounds among the dry thorny shrublands make dens for **aardvarks, warthogs** and **bat-eared foxes**, and lookouts for **cheetahs** – the latter are commonly sighted in the open woodland of Buffalo Springs. Succulent aloes, euphorbias and desert roses grow on rocky ridges in Shaba and Samburu that shelter **hyraxes, klipspringers** and **leopards**. Shaba is famous for large prides of **lions**, which during the day laze under dense thickets of the leathery mswaki bush – used by Africans as a toothbrush. Nocturnal predators such as **golden** and **black-backed jackals**, and both **striped** and **spotted hyenas** live in all three reserves; and **aardwolves** are occasionally seen. **Common genets** scrounge around campsites; and **banded** and **dwarf mongooses** charge around in packs looking for small prey. **Unstriped ground squirrels** and **Cape hares** make tasty snacks for small cats and large raptors.

Giraffes, gazelles and giraffe-gazelles

Browsers of the thorny shrubs include **common elands, impalas, Bright's gazelles** (the pale northern race of Grant's gazelle) and **gerenuks** (also called giraffe-gazelles). **Reticulated giraffes** also live here and browse even higher up the trees. Both **Grevy's** and

The dangers of dining on thorny crowns

Acacias – the distinctive thorn trees of Kenya – grow in profusion in Samburu, Buffalo Springs and Shaba NRs, shading animals and supporting hanging colonies of weavers. During dry seasons many acacia species shed their leaves, quickly bursting into green again when their shallow, densely matted roots absorb the first rains. Most acacias are armed with sharp thorns, and stinging ants that take up residence in their branches are a further hazard to would-be browsers. Nonetheless, olive baboons feast on young pods, the protein-rich leaves are sought by antelopes such as gerenuks, impalas and dik-diks – and giraffes and rhinos hardly seem to notice the thorns as they munch away. Perhaps the most easily recognisable species is *Acacia tortillis*, the flat-topped umbrella acacia, which grows in large stands which provide shade for oryxes, giraffes, zebras, gazelles and cheetahs. *Acacia elatior* attains 20m or more in height and is the most common tree along the Ewaso Nyiro river.

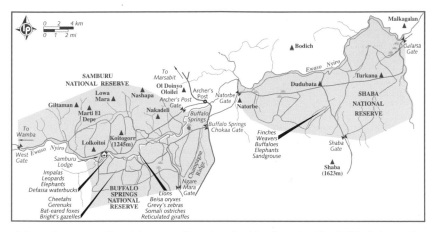

plains zebras graze the plains, sometimes in mixed herds: Grevy's lives in all three parks, but plains is rarely seen north of the Ewaso Nyiro. **Warthogs** root for bulbs and **beisa oryxes** graze on short grass throughout the reserves; and both **lesser** and **greater kudus** are seen in small numbers on the densely vegetated slopes of Lowa Mara and Koitogor in Samburu. The scarlet rump of **white-headed buffalo-weavers** in flight is a common sight; other conspicuous birds include **Somali ostriches**, **secretary birds** and **vulturine guineafowl**, which explode in a puff of red where they've been dustbathing. **Red-billed** and **Von der Decken's hornbills** are common, and **sandgrouse** drink at the Ewaso Nyiro river in the evening.

River traffic

The Ewaso Nyiro is the lifeblood of **hippos**, which can usually be seen in the lower reaches near tributaries, and **Nile crocodiles** – some large specimens bask on exposed sandbars. **Buffaloes** shelter in dense riverside thickets, and **impalas** and **common waterbucks** also stay close to the permanent greenery. **Storks** feed along the banks, and **Verreaux's eagle-owls** and **martial eagles** hunt from large trees. **Kirk's** and **Günther's dik-diks** – both favourite prey of leopards – hold territories in the dense bush but are also found far from water. Large animals which can negotiate the Ewaso Nyiro (and its crocs) pass freely between Samburu and Buffalo Springs. In the late afternoon **elephants** – red from dust-bathing – often file down to the river to drink or spray themselves with sand. Giant figs, acacias, Tana poplars and 20m-high doum palms line the banks and mark the course of the river to the horizon. The fruits of the palm are eaten by **elephants**, **vervet monkeys** and **olive baboons**; troops of vervets and baboons raid unattended camping grounds and rest under riverside trees during the heat of the day. **African orange-bellied parrots** also feed on the doum fruits and nest in old palms. The **palm-nut vulture** also feeds on palm nuts; more conventional, carrion-eating **vultures** wait on large boughs for thermals to carry them over the plains. Quick-flying **African palm swifts** are active along the river at dawn and dusk. ∎

Location Buffalo Springs main gate 20km north of Isiolo, 355km north of Nairobi; 4WD recommended in wet seasons.
Accommodation Camping grounds, tented camps and lodges in all parks.
Wildlife rhythms Vegetation dies back in dry seasons (June to October and December to April), and large animals concentrate near springs and the Ewaso Nyiro river, dispersing across the parks soon after rain.
Contact Samburu NR, PO Box 519, Isiolo; Buffalo Springs NR, PO Box 36, Isiolo.
Ecotours EAOS (☎ 02-33 11 91), Gametrackers (☎ 02-33 89 27), UTC (☎ 02-33 19 60) and Abercrombie & Kent (☎ 02-22 87 00) can organise safaris from Nairobi.

Watching tips

Nile crocodiles are fed at various lodges along the Ewaso Nyiro river. Leopards lie up in tall acacias or dense vegetation near the river. Klipspringers may be seen on outcrops near Dakadima Hill in Shaba. Caracals are most frequently encountered in Shaba and northern Samburu.

ABERDARE NATIONAL PARK

Salt lick city

Location 160km north of Nairobi; 20km west of Nyeri.
Facilities Walking trails.
Accommodation Camping grounds, cottages and lodges in park; hotels in Nyeri.
Wildlife rhythms Elephants and some antelopes disperse to higher altitudes during dry seasons, retreating to forested slopes in wet seasons.
Contact Aberdare NP (☎ 0171-55024), PO Box 22, Nyeri.
Ecotours Organise game drives with The Ark (☎ 02-21 69 40) and Treetops (☎ 02-54 07 80), or EAOS (☎ 02-33 11 91) from nearby Sangare Ranch; and from Outspan Hotel, Nyeri (☎ 0171-2424).

Watching tips

Black rhinos sometimes wander onto lawns at Tusk Camp. A black serval is a permanent resident around Kiandongoro Fishing Lodge.

ELEPHANTS and **buffaloes** are common in the densely forested Salient (the park's eastern extension), but the quickest way to see them is at the park's two game lodges. **Bushbucks, defassa waterbucks, warthogs, giant forest hogs** and **olive baboons** are also regular visitors; and the night shift can include **lions, leopards, spotted hyenas, bushpigs, genets** and **white-tailed mongooses.** A few **ducks, herons, storks** and **coots** usually linger at the lodges' waterholes; and **vervet monkeys** forage in open areas during the day. **Black-and-white colobus,** the park's most common monkey, and **blue monkeys** can usually be seen feeding along the roads to the high plains.

Elephant and **buffalo** dung litters the tracks, attracting fly-snapping **yellow wagtails.** A few **buffaloes** can generally be seen around the Salient's waterholes – **cattle egrets** often indicate their whereabouts. About 50 **black rhinos** live in the park – sightings are rare, but one occasionally visits a lodge's salt lick. **Defassa waterbucks** and **bushbucks** graze along ravines; other **antelopes** – **common elands, sunis** and **Harvey's duikers** – are less likely to be seen in the open. **Caracals,** and melanistic (black) forms of **leopards** and **servals** inhabit the Salient; **African golden cats** have been seen near camping grounds at the eastern end. Large **forest birds** include **silvery-cheeked hornbills, Hartlaub's turacos** and the monkey-eating **crowned eagle.**

Vegetation grows in distinct horizontal bands as altitude increases: **bongos** (now rare) inhabit dense bamboo thickets and moss-encrusted *Hagenia* glades above the tall forest; giant heather grows at still higher elevations and, on the highest plateaus, giant fleshy lobelias and groundsels punctuate broad swathes of tussock grass. **Common elands, lions** (hairier and more spotted up here) and **leopards** venture above the treeline, and **servals** are regularly seen hunting rodents or **Jackson's francolins. Mountain buzzards** soar over moorlands; and **alpine chats** perch at arm's length around picnic sites. ∎

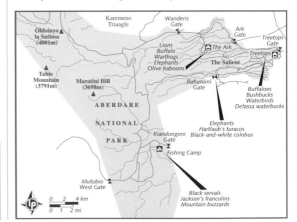

HELL'S GATE NATIONAL PARK

Walking among geysers and grazers

OL Njorowa Gorge (Hell's Gate) makes a natural highway for both plains animals and people: since it's lion-free it's possible to walk or cycle among herds of **plains zebras** and **kongonis** (Coke's hartebeests) that share the flat grasslands with lesser numbers of **impalas**, and **Grant's** and **Thomson's gazelles**. **Warthogs, secretary birds** and **common ostriches** also strut about on the valley floor and **cheetahs** are sometimes encountered. **Masai giraffes** are breeding residents and **defassa waterbucks** might be seen where the gorge narrows towards steaming volcanic vents at the park's centre and west end. **Jackals** or **spotted hyenas** sometimes scavenge around camping grounds at night.

    Rock hyraxes bask on Fischer's Tower, a 25m-high volcanic plug that commands the eastern entrance to the gorge, bolting into crevices should a **Verreaux's eagle** cruise past. **Augur buzzards** perch conspicuously on top of the pillar and both raptors nest on the cliffs nearby. Five other species of **birds of prey** nest on the 120m-high cliffs and there are plans to reintroduce the mighty **lammergeier**, which formerly bred here. **Olive baboons** lounge about on rocks at the base of the pillar, attracted to the fig trees growing from cracks near its base; **Chanler's mountain reedbucks** may sometimes be seen grazing on the slopes nearby in the late afternoon.

Whitewashed cliffs

Coarse grass on the slopes and cliff tops is favoured by **steinbucks** – look for their black nose stripe – and **klipspringers**, although the latter are never far from protective rock faces. **Common elands, buffaloes** and **Kirk's dik-diks** shelter among stands of dense *Croton* bushes. The cliffs themselves provide nesting sites for thousands of **Nyanza** and **mottled swifts**; their chief predators – **lanner** and **peregrine falcons** – perch on high ledges and cut swathes through the flocks. Colonies of nesting **Egyptian** and **Rüppell's griffon vultures** have whitewashed the walls near the western end of the gorge – the birds often sun themselves with outstretched wings. You'll need sharp eyes to spot **Cape eagle-owls** on the cliffs, but they also nest in the gorge. ∎

Wildlife highlights
The herbivore line-up includes plains zebras, common elands, impalas, waterbucks, kongonis, Masai giraffes, buffaloes, Grant's and Thomson's gazelles and warthogs; predators include spotted hyenas and (rarely) cheetahs; good for small antelopes such as steinbucks and klipspringers. Nesting birds of prey a highlight, and include colonies of Rüppell's griffon and Egyptian vultures.

Location 100km north of Nairobi; 18km west of Naivasha. Unsealed roads.
Facilities Visitors Centre.
Accommodation Camping grounds in park. Camping grounds, bandas and hotels at Lake Naivasha.
Wildlife rhythms Grass shorter and animals more visible during dry seasons. Swifts breed on cliffs March to May.
Contact Hell's Gate National Park (☎ 0311-20284, fax 20577), PO Box 234, Naivasha.
Ecotours UTC (☎ 02-33 19 60) can organise tours from Nairobi.

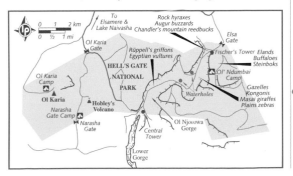

Watching tips
Klipspringers may sometimes be seen on high cliffs near Elsa Gate. Stake out artificial waterholes in the gorge for mammals – the park is otherwise virtually waterless.

LAKE BARINGO

Excellent birding in semiarid ecosystem

Wildlife highlights

Hippos, Nile crocodiles and brilliant birding (460 species recorded). Waterbirds a strong suite including flamingos, ducks, storks, herons and pelicans; African fish eagles are common and local specialities include lesser moorhens, giant kingfishers and, at the nearby escarpment, white-faced scops owls, Hemprich's hornbills and brown-tailed rock chats.

Location 110km north of Nakuru; 266km north-west of Nairobi. Sealed roads.
Facilities Expert guides, boat hire and daily bird walks at Lake Baringo Country Club. Boat hire at Kampi ya Samaki.
Accommodation Lakeside camping, cottages and hotel. Hotels in Kampi ya Samaki.
Wildlife rhythms Migratory waders and ducks arrive October to November. Many local birds breed April to June.
Contact Lake Baringo (☎ 037-40746, fax 40748), PO Box 64, Marigat.
Ecotours EAOS (☎ 02-33 11 91) and UTC (☎ 02-33 19 60) can arrange tours from Nairobi.

Watching tips

Verreaux's eagle-owls are resident in the grounds of Lake Baringo Country Club, where feeding stations attract weavers, starlings, buffalo-weavers and finches.

SPARSE vegetation around this large freshwater lake belies great birdwatching. Abundant **waterbirds** and **African fish eagles** compete with **Nile crocodiles** for fish; and **hippos** that graze on the western shore at night loll in the shallows in the early morning – a bow wave shows when a male is charging you underwater. Colourful – and easily seen – bird species include **red-and-yellow barbets,** and an assortment of **starlings, hornbills** and **sunbirds.** The nocturnal **Heuglin's courser** lives in scrub north of Kampi ya Samaki – ask a local guide to help find them.

Drowned trees fringing the western shore make ideal perches for waterbirds such as **long-tailed cormorants;** and oodles of **pied kingfishers** – plus an occasional **giant kingfisher.** But it's not just fish eaters: **Madagascar bee-eaters** hawk from these drowned trees between May and October – **blue-cheeked bee-eaters** take over the same

perches from November to April. South along the shore, **lesser moorhens** and **African jacanas** pick their way over lily pads and mats of Nile cabbage; **flamingos** sweep their bills through the shallows joined by **yellow-billed storks** and **African spoonbills;** **pelicans** feed in deeper water; **ducks** and **geese** loaf on muddy shores; and **glossy ibises** and **grey herons** are dwarfed by **goliath herons** – the latter breed year-round on rocky islands in the lake.

At the cliff face

Acacia-Commiphora woodland 3km west of the shoreline at the foot of 100m-high cliffs has a rich bird diversity. For good birdwatching walk north along the cliffs from the lake turn-off in the early morning (bird activity dies off after about 9 am). **Bristle-crowned starlings** perch high up and **rock hyraxes** bask on trees on top of the cliff. The fluting call of **white-shouldered cliff chats** echo across rock walls; **white-faced scops owls** roost in rocky ravines; and fig trees attract **speckled pigeons** and **hornbills** – Jackson's and Hemprich's are two local specialities. Colourful **finches** in the undergrowth include **purple grenadiers, green-winged pytilias** and **red-cheeked cordon-bleus. Common kestrels** and **lanner falcons** nest on the ledges, and **pygmy falcons** are common in woodland. ∎

LAKE BOGORIA NATIONAL RESERVE

Hot viewing – flamingos, kudus and geysers

AN unbroken, pink collar of **lesser flamingos** (and many **greater flamingos** – standing almost twice the lesser's height) rings the lake's shores. Some 200 to 250 **greater kudus** live in dense woodland on the steep hillsides, but most large animals concentrate south of the hot springs and geysers that erupt from the lake's margins: **impalas, Thomson's** and **Grant's gazelles, plains zebras** and **warthogs** all graze near the shore. A small herd of **buffaloes** inhabits the park, and **klipspringers** and **rock hyraxes** live on steep rock faces and **leopards** are present though rarely seen. **Abyssinian ground hornbills** sometimes forage along wooded gullies near the lake's southern end.

Walking boulders and termite chimneys

The shores are strewn with volcanic boulders – if one moves it's probably a **leopard tortoise** (there are many in the park). Tall hollow towers built by termites on flat ground – like earthen chimneys – are used as lookouts by **grey-headed kingfishers, common fiscals** and **lilac-breasted rollers**. Since there aren't any fish to eat, **African fish eagles** harass the flamingos by sweeping low and snatching stragglers. Late in the afternoon **Kirk's dik-diks** step out of the shelter of thorn bushes and a few **greater kudus** descend from the slopes to drink at springs near the lake – anywhere south of the (usually) dry river bed is a good spot to wait.

Common ostriches and **grey crowned cranes** visit the plains north of the lake. The lake's high salinity offers limited feeding opportunities for waterbirds, but a few **Cape teal, Egyptian geese** and **black-necked grebes** are usually present; and **hamerkops** and **storks** loiter at the water's edge. Otherwise it's **flamingos** all the way: sweeping their bills through shallow water; roosting on one leg; floating motionless like giant blossoms; and upending in deeper water, their skinny legs kicking with the effort. Slow processions form long lines along freshwater streams; in the late afternoon some wander onto the road to drink or bathe in puddles. ∎

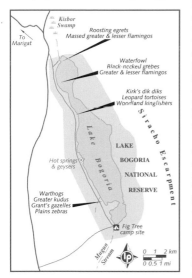

Map of Lake Bogoria National Reserve showing Kisbor Swamp, To Marigat, Roosting egrets, Massed greater & lesser flamingos, Waterfowl, Black-necked grebes, Greater & lesser flamingos, Kirk's dik diks, Leopard tortoises, Woodland kingfishers, Lake Bogoria, Hot springs & geysers, LAKE BOGORIA NATIONAL RESERVE, Warthogs, Greater kudus, Grant's gazelles, Plains zebras, Siracho Escarpment, Fig Tree camp site, Mugun Stream. Scale 0 1 2 km / 0 0.5 1 mi.

Wildlife highlights

An estimated two million lesser flamingos – forming one of the great ornithological spectacles of East Africa – and the best place in Kenya to see greater kudus. Other wildlife includes plains zebras, buffaloes, impalas and warthogs; and 375 bird species have been clocked up, including lilac-breasted rollers, common ostriches and grey crowned cranes.

Location 38km north of Nakuru (southern end – 4WD essential; 150km to northern end (sealed road).
Facilities Guards can be hired for game walks.
Accommodation Camping grounds in the park. Hotels just outside northern gate and in Marigat.
Wildlife rhythms Migrant waterfowl, waders and swallows arrive October to November, leaving again between April and May.
Contacts Lake Bogoria NR (☎ 037-40746, fax 40748), PO Box 64, Marigat.
Ecotours EAOS (☎ 02-33 11 91) and UTC (☎ 02-33 19 60) can arrange tours from Nairobi.

Watching tips

Buffaloes are usually seen in woodland at the park's southern end. Swamps at the north end support a higher diversity of waterbirds than the lake itself.

LAKE NAIVASHA
Fluctuating waters and birdlife

Wildlife highlights
Hippos in the lake; and black-and-white colobus, olive baboons and vervet monkeys are resident on the wooded southern shore, also frequented by buffaloes, Masai giraffes and antelopes such as kongonis, impalas and gazelles from nearby reserves. Waterbirds a highlight, and include African fish eagles, pied kingfishers, yellow-billed storks, flamingos and waterfowl.

Location 89km north-west of Nairobi. All sites except Crater Lake accessible by matatu.
Facilities Boat hire at Elsamere, Fisherman's Camp and Lake Naivasha Country Club.
Accommodation Camping grounds, bandas, hotels and lodges along lake shore. Hotels in Naivasha.
Wildlife rhythms Northern migrants – waterfowl and waders – swell bird numbers October to March.
Ecotours Elsamere has guides. Bird walks at Lake Naivasha Country Club and Crater Lake. EAOS (☎ 02-33 11 91) can organise tours from Nairobi.

Watching tips
Black-and-white colobus visit the lawns at Elsamere most Sunday afternoons. Hippos and good birdwatching can be enjoyed from the dock at Fisherman's Camp.

LAKE Naivasha is a freshwater Rift Valley lake – the level of which fluctuates periodically – that supports resident **hippos** and at times the largest **waterfowl** population in Kenya. **Vervet monkeys** and **olive baboons** live in woodland adjoining the south-western shore; and game corridors from nearby Hell's Gate NP allow **buffaloes**, **kongonis** (Coke's hartebeests), **antelopes** and **Masai giraffes** access to browse and grazing areas. Fish attract good numbers of **fish eagles**, **cormorants**, **pelicans** and **herons** – birdwatching is a highlight although populations of both predators and prey fluctuate. Mats of waterlilies and Nile cabbage on the southern shore attract **jacanas** and **long-toed plovers**, and **weavers** and **warblers** breed in papyrus reed beds.

Crater Lake, an extinct volcanic crater at Naivasha's western end is thickly wooded with yellow fever trees on which troops of **black-and-white colobus**, **vervet monkeys** and **olive baboons** drape themselves. A total of 38 mammal species has been recorded here; **buffaloes**, **warthogs**, **defassa waterbucks**, **bushbucks**, **Thomson's gazelles** and **impalas** can be seen by walking around the crater; and spotlighting on night drives may reveal **springhares**, **Senegal galagos**, **common genets**, **white-tailed mongooses** or predators such as **servals** and **bat-eared foxes**. Antelopes sheltering in the dense vegetation include **Kirk's dik-diks**, **steinbucks** and **common elands**. **Lesser flamingos**, and various **ducks** and **grebes** feed in the flooded crater.

At Elsamere Conservation Centre **hippos** graze on the lawns at night, **black-and-white colobus** frequent huge yellow fever trees in the gardens, and **African fish eagles** and **Verreaux's eagle-owls** feature among 200 bird species.

Crescent Island is the exposed lip of a submerged volcanic crater whose area changes with the lake's water level. **Plains zebras**, **defassa waterbucks** and **Thomson's gazelles** were all introduced and wander free; **herons**, **storks** and **waterfowl** puddle around the edges, and **pied kingfishers** are abundant. ∎

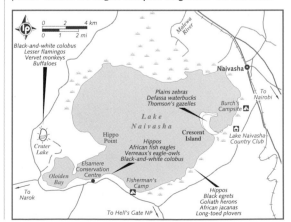

LAKE NAKURU NATIONAL PARK
Sanctuary for rarities

HIPPOS wallow near the northern and southern ends of this shallow alkaline ('soda') lake which usually has a few hundred **flamingos** feeding on its edges. Rarities are a feature: **Rothschild's giraffes**, and **black** and **white rhinos** were all introduced and are now breeding – black rhinos favour acacia thorn scrub in the south. Rogue (ie, stock-killing) **leopards** translocated from other parts of Kenya have boosted the local population – this is one of the best parks to see this big cat. A small population of **lions** is also present, and typically seen lounging about in thickets of fever trees during the day.

The great plains in miniature
Grasslands on the southern and western shores are grazed by **defassa waterbucks** – the most common antelope – and **white rhinos**; **grey crowned cranes** and **warthogs** forage among **plains zebras**, **Thomson's** and **Grant's gazelles**, **bohor reedbucks** and **buffaloes** – **oxpeckers** picking parasites off their backs; and **olive baboons** fan out from cover while raptors such

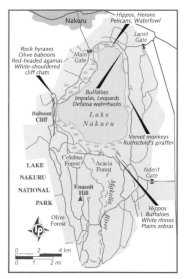

Map labels:
- Nakuru — Hippos, Herons, Pelicans, Waterfowl
- Lanet Gate
- Rock hyraxes, Olive baboons, Red-headed agamas, White-shouldered cliff chats
- Main Gate
- Buffaloes, Impalas, Leopards, Defassa waterbucks
- Baboon Cliff
- Lake Nakuru
- Vervet monkeys, Rothschild's giraffes
- LAKE NAKURU NATIONAL PARK
- Colobus Forest
- Acacia Forest
- Nderit Gate
- Enasoit Hill
- Makalia River
- Olive Forest
- Hippos, Buffaloes, White rhinos, Plains zebras
- 0   2   4 km
- 0   1   2 mi

as **bateleurs** and **vultures** cruise overhead. **Waterbirds** are abundant at the southern end including both **great white** and **pink-backed pelicans**, **greater** and the more abundant **lesser flamingos**, and many **storks**, **egrets** and **herons**. Rock hyraxes, **rock pythons** and **agama lizards** frequent the Baboon Cliff where **olive baboons** loiter for picnic scraps.

Tall yellow fever trees growing thickly at the water's edge bubble with the calls of **tropical boubous** and **white-browed coucals**. **Leopards** are often seen draped over large boughs – the corner near the Lanet Gate is a good place to look; **impalas** also favour this sheltered area and **Rothschild's giraffes** browse on trees along the eastern shore. At the water's edge **ducks** dabble among **herons** stalking in the shallows while **cormorants** rest on branches overhead. **Black-and-white colobus** forage in the dense stand of candelabra euphorbias near the south-eastern corner and **vervet monkeys** may be seen virtually anywhere among fallen timber and in trees. ∎

Wildlife highlights
Large animals such as black and white rhinos, hippos, Rothschild's giraffes and buffaloes are easily seen. Lions and leopards head the predator list while plains zebras, defassa waterbucks and gazelles are common. Primates include vervet monkeys, olive baboons and black-and-white colobus. Flamingos, pelicans and other waterbirds feature on a bird list topping 400 species.

Location 155km north of Nairobi; 5km from Nakuru.
Accommodation Camping grounds, bandas, hostel and lodges in park. Lodges outside park and hotels in Nakuru.
Wildlife rhythms Antelopes and hippos have young in March. Lion cubs born April to May. Migratory waterfowl and waders swell bird numbers from October to April. Lake waters contract during dry seasons forcing waterbirds to feed at other Rift Valley lakes.
Contact Lake Nakuru NP (☎ 037-45287), PO Box 439, Nakuru.
Ecotours EAOS (☎ 02-33 11 91) can organise guided tours from nearby Delamere's Camp.

Watching tips
White-shouldered cliff chats frequent Baboon Cliffs. A freshwater spring at the north-east corner of the lake attracts mammals and birds.

LAKE TURKANA

Ancient relics of the great lake

Wildlife highlights

Africa's largest population of Nile crocodiles; large animals of arid plains including plains and Grevy's zebras, Jackson's hartebeests, topis, beisa oryxes and lesser kudus; gerenuks and Günther's dik-diks in thorny scrub; and predators such as lions, cheetahs and spotted hyenas. Waterbirds, including large flocks of flamingos, feature among 350 recorded bird species.

Location Loyangalani/Koobi Fora 665km/845km north of Nairobi.
Facilities Museum and KWS guides at Koobi Fora (contact KWS HQ ☎ 02-50 10 81).
Accommodation Camping and bandas at Koobi Fora, camping at Allia Bay. Camping and lodges at Loyangalani.
Wildlife rhythms Crocodiles hatch April to May.
Contact Sibiloi NP, PO Box 219, Lodwar.
Ecotours Gametrackers (☎ 02-33 89 27): overland trips. Excel Aviation (☎/fax 02-50 17 51): flights to Koobi Fora. Jade Sea Journeys (☎ 02-21 83 36): boat from Kalokol to Koobi Fora and Central Island.

Watching tips

Migrating warblers and wagtails shelter in scrubby *Salvadora* bushes on Central Island; the northward migration (March to April) is better.

HOT winds scour ancient lava flows where **ground squirrels, crested larks** and **lizards** dart among sparse grass and hardy acacias. Rains bring on a flush of green and, despite treacherous roads, the wet season is the best time to visit: wildlife is abundant in Sibiloi NP – a World Heritage site with fossil beds and a petrified forest on Mt Sibiloi. Central and South Islands are also national parks, and Central Island and Ferguson's Gulf are important staging posts for **migrating birds** (October to April). Birdwatching in Sibiloi NP is excellent, and highlights include **Somali ostriches, kori** and **Heuglin's bustards, northern carmine** and **Somali bee-eaters, chestnut-bellied sandgrouse** and **fox kestrels.**

Thick avenues of *Acacia-Commiphora* scrub growing along Sibiloi's luggas shelter **greater** and **lesser kudus, gerenuks, warthogs** and **Günther's dik-diks**. **Reticulated giraffes** browse the tallest acacias, and grazing the adjoining plains of spear grass are **beisa oryxes, Jackson's hartebeests** and **tiangs** – a local race of topi. Large herds of **zebras** (both **plains** and **Grevy's**) and **Grant's gazelles** are stalked by **lions, cheetahs** and **leopards**, while **caracals** and **servals** chase **hares** and **ground squirrels**. Other predators include **striped** and **spotted hyenas, jackals** and **bat-eared foxes; scorpions** are abundant after rain.

Islands of birds and crocodiles

Puffer fish, a group normally found in sea water, indicate Turkana's prehistoric connection to the Red Sea. But the lake's most famous inhabitants are **Nile crocodiles** and up to 12,000 have been estimated to breed on Central Island. Some large crocs can usually be seen at Allia Bay, where **hippos** and at times hundreds of thousands of **flamingos** congregate; **African open-billed storks, ducks** and **gulls** feed along the shores, and **African skimmers** are usually present (they and **goliath herons** breed on Central Island, where volcanic lakes attract **lesser flamingos**). ∎

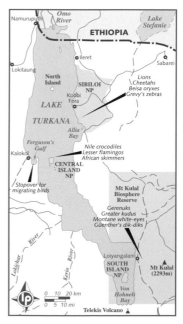

MALINDI & WATAMU MARINE NATIONAL PARKS

Kenya's snorkelling and scuba hotspots

BOTH small parks protect fringing coral reefs that hug the shoreline and are ideal for novice snorkellers. For best results, time boat trips to goggle two hours either side of low tide; the tidal range can be as great as 4m so low tide will expose the greatest number of fish and other animals. Scuba dives entail a boat ride to reefs further out, but are typically shallow, non-decompression dives.

Malindi offers more snorkelling opportunities and the action inevitably begins at the coral gardens on North Reef. Glass-bottomed boats crowd the area, but the fishes are used to being fed so you'll encounter lots of friendly **snappers, parrotfish, rubberfish, zebras, surgeons, sergeants** and **butterflyfish**. Other good snorkelling spots are Stork Passage; and Tewa Reef, which is good for **corals** and smaller **fish**, and is probably the best place for watching **octopuses**. On the way out you may see **barracudas** in the Barracuda Channel (they are present most of the year) – if not, sightings are guaranteed at Stork Passage (this is also a good place for **turtles** and **stingrays**). Generally the eastern side of North Reef has the best corals, and this is where you'll find higher numbers of the larger fish. Sometimes **reef sharks** can be spotted idling on the sandy bottom, facing into the current; **rays** and sharks are most common from September to May.

While Watamu's 'coral gardens' are good for snorkelling and glass-bottomed boat rides, the big draws here are **whale sharks** and **manta rays** – sightings are almost guaranteed in January and February (the current carrying krill from Antarctica is deflected by the coast at Watamu and lies 2km offshore at Malindi – thus these big fish are not seen inshore at Malindi). Watamu is especially good for scuba diving and Turtle Reef is the most species-rich area in the park.

Further south at the entrance to Mida Creek, are whopping big **groupers** (rock cods) – one rare species grows to over 3m and weighs 500kg. Groupers stick to the same spot for years and Mida Caves are a favourite site. This is a tricky spot to dive and you must get permission from the warden. ∎

Wildlife highlights

Kenya's top spots for snorkellers – glass-bottomed boating is available. Hundreds of species of tropical fish and mollusc in coral gardens, plus pelagic animals such as turtles, rays, sharks and barracudas. Manta rays and whale sharks are commonly seen inshore at Watamu, and large groupers live at Mida Caves.

Location Both parks adjacent to their namesake towns.
Facilities Glass-bottomed boats; several dive shops (most are closed May to July).
Accommodation Plenty in Watamu and Malindi.
Wildlife rhythms Malindi best October to November and March to April (silt decreases visibility December to March). Watamu is best November to March – access to dive sites is restricted at other times.
Contact KWS (☎ 0123-20845), PO Box 109, Malindi.
Ecotours Malindi. Juspho Tours & Safaris (☎ 0123-20140). Watamu: big hotels and Mrs Simpson's Guest House run snorkelling trips; Aqua Ventures (☎ 0122-32008, fax 32266, e aquav@africaonline.co.ke), PO Box 275, Watamu runs dive courses.

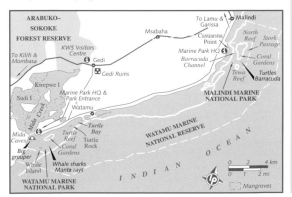

Watching tips

Make sure your boat operator will take you to Stork Passage at Malindi.

MARSABIT NATIONAL PARK

Descendants of a famous elephant

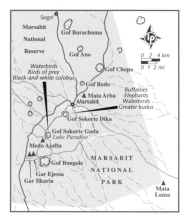

Wildlife highlights

Densely forested mountain with elephants, buffaloes and greater kudus, surrounded by semiarid plains with oryxes, zebras, giraffes, various antelopes and lions. Black-and-white colobus and blue monkeys in forest, vervet monkeys and olive baboons in savanna. Birdlife prolific – 350 species including 52 birds of prey, waterbirds in crater lakes and forest pigeons.

Location 310km north of Isiolo; 560km north of Nairobi. 4WD recommended.

Accommodation Camping on shores of Lake Paradise and at park HQ. Hotels in Marsabit.

Wildlife rhythms Large animals more abundant in forest during dry seasons, dispersing to surrounding plains during wet seasons.

Contacts Kenya Wildlife Service (☎ 0183-2028), PO Box 42, Marsabit.

Ecotours Gametrackers (☎ 02-33 89 27) includes Marsabit on its regular safaris to Lake Turkana.

Watching tips

Elephants, buffaloes and small numbers of greater kudus emerge from the forest surrounding Gof Sokorte Dika in the late afternoon to drink.

ONCE the abode of Ahmed, Kenya's most famous tusker (by the time he died at an estimated age of 62, Ahmed stood 3m at the shoulder and had 3m tusks; during his last years he was honoured with a 24-hour guard by Presidential decree), Marsabit's extinct volcanic craters are cloaked in aromatic, moss-encrusted forests. Watch for mammals along roads: the dense forest is home to herds of **elephants** and **buffaloes**, and troops of **black-and-white colobus** and **blue monkeys** – these agile primates sometimes feed together. **Antelopes** such as **bushbucks** and **sunis** might be seen bolting into the undergrowth, and you might be lucky enough to see a **leopard** by spotlighting along the road (but seek permission first). Clouds of **butterflies** swirl in pools of sunlight; **emerald-spotted wood doves** and **tambourine doves** clatter off the roads; and **olive pigeons** and **Hartlaub's turacos** – the latter's crimson wing flashes are a giveaway – feed among trailing beard moss.

Volcanic oasis

High cliffs at the northern end of Lake Paradise (in Gof Sokorte Guda) make perches and nest sites for **birds of prey** – especially **Rüppell's griffon vultures** – but **peregrine falcons**, **mountain** and **common buzzards**, **black kites** and **African fish eagles** may be seen wheeling over the lake. The freshwater lake attracts **ducks** – **southern pochards**, **garganeys** and **teals** – which mingle with **little grebes** and rafts of **red-knobbed coots**. **Hamerkops**, **ibises**, **purple herons**, and **saddle-billed** and **yellow-billed storks** feed in shallow water; and **darters** and **cormorants** rest with wings outstretched on overhanging branches. Surrounding forest is inhabited by **black-and-white colobus**.

On Marsabit's lower slopes the forest peters out into thorny scrubland and savanna – inhabited by **olive baboons** and **vervet monkeys** – where **Peters' gazelles** (a local race of Grant's gazelle), **reticulated giraffes**, **beisa oryxes** and **plains zebras** are hunted by **lions** and **cheetahs**. Less common predators include **striped hyenas**, **aardwolves** and **caracals**. Birds of the semiarid plains surrounding the massif include **Somali ostriches** and **vulturine guineafowl**; various **larks** such as **masked** and **Williams'** (endemic to northern Kenya), plus **Somali bee-eaters**, **Heuglin's bustards** and **cream-coloured coursers**. ∎

MERU NATIONAL PARK

Pride of the plains

WILDLIFE-VIEWING is best on Meru's northern plains, such as Murera, Bisandi and Rojewero: **elephants** come and go, migrating as far as 60km away, but both species of **zebra**, **Grant's** and **Thomson's gazelles**, **impalas**, **beisa oryxes**, **kongoni** (Coke's hartebeests) and **reticulated giraffes** are easily seen. Further south, **gerenuks** browse dense *Commiphora-Acacia* woodlands that also shelter **common elands**, **Kirk's dik-diks** and **warthogs**. This is ideal habitat for **lesser kudus** – one of the park's highlights – but getting a good view of one takes luck and patience (you could come across one nearly anywhere). **Unstriped ground squirrels**, **vulturine guineafowl** and **yellow-necked spurfowl** scuttle off the roads where the mounds of industrious **naked mole-rats** puff up dirt like miniature volcanoes from the rodents' digging inside.

Baobabs, buffaloes and palms

Lions are commonly seen on the plains – once the stomping ground of Joy Adamson – and there's a fair chance of **cheetahs**. **Baboons** and their arch-enemy, **leopards**, lurk among the boulders of euphorbia-draped kopjes. Honking groups of **hornbills** – sometimes several species together – feed among the woodlands and pot-bellied baobabs. Several species of palm line the 15 permanent waterways that dissect the park, providing sustenance for **palm-nut vultures** and lookouts for other **birds of prey**. The nuts of doum palms – look for their forked trunks – are a favourite of **elephants**, **vervet monkeys** and **baboons**.

Swampy grasslands are grazed by **defassa waterbucks** and (sometimes large) herds of **buffaloes**. **Hippos** are common in slower streams and in the broad Tana River, which is accessible at Adamson's Falls; **Nile crocodiles** also cruise the Tana and some large specimens travel far along its many tributaries. **Baboons** and **vervet monkeys** loiter in and around the giant fig trees which line the banks; tracks in the sand show where **impalas** and **lesser kudus** – or nocturnal **leopards** and **spotted hyenas** – have drunk, and where basking **crocs** haul themselves out. Common river birds include **ibises**, **herons** and **African fish eagles**. ∎

> **Wildlife highlights**
> Reticulated giraffes, buffaloes, abundant lions and seasonal elephant herds the main draw; beisa oryxes, lesser kudus and gerenuks star in the antelope line-up; cheetahs frequently encountered, and other predators include spotted hyenas and leopards. Olive baboons and vervet monkeys common. Hippos, Nile crocodiles and waterbirds along Tana River; 300 bird species in all.

Location 60km east of Meru; 355km north of Nairobi. 4WD advisable.

Accommodation Bush camping grounds, public camping ground with bandas, and lodges in park.

Wildlife rhythms Grass is shorter and animals are easier to see in dry seasons; elephants use Meru as a dry season refuge, wandering from the park in wet seasons.

Contact Meru National Park (☎ 0164-20613), PO Box 11, Maua.

Ecotours Cheli & Peacock (☎ 02-74 83 07) organises tours from Nairobi.

> **Watching tips**
> Lesser kudus, Kirk's dik-diks and gerenuks feed near roadsides at dusk. Pel's fishing owls hunt at night along the Tana River.

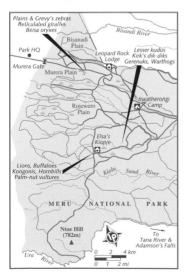

Plains & Grevy's zebras
Reticulated giraffes
Beisa oryxes

Bisanadi River

Bisanadi Plain

Park HQ

Leopard Rock Lodge

Lesser kudus
Kirk's dik-diks
Gerenuks, Warthogs

Murera Gate

Murera Plain

Bwatherongi Camp

Rojewero Plain

Elsa's Kiopje

Lions, Buffaloes
Kongonis, Hornbills
Palm-nut vultures

Kiolu Sand River

MERU NATIONAL PARK

Ntoe Hill (782m)

To Tana River & Adamson's Falls

Ura River

0 2 4 km
0 1 2 mi

MT ELGON NATIONAL PARK

Home of cave-digging elephants

Wildlife highlights

Salt-mining elephants are the most famous attraction, but dense forest hides buffaloes, bushbucks, defassa waterbucks and giant forest hogs; four species of primate – black-and-white colobus is most common; and predators such as spotted hyenas and leopards. Birds (240 species) most abundant and diverse in forest, although alpine specialities include lammergeiers.

Location 408km west of Nairobi.

Accommodation Camping grounds and bandas in park. Camping and bandas 5.5km east of Chorlim Gate. Hotels in Kitale.

Wildlife rhythms Animals mine salt year round. Antelopes graze on higher slopes in dry seasons.

Contacts Mt Elgon NP (☎ 0325-31456/7), PO Box 753, Kitale.

Ecotours Escorted walks with rangers; guides for caves at park gate. Sirikwa Safaris (☎ 0325-20061 c/o Soy Trading), PO Box 332, Kitale, arranges a guide. Delta Crescent Farm (☎/fax 0325-31462) takes travellers to the park.

Watching tips

Stake out Kitum or Mackingeny Cave before dawn for a chance of seeing elephants. The largest stands of giant groundsel and lobelias grow in the caldera.

ELEPHANTS and more commonly **buffaloes, bushbucks** or **defassa waterbucks** are seen along roads through Elgon's densely forested lower slopes; **duikers** and **giant forest hogs** frequent dense undergrowth. Large troops of **black-and-white colobus** and **blue monkeys** share the canopy with **red-fronted parrots** and **Ross' turacos**; **olive baboons** loiter at forest edges near cultivation; and a small population of **de Brazza's monkeys** inhabits the park. Caves riddle the sheer, steplike cliffs; thousands of small **insect-eating bats** cling to petrified trees lining the roof of Kitum Cave; and **roussette bats** – a type of fruit-bat – roost in the back reaches, their tongue-clicking sonar clearly audible.

Elgon's high rainfall encourages prolific plant growth, but leaches soluble mineral salts from the soil; salt-deficient food plants force most of Elgon's large mammals – including primates – to eat or lick salt-rich rocks from the caves. The most famous visitors are **elephants**, which make nightly forays deep into the caverns to tusk off and eat bits of the soft rock. This has been going on for hundreds of generations and some researchers believe elephants actually excavated some of Elgon's caves. **Spotted hyenas** shelter in remote caves and **leopards** stake out the entrances for salt-hungry visitors; **servals** have been seen near Rongai camp.

Black-and-white colobus forage as high as dense bamboo thickets where the forest peters out. Moss-covered *Hagenia* trees and giant heather grow higher still, replaced on the peaks by alpine moorland dotted with giant fleshy herbs – groundsels and lobelias – that can grow 6m high. Wildflowers (such as everlastings) grow on rocky slopes above the treeline, where **Verreaux's eagles** pick **rock hyraxes** off outcrops and **leopards** stalk **rodents, hyraxes** and **duikers. Scarce** and **alpine swifts,** and huge **lammergeiers** cruise the thin air; **white-naped ravens** forage up to about 4000m and **moorland francolins** are common in the tussock grasslands even higher. ∎

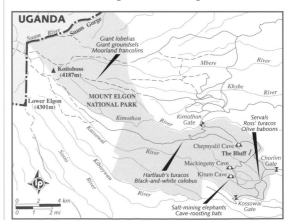

SAIWA SWAMP NATIONAL PARK

Sanctuary for a remarkable antelope

COVERING only 3 sq km, Kenya's smallest national park was established primarily to protect a population of **sitatungas** in a reed-choked stretch of the Saiwa River. Walking trails skirt the swamp – home to a selection of **marsh birds** – through riverine and savanna woodland inhabited by **monkeys**. For the best chance at **sitatungas** look down into the reeds from the eastern shore in the early morning, when these shy antelopes feed and bask. **Defassa waterbucks**, **bushbucks** and **bohor reedbucks** frequent grassy swamp edges; **pottos**, **African civets** and **common genets** could be spotlit; and **leopards**, **ratels** and **aardvarks** are occasional visitors.

Swamp with a view

Vervet monkeys are most likely to be seen in drier parts of the park and near the camping ground. **De Brazza's monkeys**, also known as swamp monkeys, are mainly active near water – the tall acacias and figs that form the canopy over the trail to observation tower 4 are a good place to look. **Blue monkeys** and **black-and-white colobus** can also be seen in this stretch. When fruiting, the fig trees attract **double-toothed barbets** (which sometimes nest in trees along the boardwalk), **crowned hornbills**, **Ross' turacos** (which exhibit raucous honking and crimson wing-flashes) and another turaco, the **eastern grey plantain-eater** (its call sounds like chimp hoots). **Grey crowned cranes** are regular visitors to the marsh.

Observation towers along the banks make ideal platforms from which to scan the reed beds for **sitatungas** and birds, and to see **red-legged sun squirrels** or **giant forest squirrels** scampering through the canopy at eyelevel. Narrow channels worn through the aquatic vegetation by sitatungas are also patrolled by **African clawless** and **African spot-necked otters**; and throughout the swamp **ibises**, **ducks** and **herons** feed in open patches of water. **Cisticolas** and **warblers** skulk at the foot of the towers; **birds of prey** – including **African fish eagles** and **long-crested eagles** – perch on the dead trees poking through the reeds; and **blue-headed coucals** sun themselves on sturdy bulrushes in the morning. ∎

Wildlife highlights
Kenya's best park for sitatungas and the localised de Brazza's monkey; other primates include black-and-white colobus, blue and vervet monkeys. Defassa waterbucks and bushbucks are commonly seen, and ratels and African civets are occasionally encountered. Birds are also a draw – 372 species, including Kenyan rarities such as Ross' turacos and blue-headed coucals.

Location 26km north of Kitale, 5km east of the highway.
Facilities Viewing platforms, boardwalks, 7km nature trail.
Accommodation Camping ground at park. Camping ground and lodge 5km north at Sirikwa Safaris.
Wildlife rhythms Most sitatunga young are born in the dry season.
Contacts KWS (☎ 02-50 06 22), PO Box 40241, Nairobi. Kipsaina Wetlands Conservation Group, PO Box 18, Kipsaina, Kitale.
Ecotours Sirikwa Safaris (☎ 0325-20061 c/o Soy Trading), PO Box 332, Kitale, can arrange an expert guide.

Watching tips
The best (and safest) observation tower is number 4, from where sitatungas, both otters and blue-headed coucals are regularly seen.

Observation tower
Ruined tower
Crowned hornbills
Red-faced cisticolas
Double-toothed barbets
Ruined tower
To Kitale & Kapenguria
Entrance gate & park HQ
Camp site
SAIWA
SWAMP
NATIONAL
PARK
Saiwa River
Ross' turacos
de Brazza's monkeys
Black-and-white colobus
Observation tower
Sitatungas
Waterbirds
Blue-headed coucals
African clawless otters

0   50   100 m
0   150   300 ft

SHIMBA HILLS NATIONAL RESERVE

Quality not quantity

Location 37km from Mombasa with all-year access; can be reached by public transport.
Facilities Three observation points, a walking trail and a waterhole.
Accommodation Two camping grounds (one with self-catering bandas), a lodge and a tented camp.
Wildlife rhythms Rains (November and late April to June) restrict walking and wildlife-viewing.
Contact Kenyan Wildlife Service (☎ 0127-4159), PO Box 30, Kwale.
Ecotours Shimba Hills Lodge conducts morning drives and afternoon walks to Sheldrick Falls.

Watching tips

Meat hung from a tree at the lodge's waterhole (to lure a leopard that never shows) often attracts fish eagles and, at night, genets.

ALTHOUGH it is one of the smallest parks in the country, Shimba Hills protects the bulk of Kenya's **black-and-white colobus** and its only population of a distinctive subspecies of sable antelope – **Roosevelt's sable**. Add to this 13 rare or restricted bird species, including the **spotted ground thrush**, **Sokoke pipit** and **east coast akalat**, about 35% (300 species) of the country's **butterflies**, and one of Kenya's richest plant diversities and Shimba Hills makes a very attractive wildlife destination.

Patches of dense forest and plantation can make viewing difficult, so a good place to start is at one of the hilltop observation lookouts. From these vantage points **elephants**, **buffaloes** and **sables** should be seen in the open glades below. The best place to search for sables is on the Marare Circuit, where you may also find **Masai giraffes**.

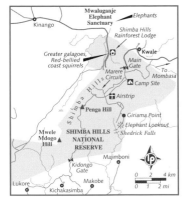

Bushbucks, **duikers** and **sunis** all occur but these shy antelopes are not easily seen.

Easily-located birds (mainly the large and noisy ones) include **Fischer's turaco** – it has a restricted distribution along the coast and Shimba Hills is one of the best places to see it. Forested areas, especially Longomwagandi Forest near the airstrip, are also good for **hornbills – trumpeter, crowned** and **silvery-cheeked**. And scrutinize any guineafowl you see – Shimba Hills is one the few places where the distinctive Kenyan race of **crested guineafowl** can be seen. Both Longomwagandi and another small forest patch, Makadara, have strong plant, bird and butterfly affinities with West African lowland rainforest, and these are great places to get out and walk (but keep an eye out for **elephants**).

The Shimba Hills Rainforest Lodge (day visitors welcome) maintains a waterhole that attracts **African fish eagles**, **elephants** and **buffaloes**. And **red-bellied coast squirrels** skittering about the restaurant tables provide reliable daytime entertainment. When the squirrels retire in the evening, **greater galagos** take over – several regularly visit the bar for their banana treat.

For the energetic, there is a 2.6km walk down to the 21m-high Sheldrick Falls. You'd be unlucky to encounter a **buffalo** or **elephant** on the trail, but an armed scout is still mandatory. On the walk down look about in the trees for **blue monkeys**. ∎

OTHER SITES – KENYA

Bisanadi NR
Savanna bounded by the Tana River serves as a wet season dispersal area for elephants and buffaloes.
60km east of Meru

Kora NR
Thornbush plains bordered by the Tana River adjacent to Meru NP – with similar wildlife: lions, elephants, buffaloes and lesser kudus. Future access to Kora – and hence Meru – may be possible from the Thika–Garissa road.
120km east of Meru

Lake Elementeita
Shallow Rift Valley lake in Soysambu Wildlife Sanctuary. Attracts sometimes huge flocks of lesser and (breeding) greater flamingos; also Kenya's only breeding population of great white pelicans (up to 5000) among 408 bird species. Night drives can feature leopards and abundant springhares.
140km north west of Nairobi,
☎ *02-33 11 91*

Lake Magadi
Kenya's most southerly Rift Valley lake attracts great white pelicans, breeding lesser flamingos, African spoonbills and chestnut-banded plovers.
100km south of Nairobi

Lewa Downs Wildlife Conservancy
Working cattle ranch and self-financing rhino conservation project in Mt Kenya's northern foothills. Main attractions are breeding black and white rhinos and some 400 Grevy's zebras. Elephants, leopards, buffaloes, reticulated giraffes and translocated sitatungas also present.
35km south of Samburu NR,
☎ *02-33 11 91*

Longonot NP
Dormant 2886m volcano with almost circular crater. Scenic walks and steaming fumaroles a feature, and artificial waterholes encourage animals including buffaloes.
60km north-west of Nairobi

Mwaluganje Elephant Sanctuary
About 150 elephants use this ancient trail through the Cha Shimba River valley as a corridor between Shimba Hills NR and Mwaluganje FR. Locals benefit financially as land use changes from agriculture to tourism; an electric fence resolves conflict and the sanctuary is gradually increasing in size. There is an information centre near the main gate and a nature trail is being established.
35km south-west of Mombasa,
☎ *011-48 51 21*

Mwea NR
Gently rolling woodland on the Kamburu Reservoir is home to hippos, elephants, buffaloes, lesser kudus and crocs.
100km north-east of Nairobi

Rukinga Ranch
Semiarid grasslands and scrub adjoining Tsavo East NP lie on the elephant migration route between Tsavo and Kilimanjaro's foothills. Permanent water attracts herds of elephants (up to 1000 visit Rukinga); other mammals include Grevy's and plains zebras, lesser kudus, gerenuks and abundant lions. Excellent dry-country birdwatching features abundant golden pipits, spotted eagle-owls and golden-breasted starlings.
50km south of Voi,
☎ *02-33 11 91*

Ruma NP
Tall grassland and acacia woodland protecting Kenya's only remaining roan antelopes. Large mammals include lions, cheetahs, leopards, buffaloes, Rothschild's giraffes and plains zebras – all little-disturbed because of tsetse flies and because locals believe the park's uranium deposits cause sterility.
34km west of Homa Bay

Solio Ranch
Working cattle ranch famous for breeding rhinos: Solio has reared 91 black and 87 white rhinos in 27 years – setting an unprecedented annual birth rate of 12%. Many have been translocated to reserves such as Lewa Downs, and Tsavo East and Aberdare NPs.
180km north of Nairobi

Taita Hills Forests
Isolated remnants (the largest only 220 hectares) of Tanzania's Eastern Arc Mountains supporting 13 endemic plants and endemic birds such as the Taita thrush and Taita white-eye. A globally important centre of plant biodiversity and source of species such as African violets.

Tana River Primate Reserve
Established to protect the endemic Tana River red colobus and Tana (crested) mangabey; and 50km of the Tana River and its adjoining plains. Other mammals include elephants, Peters' gazelles (a race of Grant's), giraffes and lions. Hippos and Nile crocodiles inhabit the Tana; and 248 birds recorded include breeding waterbirds and the rare Tana River cisticola.
160km north of Malindi

ZANIA

Highlights

- The vast plains of the Serengeti, dotted with thousands of animals
- A pink mass of flamingos feeding in the lake in Ngorongoro Crater
- Boating down the Rufiji River in Selous GR, surrounded by crocs, hippos and waterbirds
- Observing cheetahs watching the Serengeti Plains from the vantage points of termite mounds
- Meeting an elephant on the path from your tent to the loo
- Diving among a swirling 'fish soup' in the warm coral seas off Zanzibar
- Tracking and finding wild chimpanzees in Gombe Stream NP

Higher, deeper, greater

IN Tanzania the sweeping plains of East Africa, with their fertile soils and flat-topped acacias, meet the nutrient-leached miombo woodlands more typical of south-central Africa. This vast country is home to diverse wildlife, including some 430 species and subspecies of mammal, 1060 of bird and 1370 of butterfly; and the famous Serengeti NP boasts the greatest concentration of large animals on earth. Tanzania also features Africa's highest mountain (Kilimanjaro), deepest and largest lakes (Tanganyika and Victoria, respectively), largest protected area (Selous GR) and the world's largest intact volcanic crater – 20km-wide Ngorongoro. About 25% of the country is protected in 12 national parks, one conservation area and 30 game reserves; and some of its coastal waters, including parts of coral-fringed Unguja (Zanzibar) and Pemba islands, are conserved as marine parks.

Most of Tanzania is high plateau (900 to 1800m) fringed by the two bowed arms of the Great Rift Fault. The course of the Western Arc is marked by the deep, isolated freshwater Lakes Tanganyika and Malawi, where hundreds of species of unique cichlid fish have evolved. The shallow alkaline lakes of the Eastern Arc, such as Lake Natron, are the birthplace of most of Africa's flamingos. Towards the plateau's eastern edge, the fragmented Eastern Arc Mountains feature many rare and unique species.

Tanzania has two rainy seasons: the short monsoon from October to December, and long rains between March and May. Between June and October – the cool, dry season – animals congregate around limited water resources. Visiting reserves in November can be tricky, though migratory birds are present and there's abundant greenery, but travel during the long rains is often impossible.

Tanzania's 'northern circuit' is comparatively crowded, but the wildlife and mountains are unrivalled: Mt Kilimanjaro not only lures trekkers, but probably acts as a navigation beacon for many of the 600 million migratory birds that overwinter in tropical Africa. Other sights include spectacular Ngorongoro Crater, Olduvai Gorge (immortalised for its hominid fossils) and the Serengeti Plains – where 1.5 million animals (wildebeests, zebras and gazelles) make a spectacular annual trek following the seasonal availability of food.

The 'southern circuit' is ideal for more wilderness-orientated travellers: it takes in the vast, almost untouched Selous GR and Ruaha NP; and Udzungwa Mountains NP, where serious birders search out local and endemic species. Other highlights include heading west to see the chimps in Mahale Mountains and Gombe Stream NPs, which requires time; and Tanzania's coastal islands – the Zanzibar Archipelago (of which Unguja and Pemba are the main islands) and Mafia – which are revered by divers and snorkellers. ■

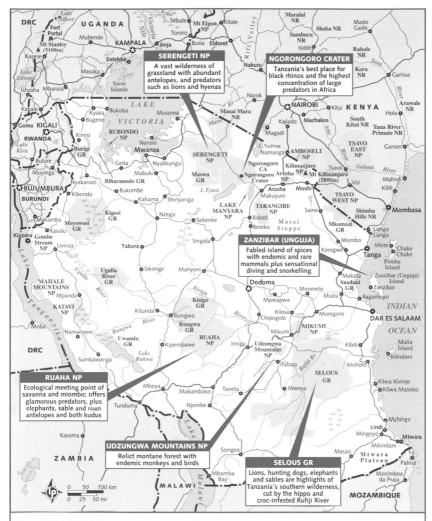

SERENGETI NP
A vast wilderness of grassland with abundant antelopes, and predators such as lions and hyenas

NGORONGORO CRATER
Tanzania's best place for black rhinos and the highest concentration of large predators in Africa

ZANZIBAR (UNGUJA)
Fabled island of spices with endemic and rare mammals plus sensational diving and snorkelling

RUAHA NP
Ecological meeting point of savanna and miombo; offers glamorous predators, plus elephants, sable and roan antelopes and both kudus

UDZUNGWA MOUNTAINS NP
Relict montane forest with endemic monkeys and birds

SELOUS GR
Lions, hunting dogs, elephants and sables are highlights of Tanzania's southern wilderness, cut by the hippo and croc-infested Rufiji River

Suggested itineraries

One week Starting at Arusha, take in both Ngorongoro CA and Serengeti NP, then visit Arusha or Lake Manyara NPs for waterbirds and hippos.

Or avoid the crowds by exploring the southern safari circuit: from Dar, overnight at Mikumi NP to sample the Selous ecosystem; head to Udzungwa Mountains NP; then backtrack for some snorkelling off Zanzibar.

Two weeks Take in the northern safari circuit, then either follow the second one-week itinerary or venture further on the southern circuit by heading into Ruaha NP or Selous GR for some spectacular large animals and a chance of seeing hunting dogs. Finish off with some snorkelling around Zanzibar or a trip to Pemba for endemic birds and the Pemba flying-fox.

One month Augment the highlights of the northern safari circuit with a trek at least some of the way up Mts Kilimanjaro or Meru, or an excursion to Rubondo Island in Lake Victoria. Take in the southern circuit and Zanzibar and/or Pemba, then consider striking out for Gombe Stream NP in the far west to see the world's most famous chimps.

NGORONGORO CONSERVATION AREA

Amphitheatre of abundance

Wildlife highlights

Ngorongoro Crater is the NCA's highlight and is fabulous for wildlife. Some 25,000 large animals enter and leave the crater at will. Lions (50), spotted hyenas (400), wildebeests (around 5000), plains zebras, gazelles and buffaloes (4000, especially during the rainy season) are abundant. This is the only place you are likely to see black rhino in Tanzania. However, impalas, giraffes, oryxes and topis are absent and only bull elephants (50) occur in the crater. The animals are used to vehicles and carry on their intimate business with total disregard for observers, so the wildlife-watching is outstanding. Some 115 mammal and 550 bird species (half of Tanzania's total), have been recorded. The NCA lakes are feeding areas for lesser flamingos, although they don't often breed here.

THE most famous feature of this World Heritage Site and Biosphere Reserve, Ngorongoro Crater, makes up only 3% of the Ngorongoro Conservation Area (NCA). NCA also protects the Crater Highlands (a chain of extinct and collapsed volcanoes) and includes the eastern part of the Serengeti Plain. Ngorongoro Crater is the largest unbroken caldera (collapsed volcanic cone) in the world. Its rim is around 2200m above sea level and the drop to the floor of the animal-rich crater is 600m. From the viewpoint on the rim you can, if the weather is clear, see right across the 20km-wide crater floor and identify the main habitat features – the Gorigor Swamp, Lake Magadi, Lerai Forest and the open plains. With binoculars you can make out

Fixed in stone

Olduvai Gorge is synonymous with the Leakey family – especially Louis and Mary – who excavated the area for 53 years and unravelled some of its evolutionary history. Erosion in the gorge exposed five geological layers in which were found fossils of numerous ancient species. Among them were tiny shrewlike animals, extinct elephants, sheep with 2m horns, rhinos twice as big as today's species and pigs with 1m tusks. But it is the finds of early hominids that put the gorge on the world stage: much of mankind's past was unravelled here at Olduvai (much also was discovered in Kenya). In addition to fossilised bones and tools, the footprints of three early hominids were immortalised as they walked away from an erupting volcano at Olduvai 3.7 million years ago. You can't visit the footprints, but a replica is on display at the Olduvai museum.

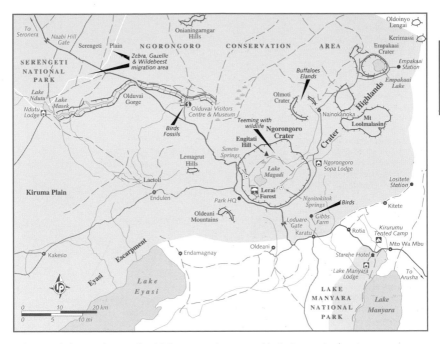

columns of **plains zebras** and **wildebeests**, and groups of **buffaloes**. Buffaloes began to use the crater floor only in the 1970s, when the Maasai moved out their livestock and ceased burning – now around 4000 use the crater.

Only one major road descends into the crater and one climbs out again; both are one-way and steep, and a 4WD is compulsory. At the bottom of the descent you will see **rufous-tailed weaver** nests dangling from acacias (this is one of the birds endemic to northern Tanzania). Near here are the Seneto Springs where the local Maasai herdsmen still bring their stock into the crater for water and salt licks.

There are 120km of roads to explore in the dry season. The freshwater pools in the Mandusi Swamp are a dry season home for **hippos**, and sometimes they can be seen out feeding during the day. The surrounding marshy grasses and reeds are worth searching for **waterbirds**, and this is one of the few places in Tanzania where you can find the **African water rail**.

The Lerai Forest, rich with fever trees (yellow-barked acacias), is the place to look for **vervet monkeys**, **olive baboons**, **elephants**, **elands**, **bushbucks** and **waterbucks**. The surrounding area is a good place to look for **black rhinos** browsing on the shrubby vegetation. Ngorongoro Crater is the only place in Tanzania where you have a realistic chance of seeing black rhinos (although present in other places, rhinos are often in-accessible). Around 20 rhinos occur in the crater and you should have little difficulty seeing one or more. Don't feed the habituated and bold vervets at Lerai ex-campsite – as you leave you will also see them sitting by the road. You'll also need to watch out for the hungry

On a clear day it is possible to see right across Ngorongoro Crater's 20km-wide floor from the rim.

Location 165km from Arusha; 4WD is required to enter the crater; access can be impossible in April to May rains; permission is required to visit other areas in the Crater Highlands.

Facilities Maps, printed material and interpretive centres at Loduare Park Gate and Olduvai Museum; most lodges have maps and books. Private vehicles must take a NP guide when entering the crater.

Accommodation Five lodges on the crater rim, one camping ground. Several special camping areas in the Crater Highlands.

Wildlife rhythms During the dry season (July to October), large animals concentrate around watercourses such as Mandusi Swamp and the Hippo Pool; migratory birds arrive November and December.

Contact NCAA HQ at Park Village Ngorongoro Crater (☎ Ngorongoro Crater 6 or 7), PO Box 1, Ngorongoro Crater. Arusha HQ (☎ 057-6091, fax 3339), PO Box 776, Arusha.

Ecotours Countless companies operate from Arusha, Dar, Nairobi and further afield.

wildlife at the packed lunchtime picnic spot at Ngoitokitok Springs: **black kites** here are as bold as baboons, and will swoop down and relieve you of your food instantly. However, Ngoitokitok is a pleasant spot at which to see **hippos**.

Roamin' circus

The crater is believed to have the highest density of predators in Africa and provides one of the best chances to see them in action. **Lions** and **spotted hyenas** are abundant, totalling around 450 altogether; **cheetahs** are occasionally seen; and **leopards** are present, though cryptic and more confined to the

Fracas at the carcass

You are more likely to encounter predators at a kill rather than witness a hunt itself, but the frenzy of feeding carnivores is a dynamic scene well worth watching as the pecking order is played out. Lions are invariably the heavyweights, but spotted hyena clans in the crater can number up to 80 individuals and can compete successfully against lions by weight of numbers. A pack of hyenas on a carcass can seem both noisy and aggressive, but hyenas don't actually fight over food. With the lions gone, a dozen or more jackals – most commonly black-backed and golden – dart into the kill when they can, even among hyenas. The golden jackal reaches the southern limit of its African range in northern Tanzania, so keep an eye out for it here (it is the most common jackal in NCA). Hyenas and jackals try to steal food from one another, while vultures wait in the wings – white-backed and hooded being the most numerous.

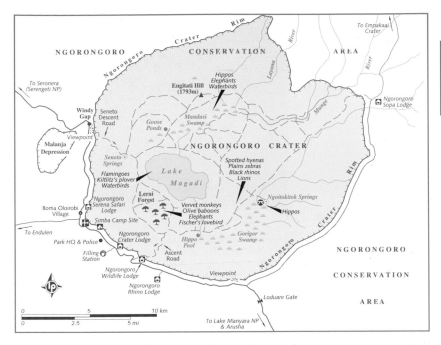

forested rim. Also, all seven of Tanzania's **vulture** species occur in the NCA – around 25% of the world's population of **Rüppell's griffon vulture** resides here and in the surrounding ecosystem. Keep an eye out for **Egyptian vultures** (usually seen singly or in pairs): they reach the southern end of their range in northern Tanzania, but nest on the cliffs of the crater rim.

Hyenas lollop across the flat grasslands, but look for them also on the edge of Lake Magadi or other wet areas, flopped in the muddy water to cool off. They sometimes hide food underwater and have been observed hunting the **flamingos** that seasonally crowd this lake.

On the crater plains you'll probably notice **Masai ostriches**, the solitary **kori bustard**, **secretary birds** and **grey crowned**

Ngorongoro Crater is one of the best places in East Africa to see predators. While lions and spotted hyenas posture over kills, black-backed jackals try to dart in and snatch morsels.

cranes (as many as 110 cranes have been recorded in a single group). One species restricted to this highland region is the **northern anteater chat**, common near areas of disturbed ground and termite mounds. On the grass plains lives **Jackson's widowbird**, which is similarly restricted to highland areas of northern Tanzania and southern Kenya. From January to April this sociable bird transforms from being a small drab job into a dark, long-tailed bird that dances about frantically to attract a mate. Jackson, after whom the species was named, described the antics of the 'Dancing Whydah' as 'a truly ridiculous sight': males set up a small area in long grass in which they repeatedly jump up and down, with jumps getting well over 50cm in height. They dance like this all day, most enthusiastically in the early morning and late afternoon.

Crowned and **blacksmith plovers** are everywhere, while **Kittlitz's plover** is limited to the water's edge. The marshy areas are home to **cormorants**, **grebes**, **herons**, **egrets** and **pelicans**. The pelicans visiting the crater are a little unusual in that they mostly live on a diet of frogs – there are no fish in the crater. Another frog-eater is the **hamerkop** – a bird that never strays far from water. In the Lerai Forest, one of the special species to watch out for is the endemic **Fischer's lovebird**. The grounds of the lodges on the crater rim are excellent places to look for forest birds – stunning **golden-winged** and **eastern double-collared sunbirds** are common.

Hotspots
Between the crater and the Serengeti is Olduvai Gorge (see boxed text). Although Olduvai is mainly about fossils, the thornbush around the museum is good for birds – two species that you won't see in Ngorongoro Crater are the **red-cheeked cordon-bleu** and the vividly coloured **purple grenadier**; the colourful **red-and-yellow barbet** is also resident. Olduvai is just 20km from the boundary of Serengeti NP, and the Serengeti Plains that fall within the NCA are seasonal home to one to two million **wildebeests**, **plains zebras**, and **Grant's** and **Thomson's gazelles** as they complete their annual 800km migration (see the Serengeti NP section).

On the southern route to Ngorongoro Crater, a stop-off or stay at Gibbs Farm, near Karatu, is highly recommended. The flower-rich garden attracts lots of birds, including **sunbirds, weavers, robin-chats, mousebirds** and **tropical boubous**. A bird list is supplied and the feeding platform in the garden is an ideal place to 'take tea'. From here there is a two-hour walk up to an enormous **elephant** salt lick (the gouged walls help explain why elephants' tusks become worn down). **Cinnamon-chested bee-eaters** have their nest holes in the red banks of the lick.

Elephants are often seen among the tall yellow fever trees in the Crater's Lerai Forest.

Other areas within the NCA are fairly inaccessible, but some adventurers hike the Crater Highlands. Just outside the NCA is Oldoinyo Lengai – Tanzania's only active volcano – and you can even go up to its rim (it last erupted in 1983). Several of these mountains are over 3000m and support diverse habitats – moorland at high altitude; dense montane forest lower on the wetter eastern sides; and acacia woodlands and plains on the drier western sides, which sit in a rain shadow. This variety gives rise to a diversity of birds and in various areas you will see mammals, including **monkeys** and **buffaloes**. Two of the peaks (Empakaai and Olmoti) are craters and their floors provide good grazing for **antelopes** such as **bushbucks**. You need to be well organised to trek in these highlands as they are off the beaten track. ■

Watching tips

To get away from the tourist crush visit the northern and eastern parts of the park during peak hour traffic: it may be less dense with animals, but offers more chance to sit quietly and watch life uninterrupted. The late afternoon is a generally quieter time to visit the west than in the morning. If you're staying at Simba Campsite, keep an eye out for habituated zebras grazing close by; after nightfall, bushpigs often snuffle through the camp. Screeching vervet monkeys in Lerai Forest may indicate the presence of a leopard or another predator: look at where they're facing, then search for movement.

SERENGETI NATIONAL PARK

Hoofbeats across endless plains

🐆 Wildlife highlights

Some of the best wildlife viewing in Africa. Because of its open plains and sparseness of sheltering trees it offers outstanding views of predators: in addition to leopards and three species of jackal, the Serengeti ecosystem is estimated to support some 2800 lions and 9000 spotted hyenas. It is the best place in Tanzania to see cheetahs, with about 250 in the park. However, hunting dogs and rhinos are now in such small numbers that you will almost certainly not encounter them. Serengeti also protects large populations of ungulates, including giraffes, topis and elands, and is famous for its migrations of wildebeests, zebras and gazelles. The park contains over 500 bird species, including Tanzanian endemics.

SERENGETI is the largest national park in Tanzania and the most famous park in Africa: a vast expanse of plains covered in wildebeests, zebras, gazelles and giraffe-trimmed, flat-topped acacias that for many of us epitomise Africa. But the Serengeti is the size of Northern Ireland and contains far more than the seemingly endless plains: the plains lie in the south-east; to the north, where the park adjoins Kenya's Masai Mara NR, the terrain becomes hilly and rocky; and to the west there is a mosaic of hills, valleys, rivers, riverine forest and plains.

Most people enter the Serengeti through the Naabi Hill Gate in the south-east. This is 20km inside the park and the real boundary is a ranch-style gate in the middle of nowhere. There is no fence and the animals graze both on the Serengeti side and in the adjoining Ngorongoro Conservation Area (NCA). In the dry season animals are scarce here because of the lack of water, but the non-water dependent gazelles – **Thomson's** and **Grant's** – are found here most of the year. From the end of the short rains until the easing of the long rains (roughly from January to April) there are abundant **wildebeests**, **plains zebras**, and **gazelles** in the area, but as there is plenty of food and

---

The smoothest ride in Africa

Serengeti is the only place in Tanzania where you can glide over a park in a hot air balloon; and the pre-dawn drive from Seronera Lodge to the launch point is the closest you will get to a 'night' drive in a Tanzanian national park. On the way you may encounter genets, civets and springhares. At the whim of the airstream and accompanied by bursts of flame, you drift over the plains. It's silent except for the burner and from the air you can spot otherwise invisible hyena dens. Everywhere tracks criss-cross the plains like some gigantic web. Groups of zebras, wildebeests, hartebeests and gazelles are visible for kilometres. You'll skim over acacias full of huddling olive baboons or vervet monkeys that have not yet risen for the day. You'll look down on vultures' nests, but in flight most birds become difficult to recognise when viewed from above. One of the biggest advantages of ballooning is that it overcomes viewing problems caused by long grass. Mammals such as bohor reedbucks, which are often obscured by reeds, and caracals, servals and African wild cats may be seen below. The balloon ride ends wherever the wind has blown you, and your champagne breakfast may be accompanied by whatever animals happen to be nearby.

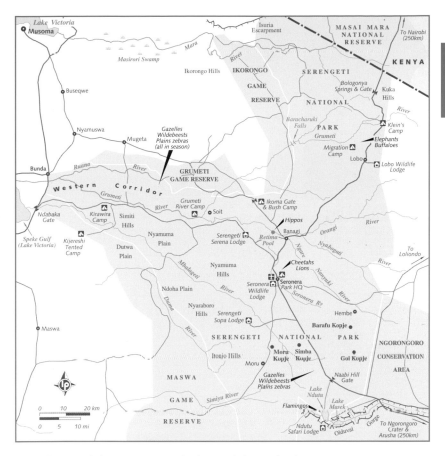

water the animals become increasingly dispersed during this time. As the area dries up (usually around May) the vast migratory herds (one to two million strong) began to form and head from the Serengeti Plains towards the Western Corridor – they won't return in numbers this far south until the following January, after the short rains finish.

The short grass plains give way to longer grass plains and the landscape becomes more varied once you pass Naabi on the way to Seronera. In addition to the gazelles, **Coke's hartebeests** (kongonis) and **topis** can be seen grazing, termite mounds and **common ostriches** (this subspecies is sometimes called the Masai ostrich) appear, and the depression at the granite outcrops of Simba Kopje may contain **elephants** and **Masai giraffes**. Around Seronera you will find many animals during the dry season: the rivers here provide a year-round water source, and the trees and shrubs provide food for browsing animals which cannot live on the plains grass. Along the watercourse of the Seronera River you may spot **elephants**, **defassa waterbucks**, **bohor reedbucks** and **lions**.

The Serengeti's many kopjes make favourite shade spots and lookouts for lions.

The Serengeti's apparently milling herds of wildebeests actually move in a recognisable order.

A great place to start

Check out the Visitors Centre at Seronera. You'll undoubtedly get distracted at the picnic tables by opportunists such as **banded mongooses**, **vervet monkeys**, **rock hyraxes** and a bevy of birds, including **superb starlings** and **d'Arnaud's barbets**. The barbets (here they are a distinctive race regarded by some ornithologists as a separate species, the Usambiro barbet) often sit on branches singing duets, facing each other while wagging their erect tails to reveal a flash of red. Nearby, an interpretive walkway winds up through a kopje. The displayed information unfolds the life, death and seasonal cycles of the Serengeti and its animals. Here, as with any kopje, is an ideal place to look out for **agama lizards** – the males have a coral-pink head and bluish tail. For those with a interest in checking out bird plumage closely, the Research Station several kilometres away from the Visitors Centre has a small museum with stuffed birds and a library.

From the Visitors Centre, you'll probably head to the Seronera Wildlife Lodge. Constructed around a kopje, **rock hyraxes** regularly run about upstairs near the dining area (book here for a unique way of seeing the Serengeti's animals – by hot-air balloon – see boxed text).

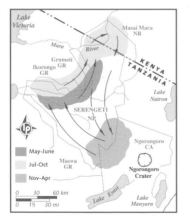

May-June
Jul-Oct
Nov-Apr

Around July the migration passes through the Western Corridor, west of Seronera, on its way north. The road follows the Grumeti River, which abounds with **hippos** and **crocs**; the crocs here are believed to be some of the largest in the world (size in crocs is related to age and food availability so the pickings on the river must be good). **Black-and-white colobus** live in the riverine forest, and can be seen about 30km from Seronera Lodge at the point where the road comes close to the river at Kimarishi Hill. The west is about the only place you can find the savanna woodland-dwelling **patas monkey** – this species is largely confined to west and central Africa, and the Serengeti's patas monkeys are a unique subspecies.

Carnivore carnival

Along with the neighbouring Masai Mara, this is one of the best places in Africa to observe the big cats. The Wandamu River area in Seronera is said to hold the

---

Wildebeest migration

Many people associate the Serengeti migration with rumbling hooves, tossing heads and thrashing tails being nipped by predators. They might think of the migration as an intense but short phase of the year. In fact, this 800km pilgrimage is an ongoing cycle of movement and dispersal that defines the Serengeti–Mara ecosystem (see map this page). Dependent on rainfall, the timing of the cycle is never totally predictable, but it is generally during May that, prompted by vanishing water and the lure of newly-watered sward, over one million wildebeests, zebras and gazelles congregate and tramp west and north from the southern plains. One column passes west to Lake Victoria, another moves north past Lobo. While on the hoof (May to June) the rut commences and wildebeests mate. They reach the north, and eventually cross into Kenya's Masai Mara NR, during July to October. During November the herds begin to reform for the return journey. By December they are dispersing among the southern grasslands; and calving starts in February. Over a million wildebeests trampling and cropping nutrient-rich grasses promotes regrowth, producing fresh graze for calving – the cycle complete.

world's greatest density of **cheetahs**. Without the obstruction of trees it is almost guaranteed that you'll see cheetahs on the plains – often alone, but sometimes a mother with young or a small bachelor group. Unlike most cats, cheetahs are daytime hunters and don't necessarily conceal themselves from their prey. They instead rely on their speed – up to 110 km/h. Watching cheetahs will give you the best chance to see big cats hunting.

Although nocturnal, **leopards** are not too difficult to spot because the big-branched trees in which they rest during the day are not common. Search the branches of sausage trees and bigger tree species along the Seronera River. But it is **lions** that most people come to see and you'll definitely see them. Lions spend most of their time laying about in shade with their paws in the air, so search the shady patches along watercourses and the shadows of big trees. Chances are your driver will be listening on the radio and will know where the big cats are (this of course often results in a traffic jam at the sighting).

Watercourses are also good places to look for **elephants**. They are dependent on water, and in the absence of green grass during the dry season are restricted to feeding on the bark and foliage of trees and shrubby vegetation along the rivers. **Hippos** and **crocs** are found along the narrow Seronera River, and good spots to check are Syd Downey's Dam and Kerr's Dam, both near Seronera Lodge. Further away and to the north is the Retima Hippo Pool – here you can get out of your car and picnic if you wish. If there has been recent rain scout about for tracks of **leopards, hippos, elephants** and other animals.

As you drive about always check termite mounds – favoured vantage points for **cheetahs**, while **topis, bushbucks** and **mongooses** use them to watch for predators. **Dwarf mongooses** also frequent termite mounds, and any shade the mound casts may be a resting spot for a **serval** or **African wild cat**.

Location 325km north-west of Arusha; access difficult during the long rains, especially April to May.

Facilities Serengeti has just about everything you need, mostly at Seronera: information centres (Naabi Hill and Seronera), maps, books and even a store. Guides can be hired at Seronera and Lobo. Ballooning available.

Accommodation About 10 lodges and camps, nine public camping grounds; some closed April and May.

Wildlife rhythms The timing of the famous migration of wildebeests, zebras and other ungulates varies from year to year, but as a rough guide the animals are in the north August to October (with most crossing into the Masai Mara during October), heading south in November and December, in the south-east of the park until May, then heading north again via the Western Corridor during June and July. The spectacular crossing by the herds of the Grumeti River (and the attendant feasting by Nile crocodiles) takes place around June. From December to February, zebras and wildebeests give birth, and provide a magnet for predators. Bird numbers and diversity peak October to April, when migratory species return.

Contact Senior Park Warden, Seronera HQ (☎ 057-622 852), PO Box 3134, Arusha; Ikoma HQ (☎ 057-622 029).

Ecotours Serengeti Balloon Safaris (☎ 057-578 578, fax 578 997), PO Box 12116, Arusha.

Two antelope species you'll often see grazing are **topi** and **Coke's hartebeest** (kongoni). They are easily confused as their body shape is similar, but their colour is clearly different: topis are brick-red, kongonis are fawn-yellow. The Serengeti protects Tanzania's greatest concentration of topis and is a stronghold for kongonis. They are especially common in the Western Corridor and northern savanna woodlands. While kongonis congregate in small groups, topis can form herds of up to 2000. Their main breeding ground is the Ndoha Plain, but this area is fairly inaccessible.

The northern part of Serengeti, Lobo, is the best place to see **buffaloes** and **elephants** in numbers, although they also occur elsewhere. The trees of this woodland area provide elephants with food during the dry season. Buffaloes are highly dependent on water, and will usually be found within 20km of a water source – and they benefit from the shade offered by the trees.

Serengeti protects the largest **giraffe** population in Africa (the race here is the Masai giraffe), although its numbers declined in the 1990s. They are dependent on acacia trees, which grow well near watercourses. The Serengeti also supports Africa's largest population of **common elands** (the subspecies here is Patterson's eland – distinguished by its rufous coat). This bovine heavyweight (males reach nearly a tonne) is unmistakable because of its great size, but its occurrence is difficult to predict – elands are great wanderers and have home ranges as big as 1500 sq km. They are a rather sociable species: calves like to get together so you may see groups of up to 50; and if a local area offers good pickings, groups of up to 1000 elands can congregate briefly.

With nearly half of Tanzania's bird total recorded, Serengeti offers some great birding. The **Masai ostrich** and **kori bustard** are readily seen, and the **lesser flamingo** is a visitor to the saline Lake Ndutu (Lagarja). Three Tanzanian endemics – **Fischer's lovebird**, the **rufous-tailed weaver** and **grey-breasted spurfowl** are locally common. The lovebird prefers mature acacia woodlands, and both the weaver and spurfowl can be spotted around open woodlands. While the lovebirds and weaver can be seen in places other than Serengeti, the grey-breasted spurfowl occurs only in the Seronera–Ndutu area of Serengeti and around Lake Eyasi in the NCA. One other species to look out for is the **brown-chested plover**, a West African migrant that sometimes turns up on the Serengeti Plains – often with **Senegal plovers**, which look somewhat similar. Migrant species are present between October and April, and include **white storks, rollers, cuckoos, swallows, Montague's** and **pallid harriers**, and **Caspian plovers**.

Some people are told that there aren't any animals in the Serengeti during the dry season. This is untrue: there are oodles of animals in the Serengeti throughout the year – there just aren't the half-million wildebeest and quarter of a million gazelles scattered across the plains. The wildebeest migration has its season and path (see boxed text), but at other times there is still ample wildlife to keep you ogling. The only time to think about avoiding is the height of the wet season, when the roads to Serengeti become problematic. You'll probably want to take in Ngorongoro Crater on any trip to Serengeti, and in the wet there may be no access into the crater. ■

Watching tips

Sharing your lion and leopard viewing with 20-odd other vehicles may not be your idea of enjoying wildlife, but you can head to the less busy Lobo or Western Corridor. Alternatively, most drivers confine their safari to the earlier and later part of the day: if you head out in the heat of the day, you'll still find the lions under the trees and perhaps even see a leopard hunting – although mostly nocturnal, they sometimes take advantage of the fact that most animals are resting (and are less alert) in the midday sun. Wear a broad-brimmed hat if going on a balloon ride – the flaming of the burner is hot stuff. Serengeti and neighbouring Ngorongoro are the places to get close-up wildlife shots, so pack far more film than you think you are going to need.

ZANZIBAR & PEMBA

Ancient connections on Africa's Spice Islands

THE Zanzibar archipelago is made up of two major islands, Unguja (usually referred to as 'Zanzibar') and Pemba, and numerous smaller islands. Accessible coral reefs have long attracted divers and snorkellers, but both main islands also have a rich diversity of land animals, including some interesting endemic species and subspecies (many of the bird species and races reflect past changes in the natural and man-made environment). The main islands are heavily populated and have been intensely cultivated for centuries – especially for cloves and other spices, which made Zanzibar famous throughout the world. Most of the original forest cover has been cleared, but the small stands that have been preserved are definitely worth exploring for wildlife.

Coral reefs, turtles and dolphins

Fringing coral reefs with a high diversity of corals, fish and other marine life bring droves of snorkellers and scuba divers to Unguja. There are countless dive sites: two of the most popular are at Ras Ngunwi village (reputed to have lots of fish) and off Stonetown itself (favoured for corals). A full day's diving off Mnemba Island is said to offer everything, but all sites offer plenty to see.

Both **green** and **hawksbill turtles** nest on Unguja: at Ngunwi you can watch female green turtles lumber ashore to lay their

The tide of destruction

The archipelago's wildlife has suffered greatly at the hands of introduced species. Apart from invasions of common pests such as the black rat, which has been spread around the world by seafarers, three species of mongoose have been introduced to the islands. These efficient predators compete with the native mongooses, which today are rarely seen, and almost certainly caused the extinction of two birds unique to the islands. But one pest animal stands out: the Indian house crow. Introduced in 1890, the crows proliferated and began to prey on small birds, eggs and nestlings. The situation became so serious that eventually a house crow eradication program was implemented by Mr Tony Archer and a team from the Commission for Lands and Environment in Stonetown. Some 45,000 crows were destroyed in the mid 1990s, but funding has since dried up and the house crow menace could yet resurface to wreak havoc on Zanzibar's native birds.

eggs; and under the lighthouse at Ras Ngunwi a dozen green turtles can be seen up close in a walled but otherwise natural lagoon, with zebra-striped **scissortail sergeants** swimming among them.

Humpback whales move north through the channel between the mainland and the archipelago in spring, and return, sometimes with families, in September. They can sometimes be seen off Unguja and Chumbe Island. **Long-snouted spinner** and **bottlenose dolphins** live in the seas around Zanzibar, and watching and swimming with dolphins has become a tourist industry off Kizimkazi. Please help the village's ecotourism venture – and the dolphins themselves – by following the guidelines that have been developed for observing dolphins.

Unguja's last stand

Jozani Park, the largest area of mature forest left on Zanzibar, is the stronghold of the endangered **Zanzibar** (or **Kirk's**) **red colobus**; **blue monkeys** (the subspecies on Zanzibar is endemic) also live here. The colobus are usually easy to see – they can occur in troops of around 100 and sometimes feed in mixed troops with blue monkeys; at midday you may see them draped over the branches of Indian almond trees having a siesta.

Jozani is also a refuge for many of Unguja's other mammals (although the **Zanzibar leopard** is almost certainly extinct). You can follow trails through several different habitats to look for them or find a fruiting tree and sit quietly nearby, especially in the early morning or late afternoon. **Red-bellied coast squirrels** scamper about in the canopy (another species, the **Zanj sun squirrel**, also lives on Ugunja) and more than 40 species of bird have been recorded in Jozani: time spent here would improve

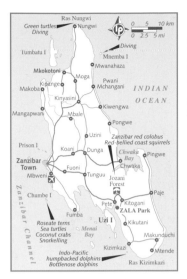

Location Unguja: about 40km north-east of Tanzania. Pemba: 50km east of the mainland and 50km north of Unguja.

Facilities Unguja: nature trails and mangrove boardwalk at Jozani Forest. Pemba: information centre and nature trail at Ngezi Forest Reserve; walking and underwater trails at Misali.

Accommodation Unguja: Plenty of choice in Zanzibar Town; resorts on Changuu and Mnemba Islands. Pemba: limited range in Chake Chake; camping on Misali Island.

Wildlife rhythms Conditions for snorkelling and diving are usually best from June to February or March.

Contact Zanzibar Protected Areas Project, Commission for Natural Resources (☎/fax 31252, **e** edgznz@twiga.com), PO Box 3950, Zanzibar.

Ecotours Unguja: CHICOP (☎/fax 31040, **e** chumbe. island@raha.com), PO Box 3203, Zanzibar runs all-inclusive tours to Chumbe. Jozani Forest accessible by public transport.

Pemba: Access to Misali through Zanzibar Protected Areas Project. Ngezi Forest accessible by public transport.

your chances of seeing gems such as the **African pygmy king-fisher, little greenbul, dark-backed weaver** and, if you're very lucky, **Fischer's turaco**. You are unlikely to encounter the critically endangered **Aders' duiker** (see the boxed text on page 102) or the Zanzibar race of **suni**; but listen for the activities of **black-and-rufous elephant shrews** during the day and **tree hyraxes** at night; traces of nocturnal **bushpigs** may also be seen during the day. Don't miss the mangrove boardwalk at the southern end of Jozani: **mangrove kingfishers** are resident and your guide can introduce you to mangrove ecology.

Unguja's bird total stands at well over 200 species and keen birders will no doubt continue to improve knowledge of the island's birdlife. During low tide at the harbour you should see a few loitering **sooty gulls** and **dimorphic egrets** (of both white and grey varieties) stalking across the mud for prey. But **crab-plovers** are the prize sighting: they feed on all Zanzibar's shores, together with **sand plovers, terek sandpipers, whimbrels** and **greenshanks**. A few could be seen at any time of year, although numbers peak between November and March.

One of Unguja's best birdwatching sites is Bwawani Marsh, at the north end of Stonetown, where **pied kingfishers, purple swamphens** and **Allen's gallinules, African jacanas** and **white-faced whistling ducks** can be seen.

Island sanctuaries

Chumbe Island, Tanzania's first official marine park (also known as Chumbe Island Coral Park – CHICOP), is a 16ha environmentally friendly resort and reserve. Money made from visitors to the reserve is used to educate local children about conservation, and Chumbe has achieved World Heritage Status. No one lives here except park staff – and lots of crabs: red **shore crabs** hide in dry pockets on the reef; thousands of orange-and-black striped **rock crabs** squeeze into crevices among the coral rag; and **hermit crabs** leave their characteristic trails everywhere.

Most of Chumbe's natural coastal forest has remained untouched and more than 60 bird species have been recorded on the island. **Little swifts** swirl over the greenery, returning to their nests under the lighthouse's window overhangs. Two islets just south-west of Chumbe supported a breeding colony of some 750 pairs of **roseate tern** in 1994. They are likely to be seen offshore from May to December when they are nesting. Some 350 species of fish have been recorded from Chumbe's almost pristine reef, and **turtles** and **dolphins** are regularly seen. Snorkelling is offered,

Zanzibar's tree hyraxes are a distinct subspecies from those of the mainland.

A snapshot of evolution

Each of the Zanzibar archipelago's islands has endemic animals, but the overlap of species between the islands and the adjacent mainland is a complex puzzle that preserves a fascinating snapshot of evolution. For example, Aders' duiker, a species that survives only on Unguja and in coastal Kenya, is a relict of ancient West African forests that once stretched right across the continent. Likewise, the subspecies of African pygmy kingfisher on Unguja is elsewhere found only in southern Africa and probably reflects past changes in the continent's vegetation. But the Pemba flying-fox is not found on Unguja or the adjacent mainland – its nearest relative is in Madagascar, 1500km to the south-east. Undoubtedly part of another wave of invading species, the flying-fox was probably isolated on Pemba before it could spread to Unguja. The Pemba Channel prevented the flying-fox's spread to the mainland and has served as an effective barrier to natural invasions of Pemba ever since.

and you can walk the forest trail or an intertidal trail (at low tide). Huge **coconut crabs** emerge after sunset – the compost heap is a good place to look.

Changuu – better known as Prison Island – supports several of Unguja's unique **lizard** species, but is far better known for another reptile: **giant tortoises**. Native to Aldabra in the Seychelles, the tortoises were transported to Changuu during the 18th century and thrived free from predation by dogs and pigs. There's also excellent snorkelling around Changuu and, even though it's only 5km away, the reef fish fauna is markedly different from that of Unguja.

Endemics with a Malagasy twist

Pemba's largest remaining patch of forest, Ngezi Forest Reserve, has been selectively logged, but the island's four endemic bird species (imaginatively named the **Pemba green pigeon**, **Pemba scops owl**, **Pemba sunbird** and **Pemba white-eye**) are reasonably common and widespread. The white-eye and sunbird are common in gardens and plantations; the green pigeon readily feeds in fruiting palms near villages; and the scops owl (more often heard than seen) inhabits woodlands and plantations.

The **Pemba flying-fox** (see the boxed text) is most common on Pemba's west coast and offshore islets, and there's also a good population at Ngezi FR (rangers should be able to point you to a camp – and watch for that cosmopolitan bat botherer, the **bat hawk**, hunting small insect-eating bats at dusk). The Pemba subspecies of **vervet monkey** and **tree hyrax** also live at Ngezi; and the **Pemba day gecko**, another Malagasy relict, should be heard scuttling among leaf litter. Other patches of forest survive at Mwitu Mkuu and Ras Kiuyu.

Misali is a small forested island just off Chake Chake that has been declared a Marine Conservation Area. **Green turtles** and **seabirds** nest on the western side, mangroves fringe the eastern side and there are underwater viewing trails through the adjoining coral reefs. ■

Watching tips

ZALA (Zanzibar Land Animals) Park is a small wildlife centre about 3km from Jozani which offers an excellent introduction to Unguja's reptiles (including the island's only species of chameleon). And in case you miss them at Jozani, Zanzibar red colobus are often heard and seen in the trees around the enclosures at ZALA Park; another small population lives near Makunduchi.

SELOUS GAME RESERVE

Tanzania's southern wilderness

> ## Wildlife highlights
> Fewer tourists and more wilderness. Some of Africa's largest populations of elephants, buffaloes, hartebeests, sables and hunting dogs. Lions, giraffes and various antelopes are well-represented; black rhinos are present but unlikely to be seen. Boating safaris on the Rufiji River are a must: the river is thick with hippos and crocs and the waterbirds are outstanding. More than 440 bird species have been recorded, including gems such as Pel's fishing owls, African skimmers and white-headed plovers. Escorted walking safaris are a highlight and this is one of the few places in Tanzania where tourists can walk in a region that contains dangerous animals.

ALTHOUGH Selous is one of Africa's largest and most important wildlife conservation areas it is largely unknown to tourists. By virtue of its size it protects vast numbers of animals: it contains the largest **buffalo** concentration in Africa (more than 110,000) and over half of Tanzania's **elephants** (57,000). The Selous ecosystem is estimated to contain Africa's largest populations of **Lichtenstein's hartebeest** (a distinct subspecies that is sometimes regarded as a full species), **common waterbuck**, and **Roosevelt's sable**. However, it is not just the reserve's size that protects the animals – the presence of tsetse flies has made it unsuitable for humans and livestock, and this has undoubtedly helped to safeguard Selous' **hunting dogs** – a species which elsewhere suffers severe persecution from livestock owners. Selous is home to 25 to 30 percent of Africa's hunting dogs and the park's population is estimated at around 1300. Furthermore, most of Tanzania's **black rhinos** inhabit Selous and the park contains large numbers of **lions**, **hyenas** and **ungulates**. The Rufiji River is packed with **hippos** and **crocs**, and more than 440 species of bird have been recorded in the area.

It's obvious why this area was declared a World Heritage site

The painted hunter

No terrestrial carnivore is more cooperative or successful at hunting than the African hunting dog. Although lions hunt together, in general females in a pride do most of the hunting; lions also have a lower success rate, catching their prey between 20 and 40% of the time. In contrast, hunting dogs in some studies hit a success rate of up to 85%. Their cooperative pack hunting and ability to run for kilometres – an average chase of a prey is between 1.3 and 3km – is the key. The dogs select one or more targets, the pack chasing them until they can go no further. Death is swift. The dogs are co-operative, tearing and tugging on the abdomen until the victims fall. Their prey is quickly eaten – then shared. Food is regurgitated to dogs that have lost the trail, are sick or injured, stayed behind to mind the pups, and to the pups themselves.

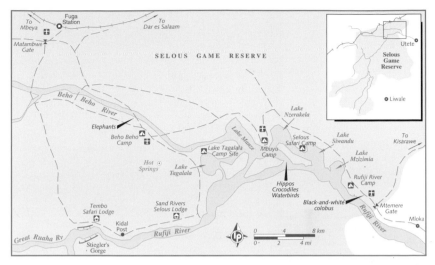

and with all the aforementioned, you'd think Selous would be thronging with tourists. But after observing the trends in Tanzania's northern safari circuit, official policy is to safeguard Selous from out-of-control tourism: only the park's northern sector is open for tourism; and only the camps and lodges are permitted to operate boats on the Rufiji River and use the tracks that hug the main waterways. In practical terms it's a place best visited on an organised trip, but in addition to the usual game drives, escorted walking and boating safaris are allowed – both rarities in Tanzania.

Along the Rufiji River

Much of the northern area is flat and dominated by grassland, miombo and *Terminalia* woodlands (the pungent, sweet smell of flowering terminalias pervades the September air). Most wildlife watching takes place on and around Selous' maze of rivers and lakes. The water is thick with **crocodiles** and **hippos**, **elephants** are a regular sight and **waterbirds** are everywhere. During the wet season the Rufiji River swells and redefines its course: the exact locations of its channels, lagoons and oxbow lakes change from year to year; and bits of lodges, camps and roads built along the river to allow great wildlife watching often end up in the drink during the wet season.

Near the Mtemere Gate the river is edged by tall, dense trees. On foot (Rufiji River Camp conducts walks here) or on the river, this is a great area for finding **black-and-white colobus** and guides should be able to lead you to them. This is also a top area to look for one of Africa's most sought after birds – **Pel's fishing owl**. Upstream from here many of the waterways are lined with sandbanks, and **African skimmers** 'plough' the water's surface and mass on the shore while **vultures** wash on the beach. Further along, *Borassus* palms fringing the water provide homes for **African palm swifts**, which can be seen darting about at sunset. Dead palms are used by **African fish eagles** as vantage

Location Park entrances 250 and 350km south-west of Dar; often inaccessible during long rains (March to May).
Facilities Boat trips, walking safaris and rough lodges.
Accommodation Camping ground, several lodges and tented camps.
Wildlife rhythms Dry season (June to October) is best as animals congregate around waterways
Contact Chief Warden, Selous GR, (☎ 051-866 064, fax 861 007), PO Box 25295, Dar es Salaam.
Ecotours About six operators have camps in Selous.

points and by **Dickinson's kestrels** as nest sites. In places along the riverbank, river combretum creates a wall of red flowers in November and December. **Crocs** in big numbers sun themselves on banks and **hippos** are often out grazing during the day. **Giraffes, waterbucks, elephants, buffaloes** and even **lions** can all be observed from the river. Interestingly, the Rufiji divides two subspecies of wildebeest: blue wildebeest is not uncommon on its northern shore, while south of the river the Mozambique (white-banded) subspecies is more often seen.

The sheer numbers of **waterbirds** on and around the river will excite even nonbirders: the **white-headed plover**, an uncommon species in East Africa, prefers the edges of waterways; the stately **saddle-billed stork** occurs in good numbers; and other treats include the rarely seen **white-backed night heron** and the migratory **squacco heron**.

Selous' mini-migration

Many animals live on the plains during the wet season and return to the waterways in the dry season, drifting down from the north to the five lakes in June and July. They can first be seen around Lakes Tagalala and Manze, then slowly move north-east to congregate around Manze, Nzelekela and Siwandu. Lake Mzizamia becomes an isolated lagoon when the river level drops in the dry season and has fewer animals than

---

To hunt or not to hunt?

Like many protected areas in Africa, Selous caters not only for photographers but also for trophy hunters. In fact, over 90% of the reserve – everything south of the Rufiji River – is given over to hunting. Ethical concerns aside (and they are considerable), it begs the question 'is hunting a legitimate part of conservation?' Hunters argue that their exorbitant safari fees are ploughed back into protected areas; if it wasn't for their money, wilderness would disappear under agriculture. In the 1980s, only about 10% of hunting revenue actually made it into Selous' coffers but the figure is now around 50%. Of course, the same argument could be made of non-consumptive tourism, one the hunters counter by claiming they actually cause less damage to Selous' ecosystem. Per person, they pay far more than wildlife watchers, so fewer of them are required to make the same profit. Fewer people means fewer lodges, vehicles, rubbish dumps and so on. Whether that's less of an impact than shooting 148 leopards (Selous' quota for 1997 – to pick one of many) is debatable.

the others, except between September and December. However, the higher tree density here makes this area suitable for **colobus** (which aren't found around the other lakes), **trumpeter** and **crowned hornbills**, and **crowned eagles**. There are also an incredible number of **hippos** and **crocs** here.

All of the lodges have local wildlife highlights in and around their grounds. Mbuyuni (Selous Safari Camp), secreted among riverside greenery, is a top spot for **elephants**, and being escorted to and from your tent is entirely necessary here (to encourage guests not to wander, management warns that certain areas are mined!). Mbuyu Camp has a baobab 20m in circumference, around which is the dining area. This tree is a hive of activity – noisy **green wood-hoopoes**, **striped ground squirrels** and **brown-headed parrots** live in the tree's hollows and carry on regardless of the people below. This is also a great bird-watching spot because of its position on the river. Rufiji River Camp has lots of bold **vervet monkeys** around the restaurant and this is the place to go on a walking safari to find **black-and-white colobus**. The riverine vegetation is ideal **Pel's fishing owl** habitat – this bird is rare in East Africa but is occasionally seen along the Rufiji.

One antelope you are unlikely to encounter elsewhere is **Roosevelt's sable**. This subspecies is restricted to Tanzania and southern Kenya, and Selous protects some 10,000 – probably the largest surviving population – Roosevelt's sables. Sables are normally sedentary but the Selous population is fairly mobile, which can make finding them frustrating at times. They are found inside the reserve mostly during the wet season (when the park is often off limits) and drift out of the reserve to the south and south-east during the dry. These selective grazers and browsers are usually found in miombo, often venturing down to drink in the heat of the day. ■

Borassus palms lining the Rufiji River make nest sites and roosts for birds such as African palm swifts.

Watching tips

Beho Beho area is good for elephants, which are often found in the galley forest adjacent to the river. Downstream, Lake Tagala's banks are covered in *Terminalia* thickets which sometimes shelter buffaloes and lions. Pel's fishing owls roost in dense, shady trees adjacent to the Rufiji: their presence is often revealed by mobbing birds, although pellets and dung littered with fish scales beneath the tree is another sign – look up!

RANGIRE NATIONAL PARK

Arid haven for migrants

Wildlife highlights
Dry season home to migratory mammals, such as plains zebras, wildebeests, gazelles, buffaloes, elands and fringe-eared oryxes. Elephants are a prime attraction along the Tarangire River during the dry season and lions occur in good numbers. One of the very few places where there is a chance to see hunting dogs in Tanzania. Fabulous for birds (more than 450 species recorded in the park and over 500 in the broader ecosystem), especially raptors; three Tanzanian endemics easily seen.

TARANGIRE is seasonally outstanding for wildlife, and is second only to Ngorongoro Crater as a dry season home for many migratory mammals. Between June and November **wildebeests**, **plains zebras**, **fringe-eared oryxes**, **common elands**, **gazelles**, **hartebeests**, **buffaloes** and **elephants** congregate around the Tarangire River, the main water source in the dry season. Once the short rains begin in November the animals start to drift out of the park, returning in June after the long rains cease. Tarangire is also a very good park for spotting **lions** and it is a stunning place for **birds**. Termite mounds can be seen throughout the park (and they are often the haunt of **dwarf mongooses**). Although only 30km from the Rift Valley escarpment, Tarangire falls outside the nutrient-rich volcanic belt and the annual rainfall is low (550mm): much of it is semiarid, and dominated by baobabs and acacias.

Enraptured over raptors

There are over 60 raptor species in Tanzania and 49 of them occur in Tarangire. The open habitat in the northern sector is peppered with leafless trees during the dry season and this provides perfect bird-watching conditions. From the tracks that wind along the high banks of the Tarangire River you'll readily get within photographic distance of tawny, long-crested and martial eagles, and black-chested snake-eagles. Pale chanting goshawks are easy to spot, and keep an eye out for the gymnogene (African harrier-hawk) in more wooded areas – these slate-grey birds can sometimes be seen probing deep in hollows with their dexterous legs in search of prey. Both augur buzzards, with their orange tails, and the striking white-winged, black-bodied, short-tailed adult bateleurs are easy for nonbirders to distinguish from below. Leggy secretary birds (yes, they are raptors too) are common and unmistakable as they walk through the bush. Vultures – lappet-faced, Rüppell's griffon, hooded and African white-backed – can all be observed massed together in trees or spiralling on thermals, often in the company of marabou storks.

Bird's-eye views

Most visitors concentrate their activity in the northern sector and around the Tarangire River. As a first port of call the patio of the Tarangire Safari Lodge is a must: it sits high on a bluff and gives a bird's-eye view over the river. Wildlife viewing from here has to be some of the best in Africa because you can sit and watch for hours as individuals or groups slowly come to water, weaving their way down through the baobabs and acacias. Some 3000 **elephants** occur in the park and come down to drink. With the aid of binoculars you can even make out that a rapidly moving column of dots is a family of **mongooses**. Early morning and late afternoon are the best times to watch the river, but the heat of the day offers great **raptor** watching as they cruise at eyelevel around the bluff.

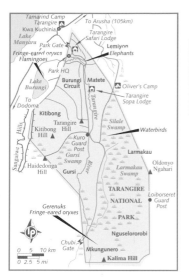

Tarangire offers great birding not just because of the diversity, but because of the excellent viewing conditions afforded by its sparse vegetation. Highlights include the birds of prey, and good numbers of three of Tanzania's endemic species – the **ashy starling**, **rufous-tailed weaver** and **yellow-collared lovebird**. Ashy (grey-brown with a very long tail) and **superb starlings** are common around lodges and camps, and noisy, twittery flocks of yellow-collared lovebirds are usually easy to locate near baobabs (they favour holes in baobabs as nesting sites). Reports of Fischer's lovebirds in Tarangire are erroneous and probably refer to escaped individuals of this popular cagebird. Rufous-tailed weavers are common in the acacia savannas throughout the park: they are bigger than most weavers (ie, they are thrush-sized), and easily recognised by their scale-like plumage, pale blue eyes and rufous tail; their large, untidy grass nests are readily seen scattered in the acacias.

Larger, ground-dwelling birds, such as **coqui**, **crested** and **Hildebrandt's francolins**, and both **red-necked** and **yellow-necked spurfowl** are regularly encountered taking dustbaths along the tracks. It's easy to see why spurfowl and guineafowl are blamed for enlarging potholes! The common guineafowl here are **crested guineafowl**, but **vulturine guineafowl** have been seen in the east of the park around Oldoinyo Ngahari – vulturines just make it into Tanzania and are right at the edge of their range in Tarangire.

Along the Tarangire River **Egyptian geese** and **crowned** and **blacksmith plovers** are common. The undersides of the fronds

Location 120km south-west of Arusha; some roads impassable in the wet season.
Facilities Maps and park booklet available at entrance. You are allowed out of vehicles in open areas.
Accommodation Several safari lodges and tented camps, and public and private camping grounds inside and outside park.
Wildlife rhythms Greatest large animal concentrations June to November. Eurasian bird migrants are present October to April.
Contact Senior Park Warden, PO Box 3134, Arusha.
Ecotours Numerous companies operating out of Arusha can take you to Tarangire – shop around.

of doum palms in the river valley are festooned with the nests of **African palm swifts**; the swifts themselves are commonly seen zooming around the palms in search of flying insects, their very long, pointed tails distinctive. For waterbirds a trip south (a full day's effort if staying in the north) to the Silale Swamp is recommended. Lush and green, this expansive swamp attracts **egrets, ibises, plovers, cormorants, storks, geese** and **ducks**. A good number of **saddle-billed storks** occurs here. **Pythons** also frequent the swamps and there is an increased chance of seeing one if the swamps are drying up – they hang in trees, so search the limbs of acacias. On the way south to Silale, pause at creek crossings and look around the river beds for **lions** and for animals digging for water. If coming from the north, you should also pass a kopje about 1km south of the Engelhard bridge across the Tarangire River – it is good for **bush hyraxes** and **klip-springers**.

Lake Burungi lies outside the park and when conditions are right, tens of thousands of **flamingos** feed in the lake. The lake shore is also a reliable place to see **fringe-eared oryxes**, which move seasonally in and out of the southern and central parts of Tarangire. Another place to find them is the Minyonyo area,

Tarangire's growing isolation

Tarangire faces an uncertain future as its migratory wildlife is almost entirely dependent on what happens outside the park – and things aren't secure. The animals are being increasingly cut off and isolated from their wet season homes. Agricultural encroachment, farming, ranching and settlements have almost severed the migratory routes north to Lake Manyara, which is an important destination for wildebeests and zebras. There are urgent calls to have a migration corridor declared between Manyara and Tarangire, but it is almost too late. To the east the pathways are being threatening by large scale agricultural developments between the Simanjiro area and the park. The Masai Steppe, and the Simanjiro and Lolkisale Game Control Areas are the most important wet season habitat for Tarangire animals (some 55,000 animals inhabit the area seasonally) and control of agriculture to the east is seen as imperative. The infertile soil and dry climate is not conducive to farming, although pastoralism (grazing) is seen as having the least impact on wildlife.

which is on the river south of Kuro guard post. South from here you will find **gerenuks**, with the Mkungonero region being the best area. The semiwilderness area south of the Silale Swamp is inaccessible in the wet season, but open to off-road driving in the dry.

Around Lake Burungi you may often find **bushbucks** or **lesser kudus** browsing in thickets. The Kitabung Hill area to the south is good for viewing **buffalo** herds, which kick up dust as they mill amid the acacias and descend to drink at dusk. **Common elands** are also seen in this region.

Tarangire is also a good place in which to see **hunting dogs**. The dogs roam the whole Masai Steppe system, so sightings are unpredictable. They den on the Steppe in the rains and are most likely to be encountered on the eastern side of the park in the dry season. Herds of antelope running and stotting without making alarm calls is one sign that hunting dogs are nearby.

The lizard buzzard typically uses an exposed perch to scan for prey such as insects and reptiles.

On the move

The movement patterns and paths of the migratory species in the Tarangire area are well known. **Plains zebras** and **wildebeests** move first, departing in October, then the **gazelles**, **buffaloes**, **elands**, **oryxes**, **hartebeests** and **elephants** move out. The bulk of these animals head north-east and some go as far as Lake Natron. **Defassa waterbucks**, **impalas**, **giraffes**, **lesser kudus**, **Kirk's dik-diks** and **warthogs** are all resident. The migratory species return in June and July – firstly the oryxes and elands, then the elephants, followed by the zebras and wildebeests; by August all the animals have returned. The migration path for many is through the Simanjiro area, so this is a good place to consider visiting once the migration begins. Operators here (who have their camps outside the parks) can offer walking safaris, driving in open vehicles, night drives and clambering about on kopjes (rocky outcrops) so the wildlife can be experienced close at hand. Night drives (a rarity in Tanzania) introduce nocturnal species such as **leopards**, **springhares**, **genets**, **civets**, **white-tailed mongooses** and **ratels**. ■

Watching tips

This is one of the best places in Tanzania to come in the dry season (July to October) if you want to see large numbers of ungulates (at this time, many ungulates in the more famous Serengeti have migrated north to Kenya). The Lemiyon region beyond the park's north-east boundary offers great photographic opportunities: it is dotted by baobabs, interspersed, in the dry season, with wildebeests and zebras.

!SHA NATIONAL PARK

In the shadow of Kilimanjaro

<table>
<tr><td>

</td></tr>
</table>

Wildlife highlights

A picturesque park where you'll see savanna animals such as buffaloes, elephants and plains zebras; hippos in permanent wetlands; and where sightings of black-and-white colobus and blue monkeys are guaranteed. Kirk's dik-diks are abundant and giraffes common near the Momela Gate. Some 420 bird species have been recorded, and the lakes are seasonally important for waterbirds and flamingos. Treks to Mt Meru's summit offer fewer people and more wildlife than Kilimanjaro, and klipspringers live on the crater cliffs.

VARYING from 1500 to over 4500m in altitude, Arusha NP protects diverse habitats and three distinct topographical features – 4566m Mt Meru, an inactive volcano and Tanzania's second highest peak; 3km-wide Ngurdoto Crater; and the Momela Lakes, which are great for birding. Arusha is easy to visit and although rhinos, elands, reedbucks and lions are no longer present, there are plenty of other mammals to see.

Just before you get to Ngurdoto Gate you'll see an acacia-fringed glade – Serengeti Ndogo (Little Serengeti) – that is always covered in **buffaloes, giraffes, warthogs** and **olive baboons**; it is also the only place where **plains zebras** occur in the park. From here the altitude rises and the vegetation alters dramatically to dense montane forest where **black-and-white colobus** (sometimes seen at the Ngurdoto Gate itself) and **blue monkeys** are certainties.

The road winding up to Ngurdoto Crater rim is flanked by tall, dense forest that is good primate habitat – look for **colobus, blue monkeys** and **olive baboons**; and large birds include **trumpeter** and **silvery-cheeked hornbills**. From several observation points you can see the pools, marshes and reedbeds that make the crater floor a favourite of **buffaloes** and **waterbirds**. Most birds are too far away to make out, but **saddle-billed storks** should stand out.

The central road from Ngurdoto Gate leads to the Momela Lakes – shallow, ground-fed lakes that seasonally attract hundreds of thousands of **lesser flamingos**, although it is impossible to predict when and where they will be present. You should also be able to see **greater flamingos** (the two often feed in separate lakes).

Feeding patterns

Arusha's lakes provide ample opportunities to witness the diverse feeding techniques of waterbirds. Little grebes cruise along the surface and dive periodically, emerging almost a minute later shaking their prey. Greater and lesser flamingos swing their beaks underwater as they filter feed with their heads down. At Momela Lodge's hippo pools sacred ibises probe the mud for molluscs with their sensitive beak, and sometimes sway their beak side-to-side in the shallows. The long legs of yellow-billed storks enable them to stand in deeper water, and snatch small fish or snails. And hamerkops can scoop up fish in midflight or shuffle in the shallows to stir up frogs then snap them up.

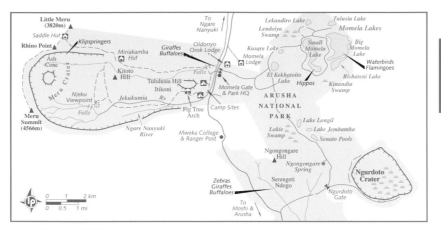

Arusha's small lakes are more seasonal, but **hippos, elephants, buffaloes** and **baboons** might be seen there. **Hippos** often use El Kekhotoito, and Kusare is a good place to spot **defassa waterbucks; Kirk's dik-diks** are common in this area. Scan the island in Small Momela Lake for **hippos** from the observation point at the edge. If you have no luck, another spot to check is about 2km along where the lake becomes swampy: this is a hippo entry and exit point. The marshes are also good for **waterbirds**, especially **little grebes**.

Some 48 waterbird species have been recorded on the Momela Lakes, but diversity varies seasonally, with Eurasian migrants present between October and April (one year it was estimated that almost the entire Tanzanian population of **Maccoa ducks** overwintered here). Unlike most Rift Valley lakes, which fill by flooding and can dry up, the Momela Lakes are fed by underground streams and always contain water.

Near the Momela Gate is an area known as 'Buffalo Ground', an acacia-fringed, swampy area at the base of Tululusia Hill that is fabulous in the dry season. **Buffaloes, warthogs, waterbucks** and countless **giraffes** reside here, and **grey crowned cranes** sometimes feed on the plain. Hire a guide and do the short walk to the nearby waterfall: it is very beautiful, and the animals are used to vehicles. Up high, you are likely to start seeing raptors including **bateleurs**, and **tawny** and **martial eagles**.

On Mt Meru (an armed guide must escort you to the top) you'll see a whole lot more wildlife and fewer people than on Kilimanjaro. The lower route to Miriakamba via Fig Tree Arch has more forest and is better for animals, including **alpine birds, olive baboons, black-and-white colobus** and **blue monkeys**. The open area at Itikoni is perhaps the best place for **elephants**, but these and **buffaloes** can occur anywhere. Above 3000m the forest peters out and the landscape is dominated by heathers and giant alpine herbs (*Senecio* and *Lobelia*) that reach well over head height. There is less wildlife, but **buffaloes** and **elephants** may also be found up here; these and **waterbucks** drink at the crater pool. **Klipspringers** can be seen on the cliffs inside the crater, and **lammergeiers** are sometimes seen soaring over the crater. ■

Location 21km from Arusha.
Facilities Small museum at Ngurdoto Gate; guides can be hired at Momela Gate.
Accommodation Lodge, NP camping grounds at both gates, one NP resthouse, two trekkers huts on Mt Meru.
Wildlife rhythms Dry season for mammals, migrating birds best during the wet season.
Contact Senior Park Warden (☎ 027-23471), PO Box 3134, Arusha.
Ecotours Most tour operators in Arusha run trips to Arusha NP – shop around. For treks hire an NP guide from park HQ.

Watching tips

Momela Lodge is a great birding site: the hippo pools teem with waterbirds, including sacred ibises, red-billed teal, African darters, grey herons, yellow-billed storks and Egyptian geese. The garden is open to nonresidents and attracts lots of birds including sunbirds. If camping at Momela Gate book site one: in the middle are two enormous trees smothered by strangler figs, and the surrounding forest is popular with colobus and blue monkeys. Elephants and buffaloes sometimes feed in the camping ground.

LAKE MANYARA NATIONAL PARK

Flamboyant rings around mirrored lake

> ### Wildlife highlights
> An outstanding park for birding: 487 species have been recorded and, depending on seasonal conditions, vast numbers of flamingos, pelicans and storks may be present. The adjacent forest is home to blue monkeys; and buffaloes, plains zebras, wildebeests, gazelles, elephants and Masai giraffes are found in the woodland and grasslands. Lions and leopards occur in small numbers and hippos reside in the lake.

MANYARA is a shallow, alkaline Rift Valley lake 40km long and 13km wide; part of the lake and its narrow shoreline make up the national park. Even if you don't visit the national park itself, you will certainly see the lake on a trip to northern Tanzania: the only road to Ngorongoro and Serengeti climbs over the 900m-high Eastern Rift Valley escarpment and from the top you look down on Lake Manyara.

Rainfall draining through aquifers at the base of the Rift Valley wall feeds Lake Manyara and groundwater forest. For such a small park, Manyara has a diverse array of habitats and supports an enormous number of bird species. Baobabs dot the Rift Valley wall, and dense forest containing large fig trees, sausage trees and mahoganies surrounds the park entrance. As this forest survives on groundwater more than rainfall, you'll notice less moss and fewer epiphytes growing on the trees. *Acacia-Commiphora* woodlands give way to a grassy floodplain before the shoreline and lake is reached. A single road traverses the park and numerous loops take in the lake's edge.

Location 120km west of Arusha; main park road is all-weather and suitable for 2WD.
Facilities Unloved museum at park entrance.
Accommodation Several hotels and tented lodges on the escarpment; self-catering bandas and camping grounds near park entrance; hostel for groups. Camping in the park may be possible.
Wildlife rhythms Most mammals resident year-round.
Contact Senior Park Warden (☎ Mto Wa Mbu 12), PO Box 12, Mto Wa Mbu.
Ecotours Any Arusha tour operator can take you to Manyara.

Disappearing waters

The lake's water level is highly changeable and can dramatically affect waterbird populations. Mudflats and sandy areas are the places to look for **chestnut-banded plovers**, a species with a very restricted distribution (it has a greyish back, but look for the chestnut slash across its white breast). In very dry years the lake shrinks to a small pool too saline for freshwater-loving birds. But if conditions are right, thousands of **pink-backed pelicans** and **yellow-billed storks**, and lesser numbers of **marabou storks** and **grey herons** congregate to breed here. **Flamingos** are an ephemeral star attraction, appearing in their hundreds of thousands one day, then leaving without warning – only to turn up at another Rift Valley lake. In very wet years the numerous streams feeding the lake can radically change the water level: dramatic flooding in 1997–98 resulted in a lake too fresh for the algal growth needed to attract flamingos. The popular Hippo Pools are currently no more: these have been consumed by the lake and lie about 1km beyond the drowned tree line.

Terrestrial animals are less affected by the waterline. **Olive baboons** and **blue monkeys** can typically be seen in the lush forest near the entrance. This is also an excellent place for locating **silvery-cheeked hornbills** – just listen for their loud, raucous grunts. **Buffaloes**, **wildebeests**, **plains zebras** and **impalas** inhabit the grassy shoreline and **Masai giraffes** can be found in the acacia woodland. The Marera River area can be particularly good for giraffes, known locally for their very dark colouring. Where acacia woodland meets open areas, look out for **rollers**, **bee-eaters** and **shrikes** hawking insects or perched in branches. The trill of **red-billed oxpeckers** may herald the arrival of a giraffe or antelope.

Once the park was famous for its **elephants** and tree-climbing **lions**, but their numbers have declined. While poaching in the 1980s drastically reduced the elephant population, the park still remains important for elephant conservation and you should encounter some – the Msasa River area is a particular favourite for mud wallowing. But you'll have to be lucky to see lions as they are scarce on the ground as well as in the trees; many of the big trees for climbing have fallen down, probably assisted by elephants. The Ndala River area is a good place to scout about for lions and elephants. If this river is low, you can go on to two hot springs (Maji Moto Ndogo and Maji Moto). These may be the place to look for **flamingos** as the hot water can promote localised algal growth. They often choose to bathe at freshwater springs, ruffling their feathers and preening themselves. ∎

Watching tips

Start looking out for wildlife about 50km from Arusha, where you'll see plains zebras; closer to the park at Makuyuni, Masai giraffes, more zebras, wildebeests, and Thomson's and Grant's gazelles appear. The trees around Mto Wa Mbu village are cluttered with marabou stork nests. Ask tour operators if big numbers of flamingos are present at the lake.

Flame birds of the Rift Valley

Why are there so many flamingos in the Rift Valley lakes? For starters, much of the water that spills into these lakes leaches through volcanic ash and lava, dissolving salts. As the equatorial sun evaporates water from the lakes, the salts become increasingly concentrated. Depending on the depth and salinity, this creates ideal conditions in which huge quantities of algae and saltwater crustaceans thrive – few other organisms can compete with them or even survive in this highly concentrated brine. However, lesser flamingos also thrive owing to their unique feeding technique: with tongue moving like a piston, they pump water through fine filters (called lamellae) inside their mandibles, catching algae and allowing most of the water to escape. With the abundance of food at certain times, it's no wonder that so many flamingos congregate.

MIKUMI NATIONAL PARK

Floodplains amid a mountainous arc

Wildlife highlights
One of East Africa's best parks for elephants, although breeding herds are scarce. Expect to see hippos, plains zebras, impalas, wildebeests, buffaloes, lions, elands and giraffes. Hunting dogs and sables are occasionally sighted. Among 413 recorded bird species are palm-nut vultures and violet-crested turacos.

MIKUMI is one of the largest and most easily visited of Tanzania's national parks, and if you're travelling between Zambia and Tanzania by road you'll get to see some of it for free – the TANZAM Hwy goes right through it. The southern border is now continuous with Selous GR, making the Mikumi–Selous complex the largest conservation area in Africa. The area is home to most species of East African large mammal, and common inhabitants include **elephants**, **giraffes**, **buffaloes**, **plains zebras**, **elands**, **wildebeests** and **lions**. Of Mikumi's primates, **yellow baboons** are common, and **vervet** and **blue monkeys** are periodically observed. Rarely seen but also present are **hunting dogs**, **greater kudus** and **sables**. This is a significant park for birds and Eurasian migrants are present from October to April.

Location 283km west of Dar on the TANZAM Hwy; 4WD essential during wet seasons (some roads impassable).
Facilities Small interpretive centre at park HQ.
Accommodation Three camps/lodges, two camping grounds, one hostel (for local students); self-contained resthouse available by special arrangement with park HQ.
Wildlife rhythms Best wildlife viewing is in the dry season, ie, June to October, but Eurasian migrant birds are present October to April.
Contact TANAPA, Mikumi NP, PO Box 62, Mikumi.
Ecotours Several Dar companies include Mikumi on their tours. Guides can be hired at park HQ.

Lots to trumpet about

Most visitors see only the northern half of the park, which is dominated by a floodplain; the hilly southern half remains virtually unexplored, but protects miombo woodlands (this is where **sables** occur). Seasonal watercourses flow onto the plain from the hills and mountains that border it on three sides. The Mkata River is a central watercourse that flows through the

Staggering trunks

Mikumi's luxuriant floodplains and waterways splay through this rocky region, providing welcome relief to many visitors. Nestled next to these waterways are clusters of palms and fruit-bearing trees, including the marula (*Sclerocarya birrea caffra*). Looking similar to the sausage tree, this thickset deciduous tree has flaky bark, broad leaves and thick foliage. Its green oval fruits are relished by monkeys, antelopes, birds and – with some notoriety – elephants. When the fruits are ripe, elephants vigorously shake the trees then 'paw' the ground with their trunk, searching for fruit. Impalas often join in, enjoying the spoils of the elephants' labour. There is considerable conjecture among scientists about whether elephants sometimes become drunk from a stomach full of fermenting fruit, but there is ample 'ear-flapping' anecdotal evidence of erratic behaviour to suggest that they can!

floodplain to the north before feeding the Tendigo Swamp on the northern park boundary.

The highway and most of the park's tourist roads run between the floodplain and the hills, and driving into Mikumi from Dar on the causeway provides an introduction to the wildlife. **Elephants, plains zebras, giraffes** and **elands** regularly feed undisturbed near the highway, and in the wet season **lions** even sun themselves on this road.

The park HQ is the best place to start. Travelling north-west into the Mkata floodplain takes you to the central hippo pools on the Mkata River, home to a large group of **hippos** and numerous **waterfowl**. Watch for **African fish eagles, long-tailed cormorants, water dikkops, African jacanas** and the **storks – saddlebilled, Abdim's** and **African open-billed**. In the dry season many large animals visit to drink or wallow: **elephants, buffaloes, zebras, warthogs** and **wildebeests** visit regularly, especially in the late afternoon. There are several large **crocodiles** and many small ones in the upper and lower pools.

Continuing west you leave the floodplain and turn north along Chamgore Rd, which runs along the edge of woodlands and crosses numerous small seasonal watercourses before reaching the Msole and Chamgore waterholes. In addition to seeing animals drinking or wallowing this is where you have a good chance of finding **blue monkeys** and **yellow baboons**. Further north the road divides into a circuit which visits the Chaga Wale – a giant grove of buttressed trees and a camping ground. Surrounding Chaga Wale are lots of *Borassus* palms and at the top of this northern route is a gigantic baobab – an ecosystem in itself, with other mature trees growing from its base or within it. There is lots of wildlife around this baobab (even **leopards** are known to use its hollow interior), but be careful of the many beehives and hornets' nests. Leaving the baobab and returning south past the waterholes, a turn across the northern part of the Mkata floodplain will bring you to open short grass areas with great views of the hills and mountains that surround Mikumi. You can do a brief side trip to Mwanambogo waterhole before returning to the park gate.

A high diversity of vegetation makes Mikumi a great place for birds, and species frequenting many different habitats occur in high numbers in a relatively small area. The circuit drive around the floodplain visits a range of habitats where birders can look for coastal species, such as **Zanzibar red bishops** and **pink-backed pelicans**; woodland specialists such as **broad-billed rollers, white-headed black chats,** and **helmet-shrikes**; and birds of grasslands (eg, **red-necked spurfowl** and **Hartlaub's bustard).** Birds of forests and mountains are represented by **purple-crested turacos** and **trumpeter hornbills**. Across the plains savanna raptors (eg, **Dickinson's kestrels** and **bateleurs)** and scavenging birds are common. Mikumi is one of the best places to see **palm-nut vultures**, and **southern ground hornbills** are abundant. ∎

Watching tips
Areas where Mikumi's floodplains abut savanna woodlands usually offer the best birding; lions are often found resting in this fringe habitat (Mikumi's lions reputedly climb trees, possibly to escape tsetse flies). Visitors interested in yellow baboon research may want to contact Mikumi's Animal Behaviour Research Unit (ABRU). Mikumi is busy on weekends – visit on a weekday.

KILIMANJARO NATIONAL PARK

Cloud-hugging mountain desert

Wildlife highlights
Although wildlife is present in the forest below 2700m it is difficult to see – black-and-white colobus, blue monkeys, turacos and hornbills are the species most commonly encountered. There's good raptor and sunbird viewing on high moorlands. The diversity of habitats (forest, mountain moorlands and desert) makes 'Kili' a botanist's delight.

AT 5895m (19,455ft) above sea level, Mt Kilimanjaro is Africa's highest mountain and lures thousands of trekkers every year. Mountains create unusual and unique conditions, and are effectively ecological islands; as a result, many of the plants and some of the animals on Kilimanjaro are endemic. The mountain's lower reaches are savanna, with montane forest above 1800m; the higher reaches change from forest to heath and moorland, then to highland desert before finally becoming glaciers, ice and snow. The national park protects the area above 2700m, starting almost at the point where the forest ends.

For every 200m increase in altitude, the temperature drops by 1°C, and near the top the temperature can be subzero at night; however, the effects of the sun are harsh and the temperature can reach 40°C or more during the day. Rainfall is at its maximum in the forest, and trekkers cover their packs with large garbage bags to prevent them becoming sodden in the dense damp forest. Above 3000m the rainfall decreases and there is little water. At the summit, oxygen is half that of sea level. This hostile environment limits plant and animal life, so the part of Kilimanjaro that is actually national park is increasingly devoid of life. The richest area for wildlife is in the forest just below.

Intent on the ascent

There are several routes up and around Kilimanjaro, and the same types of plant, bird and animal will be seen at the same altitudes on each. The vast majority of visitors tear up and down the mountain, with around 58 people per day on the popular 'Coca Cola' (Marangu) route. If you take the Forest

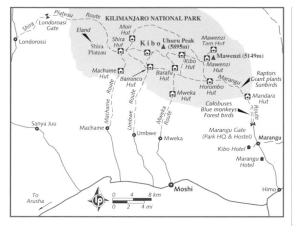

KILIMANJARO NATIONAL PARK

Plateau Route

Shira / Londorossi Gate

Londorossi

Eland

Moir Hut

Shira Hut

Shira Plateau

Kibo

Uhuru Peak ▲ (5895m)

Mawenzi Tarn Hut

Mawenzi (5149m) ▲

Kibo Hut

Mawenzi Hut

Machame Hut

Barafu Hut

Marangu

Raptors

Giant plants

Sunbirds

Barranco Hut

Horombo Hut

Mweka Hut

Mandara Hut

Machame Route

Umbwe Route

Mweka Route

Marangu Route

Colobuses Blue monkeys Forest birds

Sanya Juu

Machame

Umbwe

Mweka

Marangu Gate (Park HQ & Hostel)

Marangu

Kibo Hotel

Marangu Hotel

Moshi

Himo

To Arusha

0   4   8 km

0   2   4 mi

Trail near Marangu Gate you'll have a better chance of encountering forest animals because it's a quieter path. In this wet forest you may see **silvery-cheeked hornbills** or hear the shrill *kaw-kaw-kaw* of **Hartlaub's turacos** (look out for the crimson flight feathers of these mainly green and purple birds). Less easily seen are **mountain greenbuls, warblers** and the **mountain buzzard** – all montane forest birds. Three of the mountain's larger primates – **olive baboons**, and the arboreal **black-and-white colobus** and **blue monkeys** – should be spotted. While the forest is home to many **antelopes**, these are unlikely to be seen in the dense vegetation. Looking around will show where some common garden plants originated: impatiens, begonia and African violets are common. One of the last large mammal species to be discovered in Africa (in 1920) – the **giant forest hog** – lives in these montane forests and is sometimes encountered.

Above 3000m the forest is replaced by heathers (*ericas*) and proteas. There is a transition to heath and moorland, which contain giant lobelias and senecios (groundsels). Here the alpine birds become apparent, including the opportunistic **white-necked raven**, the **streaky seedeater** and the **alpine chat** (which commonly perches on the giant lobelias). The lobelia flowers are also a favourite with one of the typical alpine sunbirds, the **scarlet-tufted malachite sunbird**. Large mammals are few up here but small rodents prosper (you'll meet the **four-striped mouse** at the Horombo Hut, where it is doing especially well). **Elands** are, however, sometimes seen on the moorland, especially at Shira Plateau. The moorlands are a favoured haunt of the **augur buzzard** because of the presence of the rodents; for the same reason, the **Cape eagle-owl** occurs in grasslands. The most sought-after bird up here is the **lammergeier** (or bearded vulture), but as a single mountain may support only one pair of lammergeiers they are rarely seen.

Above 4000m the intense solar radiation, cold and lack of water make conditions tough for plants and animals alike, with visible life largely reduced to lichens, mosses and everlastings. ∎

Location NP HQ 45km from Moshi (60km from Arusha).

Accommodation Huts and camping grounds on the mountain.

Facilities Maps and printed materials at park HQ.

Wildlife rhythms Most trekkers don't attempt Kilimanjaro during the long rains (March to June) because it is too dangerous; climbing during the short rains (October to November) is also difficult.

Contact Kilimanjaro NP HQ (☎ 055-53195), PO Box 96, Marangu.

Ecotours About a dozen reliable companies – shop around. On the mountain you must be accompanied by a licensed guide.

Kilimanjaro's peak is permanently covered in ice, snow and glaciers.

Watching tips
If you are here only to see the wildlife, go to Mt Meru in Arusha NP instead – there is more wildlife and fewer people.

RUAHA NATIONAL PARK

B a o b a b s ,   r o c k y   h i l l s   a n d   v a n i s h i n g   r i v e r s

---

> **Wildlife highlights**
> Giraffes, elephants, buffaloes and a good number of lions are prominent among some 60 recorded species of large mammal; also the best chance to see hunting dogs in Tanzania. Antelope attractions include elands, sables and roans, and this is one of the few places where greater and lesser kudu occur together. With 425 bird species and plenty of open habitat, Ruaha is a great birding destination.

RUAHA, Tanzania's second largest national park, is good **lion**, **elephant** and **buffalo** country, and probably the best place to spot **hunting dogs** in the country: this endangered but mobile species can often be seen here, and hunting dogs have even been seen chasing **impalas** through Mwagusi Camp. Finding hunting dogs can be pot luck, but they are usually seen for a few days in every fortnight.

Ruaha encompasses a mixture of vegetation types and habitats, and these dictate where you will most likely encounter certain species. Ruaha is located on a dry, central plateau with its central highest point forming a watershed for the park's two main rivers – the Mzombe, which forms the northern boundary, and the Ruaha, which forms most of the southern. Few visitors venture north and most confine their activities to around the Ruaha River and other sand riverbeds. This area is a centre of animal activity during the dry season (June to December) when the drying rivers may leave only isolated pools. The first of these you will encounter are the hippo pools, which lie just over the bridge as you enter the park from south. From here you can head to the park HQ (a popular area for **elephants**) or north to Kimiramatonge Hill. This rocky area is a good place to view pairs of **klipspringers** and also **bush hyraxes**, which form large groups and can be seen sprawled on the rocks. **Tree**

The meeting point

Ruaha is an ecological meeting point of south, west and east Africa. Here the *Acacia-Combretum* vegetation of northern Tanzania merges with the miombo (*Brachystegia*) woodlands of south-western Africa and some animals are at the edge of their range. It is the most southerly area that you can encounter Grant's gazelles and lesser kudus, but one of the most northerly inland areas you can see sable antelopes. Roan also reach their eastern limit around here, and Lichtenstein's hartebeests are unlikely to be encountered east of here except in the Selous. Even the threatened pancake tortoise, which is endemic to East Africa, reaches its southern limit in Ruaha. The striped hyena, a species that once ranged from Britain to China and down through Africa, reaches its natural limit here in central Tanzania. Even the local zebras represent the meeting point of different areas – they are a cross between the subspecies of Mozambique and East Africa.

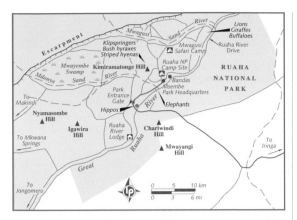

Location 124km west of Iringa; year-round access, although some park roads impassable in wet seasons (4WD recommended).
Facilities Booklet usually available at the gate. NP guides must be hired for walks.
Accommodation Lodge and tented camp; basic NP bandas and two camping grounds.
Wildlife rhythms July to October offers greatest wildlife concentrations; migrant birds arrive October and November, and the best birding is between January and April.
Contact Chief Park Warden, Ruaha NP, Box 369, Iringa.
Ecotours Ruaha River Lodge and Mwagusi Safari Camp conduct game drives; the latter also does walks. This is the only Tanzanian national park containing dangerous animals where walking is allowed.

hyraxes also occur in the park, but they are nocturnal and are most likely to be encountered around dusk. Another species to look for around rocky hills at dawn and dusk is the **striped hyena**, although they are less commonly seen than the larger and more social **spotted hyenas**.

Monkeys by the Mwagusi

The popular Ruaha River Drive takes in the Ruaha River, from where you can carry on along the Mwagusi River. In the dry season the Mwagusi is a sand river; water lies just beneath the surface where granite rocks prevent it from sinking further. In parts the sandy riverbed is sparsely fringed by tall *Borassus* palms, and some areas support large trees such as figs, tamarinds and acacias – good places to look for **vervet monkeys** and **yellow baboons**, and for **lions** resting in the shade. **Elephants** dig for water in the riverbed and excavated holes may attract **antelopes** and other species. Travelling throughout this area you should encounter **giraffes**, **buffaloes** and **impalas**, and **lions** can usually be seen daily during the dry season.

Much of the area away from the river is studded with baobabs (leafless during the dry season). Baobabs are always worth close scrutiny because they provide hollows for many species, such as **hornbills**, **lovebirds**, **squirrels** and **parrots**. Ruaha supports eight of Tanzania's 10 hornbill species, including **von der Decken's hornbill** and the **pale-billed hornbill**, which is found mostly in neighbouring Malawi and Zambia. Tanzania's endemic **yellow-collared lovebird** has a stronghold in this area. The baobab branches are also a favourite site for **red-billed** and **white-headed buffalo-weavers'** nests. At dusk, baobabs provide an ideal perch for retiring **marabou storks**, which can be seen silhouetted against the sky. They are occasionally joined by **pink-backed pelicans**, which seem entirely out of place in this semiarid environment. Among the more uncommon birds at Ruaha, **Eleonora's falcon** is a migrant that turns up during October and November before the rains begin. The **yellow-necked spurfowl** reaches the southern edge of its range around Ruaha and is frequently seen in the park. ■

Watching tips
Ruaha is earmarked for limited development of walking safaris, so check the current situation if planning a visit – walking provides the greatest opportunity for birding. At dusk the wild figs, tamarinds and baobabs lining the Ruaha River are buzzed by fruit-bats, some of which pollinate baobabs. During the day, watch for great white egrets cracking open freshwater oysters on the riverbanks. For sables, take an early afternoon game drive upstream along the Ruaha River: usually confined to woodlands at the foot of the escarpment, they come to drink at the river during the dry season.

UDZUNGWA MOUNTAINS NATIONAL PARK

An 'island' of diversity and rarities

🐆 Wildlife highlights

Renowned for Tanzanian and locally endemic animals. Local endemics include three primates (Iringa red colobus, Sanje crested mangabey and Matundu galago), birds, reptiles, amphibians, and many plants and invertebrates. Large animals are scarce in dense montane forest, but vervet monkeys, black-and-white colobus and red-legged sun-squirrels are easily seen. Of more than 400 bird species recorded, many are restricted to the mountains of Tanzania or are near-endemics found elsewhere only in areas such as Zimbabwe's Eastern Highlands. There are no roads and the park must be explored on foot.

UDZUNGWA is Tanzania's newest national park and is destined to become a hotspot for hikers and birders. It is the largest of the 11 Eastern Arc Mountains and rises from the surrounding flats through a range of different habitats – lowland and submontane forest giving way to montane forest, and finally peaking at around 2500m in short mountain grasslands covered with ericas.

While Udzungwa has many large animals, they generally inhabit areas away from walking paths. Of the smaller antelopes you may see **duikers** or **sunis** through the forest understorey, but the creatures to get excited about here are the primates and birds: the isolation of the Eastern Arc Mountains has given rise to a large number of endemic species. Much of the park is inaccessible, but you will see plenty of birds and smaller mammals by exploring the trails around the base near the park HQ and entrance at Mangula, or by walking up to the nearby 170m-high Sanje Falls on the Sanje River.

Ark of unique mountain life

Udzungwa's high number of unique species is owed partially to the region's constant climate over millions of years. In its continuous carpet of forests, ranging from 250m to over 2500m in altitude, over a quarter of its plant species are endemic. There are numerous similarities between these forests and those of Madagascar, West Africa, Zimbabwe's Eastern Highlands and the Usambara Mountains, suggesting that these regions may have been geographically linked 165 million years ago. It is surmised that they became isolated 'islands', with species once common to the linked region subsequently evolving separately. Usambara and Udzungwa, it is estimated, have been separated for five million years. Unfortunately, there is a downside to this high level of endemicity: disturbance on even a relatively small scale can have disastrous impacts on an entire species, for example, during the 1970s habitat destruction through forest clearing and construction of the TAZARA railway led to a decline in the numbers of Iringa red colobus.

Ascent through chattering forest

By wandering around the lower paths you'll invariably see **vervet monkeys, banded mongooses** and perhaps be scolded from a branch by a **red-legged sun squirrel**. On the way up to Sanje Falls look out for **blue monkeys** in the canopy – troops frequently occur together with troops of **black-and-white colobus**, so search the trees carefully for the colobus. The special species on this route – one of Udzungwa's endemics – is the endangered **Iringa red colobus**; you should be able to find it without too much trouble. Another even more endangered primate endemic to Udzungwa – recent surveys suggest it has a population of less than 1500 – is the **Sanje crested mangabey**, aptly-named

for its sagittal crest. However, these are typically found higher than the falls so you are unlikely to encounter them unless you hike higher up. Several species of bushbaby live at Udzungwa, including the endemic **Matundu galago**.

If you stay overnight in one of the camping grounds look out for the strictly nocturnal **giant pouched rat**. It is nearly 1m long (including tail), but will do nothing more treacherous than scout about for vegetable matter, which it stores in its cheek pouches to take back to its burrow. The background noises of the night may include some unfamiliar 'pinging' – caused by the resident **epauletted fruit-bats** – and the loud screams of **eastern tree hyraxes**.

Peak birding

Udzungwa attracts birdwatchers from far and wide who come to search for the many species that occur only in the Eastern Arc Mountains; the park is also one of the best places to see a variety of near-endemic and rare birds. Most are hard to see in the thick vegetation, but easy ones to locate on the falls walk are the large and noisy **Livingstone's turaco, trumpeter hornbill** and, above the falls, the **silvery-cheeked hornbill**. Those wishing to see more of Udzungwa's unique birds should take a specialised trip because you need to get off the beaten track (the **Udzungwa partridge**, only described in 1992, is restricted to one locality in an inaccessible part of the park). You might be lucky and spot the **rufous-winged sunbird** (another relatively recent discovery restricted to the Udzungwa Mountains) around or below Sanje Falls when it descends lower on the mountain in winter. The **Iringa akalat** typically lives above 1500m and the **dappled mountain robin** (one of Africa's rarest birds) lives above 1200m. Although they are not restricted to Udzungwa, this area is also one of the best in which to observe **Swynnerton's robin** and **white-chested alethe**. Armed with playback, **Kretschmer's longbill** can be called out from the viney tangles right at the park HQ.

On top of all this Udzungwa boasts a number of local **centipedes, butterflies**, and even a unique snake, the **Udzungwa wolf snake** – a nonvenomous, 30cm black snake with a red nose. Researchers here and in other parts of the Eastern Arc Mountains continue to turn up new animal (including birds) and plant species. ∎

Location 75km from Mikumi NP. Local transport is available between Mikumi and Ifakara.
Facilities Five walking trails; guides must be hired from park HQ to go to Sanje Falls or to venture off the beaten track. A canopy walkway is proposed.
Accommodation Two camping grounds (near park HQ and at Sanje Falls); Twiga Hotel has camping and other accommodation; guesthouses in village.
Wildlife rhythms Animals start breeding and migrant birds are present late September to mid-December; highland forest birds may come lower to escape the cold late May to early August.
Contact Senior Park Warden (☎ Ifakara 24). Wildlife Conservation Society in Tanzania (e wcs@twiga.com) can provide information on the area. Ecotours Birding and Beyond (e info@birdingandbeyond. co.uk), PO Box 11500, Arusha can take you to the park; long hikes are possible by arrangement with park HQ.

Watching tips
The best place to see the common birds is just outside the park while walking near the main road, or at the park HQ, where visibility is better in more open terrain. If you visit from January to March consider taking a tent and camping at Sanje Falls – this will give you some relief from the heat.

SAADANI GAME RESERVE

Tracks on the beach

Location 225km from Dar via Chalinze; park closed March to May.

Facilities Tree hide.

Accommodation Tented camp at Tent with a View; simple accommodation and camping at GTZ residence – see the GTZ office in Saadani village.

Wildlife rhythms Dry June to January is best; very hot November to February.

Contacts Wildlife Division of the Game Dept of Tanzania (☎ 0811-866 064, fax 861 007), The Ivory Room, Pugu Rd, Dar.

Ecotours Tent with a View (☎ 0811-323 318 or 151 106) offers walks, drives and boat rides. Self-drive visitors must hire a game scout.

Watching tips

Don't expect elephants and lions on the beach as per the old, romantic promotions of Saadani. Hundreds of lesser flamingos visit the processing lakes of the saltworks in season.

AT 30km long and just 7km wide, Saadani is Tanzania's smallest reserve and one of its least known. It is also the only reserve in East Africa where you can stroll along the beach between wildlife viewing activities.

In the dense coastal thickets and palms that fringe the beach, the day begins with the morning chorus – **tropical boubous, common bulbuls** and **white-browed coucals** all join in. An early walk along the beach will probably reveal **antelope** tracks, and you'll usually see **storks, sandpipers, fiddler crabs** and a few local fisherman. On foot (escorted walks are permitted) or from a vehicle you should readily find antelopes such as **reedbucks, common duikers** and **common waterbucks**, as well as **yellow baboons** and **warthogs**. The airstrip and the tracks south of the village are good open areas for **Masai giraffes, Coke's hartebeests, plains zebras** and **wildebeests**. With luck you could also see **common elands** – often found on the flats near the salt-

works. To the north a circuit of tracks passes waterholes and these are the areas to look for **buffaloes**. However, most **buffaloes** and **elephants** are concentrated along the Mligazi River and in the Madete Forest of the Mkwaja Ranch South (this area is to become part of the reserve so may become accessible in future). **Lions, elephants, Roosevelt's sables** and **greater kudus** all occur in the park but are rarely seen (the lion population is estimated at 15).

On drives or walks you'll see common grassland and woodland birds, but don't miss birding by boat on the Wami River. The river entrance is surrounded by mangroves and, further upstream, palms and riverine forest line the banks. In the river are a smattering of **hippos** and **crocodiles**, and in the trees **blue monkeys** and **black-and-white colobus**. Perched along the water's edge are **kingfishers – pied, giant** and the diminutive but vivid **malachite kingfisher. Egrets, grey herons, hamerkops** and **whimbrels** feed along the banks and sandbars, and by scrutinising the riverside vegetation you may see a **green-backed heron**. An hour upstream is a sandbank that is nearly always feather-to-feather with a mass of **African open-billed** and **yellow-billed storks**. ∎

OTHER SITES – TANZANIA

Gombe Stream NP
Gombe is famous for chimpanzees – the study of chimps started here by Jane Goodall in 1960 is the world's longest ongoing study of a population of wild animals. There are about 100 to 120 chimps in the park, and you can visit the chimp feeding station and walk along the trails in order to find them. Gombe also has about 3000 olive baboons (which have been studied since 1967), red colobus, and red-tailed and blue monkeys. Highlight birds of the area include the palm-nut vulture, Ross' and Livingstone's turacos, crowned eagles and various barbets. Lake Tanganyika teems with over 200 species of cichlids, and you can snorkel and walk along the shore unescorted. Baboons also come here to play, swim and scavenge for fish. The easiest time to visit is the dry season (June to September); conditions are pretty tough in the rainy season (October to May).
20km north of Kigoma,
☎ *0695-4435*

Kilombero Valley
Featuring a major river and floodplain, you can take a boat from Ifakara to venture up and down the Kilombero River – lots of hippos and crocs, African skimmers, white-headed plovers (which breed in June and July), coppery-tailed coucals, goliath herons and saddle-billed storks. The Kilombera weaver is found only here – and only between Ifakara town and the ferry. Pukus (otherwise mostly confined to Zambia) are readily seen in this area.
80km south-west of Udzungwa

Lake Natron
This Rift Valley lake is difficult to get to, but is the world's most important breeding area for

lesser flamingos. About 3.5 million live in the Rift Valley areas of Tanzania and Kenya, and when conditions are right they arrive to breed here. The tricky thing is that they breed in the middle of the lake which you can't see because of the mirages that the lake creates. Even when not breeding there are always some flamingos present. The slopes of an active volcano south of Natron, Oldoinyo Lengai, offer a good chance to see fringe-eared oryxes.
25km north of Oldoinyo Lengai

Mahale Mountains NP
Although less well-known than Gombe, Mahale has been a centre of chimpanzee research since the 1960s. Being 30 times the size of Gombe and in a virtually uninhabited mountainous area, Mahale has a much greater diversity of plant and animal species. Like Gombe, there are no roads. In addition to the chimps, which number around 700, the park is home to an array of mammals now largely absent from Gombe (elephants, buffaloes, roans, plains zebras and giraffes) including two mammal species which are classically West African – the giant forest squirrel and the brush-tailed porcupine. It is also home to six endemic subspecies of birds – yellow-streaked and mountain greenbuls, Bocage's akalat, yellow-bellied wattle-eye, yellow-throated woodland warbler and brown-chested alethe – and is the only place in Tanzania you'll find Stuhlmann's starling and the bamboo warbler. Being on the shores of Lake Tanganyika, take your snorkelling gear so you can check out the cichlids and aquatic life.
130km south of Kigoma,
☎ *057-3629*

Mkomazi GR
This reserve is contiguous with Kenya's Tsavo NP and shares its same semiarid features and the species found in that park (including gerenuks and the large numbers of dik-diks that characterise Tsavo). Mammal numbers are not high, but the birding is fantastic. Black rhinos and hunting dogs have been reintroduced to the reserve. There are no facilities, but walking is possible if you arrange an armed guide with the reserve.
25km east of Same.

Rubondo Island NP
Aquatic mammals and birds that are difficult to see elsewhere are a highlight. Sitatungas are readily seen, the best spots being the Mamba walking trail and its hide. Spot-necked otters swim past the island's one camp daily. A variety of mammals were reintroduced to the island in the 1960s and 70s, including elephants and giraffes – both now found in the south of the island. About 35 chimpanzees were also introduced to Rubondo and the park offers chimp tracking. Other wildlife includes bushbucks, hippos, vervet monkeys, black-and-white colobus, genets, sunis, marsh mongooses, crocs and monitors. Rubondo is a bird-watcher's dream: a single bay on the east side of the island supports 166 fish eagles. Other birdlife includes goliath herons, weaver colonies and banded snake-eagles. Bee-eaters, flycatchers and kingfishers are common. Boating safaris can take you to cormorant nesting areas. Lake Victoria is home to endemic cichlids, but visibility is not good for diving.
120km west of Mwanza,
☎ *057-6963.*

UGANDA

Country faunal emblems

Grey crowned crane Unmistakably adorned marsh bird with haunting, trumpeting call and elaborate courtship displays. Common and easily seen throughout rural Uganda and in most national parks.

Uganda kob Stately antelope that walks with head held high, abundant in Queen Elizabeth NP. Bucks spar in communal arenas for the right to mate with does. Appears on Uganda's coat of arms.

Highlights

- Tracking mountain gorillas – the greatest apes of all – in their volcanic strongholds
- Excited hoots of chimpanzees – boisterous drama queens of the forests with disturbing human traits
- Cruising the Victoria Nile to Murchison Falls among crocs, waterbirds and roaring hippos
- The shoebill of papyrus swamps, a bird whose uniqueness stands out among many unique animals
- Clouds of butterflies swirling through sun-dappled forests and drinking from roadside pools
- The magic of Kidepo Valley, a remote wilderness and refuge for arid-zone mammals and birds
- Giant herbs towering 6m high on the misty slopes of the Mountains of the Moon

The best of everything

ITS frontiers marked by the highest mountain range (the Rwenzoris) and the largest lake in Africa (Lake Victoria), landlocked Uganda straddles the transition from the vast savannas of Kenya and Tanzania to the even vaster, biologically rich rainforests of the Zaïre River basin. Diverse, abundant and easily accessible wildlife offers the best of everything from East and West Africa: herds of large animals in Queen Elizabeth, Murchison Falls and remote, semiarid Kidepo Valley NPs; gorilla and primate tracking in the western rainforests; and 1017 bird species, including gems such as shoebills and African green broadbills.

Uganda lies entirely within the tropics, and experiences high rainfall in two wet seasons (April to May and October to November), except in the north, where it is dry for much of the year but wettest between April and October. Wildlife is easier to see during dry seasons when the animals congregate around water, but don't let the wet season put you off: it attracts fewer human visitors and triggers breeding activity for some animals, especially birds. Cruises on the extensive wetlands surrounding many of Uganda's great lakes are a wildlife highlight on which you'll see hippos, sitatungas, crocodiles and many waterbirds.

Pristine rainforests in the south-west support Uganda's greatest biodiversity, and most visitors head straight for the justly famous mountain gorilla tracking at Bwindi Impenetrable or Mgahinga Gorilla NPs. But chimpanzee tracking at various locations is a growing attraction, and aficionados seek out solitude and other delights of the Semliki Valley, where the vast rainforests of the Zaïre River basin poke a toe over Uganda's western border.

The towering, often mist-shrouded 'Mountains of the Moon' – the glacier-capped Rwenzoris – are a vast watershed on whose high slopes grow East Africa's largest and most extensive stands of the so-called 'big game plants' (fleshy herbs that attain enormous size). Similar species grow in the caldera of Mt Elgon – a massive extinct volcano on the Kenyan border.

Uganda is a great wildlife destination made better by a strong reserve network, enlightened conservation policies and friendly, hospitable people. Wildlife is recovering well after decades of poaching and war, and exemplary community-based ecotourism projects are showing the way to the future. ∎

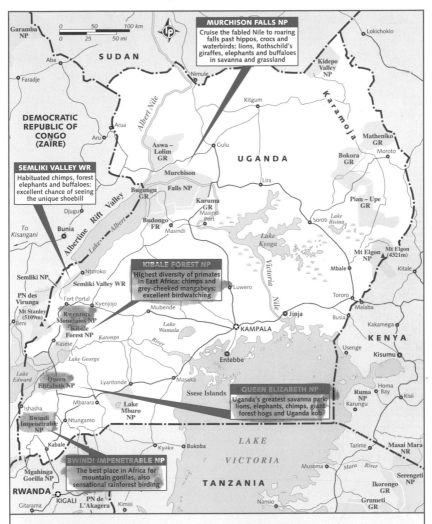

MURCHISON FALLS NP
Cruise the fabled Nile to roaring falls past hippos, crocs and waterbirds; lions, Rothschild's giraffes, elephants and buffaloes in savanna and grassland

SEMLIKI VALLEY WR
Habituated chimps, forest elephants and buffaloes; excellent chance of seeing the unique shoebill

KIBALE FOREST NP
Highest diversity of primates in East Africa; chimps and grey-cheeked mangabeys; excellent birdwatching

QUEEN ELIZABETH NP
Uganda's greatest savanna park; lions, elephants, chimps, giant forest hogs and Uganda kob

BWINDI IMPENETRABLE NP
The best place in Africa for mountain gorillas, also sensational rainforest birding

Suggested itineraries

One week Drive to Lake Mburo NP and explore the lakeside tracks; overnight then head for Bwindi Impenetrable NP. With luck you'll be able to track mountain gorillas the following day, but allow at least two days and three nights to avoid disappointment. Head for Queen Elizabeth NP; work the tracks north of Kazinga Channel and cruise the Channel itself.

Two weeks A fortnight will allow longer to explore Lake Mburo NP (two nights), Bwindi Impenetrable NP (three nights); and either push further south to Mgahinga Gorilla NP for more mountain gorillas, or to take the slower route through the southern Ishasha sector of Queen Elizabeth NP to Mweya. After enjoying QE, head for Kibale Forest NP for chimp tracking.

One month Take a fortnight to cover the many attractions in Uganda's south-west corner. After enjoying the chimps at Kibale Forest NP, head up to Semliki Valley WR for more wildlife viewing on foot; and then on to Murchison Falls NP for a cruise on the Victoria Nile. Only with a full week to spare can Kidepo Valley NP be reached and enjoyed – it's worth it.

KAMPALA

Intact habitats and wildlife conservation projects near the capital

THE roof of every large building in downtown Kampala seems to have a **marabou stork** sitting on it like an animated surveillance camera eyeing the streets below. Sinister associations aside, the storks do most of their foraging in dumps and drains further afield, returning to their nests in large trees along Nile Ave outside the *Sheraton Hotel*. The gardens of this hotel are a good spot to wander and see a few birds, including **sunbirds, eastern grey plantain-eaters** gibbering like chimps, and thoroughly urbanised **pied crows** that have been known to make nests from strands of wire. The chortlings of the ubiquitous **common bulbul** are among the first calls in the morning and often continue well after the flocks of **cattle egrets** have crossed the evening sky to roost. Squabbling **epauletted fruit-bats** hang in another roost in a grove of trees near the *Uganda Tourist Board Office*, preparing to take off for a night's feasting.

Apart from bats, mammals are scarce in Kampala, but troops of **black-and-white colobus** and **vervet monkeys** are resident in the fine *Entebbe Botanic Garden* at quiet Entebbe, half an hour south of the city on the shores of Lake Victoria. **Ross'** and **great blue turacos**, and noisy **black-and-white-casqued hornbills** feed in fruiting trees in the garden's remnant patch of rainforest; and a variety of **sunbirds** and **weavers** fuss about in vegetation beside the lake, where **waterbirds** are profuse: **hamerkops**, various **herons** and **storks**, and **cormorants** (the latter sitting with wings outstretched). **Pied kingfishers** are common and a good spot to see **giant kingfishers** is on the dock where police launches berth. **Eastern grey plantain-eaters** are common in Entebbe gardens and **vultures** mope about on trees lining the streets.

Vervet and **de Brazza's monkeys** also range free at the nearby *Uganda Wildlife Education Centre* (☎ 042-32 05 20), where **hippos** can be seen from the lake's shores. UWEC offers

Although a few common bird species can be seen in Kampala's parks and gardens – marabou storks perch conspicuously on tall buildings – there's great wildlife watching a short trip out of town in lowland rainforests.

a chance to get close and photograph **lions** and **leopards**, plus some of Uganda's more elusive animals, including **shoebills**, **patas monkeys**, **bushpigs** and **common duikers**; other attractions are an outstanding medicinal plant garden and an interpretive forest walk.

Ngamba Island Chimpanzee Sanctuary is a rainforested island 23km south of Entebbe, purchased by an international conservation trust for the release and rehabilitation of **chimpanzees** orphaned or confiscated from the illegal wildlife trade. To date 21 chimps of varying ages have been released and are free to explore the island, nest in the forest or return to a night house. Professional staff study how the chimps learn about new surroundings, and guide visitors during morning and afternoon visits to a supplementary feeding area. Viewing platforms offer great photo opportunities and there is a visitors centre with interpretive graphics. The project works with local communities who will eventually supply food for both chimpanzees and visitors. A boat trip around the island is highly recommended – chimps sometimes play at the water's edge, and sightings of **hippos**, **otters** and **waterbirds** are a feature. Visits to Ngamba Island can be arranged through the Jane Goodall Institute (☎ 041-32 00 73) or G&C Tours (☎/fax 041-32 14 79).

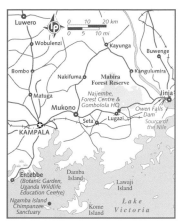

Mabira Forest, the largest tropical forest in the Lake Victoria region, crowds the highway 54km east of Kampala and is easily accessible from the capital. Among Mabira's rich diversity have been recorded 200 species of tree, 218 of butterfly and 302 of bird. **Black-and-white colobus, grey-cheeked mangabeys** and **red-tailed monkeys** are all easily seen along an extensive trail network leading deep into the forest. Monkeys also loiter near the camping ground – watchful of **African crowned eagles** soaring over the canopy where **Boehm's bush** and **giant forest squirrels** rustle about, but are hard to track along limbs and branches (the raised viewing platform at the visitors centre will help get you on their level). Another tree-dweller, the **western tree hyrax**, is nocturnal and unmistakable with its screeching calls. Spotlighting could also locate an **African wood owl** or **African civet** near the camping ground, and **leopards** are seen occasionally. **Blue duikers** might be startled along trails – although they normally freeze to avoid detection. The 3km Grassland Trail offers good birdwatching through edge vegetation, tall forest and glades where **African pied hornbills, great blue turacos** and a variety of **barbets** can be seen – Mabira Forest Pond is another good birding spot. Forest guides can be hired at Najjembe Village Ecotourism Centre, where bandas and meals are available.

A profusion of **waterbirds** feeds and roosts around the *Source of the Nile*, 30km east at Jinja. Highlights include **African fish eagles**, and abundant **pied kingfishers, cormorants** and **grey-headed gulls**; **cattle egrets** line up along the dam wall and a variety of **swallows** and **swifts** hawk insects over the water. During the April to May wet season marshy grasslands are dotted with male **bishops** in scarlet and black breeding plumage. ■

BWINDI IMPENETRABLE NATIONAL PARK

Great biodiversity in Uganda's pearl

Wildlife highlights

Pristine rainforest, the richest faunal community in East Africa and Uganda's most reliable locality for mountain gorillas. Other possibilities among 120 species of mammal are seven species of diurnal primate including chimpanzees (often heard but rarely seen) and l'Hoest's, red-tailed and blue monkeys, black-and-white colobus and olive baboons. Other forest denizens which might be encountered include bushpigs, forest duikers and six species of squirrel. The bird list stands at 360 (190 have been recorded at Buhoma alone), including 23 localised species found only along the Albertine Rift Valley and 14 found nowhere else in Uganda. Gems include black bee-eaters, black-billed and great blue turacos, and many species of sunbird, weaver, barbet, cuckoo, kingfisher and starling along forest trails. Butterflies, colourful fungi and flowers including orchids are other attractions.

APTLY named World Heritage Area where isolation, rainfall and terrain have ensured the preservation of large tracts of pristine rainforest most famous for its **mountain gorillas**. Continuous stands of both lowland and montane rainforest with a dense understorey of herbs, vines and shrubs (Bwindi means 'dark' in the local dialect) support 150 to 250 **chimpanzees** and six other diurnal **primates**; 251 species of **butterfly** and 360 of **bird** (23 of which are endemic to the Albertine Rift Valley and eight are not recorded anywhere else in East Africa).

Gorilla-tracking is the main attraction and it is estimated that half the world's population of **mountain gorillas** – some 300 individuals in 23 family units – live in Bwindi. Two groups – named Mubare and Katendegyere – have been habituated to humans and a third is being habituated; the chances of tracking Bwindi's gorillas to a visible distance are almost 100%.

In the shadow of Mubare

Habituated groups of mountain gorillas occasionally spend time in or around the camping grounds that border the national park. I was there on one such occasion and was amazed by the somewhat cavalier attitude of a silverback, Mubare, who let his group wander among the tents as they made their way into a nearby gully and a local banana grove. I first realised what was going on when I awoke to a terrific ruckus in front of my tent and a dark shadow filled the moonlit doorway. The image made me feel both excited and a little frustrated since we had hiked for six hours to track one of the groups earlier that day! Thrilling though they are, such private and unexpected viewings are not as good for gorillas as they are for people, and the national park's staff discourage such encounters to reduce risks for both.

Dedee Woodside, Environmental Educator

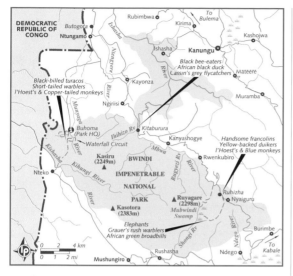

Location 108km north-west of Kabale (Buhoma); 514km south-west of Kampala. Access to Ruhizha by 4WD only.
Facilities Information board at Buhoma.
Accommodation Camping, bandas, cabins and tented camps at Buhoma. Camping and Institute for Tropical Forest Conservation guesthouse at Ruhizha.
Wildlife rhythms Gorillas are tracked year-round. Rain, and bird courtship and breeding peak in March to May and September to November, when the air is also clearer. Bird-watching is best September to March. June to July is best for butterflies emerging after heavy rains. Many orchids flower in September to October.
Contact Bwindi Impenetrable NP, PO Box 862, Kabale. Uganda Wildlife Authority (☎ 041-32 01 52, fax 34 62 91), PO Box 3530, Kampala.
Ecotours Local porters, gorilla guides and trackers plus expert bird guides can be hired at Buhoma. All major tour operators visit Bwindi – see listing in the Resource Guide.

Other wildlife – especially birds – is encountered on forest trails and the rainforest is magnificent: 200 species of tree – including some giant buttressed mahoganies – and 105 species of fern have been recorded; orchids (86 species are known from Bwindi) and ferns sprout from deep cushions of moss on branches and rocks; red balsam flowers and begonias splash colour into the undergrowth; and myriads of fungi sprout from trunks and rotting logs. Streams and pools echo with the *tik-tik-tik* of tree frogs and the canopy constantly rustles with movement of **monkeys**, **squirrels** and **birds**. Patches of sunlight on the ground swirl as sunning butterflies take off; highlights include the iridescent **blue mother-of-pearl butterfly**; various large, fast-flying **charaxes** (there are 35 species in Bwindi alone); and huge swallowtails, such as the endemic **cream-banded** and **East African giant swallowtails**.

Worth the charge

Mountain gorilla groups move daily, and may be as close as 15 minutes from the park entrance to several hours hard walking away. Altitude is not a problem – the park HQ (Buhoma) is at 1450m and the gorillas are usually seen between there and 2000m – but there can be a lot of steep hills and narrow valleys in between. Guides watch the gorillas daily and note where they nest for the night; leaving early next morning, a beeline is made for the nest sites and the tracking begins. Bwindi's gorillas sometimes feed close to the plantain and maize crops growing on the hillsides below the park, and are not averse to raiding fields now and then (realising the importance these animals now play in the local economy, retribution is rare and farmers are usually compensated for their losses).

If you're lucky, tracking may involve negotiating only a few plantations; more often, however, it's a scramble up hillsides and along slippery paths. Once the previous night's nests are

Bwindi's dense undergrowth earned it the name 'Impenetrable', but cultivation cuts dramatic swathes right up to the park boundary.

located the going can get difficult; gorillas move easily through the dense undergrowth but people with bags and cameras generally don't. Trackers cut a path following the trail, 'talking' frequently to the gorillas as you get closer with soothing belches to let them know people are about and mean them no harm.

Despite his massive size, an adult male – the silverback – is usually placid and gentle unless he feels threatened. His reaction to danger – and sometimes strangers – is to scream loudly and charge at the intruder. A charge is very exciting, but it is important not to lose your nerve – stay still and look away from the silverback. He may come close but the chances of him actually harming you are very small.

Silverbacks on slippery slopes

The Mubare group is composed of a silverback, five females and six juveniles or infants; the Katendegyere group comprises five animals: one silverback, two females, a juvenile and a youngster. 'K' group's silverback behaves unpredictably, and the group is sometimes off limits; in contrast, Mubare's silverback is known as Ruhondeza – 'one who sleeps a lot' – and his group is often very approachable. Ruhondeza is enormous, and signs of his resting spots – flattened vegetation – are usually obvious. When glimpsed through a curtain of leaves his bulk is difficult to assess; the black fur of what appears to be his torso from a distance turns out to be his massive head and sagittal crest. In gorilla body language, staring can be taken as a threat, but Ruhondeza is a gentle giant and an approach to within 5m is usually possible. Despite their bulk, gorillas can easily move through the dense vegetation and pass with hardly a rustle. Your allotted hour of viewing time may involve more slipping and scrambling on the slopes to get into a good position to photograph various family members or to keep up with playful juveniles.

Feeding party animals

Excellent birdwatching is second to the great apes among Bwindi's attractions. First-timers can expect to see dozens of new species in a day, and the secondary growth surrounding camps at Buhoma is a great place to start: **cinnamon-chested bee-eaters** hawk from exposed perches and **black-and-white-casqued** and **white-thighed hornbills** flap noisily across the canopy; **black-faced rufous warblers** call stridently from the

Identifying gorillas

Members of a gorilla group tend to resemble one another, especially along matrilineal lines. But just as the fingerprints of every human being are unique, no two gorillas have the same 'noseprint' – each has a distinctive pattern formed by the indentations above the nostrils and the shape of the nose itself. Once a group is contacted, researchers sketch the noseprints of more forward individuals with the aid of binoculars. These simple line drawings are an invaluable aid to identifying group members, especially when they are similar in size, and are refined as habituation progresses until close-up photos are possible. Noseprint sketches are supplemented by written notes on variations in behaviour and vocalizations – traits that also help to identify individuals.

forest edge; **blue-headed coucals** bounce down the path near tall grass; and **sunbirds, African paradise flycatchers** and **finches** all dart among the undergrowth.

To get the most out of the forest spend a day on the Waterfall Circuit or one of the park's other trails (one follows the Munyaga River below Buhoma) with one of the knowledgeable local guides. The variety is almost overwhelming – feeding parties, known as bird waves, comprising many species and perhaps dozens of individuals – move through the foliage at all levels from ground and trunk to canopy. It's a visual scramble to find and identify the procession of **flycatchers, barbets, sunbirds, cuckoos, weavers, starlings** and **warblers. Fruit-eating pigeons,** such as **African green** and **eastern bronze-naped,** call from high perches but are well-camouflaged and are among the hardest birds to spot. **Squirrels** or **monkeys** attracted to fruiting trees also rustle about and add to the confusion. Forest **weavers** (several species) in bold black and yellow feed next to **montane orioles,** and star attractions are **black-billed turacos** and the splendid **black bee-eater** – look for the latter high up where fallen trees have created clearings.

Undergrowth along streams that cut the Waterfall Circuit near Buhoma is home to skulking warblers.

Africa's most wanted

Red-tailed monkeys crash through the foliage and **l'Hoest's monkeys** – common near the forest edge – often travel along the ground and might streak across your path in a line. Up to six species of squirrel include **Boehm's bush** and **Carruthers' mountain tree squirrels** scampering through the canopy; Bwindi's largest, the **giant forest squirrel,** is partly nocturnal. **Bushpigs** are sometimes seen around Buhoma; less frequently seen forest mammals include **giant forest hogs** and antelopes such as **bushbucks,** and **black-fronted** and **yellow-backed duikers. African civets** and **servaline** or **large-spotted genets** might be seen by spotlighting around Buhoma; rarely seen predators include **African golden cats** – melanistic (black) individuals have been reported – and **side-striped jackals,** and other possibilities are nocturnal primates – **dwarf** and **Matschie's** (or **needle-clawed**) **galagos** have both been recorded.

To really winkle out Bwindi's bird gems, try to get to Ruhizha. This forest sector lies at a considerably cooler and wetter 2300m, where **l'Hoest's** and **blue monkeys** and **black-and-white colobus** occur, and spotlighting could reveal a **potto** and dwarf or **Matschie's galagos.** The 6km-walk to the bamboo zone south-east along the road to Kabale is highly recommended for birdwatching: dense secondary vegetation is frequented by **finches** such as **Shelley's crimsonwing,** and the ground-loving **handsome francolin** is sometimes seen on the track catching early sun; **Peters'** and **yellow-backed duikers** might also be seen on tracks in the early morning. Bwindi's 20 to 30 **elephants** frequent an extensive stand of bamboo at Mubwindi Swamp near Ruhizha and for the avid birder a walk to the swamp is a must: this wetland is the number one location for the **African green broadbill,** possibly the most difficult-to-find bird on the continent. The extensive reed beds are home to other localised species, such as **Carruthers' cisticola** and **Grauer's rush warbler.** ■

Watching tips

When tracking gorillas take gloves for grasping nettles and branches. Despite the discomforts of tracking in the wet season, better photographic opportunities may present themselves because gorillas love to sunbathe after showers and may spend more time in open ground (they often seek shade in hot weather). Butterflies are attracted to damp places on trails, and especially to animal urine or dung. Allow at least two days at Buhoma – one for gorilla-tracking and another to explore the forest trails.

KIBALE FOREST NATIONAL PARK

Chimpanzee playground

KIBALE is both a stand of pristine rainforest of rich diversity where several vegetation zones overlap and a successful ecotourism project involving local people. The main attraction is the high density of **primates** that inhabit the forest (in particular, a large community of **chimpanzees**), but **birdlife** is prolific and a nature trail has been developed at Bigodi Wetland (a nearby swamp). Some 250 tree species have been recorded in the park, all festooned with dense mats of moss on crooks and boughs. Massive fruiting figs attract birds, chimps, monkeys and other primates; bracket fungi cling to broad tree trunks; and orchids grow high up in the canopy. Permanent streams cut through the forest and swamps fill low-lying areas; the northern and southern boundaries support stands of grasslands and west of the park is a scenic 'field' of volcanic craters.

Elephants, **buffaloes** and **giant forest hogs** live deep in the forest, although are seldom seen; antelopes such as **bushbucks** and three species of **duiker** are more commonly encountered; and two squirrels – **montane sun squirrels** and **giant forest squirrels** – scurry through the canopy. An estimated 600 **chimpanzees** in several communities live in Kibale and are the subject of long-term studies. The community at Kanyanchu has been habituated and Primate Walks (essentially chimpanzee tracking) are conducted daily; organised Night Walks from Kanyanchu search out nocturnal primates such as **galagos**.

Buttress bongos
Entering the forest you might come across **red-tailed monkeys** or **grey-cheeked mangabeys** at the edge, or **olive baboons** loitering on the ground – sometimes all three species may be seen together. **Bushpigs** also favour forest edge and you'll probably see their rootings in the undergrowth; small, pellet-shaped dung indicates where **duikers** have been. Birds are hard to see in the gloom, but **eastern nicators** and **little greenbuls** complain stridently from the foliage.

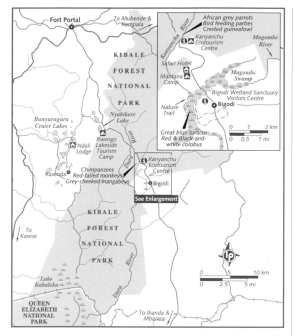

Location 35km south of Fort Portal (4WD recommended in wet seasons); 320km west of Kampala. Accessible by matatu from Fort Portal.

Facilities Visitors Centres (with binocular hire) and forest lookout towers at Kanyanchu and Bigodi. Self-guided walk (1km) at Kanyanchu Eco-tourism Centre.

Accommodation Camping and bandas at Kanyanchu. Tented camp and basic hotel near Bigodi. Lodges in crater fields west of Kibale. Hotels in Fort Portal.

Wildlife rhythms Chimps can be tracked year-round. Elephants move into the Kanyanchu area during the wet seasons, ie March to May and September to November – also the best times for birding.

Contact Kanyanchu Ecotourism Centre (☎ 0483-22636), Kibale National Park.

Uganda Wildlife Authority (☎ 041-32 01 52, fax 34 62 91), PO Box 3530, Kampala.

Ecotours Daily primate walks (8 am and 3 pm), night walks (7.30 pm) and 12km forest hike, all led by knowledgeable guides at Kanyanchu. Local guides at Bigodi Wetland. All recommended tour companies can arrange travel to Kibale – see the listing in the Resource Guide.

Although at times they can be silent and difficult to locate, **chimps** are by far the noisiest of African primates. From the time they leave their nests in the early morning – which they often announce by drumming on a tree buttress – until settling again at night, the forest echoes with their hoots and screams. Tracking these 'drama queens' is largely a matter of following their sounds, but chimps can move at a fair pace on all fours, and by swinging from vine to trunk, shimmying up trees and jumping across clearings. Telltale signs of their progress include knuckle prints in the mud along the trails, abandoned nests, broken branches, and discarded fruits and seeds. First glimpses are nearly always tantalising – the back of a head as a chimp lopes off through the undergrowth or seeing those huge, muscular arms propelling their owner along; sometimes the noise is deafening but the chimps remain hard to see. Despite their great

Poachers' legacy

We had spent all morning following the sounds and clues of chimpanzees. Some treated us to a fascinating performance as they charged through the forest, occasionally drumming on the biggest and most resonant of the buttressed trees. We heard noisy arguments between two parties, presumably young males, and saw many other primates moving through the canopy. Later we came across a couple of female chimps with infants high up in the trees. One, who had been severely injured in a snare and lost a hand, had us spellbound as she demonstrated how she compensated for being one-handed. Somehow she still gathered food, climbed trees, groomed, built nests, ran on all fours and cared for an infant from time to time. It was hard not to admire the extra effort this ape had to put into everything she did and wonder how difficult her life would be.

Dedee Woodside, Environmental Educator

Look along the main road through Kibale Forest NP for a chance to see monkeys, crested guineafowl and even chimps.

size, immense strength and agility, chimps are wary of people; if your tracking is rewarded with prolonged views, it is a rare privilege.

Relaxing on the evolutionary tree

Chimpanzees are engaging animals whose antics are deservedly famous. If you are lucky enough to locate a party that can sit still awhile, your hour will be memorable and highly entertaining. A big male – the Kibale chimps are large, healthy animals – hunkered down on a fallen trunk may be joined by a couple of subordinates who sift through his coat for salt particles and parasites. High above, the canopy rings with bird calls: the liquid whistling of the **black-headed oriole**, the metallic *tonk-tonk-tonk* of **yellow-rumped tinkerbirds**, the *'it will rain'* call of the **red-chested cuckoo** and the chortling of **Ross' turacos**.

The chimps settle down to feed, groom and relax. The sun picks out flecks of colour in their fur and markings that make every chimp unique: individuals can be told apart by face colour – some are black and some pink, some have freckles or scars, and others are missing digits or even a hand. Researchers are trying to monitor and name each individual in the Kanyanchu community – no easy task when there are estimated to be 70 animals in the group (relationships are complex and new individuals are still being identified). Grooming over, the big male might swing his legs like a child at a playground, stretch back with hands folded behind his head and doze off, or climb a tree and make a day nest for a siesta.

A rich swamp community

A nature trail has been developed at Bigodi Wetland a few kilometres south-east of Kanyanchu Ecotourism Centre. This is the best place in Kibale to look for **Central African red colobus**, although seven other primate species (including occasional **chimps**) visit the swamp, and Bigodi also offers very good bird-watching – 140 species have been clocked up. This papyrus-choked wetland is ringed by a walking trail through farmland and dense stands of figs and palms. Arrange a guide at the Bigodi Visitors Centre and start as early in the morning as possible. **Great blue turacos** and **silvery-cheeked hornbills** fly

Community-based ecotourism

Local communities have traditionally harvested an array of native plant and animal foods, medicines and plant products from Kibale Forest. The forest is under even more pressure now from some 900 communities that surround it, but hunting and indiscriminate harvesting are no longer allowed in Kibale. Instead, the national park assists communities by employing local people as rangers, guides and receptionists. In 1992 a community-based environmental organisation was formed – Kibale Association for Rural Environmental Development (KAFRED) – to promote social and economic development of local communities through the wise use of natural resources. KAFRED's main activity is ecotourism at Bigodi Wetland Sanctuary: locals are trained as wildlife guides and accompany visitors on walks; handicrafts are made from local plants and sold as souvenirs; and funds raised have paid for community facilities. Both the Bigodi Wetland Sanctuary and the Kanyanchu Ecotourism Centre now generate revenue and employ some 90 local people.

between fruiting figs in the swamp and tall trees among the surrounding crops; stands of rank grass attract **mannikins** and other **finches**; and parties of **weavers** fly over to their feeding grounds. A lookout on the edge of Bigodi is a good place to look for some of the specialised papyrus birds, such as **papyrus gonoleks** – often heard but rarely seen – and **papyrus canaries**. **Bushbucks** and **sitatungas** live in the dense vegetation, and **Congo clawless otters** patrol the waterways; **marsh mongooses** might be seen at night. **Black-and-white colobus** are common at Bigodi and **olive baboons** raid surrounding crops.

With luck, your allotted hour of watching Kibale's chimps will include interactions such as grooming.

Night stalkers

What is seen while spotlighting along the main access road near Kanyanchu and on jungle trails during Night Walks is always a matter of chance, but four **nocturnal primates**, a variety of **owls** plus the possibility of predators such as **African palm civets**, **small-spotted genets** or even a **leopard** should be temptation enough to try. A **frog** chorus from streams and ditches after sundown adds to the already strident insect calls. A **potto**, that slow-moving relative of the monkeys, might be seen stalking insects hand over hand along branches. In contrast, galagos or **bushbabies (needle-clawed, dwarf** and **Thomas' galagos** live in Kibale Forest) leap about in the foliage with great agility. **Lord Derby's anomalure** glides between trees by extending the loose folds of skin between its front and rear legs. Owls include **Verreaux's eagle-owls, African wood owls** and **red-chested owlets**; and **fiery-necked** and **pennant-winged nightjars** hawk insects around clearings in the forest at dusk.

Colourful and diverse forest birds

Birdwatching is superb at Kibale. **Black-necked** and **Vieillot's black weavers** construct nests around Kanyanchu, where **African pied wagtails** strut about on rooftops and open patches of ground and **grey parrots** fly over – their scarlet tail and silvery-grey plumage reflecting the sun. **Sunbirds** are attracted to flowering trees, and figs attract a profusion of **pigeons, hornbills, barbets** and **starlings**. Along the road to Fort Portal (the main entrance road) **crested guineafowl** scuttle across the road in the early morning, their heads adorned with a mop of black feathers; seed-eaters such as **francolins, waxbills** and **mannikins** feed in the rank grasslands and clearings along the road; **pigeons** sun themselves in treetops and the dazzling **black bee-eater** watches for its favourite prey from exposed branches. Birds of prey might include an **African goshawk** gliding across a clearing or an **African crowned eagle** looking to snatch a monkey from the canopy for breakfast. Encounters with any or all of Kibale's primates, including **chimps**, are possible along the Fort Portal road. The trails around Kanyanchu are also worth exploring for forest birds, such as **thrushes, robins,** and both **African** and **green-breasted pittas**. **Butterflies** are abundant, especially on the forest edge, gliding through sunny clearings, or settling on animal dung and urine. Among the 250 species recorded are many **charaxes** and **swallowtails**, the latter including **giant swallowtail**, which is mimicked by the **mocker swallowtail**. ■

Watching tips

A forest observation tower near Kanyanchu overlooks a clearing in which elephants are sometimes seen. Butterflies and monkeys become more active as the forest warms up, reaching a crescendo in the late morning. The northern side of Bigodi Wetland is best for seeing Central African red colobus.

MURCHISON FALLS NATIONAL PARK

Big herds at the meeting of the waters

Wildlife highlights

Large herbivores such as elephants, buffaloes and Rothschild's giraffes; antelopes including Uganda kobs, Jackson's hartebeests, defassa waterbucks, bushbucks and oribis; also warthogs and lions. Primates are represented by chimpanzees, vervet, red-tailed and patas monkeys, olive baboons and black-and-white colobus. Bird list stands at 450, including 53 birds of prey; highlights include red-throated, northern carmine, swallow-tailed and seven other bee-eater species, abundant waterbirds along the Albert and Victoria Niles, and rarities such as shoebills (there are an estimated five pairs in the park) and Denham's bustards.

THE mighty Victoria Nile bisects the park – Uganda's biggest NP – squeezing through a 7m-wide rocky cleft and dropping 43m over the western edge of the Albertine Rift Valley at Murchison Falls before continuing to Lake Albert at the park's western boundary. Large animal viewing opportunities and birdwatching are excellent in rolling grasslands, savanna and vast swamps along the Victoria Nile, and in dense stands of papyrus where it empties into the Lake Albert.

Murchison's once-famous wildlife herds are still recovering from the devastation of war: from an estimated 14,500 **elephants** 30 years ago there are now only about 1000 left in the park. However, signs of recovery are apparent and numbers of large animals are slowly building up again: **buffaloes** number about 1,000; there are some 300 to 500 **Rothschild's giraffes**; and antelopes (including **Uganda kobs**, **Jackson's hartebeests**, **defassa waterbucks** and **oribis**) are more abundant and collectively number in the thousands.

Jumbo landscape gardeners

Appealing though they are, elephants can be incredibly destructive animals, and Murchison's once-huge herds helped shape the park's modern landscape. An average elephant eats some 100 tonnes of grass, herbage and other vegetation annually, and in the 1960s Murchison's 14,500 elephants consumed an awful lot of greenery. Grasses are favoured during wet seasons, but during dry seasons elephants strip leaves, branches and insulating bark from trees and bushes. By pushing down trees and trampling saplings and small bushes their activity opens up woodlands and thickets, allowing grasses to invade and making them vulnerable to fire. Hemmed in by the protection of the national park, the damage was compounded and eventually Murchison's dense woodlands became grasslands.

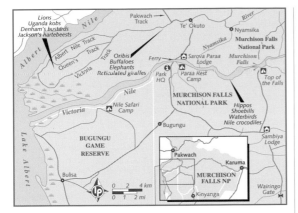

Life floating down the Nile

A boat cruise to the foot of Murchison Falls is a must. Most of the park's 1200 or so **hippos** live downstream of the falls and line the shallows by the dozen: roaring, dozing, feeding and wallowing; females are usually seen with young in February and March. Hugging the bank for part of the way, the vessel passes some fine specimens of **Nile crocodiles** basking on sandy shelves; newly hatched crocs are sometimes seen in March. **Elephants** and **buffaloes** venture down to the water's edge to soak or drink; small parties of **warthogs** – wary because of the large crocs in this reach – join **defassa waterbucks** and **bushbucks** for a drink. About halfway along the cruise to the falls a sheer sandbank holds colonies of **red-throated bee-eaters** (which nest between January and March) and **pied kingfishers**; the smaller, blue and orange **malachite kingfisher** perches on low vegetation, especially reeds.

As the cruise continues look out for the usually dry Nyamsika River which wildlife use as a highway – **elephants**, **lions** and **spotted hyenas** are sometimes seen in its sandy mouth; bird-watching can also be good here and the rare **Egyptian-plover** has been recorded. Papyrus and water hyacinth-fringed islands upstream support – literally – **weavers** and waterbirds such as **jacanas**, **gallinules**, **herons**, **ducks** and **plovers**; **shoebills** are regularly seen on a large papyrus island about halfway to the falls. **Darters** nest on fallen trees and perch along the banks of the Victoria Nile, their wings held outstretched; **black crakes** scuttle among the vegetation, even clambering up into riverside branches; and **African fish eagles** – in rich mahogany and black, with white underparts – sit atop euphorbias and acacias, calling stridently. **Olive baboons** and **vervet monkeys** forage along the banks and in large trees near the falls.

Tracking primates and birds on foot

Animals encountered south of the Victoria Nile might include **defassa waterbucks** and **warthogs**, and birding is good: **Heuglin's francolins** feed along the tracks and flocks of **northern carmine bee-eaters** are present seasonally. Walking trails from the top of Murchison Falls follow the southern bank of the

Location 97km north of Masindi; 354km north of Kampala. 4WD recommended in the park.

Accommodation Bandas and camping grounds at Paraa and Rabongo. Camping grounds at Top of the Falls. Lodges and tented camps inside and outside park.

Wildlife rhythms Grass shorter and wildlife easier to spot in dry seasons (January to February and June to July), when mammals concentrate near permanent water. Grazers establish territories on higher ground with the onset of the wet (March to May).

Contact Uganda Wildlife Authority (☎ 041-32 01 52, fax 34 62 91), PO Box 3530, Kampala.

Ecotours River cruises (9 am and 3 pm daily) upstream to Murchison Falls (also downstream by arrangement). Guided game drives and walks (at Paraa, Rabongo Forest and Top of the Falls). Cross-river ferry at Paraa. All reputable tour companies can arrange travel to Murchison Falls – see the Resource Guide.

Abyssinian rollers perch conspicuously – especially north of the Nile – and can usually be recognised by their long tail.

Jackson's hartebeests are common and share Murchison's grasslands with many other grazing animals.

On a cruise along the Victoria Nile to the foot of Murchison Falls you will see many hippos, crocs and waterbirds.

river. **Red-tailed monkeys** live in the forest near the cliffs, and **black-and-white colobus** sometimes sit over the water high on branches. **Rock pratincoles** sitting on flat rocks – particularly at the top of the falls – periodically hawk for insects; thousands of **swallows** and **swifts** of several species also feed over the water and cliffs.

Thousands of **bats** roost just below the falls on the southern bank at the so-called Bat Cliffs, emerging at dusk to feed; birds of prey such as **bat hawks** and **falcons** wait for the feast, while **black kites** can usually be seen wheeling about at any time of day. Overhanging branches are also used by **giant kingfishers**, which patrol this reach of the river, and at night by **Pel's fishing owls**. These large, rare owls are sometimes seen roosting in large trees along a dry stream bed that enters the southern bank near the bottom of the falls. **Pennant-winged nightjars** pass through the park from November to February and may be seen around the Top of the Falls camping ground. A network of trails through Rabongo Forest, a stand of ironwood in Murchison's south-east, can also be explored on foot: **black-and-white colobus, red-tailed monkeys, olive baboons** and sometimes **chimpanzees** may be seen here, and **buffaloes** are common; birds along the waterways include **shining-blue kingfishers**.

The best of Murchison

The best wildlife viewing is by vehicle north of the Victoria Nile, where most of Murchison's **elephants, buffaloes** and **Uganda kobs** are found, and sightings of **patas monkeys** are most frequent. Take at least an afternoon to explore the Queen's, Pakuba, Victoria Nile and Albert Nile Tracks through tall grass-

lands and savanna woodland, and papyrus swamps at the river delta. The Nyamsika Cliffs – up to 30m high in places – are a good spot to look over grassland for large mammals (**elephants** can often be seen from here) and birds such as **bee-eaters**.

To the west, **oribis** are abundant among the grass and regenerating acacias, grazing among **Grant's gazelles** and **Jackson's hartebeests**; the remaining tall acacias are browsed by **Rothschild's giraffes**. **Buffaloes** feed in marshy hollows and there is a large resident herd here; if you can't spot them, the telltale calls of the **piapiac** (its call sounds like its name is spelled) should give them away – flocks of this long-tailed member of the crow family often associate with buffaloes and elephants. Swathes of grassland are dotted with sausage trees, their bloated fruits swaying in the breeze coming off Lake Albert, and hundreds of distinctive *Borassus* palms make lookouts for **martial eagles** and **red-necked falcons**. **Abyssinian ground hornbills** – the female has a blue face – waddle along looking for small animals and **secretary birds** hunt snakes. **Lions** hunt **antelopes** and **warthogs** in the rolling grasslands, and **Uganda kobs** lek on flatter ground nearer the rivers: bucks spar on the short turf among bushes and termite mounds. **Butterflies** sip moisture in huge swirling flocks; and birdlife is abundant and varied: several sorts of **bee-eaters**, including **swallow-tailed** and **little bee-eaters**, perch on low shrubs and wait for insects; and look out for **Denham's bustards**, large, powerful birds with a reddish hind neck – Murchison is one of the best places to see these rare birds. ■

Buffaloes graze with attendant cattle egrets among Borassus palms north of the Victoria Nile

Watching tips
Take the first boat cruise in the morning to get the best light and sit on the left hand side; if you miss shoebills on the cruise search the dense papyrus beds of the Victoria Nile delta area from the north bank. Leopards are sometimes seen in trees along the Pakuba Track and the road to Pakwach. Patas monkeys are most often seen in grassland south of the Victoria Track.

QUEEN ELIZABETH NATIONAL PARK

Giant hogs and fighting kobs

Wildlife highlights

Uganda's finest selection of large animals: 95 mammal species with a West African spin include good numbers of elephants, buffaloes, hippos and Uganda kobs; antelopes such as defassa waterbucks, bohor reedbucks, bushbucks and topis; and healthy populations of lions plus a good chance of seeing leopards and spotted hyenas. A chimp community is resident in Kyambura Gorge and other common primates in the gorge include olive baboons, vervet monkeys and black-and-white colobus. Warthogs and banded mongooses are abundant and this is the best place in Uganda for giant forest hogs. Birds are a highlight and total 550 – one of the highest for any national park in the world – including 53 raptors, many waterbirds and gems such as shoebills, black bee-eaters and 12 species of kingfisher.

MUCH of QE, as it's universally known, sits between Lakes Edward and George, which are connected by the broad, 34km Kazinga Channel. The tracks traversing the north side of the Kazinga Channel provide good wildlife-viewing in savanna with thickets dominated by candelabra euphorbias: **defassa waterbucks** and **buffaloes** are common, **hippos** wallow in shady mudbaths, and **warthogs** can only be described as abundant. Dense thickets in this area are also probably the best place to look for **leopards**; **spotted hyenas** and **large-spotted genets** scavenge around Mweya some nights. **Giant forest hogs** are easy to see along the Royal Circuit, especially late in the day when they venture out of thickets; **banded mongooses** – some the subject of long-term studies – charge about looking for prey; and the solitary **ichneumon** (or **Egyptian**) **mongoose** also frequents this area.

Further north, herds of **elephants** and **buffaloes** graze on the grassy slopes of volcanic craters that rise towards the distant Rwenzori Mountains. Crisscrossing tracks of buffaloes and antelopes show where they descend to the shores of saline lakes in the craters; several lakes, such as Nyamunuka, are frequented by **flamingos**, **storks** and other **waterbirds**. The so-called Baboon Cliff, the lip of another crater, is a good spot to watch

---

Queen Elizabeth Bird Observatory

With a bird list topping 550 species it is not surprising that a permanent ornithological research facility should be set up, and in 1997 the QE Bird Observatory was established to study resident and migratory birds in the park (such as African skimmers, pictured here, which are present from December to May). Bird observatories are centres for the collation of data and the coordination of field observations; at QENPBO staff are particularly interested in a long-term study of annual bird migration along the Albertine Rift Valley, but are also involved in raising local awareness, training guides, and developing facilities such as hides, walkways and trails in the park. QENPBO is located next to the Institute of Ecology Hostel at Mweya and visitors are welcome to drop in.

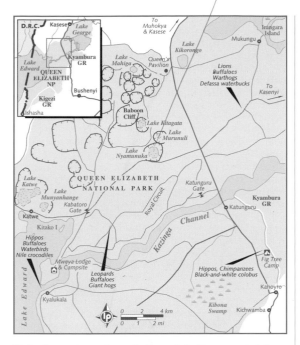

birds of prey. Across the main Kampala to Kasese road, **defassa waterbucks** and **lions** are common along the Kasenyi Track, and most of QE's 31,000 **Uganda kobs** are concentrated in this area. Extensive leks (combat arenas where kob bucks stake out territories and challenge all comers for the right to mate with females) near the track are recognisable by dozens of bucks resting and sparring where the grass is worn short like a playing field. Chattering groups of **grey-backed fiscals** glide in single file from branches; flocks of **Abdim's** and **woolly-necked storks** feed in marshes; and **Temminck's coursers** run low and fast when approached. **Flappet larks** high in the sky are difficult to see but the drumming of their wings is easily heard.

Lions roaring as the sun sets over Lake Edward add to QE's magic.

Queen Elizabeth NP is the best place in Uganda to see giant forest hogs.

Hippo channel

Water is a feature of QE: **hippos** are abundant, **waterbirds** a highlight and **sitatungas** live in papyrus swamps fringing the lakes. A boat trip along the Kazinga Channel is a must. In the late afternoon **elephants**, **buffaloes** and **Uganda kobs** drink from the shores; some of the **buffaloes** might also be lolling about in the water. **Hippos** are always present (most of QE's hippos are concentrated in this stretch), and late in the day there's a chance some will be grazing up on the bank. **Nile crocodiles** – including some large specimens – bask on the banks, although they usually slide into the water when approached (crocodiles have only recently colonised this part of the park).

The Kazinga cruise offers great birdwatching: mixed flocks of waterbirds – **ibises**, **spoonbills** and **storks** – feed in the reed beds and shallows; **ducks** and **geese** loaf on exposed mud; the nests of **Jackson's golden-backed weavers** dangle from tall papyrus stems; and dozens of **pied kingfishers** perch on overhanging branches. Birders should watch carefully in the reed beds for skulking **warblers** and the **papyrus gonolek** (though you'd probably need a tape recorder to entice it from hiding).

Near the entrance to Lake Edward a sand bar on the south bank is a favourite hangout of **buffaloes**, **hippos** and hundreds more **waterbirds**: **African skimmers** – black and white ternlike birds with a scarlet and yellow bill; **great cormorants** vibrating their throats to keep cool; and **pelicans** of both species loafing about among **terns** and **grey-headed gulls**. Hundreds of **swallows** and **martins** hawk for insects a few feet above the water.

Tree-climbing lions

The largest herds of **buffaloes** and **elephants**, some of which have probably moved across from the DRC to escape poaching, and nearly all the **topis** are concentrated in the southern, or 'Ishasha', sector of the park. This seldom-visited area of

Tracks north of Kazinga Channel are reliable for sightings of leopards – look near dense thickets late in the day.

A cruise along the Kazinga Channel is a must – expect to see hippos, crocs and plenty of waterbirds. Elephants and buffaloes drink from the channel near Mweya.

savanna woodland has QE's highest diversity of mammals and excellent birdwatching. **Defassa waterbucks, bushbucks** and **warthogs** are abundant, and **giant forest hogs** might be seen in wooded areas. **Hippos** and **crocs** live in the Ishasha River, where gallery forest supports **black-and-white colobus**. A community of **chimpanzees** lives along the forested Ishasha River Gorge, but they are not habituated and the area is only accessible on foot. Large numbers of lekking **Uganda kobs** attract Ishasha's most famous inhabitants: tree-climbing **lions**, best seen by driving along the Northern Circuit. **Kingfishers** patrol the Ishasha River and birdwatchers should also work the forest and adjacent savanna; **bee-eaters** and **snake-eagles** use exposed snags as lookouts for their respective prey.

Valley of the apes

Dropping dramatically from the surrounding plain, Kyambura Gorge marks the boundary of the Kyambura Game Reserve, which adjoins the eastern side of QE. About 1km across at its widest point, the 100m-deep gorge is drained by the Kyambura River (with resident **hippos**) and the permanent water supports a dense forest that is home to **chimpanzees, red-tailed monkeys, black-and-white colobus** and **giant forest hogs**. Looking over the canopy from the gorge rim, it is sometimes possible to see chimps in the trees – and even occasionally venturing out to fruiting figs on the adjoining savanna (the sight of chimps standing semi-erect to see above the grass is one you'll never forget). Chimp tracking is conducted daily along the gorge, which is also excellent for birdwatching: prize sightings could include **black bee-eaters** or **blue-breasted kingfishers**. Crater lakes east of the gorge support large numbers of **flamingos** of both species plus other **waterbirds**. The Maramagambo Forest is a large area of dense forest stretching up the escarpment of the Albertine Rift Valley into QE's southern reaches. Walking trails from the ranger station at Nyamasingiri lead through the forest, where **l'Hoest's, blue**, and **red-tailed monkeys** may be seen as well as **chimps**, and forest birding is excellent. Five species of forest **duiker** and numerous **squirrels** live in Maramagambo; and **fruit-bats** emerge at dusk from a cave near the camping ground. ∎

Watching tips

Sit on the left hand side of the boat on the Kazinga Channel cruise for best viewing and photo opportunities as it heads towards Lake Edward. Warthogs can be approached on foot around Mweya, where banded mongooses charge through camp daily. Shoebills are sometimes seen in seasonal swamps along the Northern Circuit in the Ishasha sector.

LAKE MBURO NATIONAL PARK

Lakes, swamps and grasslands

Wildlife highlights
Wildlife of the plains and freshwater swamps are the main attractions: plains zebras, impalas, buffaloes, common elands, defassa waterbucks, topis and warthogs highlights roam the former; and sitatungas, hippos, Nile crocs and three species of otter inhabit an extensive system of lakes and swamps. Predators include leopards and spotted hyenas, and primates are represented by olive baboons and vervet monkeys. Waterbirds feature among 315 recorded bird species; among the prize sightings are shoebills (rare) and African finfoots.

HERDS of **common elands, buffaloes** and **plains zebras** graze among **impalas** (Lake Mburo is the only Ugandan park where impalas survive), **topis, bohor reedbucks** and **defassa waterbucks** in rolling grassland; acacia woodland pierced by candelabra euphorbias harbours **warthogs** and small antelopes such as **common duikers, oribis** and **bushbucks**. The savanna is broken by kopjes, but permanent and seasonal wetlands are the park's main focus for wildlife-watching: a vast swamp fed by the Ruizi River links Lake Mburo and five other lakes, and seasonal rains fill adjoining temporary swamps. During the rainy seasons temporary swamps in low-lying areas attract birds such as **rufous-bellied herons** (not recorded in any other Ugandan park) and the rare **saddle-billed stork**.

Bushpigs scavenge around Rwonyo Rest Camp at night and spotlighting along the tracks nearby could reveal opportunists like **side-striped jackals, African civets** or **large-spotted genets**; and **lesser galagos** in trees. Other lucky sightings could include **spotted hyenas** or **leopards**. Birders should listen for **fiery-necked nightjars**, and owls such as **African scops owls** and **Verreaux's eagle-owls** in this area. **Olive baboons** are found in savanna near Rubanga Forest (west of Lake Mburo) and a ranger can guide you on foot through the forest itself for birdwatching.

The Zebra and Ruroko Tracks pass through some of the best areas to search for wildlife. Clouds of yellow, white and blue **butterflies** of a half-dozen species drink at puddles in wheel

---

In the thicket of things

The flat river valleys of Lake Mburo NP feature dense thickets of vegetation that can offer productive wildlife viewing. They usually grow where a pioneering *Euphorbia* becomes established on an abandoned termite mound, where it escapes the worst of wet season flooding or a dry season grassfires. Other plants, such as climbing vines, succulent aloes and sansevierias, soon sprout beside the *Euphorbia*; and seeds from fruits carried by birds from other thickets take root and thrive in the shade of any emergent trees – such as olives – which also become established.

The mounds become thickets – dense islands of vegetation – which become sizeable enough to shelter large animals such as buffaloes and bushbucks. They also make a home for a host of smaller creatures such as rodents, mongooses, reptiles and insects; and provide nest sites for birds such as white-browed robin-chats, tropical boubous, white-browed coucals and black-headed gonoleks. Thickets live and die over many years; eventually the old euphorbias and trees die off, letting in more light and grass, and fire sweeps through once again.

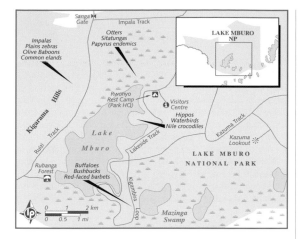

Location 121km south-west of Masaka; 230km south-west of Kampala. 4WD recommended in park.
Facilities Visitors Centre and boat hire at Rwonyo Rest Camp.
Accommodation Bandas and camping at Rwonyo Rest Camp. Camping grounds beside Lake Mburo. Tented camps inside and outside park.
Wildlife rhythms Mammals stay close to lakes and permanent swamps during dry seasons. Impalas, zebras and waterbucks disperse during wet and elands move into southern and eastern parts of the park.
Contact Uganda Wildlife Authority (☎ 041-32 01 52, fax 34 62 91), PO Box 3530, Kampala.
Ecotours Guided walks at Rubanga Forest. Lake Mburo is close to Kampala and all recommended tour companies can organise a visit – see the listing in the Resource Guide.

ruts; an assortment of **doves** – chiefly **red-eyed**, **laughing** and **ring-necked** – explode into flight from just under the wheels; and **crested francolins** make suicidal dashes across the track. **Oribis** emerge from cool grassy hollows in the late afternoon to graze in pairs among bigger animals – approach too closely and they usually whistle an alarm before bounding off with a peculiar rocking horse gait (better seen than described).

Waist-high termite mounds (like red earth milestones next to the track) are used by **red-necked spurfowl** as lookouts and by male **topis** watching for predators, although Mburo's lions were killed off long ago by local farmers. **Plains zebras** mingle with **impalas** and **topis** – and with Ankole cattle grazing illegally in the park; **common elands**, although abundant, prefer the shelter of wooded hillsides; and **klipspringers** stake out their territories on high kopjes. The twisted, pale trunks of *Boscia* trees make nest shelters for **barbets** and **hornbills**, including the **red-faced barbet** – the Kigambira Loop is the best place in Uganda to see this localised species.

Healthy populations of **hippos** and **crocodiles** inhabit the wetlands – both can usually be seen from camping grounds on Lake Mburo's shores (watch for **buffaloes** in adjacent woodlands) – and three species of **otter** (**African** and **Congo clawless**, and **African spot-necked**) patrol the lakes and swamps, but **waterbirds** are the most abundant inhabitants. The evocative call of the **African fish eagle** carries through morning mist – pairs nest in tall trees where **darters** and **long-tailed cormorants** loaf with wings outstretched. **Hamerkops** and **water thick-knees** feed along the shore; **pied** and **malachite kingfishers** dive for tilapia and tadpoles; **pelicans** – usually **pink-backed** but occasionally **great white** as well – dip for fish further out; and a variety of **herons** ranges from the skulking **green-backed** to the **goliath** – the biggest of all – spearing fish in deeper water. A dense papyrus swamp choking the northern end of Lake Mburo is ideal habitat for **sitatungas** and home to **papyrus yellow** and **white-winged warblers**, **papyrus canaries** and the **papyrus gonolek**. Prized bird sightings have included **shoebills** and **African finfoots**. ■

Watching tips
Hire a canoe to explore the papyrus swamps for sitatungas. Arrange with the warden to do a night drive along one of the tracks. Lake Mburo itself is one of the best places to see the African finfoot; scan the water from breaks in the dense lakeside vegetation in the early morning.

BUDONGO FOREST RESERVE

Ironwood forest with abundant chimps

Wildlife highlights

The largest population of chimpanzees in Uganda. Black-and-white colobus and red-tailed and blue monkeys are common, and seeing a chequered elephant shrew is a possibility, in a list of 25 mammal species. First-class forest birding, with 350 species recorded; highlights include francolins, pittas, spinetails, nine species of kingfisher, 11 of barbet, plus forest starlings and hornbills.

Location Kaniyo Pabidi 29km north and Busingiro 40km west of Masindi.
Facilities Information centres and walking trails.
Accommodation Camping grounds and bandas at Busingiro and Kaniyo Pabidi. Hotels in Masindi.
Wildlife rhythms Bird breeding and activity is highest during rains (February to April).
Contact UWA (☎ 041-32 01 52, fax 34 62 91), PO Box 3530, Kampala.
Ecotours Chimp tracking with trained guides at Busingiro and Kaniyo Pabidi; guided bird walks on Royal Mile.

Watching tips

Kaniyo Pabidi is the only known site in Uganda where Puvel's illadopsis can be seen.

TRACKING **chimpanzees** in East Africa's largest remaining stand of ironwood forest is the main attraction at Budongo: there's a good chance of contacting one of the five habituated groups in a population estimated at 600 to 800 individuals (morning tracking at Busingiro Ecotourism Site is generally more successful than afternoon walks). Parts of the forest have been logged, but biodiversity remains high (for example, some 289 species of **butterfly** have been recorded) and, ironically, **black-and-white colobus** and **red-tailed** and **blue monkeys** seem more abundant in logged forest near Busingiro. Savanna woodland abuts Budongo to the north, and **elephants**, **defassa waterbucks**, **Uganda kobs** and **buffaloes** might be seen from the road into Murchison Falls NP.

Walks along the Royal Mile, a 15km drive east of Busingiro, offer what is probably Uganda's best forest birding. **Chocolate-backed, blue-breasted** and **African pygmy kingfishers** are particularly common; **greenbuls, sunbirds** and **apalises** keep birders looking into canopy flocks; fruiting trees attract a variety of **hornbills, barbets** and **starlings**; and **crested guineafowl** and skulking **Nahan's francolins** are sometimes seen crossing the road.

Trails around Busingiro are also productive: both **African** and **green-breasted pittas** occur (green-breasted pittas breed in Budongo from April to May – listen for their bell-like whistling); various **illadopses** are common in undergrowth; and swifts, such as **Sabine's** and **Cassin's spinetails** soar over forest clearings. Mammal encounters at either site could include **chequered elephant shrews** bustling through leaf litter; and spotlighting could yield **pottos, tree pangolins, hammer bats** or any of five **owl** species.

The stand of ironwood and mahogany at Kaniyo Pabidi Ecotourism Site have never been cleared – a 300-year-old mahogany grows near the entrance. Apart from **chimps**, the network of forest trails is good for sighting **black-and-white colobus**, and more good birding includes **blue-throated rollers** perched on topmost branches; **tambourine doves** feeding on the ground; **black-billed turacos** and cackling **black-and-white-casqued hornbills** in the canopy; and **forest francolins** and **crested guineafowl** in undergrowth. **Olive baboons** and **Abyssinian ground hornbills** feed along the road to Murchison Falls in the early morning. ∎

[Map] BUGUNGU GR · Olive baboons · Abyssinian ground hornbills · Weiga Swamp · MURCHISON FALLS NP · Kaniyo Pabidi Ecotourism Site · Lake Albert · Chimpanzees · Blue-throated rollers · Black-and-white colobus · BUDONGO FOREST RESERVE · Murchison Falls NP Gate · Sonso River · Biso · Spinetails · Crested guineafowl · Green-breasted pittas · Busingiro Ecotourism Site · Great forest birding · Masindi · The Royal Mile · Nyabyeya Forestry College · 0 5 10 km · 0 3 6 mi

KIDEPO VALLEY NATIONAL PARK

Magic of remote arid-zone wilderness

HERDS of **elephants** (about 350 remain) and **buffaloes**, and smaller numbers of **common elands, plains zebras** and **Rothschild's giraffes** are easily seen amid thorny savanna scrub of the shallow Narus River valley and around Apoka Rest Camp. **Antelopes** include **Jackson's hartebeest, defassa waterbucks** and **bohor reedbucks**; oribis and both **Kirk's** and **Günther's dik-diks** shelter in dense thickets on stony ridges; and **olive baboons**, and **patas** and **vervet monkeys** forage over the savanna. **Bright's gazelles** – a race of Grant's – have recently been seen near Moru Apol and rumours of **black rhinos** persist around Mt Zulia.

The predator list includes **Nile crocodiles** in the Narus River; **lions, leopards, spotted hyenas** and **bat-eared foxes**; **caracals** stalk **striped ground squirrels** and ground birds; and **hunting dogs** have been reported from near Mt Lomej. A ruined lodge on a ridge at Katurum makes a good vantage point from which to scan for animals during dry seasons, when the Narus is the source of the park's only permanent water. Spotlighting near Apoka could reveal **Senegal galagos, side-striped jackals** or a **white-tailed mongoose**, and **elephants, buffaloes** and sometimes **lions** are nocturnal visitors to a nearby waterhole.

Birdwatching is sensational: **piapiacs** and both **oxpeckers** hang around grazing herds; **secretary birds** and good numbers of **Somali ostriches** strut among **Abyssinian ground hornbills, helmeted guineafowl** and five species of bustard including **Denham's bustard**. **Abyssinian rollers, yellow-billed shrikes, Clapperton's francolins** and **black coucals** live in grasslands around Apoka; and **fox kestrels, white-shouldered cliff chats** and various **swifts** frequent the cliffs at Katurum. *Kigelia* woodland along the Narus attracts **northern carmine bee-eaters, rollers** and **rose-ringed parakeets**; and the Kidepo River valley offers exceptional dry-country birding, with **pygmy falcons, white-bellied go-away-birds** and **little green bee-eaters** (the latter at the southern limit of their distribution). ■

Wildlife highlights

Seldom-visited wilderness and Uganda's only park with cheetahs. High mammal diversity includes elephants, plains zebras and buffaloes with arid-zone antelopes such as Bright's gazelles and Günther's dik-diks; lions, spotted hyenas and leopards head predator list. Exceptional birding (475 species) with many highlights, including Somali ostriches, bustards, little green bee-eaters and Abyssinian ground hornbills.

Location 840km north of Kampala (4WD essential); access by aircraft is recommended.

Accommodation Cabins and bandas at Apoka Rest Camp. Camping ground at nearby Kakine.

Wildlife rhythms Mammals and waterbirds concentrate near pools in the contracting Narus River during dry seasons.

Contact Uganda Wildlife Authority (☎ 041-32 01 52, fax 34 62 91), PO Box 3530, Kampala.

Ecotours Guided game drives and walks; night drives by permission. G&C Tours (☎/fax 041-32 14 79) and Semliki Safaris (☎/fax 041-25 97 00) can organise transport and accommodation. Charter flights through CEI Aviation, Metropole House, 8–10 Entebbe Rd, Kampala (☎ 041-25 58 25).

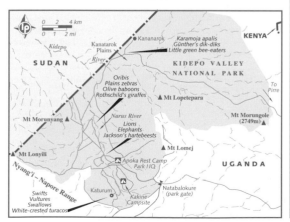

Watching tips

Stone partridges inhabit a rocky outcrop at the Imilliny Ranger Station. Karamoja apalis (an endemic warbler) occurs on the Kanatorok Plains north of Kidepo River.

MGAHINGA GORILLA NATIONAL PARK

Peak forest viewing

Wildlife highlights
Mountain gorillas head the bill, but dense forests also support golden monkeys, black-and-white colobus, elephants, buffaloes, bushbucks and giant forest hogs. One of the most accessible places to see localised birds (115 species recorded) such as Rwenzori turacos and scarlet-tufted malachite sunbirds.

Location 14km south of Kisoro (4WD necessary); 510km south-west of Kampala.
Facilities Information board and scenic viewing platform.
Accommodation Bandas, dorm and camping grounds outside park entrance. Hotels in Kisoro.
Wildlife rhythms Mountain gorillas usually present March to May and September to December. Alpine birds may move to lower slopes during wet seasons.
Contact Uganda Wildlife Authority (☎ 041-32 01 52, fax 34 62 91), PO Box 3530, Kampala.
Ecotours Guided bird, nature and mountain walks can be organised at park HQ. See the Resource Guide for a list of tour operators.

Watching tips
The deep gorge on Mt Sabinyo is good for Rwenzori turacos. Stake out Rugezi Swamp late in the day for the chance to see elephants and giant forest hogs.

TRACKING mountain gorillas that live on the slopes of extinct volcanoes is the main attraction, but other primates that can be seen among a modest mammal list are **golden monkeys** (a localised form of the blue monkey) and **black-and-white colobus**. Elephants, **buffaloes** and **giant forest hogs** also inhabit the densely forested slopes and may be encountered along walking trails, as may **black-fronted duikers** and **bushbucks** live in Mt Gahinga's swampy crater. Traces (usually dung) of nocturnal hunters like **African civets**, **servaline genets** and **spotted hyenas** may be seen on the lower trails, and other predators – which are rare in the park – include **leopards**, **side-striped jackals**, **servals** and **African golden cats**.

Gorilla positioning systems

About 50 **mountain gorillas** in five groups inhabit the park; a habituated group of nine, which includes two males, is tracked daily and its position recorded with a GPS (global positioning system) – a device that uses satellites to pinpoint an exact location. Gorilla-tracking is generally less physically demanding than at Bwindi Impenetrable NP, but Mgahinga's gorillas are international travellers that wander seasonally into neighbouring Rwanda and the DRC – probably to search for preferred foods, or to eat medicinal plants for a deworming session. Mt Sabinyo supports good stands of bamboo and wild celery, much favoured by gorillas, and a chance encounter with a solitary male is possible; **golden monkeys** are often seen here.

The once-cultivated slopes leading to the foot of Mts Muhavura, Gahinga and Sabinyo support abundant birdlife: **common stonechats** flit among the volcanic boulders; **augur buzzards** perch on dead branches; and **regal**, **bronze** and **malachite sunbirds** dip their bills into the flowering spikes of red-hot pokers. Crossing fast-flowing streams you enter thick bamboo and moss-festooned forest, about 1km above the park entrance, where **golden monkeys** and forest squirrels – **Boehm's bush**, **Carruthers' mountain tree** and **montane sun squirrels** – may be seen; **buffaloes** are also quite common. The localised **Rwenzori turaco** inhabits dense forest and **scarlet-tufted malachite sunbirds** sometimes feed alongside other **sunbirds** on lower slopes. ∎

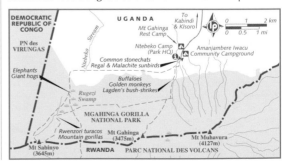

MT ELGON NATIONAL PARK

Monkeys and antelopes on forested slopes

MOST of the mountain's **elephants** have disappeared, although some were sighted near the Kenya border during the 1990s; **bushbucks** and **buffaloes** live deep in montane forest, and are generally seen far from the intensively cultivated lower slopes. Apart from rodents and shrews, which in a recent survey were found to be common and diverse, primates are the most common mammals. **Olive baboons** raid crops on the lower slopes, retreating to the forest above the park's boundary – where **blue monkeys** and **black-and-white colobus** might be encountered. Colobus also forage at higher altitudes. The mountain's swamps are frequented by **defassa waterbucks**, **sitatungas** and **de Brazza's monkeys**, and with luck you could startle a **bush-pig** or a **common duiker** in the undergrowth along one of the trails. Predators include **spotted hyenas** and **leopards** but are rarely encountered. The three marked trails radiating from the Forest Exploration Centre offer good birdwatching, while **tree hyraxes** (active and noisy at night) and **red-legged sun squirrels** also live in the canopy. **Swallows** wing over valleys where iridescent **tacazze** and **golden-winged sunbirds** stand out among several other bird species competing for nectar. Fruiting figs attract various **pigeons** and **starlings**, **Hartlaub's** and **Ross' turacos**, and **crowned**, **African grey** and **black-and-white-casqued hornbills**; **cinnamon-chested bee-eaters** hawk from perches; and tail-bobbing **mountain wagtails** flit along streams.

Stunted heath and moorland grow above 3000m and are accessible only by hiking overnight. Up here grow the so-called big game plants – giant fleshy herbs such as lobelias and groundsels – which can reach 6m in height and are most profuse in Mt Elgon's vast caldera. There are few mammals at these heights, but **Chanler's mountain reedbucks** are sometimes seen near the caldera rim. Most outstanding of the birds of prey is the **lammergeier**, but other raptors include **Verreaux's eagles** picking **rock hyraxes** off the outcrops, and **mountain buzzards** that swoop on rodents. **Scarce** and **alpine swifts** range widely after insects, and **moorland francolins** feed among grass tussocks. ∎

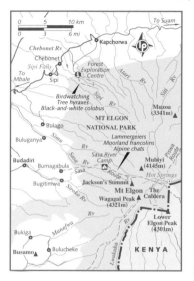

Wildlife highlights

Mammals include olive baboons, black-and-white colobus and blue monkeys – all common in tall forest – and rock hyraxes at higher altitudes. Defassa waterbucks and bushbucks are the most common antelopes. Mammals generally not easy to see but birdwatching is good: alpine and montane forest birds a speciality among 300 species including pigeons, turacos, hornbills and birds of prey (especially lammergeiers).

Location 78km from Mbale to Forestry Exploration Centre
Facilities Guides and marked trails from FEC.
Accommodation Camping, dorms, bandas and meals at FEC. Wide range near Sipi Falls. Camping on mountain trails.
Wildlife rhythms High-altitude birds may move lower down slopes during wet seasons.
Contact Mt Elgon NP (☎ 045-33720), PO Box 135, Mbale.
Ecotours Volcanoes (☎ 041-34 64 64) can organise walking on alpine trails.

Watching tips

The Sasa and Piswa Trails above 3000m give the best chance of seeing lammergeiers.

RWENZORI MOUNTAINS NATIONAL PARK

Distinctive vegetation at all altitudes

BLUE **monkeys** and an endemic race of **black-and-white colobus** are common along the trail through the densely forested slopes of the Mubuku Valley; **l'Hoest's monkeys** are less frequently seen and **chimpanzees** usually only heard. Stands of distinctive *Symphonia* trees, with straight, silvery trunks and scarlet blossoms, and aromatic evergreen *Podocarpus* (another tree species) tower over an understorey – thick with giant tree ferns, wild ginger, hibiscus, begonias, balsams and arum lilies – where **black-fronted duikers, bushpigs, giant forest hogs** and **bushbucks** may be startled if you walk quietly along the trail.

Giant earthworms in shades of pink and green – some stretching to 45cm in length – cross the trail; and excellent forest birdwatching features the conspicuous **regal** and **purple-breasted sunbirds**, skulking **handsome francolins**, **olive pigeons** and 'click-cawing' **Rwenzori turacos** (these localised birds feed on the mauve cones of *Podocarpus* trees). Spotlight for **southern tree hyraxes**, easily located by their nocturnal screeching, and for **Rwenzori otter shrews** feeding in mountain streams.

Forests of bonsai gone mad

The endemic **Stuhlmann's double-collared sunbird** is common in the bamboo zone above 2500m; beyond grow glades of *Hagenia* (African rosewood) with stout, contorted limbs ornately encrusted with trailing beard moss and cushions of moss, like bonsai plants gone mad. Between heavy showers, **black-fronted duikers** pick their way over soggy ground covered with deep mosses, through which sprout metre-high spikes of pink orchids. Calls of **white-naped ravens** pierce the misty silence and, at dusk, endemic **Rwenzori nightjars** flit about the clearings.

Giant groundsels and lobelias become more common in the zone dominated by 15m-high giant heather between 3000 and 3800m. Extensive stands of *Helichrysum*, giant groundsels and giant lobelias are most common above 3800m. **Scarlet-tufted malachite sunbirds** pick insects from the 7m-high, powder-blue flower spikes of Wollaston's lobelias – even probing though dustings of snow. **Rwenzori red duikers** (which replace black-fronted duikers at these heights) live among the vegetation that grows thick to the edge of alpine lakes. The tarns themselves are frequented by **African black ducks**; and **swifts, mountain buzzards, Verreaux's eagles** and **lammergeiers** cruise at the greatest heights. ■

At the time of publication Rwenzori Mountains NP was off limits to travellers owing to military unrest. The situation could change in this popular mountaineering destination, but we urge you to contact the Uganda Tourist Board (☎ 041-34 21 96) before venturing into the area.

SEMLIKI NATIONAL PARK

Rainforest with a Congo rhythm

A finger of the vast Ituri Forest, stretching from the Zaire River over the Ugandan border into Semliki NP, offers sensational lowland rainforest birdwatching with a West African flavour. Among the mammals there's a chance of encountering any of eight species of **primate**, or larger species such as **elephants, buffaloes, hippos** and **leopards**. Animal lists total 400 birds (including 12 **kingfishers**) and 53 mammals – a high percentage of both are found nowhere else in Uganda. Mammal enthusiasts could spotlight for West African nocturnal specialities such as **water chevrotains** (small, deerlike animals whose closest relatives live in South-East Asia), **Zenker's flying mice** and **Beecroft's flying squirrels**. **Chimpanzees** have been recorded, but are rarely heard or seen, and okapis once occurred in the area but have almost certainly been poached to local extinction.

Birds running hot and cold

Primates and birds are attracted to fruiting trees along the main road: you'll almost certainly see **black-and-white colobus** here; **Central African red colobus** are rare, but other possibilities include **grey-cheeked mangabeys**, and **red-tailed, blue** and **de Brazza's monkeys**. **Olive baboons** and **vervet monkeys** prefer grassland adjoining the forest. Birding is excellent along the main road: fig trees attract **turacos** – including the spectacular **great blue** and **Ross' turacos** – **pigeons, starlings** and up to eight of the park's nine species of **hornbill**. The forest also shelters **bushpigs, white-bellied duikers** and **pygmy antelopes**, but you are more likely to see the tree-climbing **fire-footed rope** and **red-legged sun squirrels**.

The hot springs at Sempaya are surrounded by forest in which both species of **colobus** live; **marsh birds** inhabit the reeds on the way to the 'male' springs at Sempaya (where **sitatungas** are sometimes seen by scanning from the observation tower); **waders** feed in the near-boiling water; and **olive** and **African green pigeons** visit the springs to drink at dusk.

A trail to the Kirumia River is excellent for birdwatching: outstanding attractions in forest and secondary growth include **rufous-sided broadbills** and **African piculets** (East Africa's smallest species of woodpecker). **Spot-breasted ibises, white-bellied kingfishers** and **Nkulengu rails** have been seen near oxbow lakes past the first river crossing; and the chance to find a **red-fronted antpecker** – and of identifying the profusion of **greenbuls, sunbirds**, forest **waxbills** and **weavers** – should gladden the hearts of hard-core birdwatchers. ∎

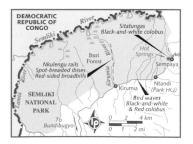

Wildlife highlights

Black-and-white colobus are most commonly seen of eight primate species. Hippos inhabit rivers and sitatungas frequent swamps; rainforest hides elephants, buffaloes and bushpigs. Peerless lowland rainforest birding – over 400 species – features nine hornbills (three found in no other Ugandan park) and Nkulengu rails.

Location 52km north-west of Fort Portal; 371km west of Kampala.
Facilities Observation tower and boardwalk to hot springs.
Accommodation Camping grounds at Sempaya and Ntandi. Guesthouse in Bundibugyo. Hotels and lodges in Fort Portal.
Wildlife rhythms Bird courting and breeding is at its peak just after drier months (January to February). Migrant waders visit the hot springs from November to April.
Contact Uganda Wildlife Authority (☎ 041-32 01 52, fax 34 62 91), PO Box 3530, Kampala.
Ecotours Semliki Safaris (☎/fax 041-25 97 00) can organise visits from nearby Semliki Valley WR.

Watching tips

African open-billed storks roost in large trees en route to the 'female' hot springs.

SEMLIKI VALLEY WILDLIFE RESERVE

Walk among elephants

Wildlife highlights

Habituated chimpanzees a draw among five other primate species; both forest and savanna races of elephants and buffaloes; savanna mammals such as Uganda kobs, bohor reedbucks and Jackson's hartebeests, plus lions, spotted hyenas and leopards. Hippos and Nile crocodiles in Lake Albert. Great birding – 350 species recorded; shoebills and other waterbirds a speciality.

Location 30km from Fort Portal to park boundary, 60km to Semliki Safari Lodge.
Accommodation Lodge in park.
Wildlife rhythms Mammals gravitate to river valleys at height of the dry season (December to February). Huge flocks of Abdim's storks arrive October to November.
Contacts UWA (☎ 041-32 01 52, fax 34 62 91), PO Box 3530, Kampala.
Ecotours Chimp tracking, night drives, game walks, boat trips on Lake Albert. Semliki Safaris (☎/fax 041-25 97 00) organises all tours, accommodation and activities in the reserve.

Watching tips
Night drives are most productive during dry seasons, when mammals emerge from their daytime shelters in riverside vegetation to forage.

GRASSY floodplains of the Semliki and Wasa rivers in the north and west are grazed by **Uganda kobs, defassa waterbucks** and **bohor reedbucks**, and thorn thickets shelter **oribis** and **bushbucks. Jackson's hartebeests** – 30 were recently translocated from Murchison Falls NP – live among stands of *Borassus* palms along the entrance road; **warthogs, olive baboons, banded mongooses** and **Abyssinian ground hornbills** also forage here, and **red-necked falcons** use the palms as a lookout from which to hunt abundant grassland birds. **Elephants** concentrate in woodland in the park's south, where they can be approached on foot with a guide.

Hooting galleries
A community of about 40 **chimpanzees** has been habituated and can be tracked on a network of trails through gallery forest along the Mugiri River (at the foot of the Kigura escarpment). Large groups – up to 30 individuals – gather at fruiting *Cynometra* trees in January and February. Chance encounters in this forest might include **elephants** or **buffaloes** (the smaller forest races of both occur), **Harvey's duikers** or **bushpigs,** but **black-and-white colobus,** and **blue** and **red-tailed monkeys** are commonly observed.

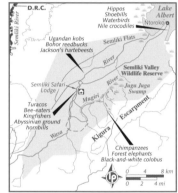

Birdwatching is highly productive, and could be rewarded with sightings of **blue-breasted kingfishers, crested guineafowl** or the vocal **leaflove.** An unhabituated community of **chimps** lives along the Wasa River.

A few **lions** survive in Semliki WR and other predators that might be seen – usually on a night drive – include **leopards, servals, spotted hyenas** and **African golden cats** (although this cat remains as elusive here as elsewhere across its range). Forest along the Wasa River shelters **buffaloes**, which also frequent adjoining marshes, and **giant forest hogs. Hippos** wallow in the margins of Lake Albert and the odd **Nile croc** basks on the bank. Boat cruises (organised by Semliki Safari Lodge) search for **shoebills** – sometimes several are seen on one trip – and other bird specialities including **red-throated bee-eaters** (breeding January to March) and **pied kingfishers** nesting in sandbanks, as well as **lesser** and **African jacanas,** and **African pygmy-geese. Goliath herons, hamerkops** and **yellow-billed storks** are all normally seen. ∎

OTHER SITES – UGANDA

Bugungu Wildlife Reserve
Savanna woodland supporting black-and-white colobus and olive baboons abuts the southern boundary of Murchison Falls NP and surrounds the Weiga Swamp (approximately halfway between Butiaba and Bulisa). Scattered herds of buffaloes, defassa waterbucks and bohor reedbucks populate the reserve, and lions, elephants, bushbucks and duikers are also seen occasionally. Plenty of habitat for hippos, sitatungas, otters and marsh birds, such as black coucals, marsh owls and yellow-mantled widowbirds.
40km north of Butiaba

Kalinzu Forest Reserve
Relatively intact rainforest on the Albertine Rift Valley escarpment, contiguous with the Maramagambo Forest. Chimpanzees are being habituated, 11km of forest trails have been developed and trained guides lead spotlighting walks to look for nocturnal primates and birds. Butterflies a highlight (262 species); highland birds include yellow-bellied wattle-eyes, Rwenzori turacos and purple-breasted sunbirds.
77km west of Mbarara

Kigezi Wildlife Reserve
A buffer between Queen Elizabeth NP's Ishasha sector, Maramagambo Forest and heavily populated areas to the south. Grassy savanna and *Acacia sieberiana* woodland with warthogs, herds of antelopes including Uganda kobs, defassa waterbucks, bushbucks, topis and oribis, plus occasional lions and giant forest hogs, and a few hippos. Dense forest contiguous with Maramagambo supports unhabituated chimpanzees, and black-and-white and some Central African red colobus. Kigezi is a refuge for elephants that move east from the Rwindi Plain in the DRC and south from Queen Elizabeth NP at the start of the wet season.
130km west of Mbarara

Kyambura Wildlife Reserve
Rolling savanna dotted with crater lakes forming a buffer between settled lands and Queen Elizabeth NP, from which it is separated by Kyambura Gorge. Plains wildlife is similar to QE, and includes Uganda kobs, defassa waterbucks, warthogs, lions, leopards, elephants and good numbers of buffaloes. Three saline crater lakes periodically attract large numbers of flamingos, which have attempted to nest at Lake Maseche. Swamps adjoining Lake George support hippos, sitatungas, otters and waterbirds.
100km north-west of Mbarara

Lakes Bisina and Opeta
Important staging area for migratory birds, contains rare residents such as shoebills (reported to nest), significant species such as rufous bellied herons and Uganda's only endemic species, Fox's weaver. Sitatungas inhabit dense reed beds.
93km east of Soroti

Lake Bunyonyi
Large freshwater lake supporting otters, sitatungas and waterbirds. Pied kingfishers, swallows and various weavers abundant around open water near Kisoro, and the papyrus-choked outflow 41km south of Kisoro is particularly good for papyrus birds, grey crowned crane and waterbirds.
10km west of Kabale

Mpanga Forest
Tiny but intact tall rainforest and swamp community with 205 tree species (two unique), eight large mammal species, including red-tailed monkeys and bushpigs, and 78 butterfly species. Highlights of 141 recorded bird species include semitame hornbills at the camping ground, blue-breasted kingfishers, grey parrots and black-billed turacos; walking trails make an ideal introduction to Ugandan forest birding.
40km west of Kampala

Pian-Upe Wildlife Reserve
The most important game reserve in the Karamoja region, with rolling plains of black cotton soil flooded by intermittent rivers draining into Lake Kyoga. The greatest animal diversity is in the south-east, between Mt Kadam and Greek River, where herds of buffaloes and Jackson's hartebeests roam among elands, giraffes, plains zebras and roan antelopes; other large animals include Grant's gazelles, bushbucks, Uganda kobs, topis, defassa waterbucks and warthogs. Bohor reedbucks are abundant north and east of Lake Opeta. The scenic southern sector of Pian-Upe has been recommended for national park status.
350km north-east of Kampala

Ssese Islands
Group of 84 mostly uninhabited islands in northern Lake Victoria. Well forested Buggala supports black-and-white colobus and vervet monkeys. Bukasa also has resident monkeys; and various papyrus fringed islands are good for otters, hippos, crocodiles, sitatungas and many waterbirds. Different colour forms of the African paradise flycatcher are abundant on Buggala and Bukasa islands.
45km south of Entebbe

RWANDA AND THE DEMOCRATIC REPUBLIC OF THE CONGO (DRC)

Highlights

- Tracking mountain gorillas through bamboo on the steep slopes of the mighty Virunga volcanoes
- Herds of antelopes congregating at sunset on the plains of PN de l'Akagera as lions start to hunt
- Huge troops of habituated black-and-white colobus at RF de Nyungwe
- Primates – especially chimpanzees – in the forests growing on ancient lava flows at Tongo, PN des Virunga
- Great pods of roaring hippos along the Rutshuru River, PN des Virunga
- Trekking to the peaks of the Rwenzoris, land of giant herbs, dripping forests and alpine wildlife

Biological riches at the edge of the Zaïre River basin

ALTHOUGH it is one of the smallest countries in Africa, Rwanda's varied topography and habitat support a biological richness well out of proportion to its size: including 170 species of mammal, 670 of bird and 400 of butterfly. Dormant, 4500m volcanoes in the north-west and montane forests on the shores of Lake Kivu slope to rolling savanna and swampy lowlands in the east, creating diverse regional climatic conditions and a highly variable annual rainfall. On the northern border, the slopes of the Virunga volcanoes support the largest remaining population of mountain gorillas – tracking these gentle animals is one of the greatest wildlife experiences on earth. Rwanda's eastern border is marked by the Akagera River and the country's largest reserve, PN de l'Akagera, where substantial herds of plains zebras, topis, impalas and buffaloes still graze the savanna. The vast swamps of the Akagera basin support important populations of sitatungas and shoebills. The RF de Nyungwe rates the highest priority for conservation in continental Africa, combining high biodiversity and endemicity, and significant threatened species. This montane forest is home to many species of primate, including large troops of black-and-white colobus, plus chimpanzees, Central African red colobus, owl-faced and l'Hoest's monkeys. Outstanding birdwatching includes the chance to look for rarities such as the Congo bay-owl, long thought to be extinct.

At the eastern edge of the Democratic Republic of the Congo (DRC – formerly Zaïre) the great plains of East Africa lap against the foot of Africa's highest mountain range (the glacier-capped Rwenzoris), the vast rainforests of the Zaïre River basin and the great lakes of the Albertine Rift Valley: Lakes Kivu, Edward and Albert. Large areas of primary forest remain intact (the DRC contains nearly half of Africa's rainforest), and a great slab in PN de Kahuzi-Biéga protects large populations of two of the world's great apes – chimpanzees and lowland gorillas – plus many animals unique to the Zaïre basin. The vast PN des Virunga is contiguous with other reserves in Rwanda and Uganda, and protects a diversity of habitats and wildlife, including mountain gorillas and chimpanzees in southern rainforests; savanna wildlife in the central section – elephants, buffaloes, topis and other antelopes, plus hippos and waterbirds; and the alpine vegetation of the Rwenzori peaks. This is wildlife adventure country, where facilities are few but the rewards great for a traveller prepared to rough it; birdwatchers in particular will find a high percentage of DRC's 1000 bird species in these two parks. ∎

Please note that civil war and poaching have taken a toll of wildlife, its habitat and the people who protect it in the DRC's national parks. It is once again safe to track gorillas in Rwanda, but although several NGOs are striving to restore normality we urge all travellers to seek competent advice before visiting any parks in the DRC.

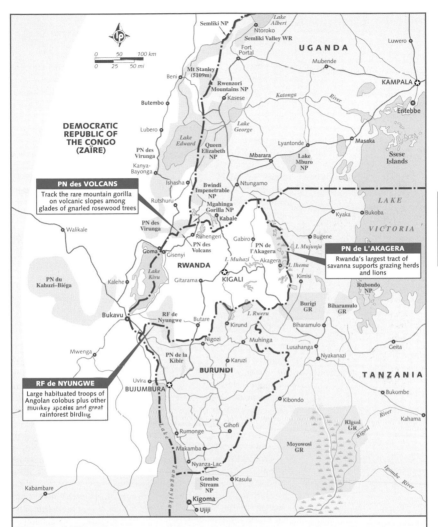

PN des VOLCANS
Track the rare mountain gorilla on volcanic slopes among glades of gnarled rosewood trees

PN de L'AKAGERA
Rwanda's largest tract of savanna supports grazing herds and lions

RF de NYUNGWE
Large habituated troops of Angolan colobus plus other monkey species and great rainforest birding

Suggested itineraries

One week Although no park is too far away from Rwanda's capital, Kigale (and the roads are good), a week will allow only a cursory look at each – and not enough time to get to the DRC (Zaïre). You'll need two days to get to PN des Volcans to see the mountain gorillas – a day to get to Ruhengeri, tracking the following morning then returning to

Kigale. Allow another day to visit PN de l'Akagera – there's plenty to see, but tourist facilities are limited so an overnight stay is unlikely. Use the rest of your week to explore the trails in RF de Nyungwe: walk down to Kamiranzovu Marsh; take a primate walk and enjoy the large troops of black-and-white colobus; then get to grips with the rainforest birds.

Two weeks Combine your exploration of the Rwandan parks with a trip over the border into the DRC – an adventure in itself (please note the safety warning opposite). In PN des Virunga, track mountain gorillas on the volcanoes or chimps in the Tongo area. Then go for the lowland gorillas in PN de Kahuzi-Biéga and get a taste of birding the Zaïre River basin rainforests.

PARC NATIONAL DE **L'AKAGERA**

Rwanda's greatest reserve

Wildlife highlights

The greatest diversity of large mammals in Rwanda: herds of topis, plains zebras, impalas, common elands, oribis and bohor reedbucks; defassa waterbucks and sitatungas share vegetated waterways with hippos and Nile crocodiles; carnivores include lions, leopards, spotted hyenas and side-striped jackals; and specialities include roan antelopes, black rhinos (introduced from Tanzania) and elephants. Waterbirds include shoebills and African finfoots, and several papyrus endemics shine among 525 recorded bird species. More than 40 raptors have been recorded, and Akagera lies on the great Nile Valley bird migration route between Europe and southern Africa.

THE Kirara and Kamakaba plains support the largest concentrations of grazers and their predators: Kamakaba is a favoured haunt of **defassa waterbucks** and **bohor reedbucks**; **buffaloes** seek permanent water on the plains during the dry season; and **impalas** (the most abundant antelope), **topis**, **plains zebras** and **oribis** graze farther from water. **Lions** and **side-striped jackals** – the park's only jackal – are commonly seen stalking at the edges of these plains (**spotted hyenas** are primarily nocturnal); jackals and hyenas also loiter near the Hôtel Akagera at night for scraps. Smaller plains animals include **warthogs**, and **white-tailed** and **marsh mongooses**; **vultures**, **bateleurs** and other **raptors**; and, especially after fires, **lilac-breasted rollers**.

Prizes of the swamps

Hippos can be expected virtually anywhere along the all-weather track that skirts the vast network of lakes, swamps and channels on the park's eastern edge; not surprisingly, Plage aux Hippos is a good spot to look. Several **lion** prides hunt Akagera's large population of **sitatungas** through the marshes between Lakes Kivumba, Hago and Mihindi; the sitatungas themselves are most active shortly after sunrise, particularly on the floating meadows adjacent to Lake Rwanyakizinga.

Crocodiles can also be seen at Plage aux Hippos, and basking at Lake Mihindi (where they breed) and Lake Kivumba. **Elephants** are rarely seen, but frequent the Rurama peninsula on Lake Ihema, and the Nyampiki peninsula between Lakes Hago and Kivumba. **African clawless otters** are sometimes seen during the day in sheltered bays, but the park's other species,

Akagera – quelle tragedie!

Tourism in reserves was once Rwanda's third-largest foreign exchange earner; Akagera protected nearly 10% of the country and was among the best reserves in Africa. But in the aftermath of the recent war, illegal farms and settlements have proliferated within park boundaries and, in response to demands from pastoralists and farmers, the park was recently downsized by 70%. The formerly grand herds have been severely depleted by hunting: of all species recently surveyed only plains zebras have maintained their numbers; others have declined by as much as 75% and some, such as giraffes, black rhinos and elephants are now rarely seen. Poaching is further whittling away the herds and common duikers are now probably extinct. As Rwanda picks up the pieces it remains to be seen how effectively the 'new' park is managed and whether tourism can again provide an incentive for local people to protect what remains of this wilderness.

the **African spot-necked otter**, is mostly nocturnal. The **shoebill**, the prize bird of the swamps, is best sought along the channels connecting Lakes Mihindi, Hago and Gishanju, or Hago and Ngerenke.

Abundant and diverse waterbirds

The many kilometres of waterside habitat support **African fish eagles**, and **malachite** and **pied kingfishers** (all abundant); an assortment of **herons, ibises, storks** and **egrets**; **crakes** and **rails** skulking in the forests of reeds; and, in open water, **cormorants, darters** and **pelicans**. Seasonal visitors include large flocks of **white-faced whistling ducks** between December and February; **carmine bee-eaters** from April to September; and **white-winged terns** passing through on migration (November to December and March to April). Lakes Ihema and Mihindi are the places to look for papyrus endemics, such as the striking **papyrus gonolek**, vocal **white-winged warbler**, and **Carruthers'** and **winding cisticolas**. **Water thick-knees** and **Gabon nightjars** nest on ground trampled by **hippos**, while **spur-winged geese** and **spur-winged plovers** live on the grassy edges. Colonies of **darters** and **cormorants** breeding on islands in Lakes Ihema and Mihindi are joined by nesting **herons, egrets** and occasionally **yellow-billed** or **African open-billed storks**.

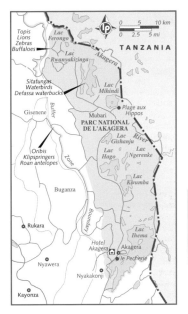

Life on the high grasslands

The high, grassy plateaus of the Mubari are grazed year-round by **oribis** and small numbers of **bohor reedbucks** during the wet seasons (especially at Mutumba). At the end of the rainy seasons (December and April to May) **buffaloes** may be seen among the sausage trees on Mutumba, and herds of **topis** and **plains zebras** gather on the plateaus; **defassa waterbucks, lions** and **side-striped jackals** also ascend the slopes of Mutumba; and small herds of **common elands** graze the plateaus of Mutumba, Mucucu and Kitabiri. This is the best part to look for the **roan antelope**, especially near its former stronghold in the Kinteko region. **Klipspringers** abound on Rurama and also on the slope leading to Lake Ihema from Hôtel Akagera. The mountain savannas are rich in grassland birds: **striped pipits** on large rocky outcrops; **ring-necked** (Kiyonza Ridge, especially after fires) and **Shelley's francolins** (Rurama); and **Souza's shrike** (Rurama and Kitabiri).

    Vervet monkeys and **olive baboons** are the only large mammals commonly seen in the woodlands growing near Lake Kivumba, although parties of **banded** and **dwarf mongooses** might be seen bounding off the track as your vehicle approaches. **Leopards** also are quite common, but like the smaller predators – **servals, genets** and **African civets** – are most likely to be seen by spotlighting. These woodlands are particularly good for birds: **red-faced, crested, black-collared** and **double-toothed barbets**; small flocks of **white-crested helmet-shrikes**; and dry season visitors including **African** and **Eurasian golden orioles, Madagascar lesser cuckoos** and **grey-headed kingfishers**. ∎

Location 75km east of Kigali.
Facilities Boat hire at le Pêcherie.
Accommodation Camping grounds and Hôtel Akagera in park.
Wildlife rhythms Grazers seek high ground during wet seasons (October to November and March to early May), moving to valleys in driest times (January to February and late May to September). Crocs nest June to July.
Contact Office Rwandais du Tourisme et des Parcs Nationaux (ORTPN) (☎/fax 070-76514), BP 905, Kigali.

Watching tips
African finfoots frequent the waters of Lake Ihema, especially where overhanging branches of ambatch trees trail in the water.

PARC NATIONAL DE **KAHUZI-BIÉGA**

Habituated lowland gorillas

Wildlife highlights
Lowland gorillas are the main attraction in the eastern sector. The western sector protects a little-explored slab of rainforest, with between 4500 and 11,000 lowland gorillas plus chimpanzees, colobus and other monkeys, elephants, and Zaïre River basin endemics such as owl-faced monkeys, giant genets and aquatic genets. Sensational forest birding; some birds (such as the African green broadbill and Congo peafowl) have affinities with South-East Asian families.

THE eastern sector of this park is a mosaic of forest, bamboo and *Hagenia* woodland – excellent habitat for some 250 **eastern lowland gorillas** that live on the slopes and saddles of Mts Kahuzi and Biéga. Four of about 25 groups have been habituated to visitors and a few solitary males also roam the forests. Tracking a group can take up to four hours (although about two hours is normal) and gorillas are usually located between 2100 and 2400m (but are sometimes found lower or as high as 2500m) – they congregate to feed on bamboo shoots from September to November. The rarely seen **owl-faced monkey** inhabits bamboo stands on Mt Kahuzi.

The western extension's rich biodiversity would amply repay the rough conditions of a visit. **Lowland gorillas** also live here, although none are habituated, and other primates include **chimpanzees** (rarely seen), **black-and-white** and **Central African red colobus**, and **blue**, **de Brazza's** and **l'Hoest's monkeys**. Large mammals include **forest elephants** (generally associated with swampy clearings), **giant forest hogs**, **bushbucks** and various **duikers**. **Thomas' tree squirrel** favours secondary growth near waterways, and **Alexander's bush squirrel** is usually seen hunting over the thick limbs of large trees. Spotlighting may yield **galagos**; and the localised **giant servaline** and **aquatic genets**, or **Rwenzori otter shrews** could be found along rivers.

A taste of birding in the Zaïre River basin could be attempted along the main road and where secondary growth abuts the forest between Miti and Kisangani. This is cutting-edge stuff (there's no field guide), but the rewards might include the endemic **Rockefeller's sunbird**, **Congo peafowl** or nocturnal rarities such as **Congo bay-owl**, **Albertine owlet** and **Rwenzori nightjar**. The area is rich in **barbets**, **hornbills**, **kingfishers** and a host of **flycatchers** and **warblers**. Forest birds common to the Albertine Rift Valley include **handsome francolins**, **dusky crimsonwings**, **stripe-breasted tits** and **red-chested sunbirds**. ∎

Location 25km north-west of Bukavu (Station Tshivanga).
Facilities Eastern sector has trails to facilitate gorilla tracking and a walking track ascends Mt Kahuzi.
Accommodation Camping ground at Station Tshivanga.
Wildlife rhythms Gorillas and chimpanzees share diet and range during dry seasons; gorillas are probably folivorous and chimps eat more insects during major rains (March to June).
Contact Institut Congolais pour la Conservation de la Nature (ICCN), 185 Avenue du Président Mobutu, Bukavu.

Watching tips
The highly localised African green broadbill has been recorded on Mt Kahuzi.

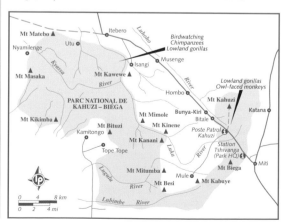

RÉSERVE FORESTIÈRE DE **NYUNGWE**

An outstanding island of biodiversity

THE region's single most important area of biodiversity and rated the highest priority for forest conservation in Africa. Half a dozen **elephants** remain, and can sometimes be seen on a guided walk to Kamiranzovu Marsh, where **marsh mongooses** and **Congo clawless otters** also live. **Giant forest hogs, bushpigs** and **duikers** are sometimes startled along the reserve's many trails, and commonly seen rainforest squirrels include **giant forest, montane sun** and **Boehm's bush squirrels. Tree hyraxes** are easily heard after dark throughout the forest; and spotlighting on a slow drive along the paved road between Butare and Cyangugu offers a chance of seeing mammals such as **side-striped jackals, civets** and **African palm civets**, and **large-spotted** or **servaline genets**.

Monkey forest

Habituated troops of monkeys – **Angolan colobus** (troops of which number up to 400), **Dent's monkey** (a local race of blue monkey) and **grey-cheeked mangabeys** (the last two often seen together) – are virtually guaranteed on guided walks from Uwinka Tourism Center. Other monkey possibilities include **l'Hoest's** (along the paved road) and **diademed monkeys**, which sometimes associate with colobus and blue monkeys. **Olive baboons** and **vervet monkeys** loiter near Nyungwe's eastern edge; and **chimpanzee** habituation is under way (you'll almost certainly hear chimps). **Golden** and **owl-faced monkeys** live in the extensive bamboo stands in the south-eastern part of the reserve, and **eastern needle-clawed** (near Uwinka) and **greater galagos** (along the Bweyeye road) are nocturnal prosimian attractions.

The dirt road leading to Rangiro (particularly on the far side of the pine plantation), and the Red, Blue and Kamiranzovu Trails are all highly recommended for birding. The paved road through the park permits viewing at all levels of the forest: expect **mountain buzzards** and **cinnamon-chested bee-eaters** perched along here, plus numerous **sunbirds, wagtails** and flocks of **waxbills. Handsome francolins** are common along the trails, and turacos include **great blue** (Green Trail) and localised **Rwenzori turacos** (Grey Trail). Other large forest specialities are **African crowned eagles**, known to nest near Uwinka, and **crowned** and **black-and-white-casqued hornbills**. Spotlighting is also recommended – **Congo bay-owl** was recently rediscovered at Nyungwe. ■

Wildlife highlights

Habituated troops of Angolan colobus, Dent's monkeys and grey-cheeked mangabeys, plus 500–1000 chimpanzee species among 13 primate species. Other mammals (50 species in total) include three duiker species (on the rebound from poaching), a few elephants, giant forest hogs and bushpigs. Rainforest bird paradise: 275 species, including 24 Albertine Rift Valley endemics, four turacos, 13 sunbirds and assorted rarities.

Location 210km south-west of Kigale. 90km west of Butare.
Facilities 50km of trails.
Accommodation Camping grounds at Uwinka, along Red Trail and at Karamba. Lodging at PCFN HQ (Gisakura).
Wildlife rhythms Most birds and mammals breed in wet season (September to May).
Contacts ORTPN (☎ 070-76514), BP 905, Kigali. Nyungwe Forest Conservation Project (PCFN), BP 1699, Kigale or BP 363, Cyangugu.
Ecotours PCFN guided primate walks (8 and 11 am, and 2 pm daily).

Watching tips

Grauer's and short-tailed warblers are sometimes seen in undergrowth along the Red Trail between the Green Trail turn-off and the first waterfall.

PARC NATIONAL DES **VIRUNGA**

Great apes and active volcanoes

Wildlife highlights
Diverse habitats supporting mountain gorillas and chimpanzees in the south. Savanna wildlife includes elephants, hippos, buffaloes, Uganda kobs, defassa waterbucks, topis and lions – plus hippos and waterbirds at Rwindi. An isolated population of mountain gorillas and other primates at Mt Tshiaberimu. Primates, alpine vegetation and birdlife on the high peaks of the Rwenzoris; and okapis, giant forest hogs, bongos and excellent bird-watching in rainforests of the Ishango sector.

Location (All distances from Goma): Kibati 13km (for Nyiragongo); Kakomero 39km (for Nyamulgira); Bukima 60km; Djomba 95km; Tongo 65km; Rwindi 125km.
Wildlife rhythms Gorillas move freely over the borders of Uganda and Rwanda though contiguous habitat.
Contact Institut Congolais pour la Conservation de la Nature (ICCN), Parc National des Virunga, BP 315, Goma.
Ecotours Make inquiries through reputable tour operators before venturing into the DRC.

Watching tips
A small population of owl-faced monkeys inhabits Mt Tshiaberimu, where Kivu ground thrushes are among the bird attractions.

SIGNS of **giant forest hogs**, **elephants** and **buffaloes** may be seen while tracking **mountain gorillas** on the slopes of the Virunga volcanoes; birdlife at this altitude includes **white-naped ravens**, **Rwenzori turacos**, and **regal** and **scarlet-tufted malachite sunbirds**. Encounters with **black-and-white colobus**, **red-tailed monkeys** and **olive baboons** are possible while tracking **chimpanzees** in forest growing in an ancient lava flow near Tongo. Giant groundsels and lobelias grow near the summit of an active volcano, Mt Nyiragongo; and look for signs of **chimps**, **elephants**, **buffaloes** and **bushbucks** while trekking on another, Mt Nyamulgira.

Savanna plains of the Rwindi sector feature **warthogs**, **Uganda kobs** and **topis** (which attract **lions**), and smaller herds of **bohor reedbucks** and **defassa waterbucks**. Concentrations of **hippos** can be seen from the track along the Rutshuru River; adjoining bush supports **waterbucks**, **bushbucks**, **buffaloes** and **giant forest hogs**. **Elephants** congregate along the Ishasha River and a track along the Rwindi River is also good for **hippos**. **Sitatungas** inhabit the shores of Lake Albert, where **waterbirds** include both species of **pelican**, **shoebills** and abundant **marabou storks**. About 14 (unhabituated) **mountain gorillas** survive between 2800 and 2900m on the slopes of Mt Tshiaberimu; the surrounding forest also supports **blue monkeys**, **black-fronted duikers** and **African civets**.

Rainforest adjoining the Semliki River in the Ishango sector supports hundreds of bird species and a rich primate fauna. The rarely seen **okapi** shares these rainforests with **giant forest hogs**, **bongos** and the small, red **'forest' buffalo**, and this is the only sector of PN des Virunga with **Nile crocodiles**.

Trekking the Butawu Route of the Rwenzori Mountains should yield **black-and-white colobus**, **blue monkeys** and **Rwenzori turacos** on forested slopes; **black-fronted duikers** and **Stuhlmann's double-collared sunbirds** above 2500m; and **swifts**, **mountain buzzards** and **lammergeiers** on the peaks. Stands of giant herbs are particularly impressive in the Rwenzoris. **Leopards** have been seen as high as 4200m, where they feed on the abundant **rock hyraxes**. ∎

PARC NATIONAL DES **VOLCANS**

Gorillas not to be missed

AN estimated 110 **mountain gorillas** inhabit PN des Volcans in groups numbering three to 20 individuals – some groups periodically straying into adjoining Uganda and the Democratic Republic of the Congo (DRC). The first half hour of tracking normally involves a steep climb and fording mountain streams, during which **bushbucks** and **black-fronted duikers** (the most common herbivores) are sometimes startled in the undergrowth. **Buffaloes, bushpigs, giant forest hogs** and **yellow-backed duikers** are encountered only rarely and large predators almost never – leopards have not been seen since 1979, although **African golden cats** and **spotted hyenas** probably still hang on in small numbers.

Mt Gahinga is almost entirely covered with dense thickets of bamboo – habitat favoured by **gorillas** and **golden monkeys**. **Elephants** climb as high as Mt Visoke's swampy crater to feast on bamboo shoots, and **duikers** are also sighted there periodically. Look for **antelopes** – and sometimes **elephants** and **buffaloes** – taking an early drink at Lake Ndezi or in Mt Muside's crater lake. Large stands of *Hagenia* form a parkland with a rich undergrowth on the Mt Visoke saddle area – prime **gorilla** habitat. Hollows in the massive, moss-clad trunks shelter **tree hyraxes, genets, African common dormice, giant forest squirrels** and **forest pouched rats** – by camping overnight and spotlighting you'll have a better chance of seeing some. The park's bird attractions include the localised, canopy-dwelling **Rwenzori turaco; handsome francolins** foraging for seeds along trails; and **Chubb's cisticolas** duetting in undergrowth. The richest bird zone is the *Hagenia* forest, in which may be seen **greater double-collared** and **regal sunbirds**, and three brilliant **waxbills: dusky** and **Shelley's crimsonwings**, and **black-headed waxbills**. Birds of prey include typical forest bird-hunters such as **rufous-breasted sparrowhawks** and, in more open country, **mountain buzzards**. Birdlife drops off at higher altitudes, although stands of giant alpine herbs (especially on Mts Karisimbi and Visoke) are notable for **scarlet-tufted malachite sunbirds**. **Maccoa** and **African black ducks** feed in crater lakes, and **buff-spotted fluff-tails** skulk in the surrounding marshes. ■

Wildlife highlights

Mountain gorillas, the number one attraction, share montane forest with golden monkeys (a subspecies of the widespread blue monkey); black-fronted duikers and bushbucks are slowly recovering from poaching, and there are a few buffaloes and elephants. Other large mammals include bushpigs, giant forest hogs and tree hyraxes. Birds number about 100 species, including the localised Rwenzori turaco, handsome francolins and scarlet-tufted malachite sunbirds.

Location 15km north-west of Ruhengeri.
Facilities Walking trails ascend the peaks.
Accommodation Camping grounds at NP HQ and throughout the park. Hotel at Ruhengeri.
Wildlife rhythms Birds and large mammals move off the high peaks during the wet season, when freezing temperatures and hail are prevalent.
Contact Office Rwandais du Tourisme et des Parcs Nationaux (ORTPN) (☎/fax 070-76514), BP 905, Kigali.
Ecotours Guides and guards must be arranged at Kinigi.

Watching tips

Gorillas frequent the giant lobelia zone on Mt Visoke's high slopes during drier months, when the high mountain vegetation retains moisture from night mists.

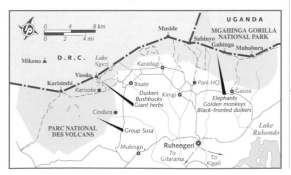

WILDLIFE GALLERY

*Recognising, understanding and
finding East Africa's key wildlife*

EAST AFRICAN MAMMALS

EAST Africa's mammals come in an incredible assortment of sizes, shapes, colours and patterns. Those that range widely through the world's oceans, such as whales and dolphins, and the night-flying insect-eating bats are well represented, but East Africa is most famous for its land mammals, including the world's heaviest (African elephant), tallest (giraffe) and swiftest (cheetah). Apart from boasting the greatest concentration of large land mammals on earth (the Serengeti migration), East Africa has one of the highest mammal diversities in Africa – some 400 of the continent's 1150 or so mammal species have been recorded here. Many groups, eg, the herbivores, have evolved into an extraordinary variety and concentration that support the region's healthy populations of carnivores – especially the big cats.

A land of milk and honey badgers

All animals classified as mammals, including ourselves, are united by several common features. From elephants to elephant shrews, all mammals are warm-blooded, ie, they regulate body temperature through internal mechanisms, rather than relying on the sun's rays – as reptiles do. Birds are the only other warm-blooded vertebrates, but only mammals have hair or fur; and whereas all birds lay eggs, all African mammals give birth to live young that have developed (gestated) for some weeks or months in the female's placenta or womb. And female mammals produce rich milk, dispensed through teats (modified sweat glands called mammae – hence the name 'mammals'), for the prolonged care of offspring until they become independent. Parental care is a trait most developed in mammals (and reaches its greatest extent in humans), but is such a labour-intensive process that only small numbers of offspring can be cared for at a time.

The arms, teeth and claws race

For a few species at the top of the food chain (like lions and leopards) and some vegetarian giants (such as elephants and giraffes), adult life can be comparatively relaxed. But every mammal at some stage in its life is vulnerable to predation, and consequently most have at least two acute senses to warn of threatening danger: hearing – its corollary being the development of complex vocalisations; and smell, which is usually developed so far beyond our own abilities that we can only guess at the wealth of information it communicates. Many mammals, particularly predators, also have acute eyesight – and others make up for any visual deficiency with strategies like having a tanklike physique (such as rhinos) or escaping underground (like naked mole-rats). Weapons of attack include some fine sets of teeth and claws, deadly speed and stealth; but despite the sometimes amazing weaponry carried by antelopes, their horns are generally used in the perpetual struggles among males for dominance.

Introducing the key players

All mammals exhibit basic behaviours, such as eating, drinking (in most cases) and resting, which take up much time but once fulfilled give way to a new agenda of courtship and mating. More subtle behaviours include play, territorial marking and displacement; and life-or-death encounters involving defence, bluff and attack. Such interactions are highlights of mammal-watching and there is no better place to begin than East Africa. A high percentage of mammals are easy to see (if you follow a few basic guidelines – see the Wildlife-Watching chapter), because they are at least partially active during the day. The following pages introduce the key players of the East African wildlife experience, how they interact and why – with as little jargon as possible (for a list of comprehensive field guides refer to our Resource Guide). ∎

*The **Zanzibar** (or **Kirk's**) **red colobus** is restricted to southern and eastern Zanzibar.*

*The **Angolan colobus** has a fragmented distribution from the Zaire River basin to coastal Kenya.*

***Yellow baboons** lack the olive baboon's thick mane and have white or off-white underparts.*

*The long-limbed **patas monkey** is an uncommon inhabitant of Serengeti grasslands.*

PRIMATES

Evolutionary cauldron

East Africa is a hotspot for primate diversity, an evolutionary cauldron from which forest monkeys spread out onto the plains, and from which the great apes and we humans developed. From an ancestral squirrel-like animal, evolutionary pressures modified a basic tree-climbing body pattern – long back, short neck and five-fingered hands and feet for clinging to trunks, branches and food (traits which can still be seen in unrelated animals such as possums) – into today's diverse primate forms. Represented in East Africa are the 'primitive' bushbabies and galagos; gorilla and chimpanzee; and two species of baboon and 17 species of monkey (primate taxonomy is complex and opinions vary on these figures, eg, some researchers regard yellow and olive baboons (inset) as subspecies of the widespread savanna baboon).

The basic monkey form (common examples among many are red-tailed and blue monkeys) speaks volumes on agility in a three-dimensional habitat: slender limbs make virtually any branch or foodstuff accessible and a long tail provides balance when jumping across gaps in the canopy. But there are also many variations of this body plan, including the arboreal colobus monkeys, which have only a rudimentary thumb; others with even longer limbs that spend much time on the ground, such as patas and vervet monkeys; and the baboons, with long, rather doglike snouts. All primates can sit and stand, and many can walk; all have furless digits, palms and soles; and, apart from bushbabies and the nocturnal owl-faced monkey, all primates are diurnal and mainly vegetarian, although insects and other small animals are eaten to varying degrees.

For primates, sight is the best-developed sense and smell the least. All species have bifocal vision and expressive faces; many, such as de Brazza's monkey, have bold facial markings that visually reinforce communication. Touch is also highly developed, an opposable thumb in most species enabling them to grip a wide variety of food morsels and groom each other (something primates do a lot of). Grooming is an important part of social

Political animals

Status is big among chimps; males constantly vie to dominate a clan for the benefits it confers. For example, being the 'alpha'

male means you get to monopolise the sex scene, scoring most of the matings (a challenge since females are promiscuous). But other male chimps may gang up and try to oust the alpha male, so he relies on a network of buddies for help and rewards them with, for example, a share of the meat taken on hunts. Squabbling among lesser ranks goes on all the time and all males must maintain allegiances and friendships throughout their lives. When two adults fight, a third party may bring the rivals together for a reconciliation, which inevitably involves mutual grooming. But (a very human twist this) they also use deception to lure a rival to a reconciliation, then punish him for past transgressions.

Rainforest-dwelling *l'Hoest's monkeys* may travel in single file on the ground between trees.

Striking *de Brazza's monkeys* shelter in and seldom stray far from waterside forests.

interaction and individuals vie for the privilege of grooming their superiors. A colobus that desires grooming stretches out in front of another, even slapping its face if the expected attention is not forthcoming; and should one desire to groom a recalcitrant, it grabs it by the forelock and smacks its head until it cooperates!

The ancestral mirror

Just as squirrels offer clues to the physical origins of primates, primate behaviour (and misbehaviour) shows unequivocally the origins of our own behaviour. All diurnal primates are highly sociable, forming troops (monkeys) or communities (chimps) where both sexes vie for dominance in hierarchies of usually shifting alliances. Social structure varies among species, but usually involves a stable core of females whose female offspring stay in the group for life; males leave to join other groups as they mature. Nearly all species forage, sleep and range together, and fundamental to primate societies is the intense care lavished on infants. Playing as a youngster with other infants and juveniles (young chimps play tag and run round in circles till they're dizzy) builds lifelong friendships and social bonds, and reinforces hierarchies. Jealousies and rivalries inevitably develop, but then there are sometimes elaborate rituals of appeasement: chimps offer a palm as supplication ('gimme five, man!') and bow to superiors; and dominants put a hand on the head of a lower-ranked member as reassurance. ■

The *blue monkey* is widely distributed in many types of primary and secondary growth.

Troops of *red-tailed monkeys* often associate with blue monkeys in rainforests.

Hotspots

Kibale Forest NP An extraordinary concentration of primates (13 species – including chimpanzee) in pristine rainforest. **RF de Nyungwe** Another centre of high diversity, including huge troops of colobus. **Kakamega Forest NR** Kenya's monkey hotspot – a relict of West African rainforests.

GREATER GALAGO

Successful 'ancestor' of primates

Galagos (or bushbabies) are 'primitive' tree-dwelling primates (called prosimians) which closely resemble 60 million-year-old fossils, but barely resemble today's more familiar monkeys and apes (prosimians are only 'primitive' in the sense that they evolved before modern primates). The 14 or so species found in East Africa range in size from squirrel galagos that could sit comfortably in a cupped hand to the largest – the cat-sized greater galago (sometimes referred to as the large-eared or thick-tailed greater galago – both are apt descriptions).

All galagos are exclusively nocturnal, waking up at dusk and emerging from their nest after dark. They can see and accurately judge distances in what to humans is almost total blackness: smaller species have enormous eyes and can leap up to 7m propelled by long, powerful back legs. Greater galagos have comparatively small eyes and typically walk along branches like a monkey, only jumping to avoid danger or to cross from tree to tree. On the ground, where they are more vulnerable to leopards, greater galagos hop on their hind legs or walk on all fours, tail held erect like a cat's.

Galagos are widespread and can live in high densities in suitable habitat. The territories of dominant males contain the home ranges of several females and their offspring. A combination of their loud, distinctive calls (some of the larger galagos' calls resemble a baby crying – hence the name 'bushbaby') and complicated scent-marking of treetop pathways helps individuals to avoid confrontation and direct competition for food. Galagos and bushbabies are readily seen by spotlighting (two or more species may coexist in some areas); most calling occurs in the first hour of night – a good time to look for them.

Galagos' slender digits cannot be moved independently – a feature which compromises grooming ability, so several lower teeth and the second toe of each hind foot are adapted for combing their woolly hair. ∎

Recognition Vaguely catlike with large, leathery ears and a bushy tail. Upperparts variable: silvery grey to brown; melanistic (black) forms occur. Belly fur paler.
Habitat Dense vegetation in woodlands, forests, savanna and cultivation, from sea level to 1800m.
Behaviour Exclusively nocturnal; can rotate head through 180-degrees when searching for prey; visits feeding stations at safari lodges. Rarely drinks. Very vocal during breeding season.
Breeding A single young born in a leafy nest or hollow (births peak in September) is weaned at three months.
Feeding Eats mainly fruit (especially figs), nectar, seeds, flowers and acacia sap; also insects and larvae, snails and occasionally eggs, nestlings and small reptiles.
Voice Very vocal. Most common contact call is a babylike crying, repeated up to 100 times per hour.
Swahili Komba mkubwa

Hotspots
Masai Mara NR, Ngorongoro CA, Kibale Forest NP

VERVET MONKEY

Agile social climbers

If any species epitomises East African monkeys it is the wide-spread, active and agile vervet. Equally at home in trees and on the ground, troops are commonly encountered foraging, playing and resting where grassland meets the trees, and can become pests at camping grounds and lodges. The savanna edge provides both rich pickings and shelter, but is shared with competing blue monkeys and baboons. Foraging some distance into the grassland, vervet troops move slowly, investigating holes and turning over dung and small rocks for insects, standing up straight or jumping above tall grass to get their bearings and ducking back to the trees should danger threaten. Crossings between trees are made in single file with little straying – this is when they are most vulnerable.

A troop is mainly comprised of females and young that defend an ancestral home range, assisted by males that compete among themselves for mating rights and dominance. Female rank is inherited and rigorously enforced – those of lower status showing obsequiousness to even juveniles of the dominant ranks (and risking chastisement if they don't). Ruling families get precedence at food, while subordinates vie to groom their social superiors and handle their infants, and to enlist their support in squabbles.

Males develop a startling blue or turquoise scrotum and scarlet penis as they mature – appendages which dominant individuals display prominently to neighbouring troops (behaviour that isn't tolerated from subordinates). Eventually young males are forced to transfer to other troops, usually during the mating season – a dangerous process that leaves them vulnerable to predation, and rejection or even fatal aggression from the new troop. But the urge to migrate is compelling, and to ameliorate the danger brothers often transfer to other troops as a group, or join a troop to which an older brother already belongs. ∎

Recognition Small, slender monkey with long tail, grizzled greenish fur, black face and hands, and bluish belly skin that shows through whitish belly fur.
Habitat A variety of wood-lands and adjoining savanna, including miombo and yellow acacias along rivers.
Behaviour Variable daily routines. Troop size averages 11–25. Babies are born black and suckle both mother's teats simultaneously. All ages expressive – 60 visual gestures have been identified.
Breeding Timing varies. A single infant is born after 165 days and clings to mother for four months.
Feeding Mainly vegetarian, especially seeds, gum, leaves and flowers of acacias, and figs and other fruits; grass and insects are eaten mainly during rains.
Voice Complex – 36 distinct sounds have been identified, including alarm calls that identify different predators.
Swahili Tumbili

Hotspots
Samburu NR, Amboseli NP, Tarangire NP, Queen Elizabeth NP

OLIVE BABOON

Savanna pioneers among monkeys

Intelligent and opportunistic, baboons appear to be expanding their range in the face of human settlement. Large troops of up to 150 olive baboons fan out to forage across the savanna, some walking on all fours, others sitting upright when they find a morsel. Infants peep out from their mothers' breast fur, juveniles play, and adults feed and watch for danger – large males standing out by their 'cape' of dense fur. A full-grown male olive baboon is a formidable animal that bares 5cm-long canine teeth in threat displays and defence; groups of males can kill a leopard and their presence in troops enables baboons to forage in lion country. The approach of a predator usually sends baboons scurrying into the trees, from where they may shower it (or a person) with liquid excrement.

Baboon social lives are subtle and complex, but fun to watch: they stare into space or avert their gaze when being submissive; shrug their shoulders when startled; and females signal their readiness to mate by presenting hindquarters, showing their eyelids and smacking their lips. Females and young form the core of a group, and stay in it for life unless the troop subdivides. Female rank is family based, inherited and strict, and juveniles from high-ranking families can threaten adults from lower ranks. Long-term alliances develop between females as they grow; and each adult female has close ties with two or three males, with whom she forages and sleeps, normally mating with the most dominant. Males that associate with females become godfathers to their infants, and will protect juveniles and mothers from bullying by other troop members. Sexually mature subadult males transfer to other troops or form loose associations ('cabals') – despite her consorts, females in oestrus tends also to be receptive to dominant male 'strangers'. All members of a troop find the black infants irresistible: females vie to handle them and males hold them out to appease attacks from bullies. ■

Recognition Large greenish monkey with shortish, broken-looking tail and bare, doglike muzzle. Mature males have a thick, erectile mane and grey cheeks.
Habitat Widespread in woodland, savanna, forest and cultivated land; has become an agricultural pest in some areas.
Behaviour The most terrestrial monkey. Diurnal with erratic daily patterns; sleeps in trees, rising late and retiring early, and foraging, resting or grooming at any time. Adult males band together to defend the troop.
Breeding Year-round after 6-month gestation. Soft black fur of newborn changes to adult colour at 6 months.
Feeding Omnivorous; mainly grass and fruit, but also seeds and animals as large as fawns; digs for roots, shellfish and crocodile eggs.
Voice A wide range of grunts and barks, becoming louder and more strident when threatened.
Swahili Nyani

Hotspots
Nairobi NP, Kibale Forest NP

BLACK-AND-WHITE COLOBUS ✓

Treetop 'matadors'

Although they are common in montane forests, the first time you see a black-and-white colobus (also called a guereza or mantled colobus) will probably be when it leaps headfirst from one tree to another – tail and long hair flowing behind and front legs extended to break the fall – before catapulting off another branch and disappearing into the foliage. Bold, pied markings stand out from a distance among the greenery and, in the early morning, troops of colobus sun themselves high up in a favourite tree where they can be seen by neighbouring groups. Flaunting tails and cape-like frills, and occasionally shaking branches, demonstrates each troop's size and prowess; the dominant male in each periodically lets loose a chorus of raucous roars that echoes around the valleys as far as 2km away. It seems an excessive performance for a vegetarian primate, but the male has good reason to show his strength: bachelor troops are watching and waiting for an opportunity to displace him and take over his harem.

Recognition Entirely black with long, white frills on flanks, and white or white-tipped tail. White brow and 'beard' surrounds naked black face.

Habitat Common and widespread in forests, from lowland rainforest and dry riverine forest to montane forest.

Consummate vegetarians

Black-and-white colobus can be seen in virtually any habitat with trees, typically sitting hunched up stripping leaves off twigs. Close-to their rather sad faces are topped by a 'matador's hat', and when their long tail hangs down the tufts look remarkably like beard moss that sways in the swirling mists of montane forests. The secret to the success of this very wide-ranging monkey is a complex digestive process that can break down old, hard and fibrous leaves; colobus may consume up to a third of their body weight daily, but must rest long periods for digestion (during which bacterial fermentation, similar to that in ruminants, breaks down cellulose and detoxifies leaves and seeds). These consummate vegetarians don't visit the ground very often, taking water from hollows on branches, but when they do they climb down trunks headfirst. The various species of red colobus are also leaf eaters, and where black-and-white and red colobus coexist each eats different parts of the same plants. ∎

Behaviour Sociable in small territories. Family groups of 6–10. Only dominant male displays and mates, although the oldest female mostly leads the troop. Infants are born white, turning dark at 3–4 months.

Breeding A single infant born during rains after a 6-month gestation becomes independent at 10 months.

Feeding Strictly vegetarian, eating a very wide variety of leaves, including old and fibrous ones, but also unripe fruit and seeds.

Voice Males roar loudly as a territorial proclamation, especially at dawn and dusk.

Swahili Mbega mweupe or Kuluzu

Hotspots
Lake Naivasha (El-samere), **Kibale Forest NP** (also Central African red colobus), **FR de Nyungwe**

GORILLA

Lord of all he surveys

Largest of the great apes, the gorilla sits comfortably on an evolutionary limb onto which it climbed just before its ancestors evolved into chimpanzees and humans. Thus, although our kinship with these gentle animals is unquestioned (gorillas are prone to colds, arthritis and heart disease, among other human ailments), they actually show more differences than similarities. These are the lifestyle apes, to whom comfort is all-important: gorillas spend more time on the ground than other apes; they are the only apes that have never been seen using tools; and they are almost exclusively vegetarian. Each family group is dominated by a large silverback: he decides when it's time to move and eats the choicest morsels, regardless of who found them (only youngsters are agile enough to climb and feed out of his reach). But when threatened this normally gentle giant will defend his impish offspring with his life. Intruders are met with roars, chest-beating, thrashing vegetation and terrifying charges which are usually enough to send any other animal packing. Of course they aren't to know that it's mainly bluff and the correct response is to do nothing – to flee would almost certainly incite his violence (and quite right, too, according to one African tradition – only a coward would run away).

Much gorilla time is spent eating and resting – males develop a massive paunch from the sheer bulk of vegetation consumed – and you'll probably encounter a group lounging about together in the undergrowth, dozing or basking during sunny spells. A silverback is very indulgent with his offspring, allowing them to crawl all over his huge bulk, and can become quietly tolerant of humans – which is why you are able to get into their formerly inaccessible habitat and enjoy one of the world's great wildlife experiences. Guides soothe the troop by imitating gorilla noises, but much harder to replicate are the loud farts which gorillas frequently vent, sometimes in answering volleys like puerile teenagers. ■

Recognition A huge ape completely covered in thick black hair except for face, chest, soles and palms; mature males have a 'silver' back. Silverbacks weigh 160kg or more.

Habitat Regenerating secondary forest, valley floors, rainforest clearings and edges, and adjoining cultivation up to 3400m.

Behaviour Lives in non-territorial harems averaging 10 members; builds nests on ground or trees at night and for siestas; older offspring are driven out, females frequently change groups or gravitate to solitary silverbacks to form new harems.

Breeding Single infant born after 8½-month gestation is nursed until 1½–2 years old.

Feeding Vegetarian; mostly leaves, shoots and stems of *Galium* vine, wild celery and thistle; also flowers, fruits, bark, bamboo shoots and occasional insects.

Voice Loud, 90% by silverback; most commonly deep hoots followed by chest beating; also screams and barks.

Hotspots
Bwindi Impenetrable NP, Mountain Gorilla NP, PN des Volcans

CHIMPANZEE

'Brother, can you spare a gene?'

Young chimps laugh, turn somersaults, tickle each other, play tag and cry real tears. Juveniles play with infants and with small monkeys – ironically, because adults mount organised hunts for red colobus and other species. The terrified victims are ripped apart and eaten; subordinate males beg with hands out and females grant sexual favours for a share of the prized meat. Monkey-hunts are everywhere among chimp communities, but food traditions and the use of tools vary greatly from area to area: famous examples include using rocks to break open nutshells and stems to extract termites from holes. Other behaviour that varies between chimp 'cultures' includes grooming leaves to get attention; using moss to soak up drinking water; using a leaf as a napkin; making cushions to sit on; and eating medicinal plants when feeling poorly. Chimps drum on tree buttresses to advertise a food source, sit and gaze at waterfalls, and break into frenzied drumming and hooting during rainstorms. But it's not all play: a baboon seen threatening a chimp with its impressive canine teeth at a food source got a quick smash in the guts for its pains, followed by an uppercut to the jaw as it doubled over. Not surprising, then, that geneticists have discovered we share 98% to 99% of our genes with chimps. Not convinced? 'Rain dances' aside, a captive group was witnessed shuffling around in a circle stamping out a rhythm. OK, it could have been one of those spontaneous rave things – but the discovery in 1974 that chimps systematically murder individuals and even whole communities in neighbouring territories sent shock waves through the scientific world. Parties on these 'lethal raids' jump and kill lone males, and drag females back to their community.

Most of the aforementioned has been revealed after decades of research at Tanzania's Gombe Stream and Mahale Mountains, and Uganda's Kibale NP. 'Chimp tourism' is still in its infancy, but watching these fascinating apes in the wild is likely to be one of the highlights of any trip to East Africa. ∎

Recognition An agile, muscular ape, blue-black to dark brown, with bare, expressive face and low brow; naked palms, soles and butt region. Adults can have silvered backs.

Habitat Primary or secondary forest, and gallery forest adjoining miombo and savanna in which they forage.

Behaviour Communities of 9-120 forage in territories protected by males that spend their entire lives on ancestral turf in shifting hierarchies; females disperse to other communities; adults weave arboreal nests for sleeping and siestas. Average group size 3-8. Watch for reciprocal grooming sessions after meals.

Breeding Infant born after an 8-month gestation is weaned at five and dependent until 6-8 years.

Feeding Opportunistic omnivores, eating fruit in season (especially figs) plus leaves, bark, insects, eggs and live animals as large as bushpigs and guineafowl.

Voice Can be incredibly noisy; 34 recognisable sounds, the loudest being pant-hoots and excited screams. Best heard in the hour after dawn.

Hotspots
Kibale Forest NP, Queen Elizabeth NP, Budongo FR

DOGS

Golden jackals are the most common of the three jackal species in Ngorongoro Crater.

Side-striped jackals den in abandoned termite mounds, aardvark holes and hillsides.

The black-backed jackal is often seen scavenging around kills, but is also a capable hunter.

Pairs or family groups of bat-eared foxes are best seen at dusk and dawn when they start to hunt.

The sociable predators

The ancestors of domestic dogs are alive and well on the plains of Africa, complete with the unmistakable repertoire of sounds and body language that humans understand instinctively (the golden jackal even barks and yelps like a domestic dog). Built for an active life, their entire body shape suggests hunting on the move (such as long legs that are suited to coursing through open country). Their pointed muzzle is full of sharp, tearing teeth (including splendid canines); and their blunt, nonretractile claws make them fine diggers.

Many dogs are social killers, eg, jackals usually hunt as resourceful pairs that also scavenge from other predators' kills. All dogs have finely developed senses: acute smell that detects food and other dogs (and its corollary, scent glands to mark out territories); keen vision to sight pack members, prey and predators; and exceptional hearing – canids have the most complex calls of all carnivores. The aural sensitivity of nocturnal bat-eared foxes is exceptional: their enormous ears act as twin satellite dishes homing in on the movement of termites up to 30cm beneath the soil.

Most distinctive of the three jackal species, pairs of black-backed (also known as silver-backed) mate for life and stoutly defend a territory marked with scats, urine and howling choruses. Sociability is central to the success of all East African species: all young are born ('whelped') underground in dens and receive intense parental care (inset: side-striped jackal) until weaned – jackal offspring may cohabit with their parents long enough to help rear another brood. As they develop, pups become lively and playful (traits that extend into adulthood); playfulness and appeasement – like showing their white belly as a sign of submission – mitigate the dangers inherent in social contact among killing animals.

But all dogs face competition and hardships: leopards in particular are well known to like dog meat. Defence consists of speed, those fine teeth, and loose, erectile fur on the back and tail that seem to enlarge their profile (body extremities such as ears, tail and back are highlighted with black in many species, which exaggerates a cornered dog's movements and size). ∎

Hotspots

Ngorongoro CA All three jackals coexist where their preferred habitats overlap (golden jackal dominates during the day, black-backed at night). **Queen Elizabeth NP** Side-striped jackal is common on the Ishasha Plain. **Amboseli** and **Serengeti NPs** Bat-eared foxes rest, play and groom from about 4.30 pm onwards.

HUNTING DOG

Team players

Despite their relatively small size compared with their prey (one antelope can be twice the weight of an individual dog), the superb pack-hunting skills of hunting dogs make them one of the most efficient predators on the plains. Unlike lions and leopards, which use their weight to help bring an animal down, hunting dogs rely exclusively on their numbers and ability to wear their victim out. Breasting a rise at full pelt they bowl into antelopes surprised on the other side, scattering the herd while the leader selects the weakest and runs it down, the others following in close order to rip it apart. Almost exclusively diurnal, hunting dogs chase prey by sight, making up for a lack of speed with endurance – coursing game in open country for several kilometres, harassing it with nips until it is exhausted, then knocking it down and swiftly devouring it. As long as it is kept in sight prey seldom escapes: in some studies up to 85% of prey chased was eventually brought down. In thicker habitat, packs may split and pursue several animals.

Sight plays a pivotal role in hunting dog society – each of these sociable dogs is uniquely marked in blotches of tan, black and white, too loud for camouflage, but thought to reinforce their inclusion in a tight, ordered hunting unit. Upon emerging from the den every dog's day begins with an elaborate 'meet' ritual, in which the pack assembles with excited, high-pitched twittering; pups try to coerce adults into regurgitating food, and adults outdo each other in elaborate shows of submission and mobbing (mobbing appears to be an important process of socialisation, reinforcing pack membership).

Karen Blixen, author of *Out of Africa*, reported seeing a pack of hunting dogs numbering 2000 early in the 20th century. Such sights are gone: modern packs can still number between 40 and 60 animals, but 10 is the average in East Africa. The hunting dog's former abundance and diurnal habits led to its prosecution by pastoralists, and canine diseases spread from domestic dogs to decimate wild packs. The end has already come for most packs and the hunting dog is now the rarest large carnivore in East Africa. ∎

Recognition Long-legged dog. Fur ochre, tan, black and white. White tail tuft. Prominent, rounded ears over black muzzle and face.

Habitat Woodland, savanna and grassland with sufficient prey.

Behaviour Most sociable and diurnal canid, with large overlapping home ranges. Packs consist of same sex hierarchies subordinate to a breeding pair; all help rear young by regurgitating meat. Females emigrate at 18 months to 3 years of age.

Breeding Up to 18 pups born during rains; follow the pack after 9 weeks.

Feeding Strictly carnivorous, running down small or medium-sized antelopes; larger and smaller animals are taken opportunistically.

Voice A repetitive, bell-like *hoo* carries over long distance as a contact call.

Swahili Mbwa mwitu

> **Hotspots**
> **Selous GR, Mikumi NP** (easiest to see when pups are in dens)

CATS

African wild cats thrive where rodents are plentiful, such as at the outskirts of settlements.

*Hunting **servals** locate rodents in tall grass with their large ears and make great leaps onto prey.*

*Mainly nocturnal, the **caracal's** 'jacked up' back legs enable it to leap 3m vertically to swat birds.*

*Servals, African golden cats and **leopards** (shown here) can occur in a black, or melanistic form.*

Variations on a theme

Cats are so well known as to almost obviate any description; there are seven species in East Africa, three of which rate among the most glamorous wild animals on the planet. The standard cat package consists of short fur, long body, rounded head, long canine teeth for gripping prey and sharp carnassial teeth (at the back of the mouth) for shearing flesh. Variations among the smaller cats include a short tail and long legs, with further refinements such as the extra long back legs of caracals for powerful leaps (up to 3m vertically!).

Although cats have a rather poor sense of smell, their other senses are highly developed: excellent bifocal vision, even in dim light; acute hearing, amplified in servals and caracals by very large ears (inset); and sensitive whiskers. All (except for the cheetah) have sharp claws which can be retracted into sheaths and pads on the soles of their feet for silent stalking; and all climb well – although the heavyweight lions don't go in for it much. Cats are at the top of the food chain and are almost exclusively carnivorous. Except for short periods of consorting and when females have young, the majority hunt and live alone to ensure an adequate share of food resources.

Cats are expert stalkers that kill by clamping their jaws around the throat of prey until it suffocates, or biting to sever its spinal cord. Most lie up for much of the day, but start hunting by late afternoon. The smaller cats aren't so easy to spot from a distance – muted colours help them blend in – but peak sighting times are early morning and evening. Watch for ears poking up over the grass (dark markings behind the ears act as signals for kittens following behind their mother); likewise, that little black bird sitting on a grass head in the distance could be the tail tuft of a lion on the prowl. A serval's prodigious leaps after prey are a giveaway; and swatting birds in flight is a caracal speciality. The African wild cat is widespread and chance sightings could occur anywhere you can spotlight. If you don't see one while on safari you won't have to go far to study one in detail, for this is the direct ancestor of nearly every household cat on earth – you can tell them apart by the unmarked, ginger-coloured backs to the wild cat's ears. ■

Hotspots

Serengeti NP and **Ngorongoro CA** Good for all savanna cats, including servals. **Aberdare NP** Servals, including black forms, are regularly sighted in alpine grasslands; the rare African golden cat is sometimes reported in the Salient forests.

CHEETAH ✓ Serengeti

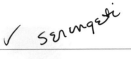

A most unusual cat

Charismatic and least catlike of the big cats, cheetahs usually hunt shortly after dawn, resting up in long grass during the heat of the day and resuming the hunt in the late afternoon. Much time is spent moving surreptitiously into position before bursting from cover and running down prey – shadowing its jinks, then tripping it up or knocking it off balance. Cheetahs do not have retractable claws (a feature which adds traction during sprints) and once prey is caught it is suffocated with a bite to the throat. The cheetah's incredible bursts of speed can reach 112km/h (during which it takes 7m-long bounds), but can be maintained for only 200 to 300m; cheetahs try to get within 30 to 50m before attacking.

The least aggressive and weakest of the big cats, cheetahs drag prey to cover before feeding and wolf it down to avoid losses to lions, hyenas and even vultures. Groups of lions, dogs and hyenas may kill an adult cheetah, and more than 50% of cubs are taken by predators within their first three months. But there's a still more insidious threat: some 30,000 to 40,000 years ago the grasslands of Africa virtually disappeared under forest and it is estimated that the cheetah population fell to only a few individuals, including perhaps only one female; today's population has a greatly diminished gene pool and inbreeding is a concern for the cheetah's long-term wellbeing. Ironically, cheetahs are often dogged by onlookers – it is not unusual to see one surrounded by safari vehicles – which sometimes forces them to hunt during the heat of day.

Cheetahs are generally solitary, although males sometimes live in small groups that can last for years. Females raise their young alone, caring for them for up to two years and even going without food to ensure they eat.

Unlike other cats, which have innate hunting skills, cubs must learn how to stalk and catch prey – females bring them dazed or half-dead young animals and teach them how to hunt. ■

Recognition Rangy cat with long tail ringed at the tip. Fawn or cream with evenly spaced spots. Black stripes between eyes and mouth.
Habitat Widespread in savanna, grassland and semiarid plains with patchy cover.
Behaviour Males and females socialise only during oestrus, but 2–3 independent males may band together to defend territory. Uses termite mounds, vehicles and leaning trees as observation posts.
Breeding Cubs (3–4) born after 3-month gestation, feed at kills after 5–6 weeks, catch prey at 9–12 months.
Feeding Hunts gazelles, impalas, oribis, hares, warthogs, duikers and calves of larger antelopes. Groups may take zebras, wildebeests or young buffaloes.
Voice Generally silent. Cubs called to feed on a kill with soft, birdlike chirps.
Swahili Duma

Hotspots
Masai Mara NR, Samburu NR, Buffalo Springs NR, Serengeti NP

✓ LION

Recognition Fawn or tawny coat. Black to golden mane. Cubs' spots fade with age.
Habitat Grasslands, savanna and woodland; uses cover to ambush prey and hide cubs.
Behaviour Prides of related females defend territories. Prey ambushed normally within 30m. Females mate 2–3 times per hour for 2–6 days to conceive; and suckle each other's young.
Breeding Cubs (2–6) born in a hidden den after 3½-month gestation, join the pride after 4–8 weeks.
Feeding Ambushes medium-large ungulates and suffocates victims by biting throat. Follows vultures to kills and steals from hyenas.
Voice Deep, far-carrying roar can carry up to 8km.
Swahili Simba

Hotspots
Masai Mara NR, Serengeti NP, Ngorongoro CA, Queen Elizabeth NP

The mane event

This is the big cat of the plains, larger and more powerful than any other predator: lions' jaws bite easily through muscle and bone, often leaving little more than the head and spine of their prey intact. Some prides specialise in toppling buffaloes, others prey on giraffes, but most usually hunt impalas, wildebeests, zebras and other common herbivores (although a curious or hungry lion will eat rodents, lizards and even ostrich eggs). A few notorious rogues have killed dozens of people (although attacks are rare and usually made by old or injured lions). While lions are active mainly at night, many hunts occur just after dawn so get out there early to see them at their best. Most of the day is spent lazing around in the shade before the hunt begins again in the late afternoon; females often play with cubs and suckle late in the day before setting out.

Two things make lions stand out from other cats: the differences between males and females (most apparent in the male's shaggy mane and size), and their sociability. Prides of about 12 lions defend territories; one or more dominant males sharing mating rights and food with several females and their offspring. Females do most of the killing, cooperatively stalking and ambushing prey, but around the kill every cat becomes a snarling, hissing competitor for the choicest meat – the adult males inevitably getting their proverbial share.

The trade-off? Resident males cooperatively ward off attacks by nomadic males looking to dominate a pride. Nomads are usually related subadult males that have been kicked out of their home pride; if they can drive off another pride's resident males they can appropriate their females and will kill as many cubs as they can catch. Females come into oestrus shortly afterwards and the victors enjoy their spoils – fatherhood and a hunting pride. New litters are usually born at the same time and the pride continues as a cooperative group once again – displaced males don't usually get a second chance. ■

LEOPARD

The cat that doesn't like to be spotted

The leopard's reclusive habits make finding it difficult and even if you do, chances are it will melt into the undergrowth or flatten itself against a branch to become less conspicuous. But it's worth the effort – they are more common than most people think and still the world's most widespread big cat. Adults are solitary most of the year, males and females associating only long enough to mate. During the day they typically lie up in a lair – such as a rock overhang, cave or dense thicket – but rarely in the same place two days running: check cliffs, kopjes and large riverine trees; and look for a twitching tail hanging from a branch or animal remains wedged in a forked bough. Listen for a rasping groan (like wood being sawed) after sundown and before dawn – often given on the move, it warns other leopards to avoid contact.

By dusk leopards are active and at night in their element, hunting by stealth and ambush, pouncing from a few metres away or leaping from a tree onto prey that can include guard dogs or domestic goats. This powerful cat can bring down a topi and drag an impala up a tree – so lions or hyenas won't steal it – and occasionally one develops a taste for human flesh. They pluck fur and feathers from small prey and drink water when available, but otherwise can survive by drinking blood and bodily fluids. Baboons are a favourite, and as primates see poorly in the dark, they are vulnerable after sundown. But by day baboon troops mob leopards and several males may gang up and kill one. Lions will kill a leopard if it blunders into a pride (leopards often climb trees to avoid other predators and to protect their kills). Female and male leopards have overlapping ranges but defend exclusive territories. A male's territory may overlap that of one or more females; he marks his turf by spraying urine on bushes, rocks and fallen branches; with secretions from anal glands; and by clawing the bark of trees. ∎

Recognition Pale yellow to tawny; dark rosettes on flanks, back and tail; solid spots on the face; whitish below. Black forms occur.
Habitat Semiarid scrub, savanna, mountains and lowland rainforest; favours riverine forest, woodlands and rocky outcrops.
Behaviour Solitary. Mainly nocturnal, hunting during day when undisturbed or when females have cubs. Suns on termite mounds or large rocks. Can swim.
Breeding Year-round; 2–6 cubs born after 90–112 days become independent at 18–22 months.
Feeding Carnivorous; hunts small antelopes, warthogs, hyraxes and monkeys; also arthropods, birds and reptiles. Individual tastes vary.
Voice Cubs contacted with a loud sniff ('prusten') or *meaow*.
Swahili Chui

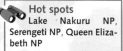

Hot spots
Lake Nakuru NP, Serengeti NP, Queen Elizabeth NP

MONGOOSES ✓

Strike like lightning

A lack of colourful markings readily distinguishes most of East Africa's 13 mongoose species from other small predators, such as civets and genets. Two or three common species (particularly Egyptian, slender, and the two social mongooses – banded and dwarf) that forage during the day are often seen slinking through long grass or pausing to stand on hind legs and sniff the breeze. Mongooses vary greatly, with basic body plans ranging from elongated, slender species with short legs that prey largely on vertebrates; to the stockier, long-legged cusimanses and 'dog-mongooses'.

*The solitary **Egyptian** or **ichneumon mongoose** is most common on grassy plains.*

Most mongooses are normally solitary; nearly all are primarily ground-dwelling (only slender and Egyptian can climb well); and many are nocturnal. However, all have in common a more or less pointed muzzle, inconspicuous ears and a grizzled, shaggy coat. Small size indicates that mongooses subsist on small prey and explains why they are East Africa's most abundant and diverse carnivores; nonetheless, that so many terrestrial mongoose species can survive side by side (and compete with genets, civets and small cats) is testament to the abundance of small prey.

*The **slender mongoose** is a solitary and agile killer of rodents, birds and reptiles.*

Mongooses feed on small animals ranging from insects and spiders to rodents and lizards, caught opportunistically or by digging, which are then chewed up on the spot; the slender mongoose is an extremely agile predator of vertebrates, including birds and hyraxes, and can leap 1m vertically to snatch prey. Mongooses are perhaps best known as fearless killers of snakes, a reputation not entirely undeserved: slender and Egyptian mongooses can overpower even dangerous cobras with lightning strikes, although the tables are readily turned if a mongoose is caught unawares.

Dwarf mongooses are widespread in savanna and can become semitame around lodges.

Good mongoose country features burrows and shelters, particularly abandoned termite mounds, but don't look too early in the morning – mongooses like to lie about in the sun (inset: dwarf mongooses) or play before heading out on the hunt. Nocturnal species, such as white-tailed mongooses are readily spotlit; watch for birds mobbing slender mongooses (they ignore most other mongooses) and for parties of hornbills feeding with dwarf mongooses (see the Hornbills section). ■

*The **white-tailed mongoose** is one of the most commonly seen nocturnal hunters.*

Hotspots

Masai Mara NR and **Serengeti NP** A variety of habitats exploited by the sociable and nocturnal species, plus slender and Egyptian mongooses. **Lake Mburo NP** Thickets, marsh and savanna support the six common species.

BANDED MONGOOSE

Comrades in arms

Solitary mongooses make a tempting treat for eagles, cats, dogs and large monitor lizards. So it makes sense to band to-gether for protection, which is what banded mongooses do (although the name refers to the stripes on their rumps). When danger threatens, the would-be predator is confront-ed with a writhing mass of mongooses snapping and spitting – one male was observed to climb a tree to force an eagle to drop one of its comrades. Yet only two species of mongoose in East Africa have adopted this behaviour (the other is the dwarf mongoose), the downside of a social life being that food resources must be spread among group members.

The banded mongoose is the most commonly seen species: family groups, sometimes numbering as many as 40 members, shuffle through the savanna with a bouncing gait, occasionally standing on hind legs to scan over the grass or climbing a termite mound for a better vantage point. A typical pack includes three or four breeding females and males, plus offspring, whose day starts well after sunrise: the usual routine is to wander around their home range foraging, scent-marking rocks, branches, termite mounds and each other. Hot spells are spent resting under bushes.

First in, first served

Nosing in burrows, crevices and under bark, banded mon-gooses snap up virtually any animal too slow to get out the way – difficult or dangerous prey is shaken or thrown against the ground to immobilise it before swallowing. But when food is encountered, it's every mongoose for itself (food is shared only with juveniles). So what other advantages are there in being a social mongoose? Breeding is synchronised within the pack so the season's young can be fed and pro-tected together: any lactating female will suckle newborn young, regardless of parenthood; all pack members groom and play; and adult males babysit the den while the pack is out foraging. Larger packs also dominate bigger territories, and thus greater food resources, hounding off smaller groups during boundary disputes. ∎

Recognition Robust mon-goose with long legs, pointed snout and long claws. Grey-brown upper-parts with dark bands on rump; paler below. Length 45–75cm.

Habitat Savanna, woodlands and grasslands, especially with termite mounds; also cultivated land.

Behaviour Diurnal. Packs typically number 15–20 and sleep in abandoned termite mounds. Forage over 3–10km a day, usually led by a senior female. Packs may produce four litters a year; many young don't survive and subadult males disperse to other packs.

Breeding Usually 4 young born in den (mostly in rains) after 2-month gestation; join foraging after 5 weeks.

Feeding Omnivorous; small animals of all types: insects, millipedes, spiders, scorpions, rodents, birds and eggs, plus fruit and berries.

Voice Constant contact calls: chirps, twitters and churrs.

Swahili Nguchiro miraba or kicheche

> **Hotspots**
> Masai Mara NR, Serengeti NP, Queen Eliza-beth NP (Mweya)

SPOTTED HYENA

Maladies of the night

Long maligned as misshapen, giggling cowards, spotted hyenas are now recognised as deadly and efficient hunters of the plains. They are certainly opportunistic scavengers and some African tribes still leave very old relatives outside at night for hyenas to finish off. But research is showing that many kills previously attributed to lions are actually spotted hyenas' kills stolen by lions. Hunts usually start with one or two hyenas that keep up that deceptively loping stride for hours at a steady 10km/h, wearing down their victim by nipping at its heels. Eventually the prey is stopped by the hyenas biting its legs and belly, and clamping their massive jaws around the victim's genitals and tail. The chase attracts other clan members, and even more when a kill occurs – the consequent squabbling also attracts lions and rival hyena clans, and pitched battles between both can end in deaths.

Spotted hyenas can intimidate cheetahs, leopards, and lions (although rarely full-grown male lions). Powerful jaws are their main weapon and tool, and those teeth can shear through bone and thick hides. Active mainly at night, they cool off by lying in puddles, but if they spot vultures homing on a kill they will quickly follow.

Male hyenas are only significant during the height of female oestrus – females have higher testosterone levels than the males themselves: they dominate males at kills, determine clan structure, protect communal dens, and initiate hunts and territorial disputes. But the females' most unusual feature, which gave rise to a hermaphrodite myth, is an enlarged clitoris that can elongate like a penis (up to 19cm long) with a foreskin and fibrous tissue that mimics a scrotum. Not only does the male mate through this 'female phallus', but the cubs are born through it. And the killer instinct is there at birth: pups are born with fully formed front teeth and, if female, the first-born tries to kill the second if it is of the same sex – in the darkness of a den it makes sense for every hyena to act like a male. ∎

Recognition The only hyena with spots. Sloping hindquarters with short black tail. Rusty or tan with dark spots. Round face and ears. Broad black muzzle.

Habitat Open savanna, thorn scrub and montane grasslands with abundant prey; dens in rocky country.

Behaviour Female-dominated but competitive clans, sometimes numbering 100 animals. Socialise before setting out to hunt. Males aged 2 years disperse to other clans. Cubs weaned in communal dens, higher-ranking offspring weaned faster.

Breeding Usually 2 cubs born in den after 4-month gestation. Suckled 8 months, weaned at 12–16 months.

Feeding Carnivorous; carrion (even desiccated corpses), human refuse; hunts large and small mammals, especially wildebeests, Thomson's gazelles and young of other antelopes; steals kills.

Voice Complex; most commonly a far-carrying, rising *wooo-up*; also eerie 'laughter'.

Swahili Fisi madoa

Hot spots
Masai Mara NR, Ngorongoro CA, Queen Elizabeth NP

STRIPED HYENA

Reclusive dog-tigers

The two East African hyena species are distinct in appearance, behaviour and food preferences. The pugnacious spotted hyena dominates the plains and is most easily seen, while the smaller striped hyena is essentially nocturnal – best sought by spotlighting, but with luck flushed accidentally by day. An opportunistic, solitary hunter, the striped hyena's behaviour is affected by the presence of its spotted cousin: where the latter is present, striped hyenas tend to keep to open woodlands – if they do meet, the striped hyena is submissive, surrendering food and making a quick exit. Although striped hyenas will drink if they can, they can live in waterless areas. Foraging alone, they most often pursue large insects (including grasshoppers, beetles and moths), but will also eat small animals such as gazelle fawns and hares if they can catch them. Striped hyenas are social creatures; several animals live together and defend the same home range or territory. It is thought that several related females (with the aid of grown offspring) cooperate to rear cubs in shared dens in kopjes, ravines and rocky hills. One to six cubs are born per litter and are fed by all family members as the adults return to the den with food. Although striped hyenas show little fear of leopards and cheetahs, they keep well away from lions. ■

Recognition Grey to golden with black stripes, long hair and large, pointed ears.
Habitat Scrub and woodland.
Behaviour Strictly nocturnal.
Breeding 1–6 cubs born after about 90 days.
Feeding Eats small invertebrates, carrion and fruit.
Voice Giggles, whines and growls.
Swahili Fisi miraba

Hotspots
Serengeti NP, Ruaha NP

AARDWOLF   Serengeti

Peg-toothed termite-eater

Lacking the massive jaws and teeth of spotted and striped hyenas, the aardwolf's small, peglike teeth are adapted to a highly specialised diet consisting almost exclusively of termites, including species that other termite specialists rarely touch because they squirt noxious chemicals as a defence. No other termite-eaters eat so many either: an aardwolf in a typical night spends up to six hours lapping up some 250,000 termites, oozing copious quantities of sticky saliva and swallowing lots of soil in the process. Watch for this usually solitary animal on heavily grazed and trampled grasslands with lots of termite mounds, walking in a zigzag with head low to the ground as it listens for termites moving about on the surface (the striped hyena also forages in a zigzag). Good signs of their presence include latrines, in which their partly buried scats (smelling strongly of ammonia) show soil and remains of termites. Aardwolves are thought to live as monogamous pairs sharing a territory with their most recent offspring. Family members enthusiastically scent-mark their territorial boundaries by smearing their anal glands on grass stems, bushes and other objects. Young are generally born during the wet season, staying at the den for three months before venturing out to hunt termites and other prey. ■

Recognition Like a small striped hyena. Buff to reddish brown. Snout bare.
Habitat Open savannas and heavily grazed grasslands.
Behaviour Nocturnal. Male babysits while female hunts.
Breeding 2–3 cubs per litter.
Feeding Harvester termites; some other small animals.
Voice Growls, barks or roars.
Swahili Fisi ya nkole

Hotspots
Serengeti NP, Masai Mara NR

RATEL

Black-and-white terror

Much the same size and shape as badgers everywhere, the ratel (also called the honey badger) has a reputation for ferocity far outstripping its size. Some Africans say they would rather face a lion than a ratel and, incredible as it sounds, ratels have been known to rob lions of their kill. And if a man should get too close, well they're just the right size to jump up and hang onto his testicles with their vicelike jaws. Normally though, they prefer to dig out scorpions, rodents and other burrowing animals, and are adept at extracting difficult items, such as honeycomb from beehives and tortoises from their shells. For a mammal that eats mainly small animals the ratel is well equipped: its forelimbs end in massive claws for digging; thick, bristly fur protects it from dangerous prey; and its skin is loose so that any overconfident hyena or leopard that grabs hold can be turned on and bitten back. And when eating stinging insects, such as ants or bees, the ratel knocks them out by releasing unpleasant secretions from its anal glands (the ratel is reputed to skunks). Ratels are reputed to break open beehives located by honeyguides (small birds that feed on beeswax) for their mutual benefit. But although greater honeyguides certainly seek out people and lead them to hives, to date there has been no authentic record of a ratel being guided. ∎

Recognition Black with white crown, back and tail. 75cm.
Habitat Forest and grassland.
Behaviour Nocturnal; hunts alone or in pairs. Climbs well.
Breeding 1–4 cubs.
Feeding Eats virtually any small animal (even deadly snakes); also eggs, carrion.
Voice Rattling roars.
Swahili Nyegere

> **Hotspots**
> Masai Mara NR, Serengeti NP, Queen Elizabeth NP

AFRICAN CLAWLESS OTTER

Water babies

The odd dour researcher may resist the idea of animals having 'fun', but it is otherwise hard to explain an otter somersaulting down a mud bank when walking would be simpler and running faster. Likewise, the African clawless otter has been known to drop a pebble into the water and catch it when it hits the bottom, and even to swim about with one balanced on its head. Just for variety they might carry a stick to the bottom, release it then race it to the surface.

But otherwise, otters are serious aquatic carnivores propelled by webbed hind feet and a long, rudderlike tail. Superb divers with waterproof fur and prominent whiskers, they locate prey by groping about underwater with unwebbed 'fingers', gripping slippery fishes or frogs with naked palms and sometimes eating while treading water. Signs of their presence include scats with broken crab shells or fish bones; smooth paths down mud banks where they habitually slide into the water; and middens where shellfish have been smashed against a rock. If you wait quietly in likely habitat, you'll probably see one break the surface to take a breath, or be able to follow its undulating progress as it swims just below the surface. ∎

Recognition Chocolate-brown to tan; white cheeks, chin and chest. 1.5m.
Habitat Hunts in freshwater.
Behaviour Excavates dens in overhanging banks.
Breeding Up to 3 cubs.
Feeding Mainly crabs.
Voice A startling *aah*.

> **Hotspots**
> Saiwa Swamp NP, Lake Mburo NP, Ngamba Island Chimpanzee Sanctuary (Lake Victoria)

AFRICAN CIVET

Fragrant bandit

For centuries people have known of the secretion made by African civets from their perineal glands (a pair of glands situated near the anus in some mammals). Known as civetone, it is still harvested, particularly in Ethiopia, from captive specimens and used as a floral scent. Civets are solitary, pugnacious animals and smell seems to play an important role in keeping them out of each other's way: civetone is used to mark a home range and is smeared on rocks, branches and trees; and civets also make conspicuous, strongly scented dung middens, called civettries. Common and mainly nocturnal, civets are usually encountered when spotlighting along trails and roads, although they may also be abroad during the early morning. Essentially ground animals, they climb and dig poorly, and rely on holes dug by other animals for nurseries and dens in which to lie up during the day. Civets wander nightly through their home range, trotting or walking with head down. Any small animals encountered are killed by lunging and biting, shaking and tossing. Perfect opportunists, they can digest poisonous plants and distasteful invertebrates, and kill dangerous snakes. When cornered they bluff by erecting a spinal crest, which increases their apparent size by some 30%, but swim well and readily take to water to escape. ■

Recognition Vaguely doglike. Black with creamy blotches.
Habitat Forested mosaics, cultivated and marshy areas.
Behaviour Young freeze until detected.
Breeding 1–4 kittens in den.
Feeding Eats roots, shoots, fruits and small animals.
Voice Contact call *ha ha ha.*
Swahili Fungo

Hotspots
Saiwa Swamp NP, Lake Mburo NP

COMMON GENET

Agile nocturnal prowler

Attractively marked, common genets are widespread, mainly nocturnal carnivores that show great variation in coloration and pattern among several regional populations. About the size of a large domestic cat, they hunt alone in trees or on the ground, patrolling up and down branches (but descending headfirst) and through undergrowth to stalk or pounce on large insects and small vertebrates. Look for these common savanna predators along roads shortly after nightfall (they are particularly active on moonlit nights) – their eyeshine is easy to pick up and when they slink into the bushes the long tail (about half the total body length) is usually distinct.

In places common genets have learned to scavenge from humans and they may become semitame around camping grounds and lodges at night. It is not known whether they hold territories – several may be seen foraging in close proximity, and females almost certainly have smaller home ranges than males. Young are born in a tree hollow, burrow or nest of leaves. They begin hunting at between 11 and 18 weeks, catching their own prey at six months of age. Common genets mark their territories with urine and scent secreted from their perineal (anal) glands, and by leaving scats on branches. ■

Recognition Catlike. Creamy-yellow with dark brown spots and banded tail.
Habitat Savanna and woodland; rocky or hilly areas.
Behaviour Mainly nocturnal; solitary; sleeps in hollow.
Breeding 2-3 young.
Feeding Eats invertebrates, small vertebrates and fruit.
Voice One or more coughs.
Swahili Kanu

Hotspots
Samburu NR, Tsavo East NP, Serengeti NP

GROUND PANGOLIN

Animated pine cones

Also known as scaly anteaters, pangolins are small (reaching just over 1m in length) and seldom seen on safari, although they are not uncommon. If you do bump into one, it's worth a closer look: pangolins' upperparts are entirely covered in broad, overlapping scales, which make them look like a huge pine cone. The weight of their ambling gait is entirely supported by the back legs and when threatened, a pangolin rolls itself up into a ball, presenting any would-be attacker with a slippery sphere of horny scales on which it can't easily get a grip. However, the pangolin's face and underparts lack scales, and lions and hyenas make a quick meal of one if they can breach its defences. Further threats come from people (some tribes use their scales as charms) and grassfires, from which pangolins can't easily escape. The wall of scales is a pangolin's primary defence: their powerful foreclaws can also be used against an attacker, but they are essentially for ripping open soil and hollow logs to get at their main prey – ants. Their narrow head is small, the snout long, narrow and toothless and their sticky tongue – as long as its head and body combined – shoots into underground passages to recoil covered in insects. Young pangolins cling to their mother's back, sidling under her tail or belly at the first sign of danger. ■

Recognition Unmistakable. Long, muscular tail.
Habitat Woodlands and savanna.
Behaviour Uses natural shelters; can climb trees.
Breeding A single offspring eats ants after 3 months.
Feeding Licks up ants and termites with sticky tongue.
Voice Hissing or puffing.
Swahili Kakakuona

Hotspots
Masai Mara NR, Serengeti NP

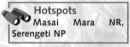

DUGONG

Sirens' swan song?

Strands of seagrass floating to the surface of shallow coastal waters are a subtle sign that dugongs are grazing below. Also known as 'sea cows', these harmless marine herbivores graze exclusively on meadows of seagrass that grow along the East African coast. They look like no other animal, but are probably most closely related to elephants, and are thought to have inspired legends about mermaids and sirens. With a face dominated by a wide, bristly piglike snout it's hard to see how, but dugongs have sweet voices that fill the water with chirping, trilling and twittering. Dugongs pose no threat to anyone or anything, yet will probably be the next large animal to become extinct in East Africa. Their habitat is increasingly being encroached by fishermen – dugongs drown when they get caught in fishing nets. Dugongs swim slowly and herds may be visible just beneath the surface, rising in unison to breathe every 80 seconds or so; sadly, many dugongs also die from injuries inflicted by propellers on boats. And their sole feeding grounds, the seagrass beds, are easily damaged by people walking across at low tide. Nobody knows how many dugongs are left, nor what long-term effects their demise will have on coastal ecology, but one thing is certain – their disappearance will go almost entirely unnoticed. ■

Recognition Bulbous, grey-brown with blunt face and no dorsal fin. Length 3m.
Habitat Sheltered waters with seagrass meadows.
Behaviour Forages and rests alone or in small herds.
Breeding Single calf accompanies mother 18 months.
Feeding Grazes on seagrass.
Voice Chirps and twitters.
Swahili Nguva

Hotspots
Mida Creek (Watamu MNP)

AFRICAN ELEPHANT ✓

Queen of breasts

Besides being the largest land animal and truly charismatic, African elephants show some amazing signs of intelligence and what looks like compassion. For example, they can use their tusks to short-circuit an electric fence to get to forbidden fruits beyond; and a sick or wounded elephant is sometimes propped up by two comrades – should it fall over they'll break tusks in their efforts to raise it up again. Elephants recognise their dead, feeling the bones while standing quietly; they cover dead kin in dirt and branches – and have been known to do the same for a human they have killed. With elephants, the key points to watch are the trunk – often nonchalantly draped over a tusk, it does the grasping, drinking, spraying and trumpeting; those huge, leathery ears – which stand out when they're annoyed; and their long tusks – which act as both tools and weapons. Also look out for breasts on females, located between their front legs.

Matriarchal herds – made up of several related adult females and their offspring – are dominated by the oldest cow (the matriarch) that leads the herd well after she stops calving at age 45 or more. Young bulls are ousted from matriarchal herds at 10 to 14 years of age and drift between family units or into bachelor herds. Herds are very sociable and vocal, greeting each other (and other herds) with trumpeting, pirouetting and placing their trunks in each others' mouths. Low frequency sounds below human perception allow elephants to maintain contact for up to 10km, and advertise to males when a female is on heat (which brings them running).

Males come into 'musth' one month per year and it's a sight: liquid oozes from the temporal gland, leaving dark stains on the side of the face; the massive penis turns green, drags along the ground dribbling and exudes a strong smell. Several bulls compete for dominance and when one eventually mounts (for a knee-trembling 60 seconds) other females gather round with much trumpeting and ear-flapping. ∎

Recognition Huge – bulls can stand 3.4m high and weigh 6300kg (forest elephants much smaller). Variably grey coloration is affected by dust-baths.
Habitat All major habitats with shade and water, from semidesert to rainforest and montane grasslands.
Behaviour Herds have huge home ranges and make seasonal movements led by the matriarch. Active 16–20 hours a day, drink and bathe daily. Large herds congregate during rains. Bulls get 'green penis syndrome' and bad-tempered in musth.
Breeding Single calf born after 22-month gestation (mostly in rains); may remain with mother 10 years.
Feeding Eclectic browsers and grazers, consuming up to 150kg in 24 hours; recycle huge quantities of vegetation and reshape entire landscapes.
Voice Herds highly vocal, with deep contact rumblings, squeals, roars and snorts; trumpeting signals annoyance and pleasure.
Swahili Tembo or Ndovu

Hotspots
Amboseli NP, Ruaha NP (dry season), **Semliki Valley WR** (forest elephant)

PLAINS ZEBRA

Recognition Stocky with variable broad black-and-white stripes extending onto belly (browner in mares) and an erect, striped mane.
Habitat Widespread in grassland, savanna and woodland near permanent water; avoids wet ground.
Behaviour Nomadic, first to graze tall grasslands (followed by wildebeests and other migrating animals). Rests in the open at night; files to water at midday.
Breeding Peaks in rains; one foal born after 12-month gestation; suckles 6 months.
Feeding Can eat tall, coarse grasses not normally consumed by other herbivores.
Voice Noisy at night, when stallions rally mares with a loud 'barking bray'.
Swahili Punda milia

Hotspots
Masai Mara NR, Ngorongoro CA, Lake Mburo NP

Why stripes?

Among the most easily recognisable of all animals, the plains zebra is also variously known as Chapman's, Burchell's and common zebra (another species, Grevy's zebra, also lives in East Africa – where their ranges overlap the two mingle freely but never interbreed). Zebras are savanna horses whose ancestors evolved in North America and spread via land bridges to Africa during the last three million years. Zebra stripes are as individual as a human fingerprint, but their function is a matter of controversy: they effectively break up a zebra's outline (even from a short distance away) and probably act as a general antipredator pattern. But they may also be a bonding feature (an attractive visual stimulus imprinted at birth that helps keep herds together) – in keeping with this theory unstriped horses, such as wild asses, are not nearly so gregarious. Another theory is that stripes are a defence against biting tsetse flies, whose great compound eyes see many different images at once and can't easily make out a zebra's outline; running in a straight line then zigzagging is said to further confuse the flies. Again, living outside the tsetse zone, wild asses are unstriped.

Hanging out with the crowd

All zebras are highly sociable with each other and other herbivores, such as antelopes (especially oryxes and elands), giraffes and buffaloes. Intelligent, fast and adaptable, zebras have been seen sliding under wire fences to reach grazing land and can be unpopular with pastoralists. A plains zebra stallion looks after up to six mares and their foals, fighting off male rivals (as many as 18 can gather when a filly first comes into oestrus) and following behind the herd when it moves – to discourage predators. Males form bachelor herds and try to abduct females from harems when they reach maturity. Watch for the mutual nibbling of legs, shoulders and neck among family members; facing in opposite directions to help spot predators; and lining up to roll in dust or rub against trees or termite mounds, which probably dislodges parasites and conditions their coats. ■

GREVY'S ZEBRA

East Africa's endangered horse

East Africa's other zebra, Grevy's, is a large striped ass of semi-arid country that commonly associates with giraffes, oryxes, elands, impalas and buffaloes. Both plains and Grevy's zebras frequently occur together in mixed herds, especially in the dry season, but seen side by side the two cannot be mistaken (Grevy's has finer stripes which do not extend onto the belly, and large, rounded ears). Evidently they have no trouble telling the difference because they never interbreed; in fact, the two have entirely different social systems: Grevy's mares associate in loose herds that share a home range while stallions stake out territories on good pasture near water. Any mares on heat are waylaid as they pass through a male's territory to drink, the stallion fending off the advances of bachelors loitering near his boundaries. But although intolerant when mares are in heat, stallions actively consort with bachelor herds on their turf at other times (unlike plains zebras).

The precocious foals are born with their mane extending along both back and belly; this is shed as they grow to resemble a more conventional mane. Foals can stand within 11 minutes and run in about 45; and their legs are so long they must splay them to touch their noses to the ground. A foal follows its mother faithfully, even suckling from behind, but stay behind in crèches guarded by an adult while she goes to water to drink.

Zebras have never been popular with pastoralists because they compete with livestock for graze and water; Grevy's zebra is a point in case whose range is fast contracting. From a population of 13,700 animals in 1977, this species has experienced a 70% decline and at the millennium its numbers hovered around some 5000 individuals (making it an endangered species). ∎

Recognition Finely striped zebra with white belly, large ears and tan muzzle; stripes wider on the neck and chest, and form a 'bull's-eye' on the rump.

Habitat Mosaics of semiarid *Acacia-Commiphora* thornbush and grassland, preferably with permanent water and pasture.

Behaviour Diurnal and nocturnal. Herds disperse during dry seasons, stallions remaining on territories where possible, digging and defending waterholes in stream beds; otherwise migrate to areas of higher rainfall. Mares foal at traditional place year after year.

Breeding A single brown-and-white foal born during rains after 13 months gestation is weaned by 9 months.

Feeding Can subsist on grass too tough for cattle, browsing when grass disappears.

Voice Most common sound is a donkeylike braying.

Swahili Kangaja

Hotspots
Samburu NR, Buffalo Springs NR, Lewa Downs WC (also plains zebra), Meru NP

WHITE RHINOCEROS

The square-lipped giant

White rhinos are no more white than black rhinos are black: the name is a corruption of *weit*, a Dutch word meaning 'wide' – referring to the shape of its mouth (white rhinos have broad, squared-off lips for grazing whereas those of black rhinos are pointed for plucking leaves). The white rhino's relatively docile nature means that in reserves where they can still be seen you should be able to get close enough to see this distinctive feature. You can also admire its great size, second only to African elephants (male white rhinos can weigh up to 3600kg, more than twice as much as the biggest black rhino). It takes practice to tell white and black rhinos apart at a distance, but both are shaped differently: the highest point on a white's back being a prominent shoulder hump; on a black it's the haunches. Also, black rhinos tend to stay closer to cover, while white rhinos often feed in the open in the company of others of their kind, even veering close to gregariousness at times.

A female white rhino shares her home range with her most recent calf (and sometimes with unrelated juveniles); her home range overlaps with those of other females and several may graze side by side. Males defend territories and can be belligerent and very vocal, especially when seeking out a female on heat. Since two charging males could do great damage, encounters on territorial boundaries often involve two males staring at each other awhile before backing off.

White rhinos were once widespread in grasslands over sub-Saharan and southern Africa. The southern African race was all but wiped out early in the 20th century, but at the eleventh hour was protected and bred back from less than 100 individuals to some 6000 animals at the millennium. The northern subspecies was not so lucky: discovered only in 1903, it was poached to probable extinction in East Africa, except where small numbers have been transported to strictly protected reserves. ∎

Recognition Massive. Long, low-slung head with wide mouth. Prominent shoulder hump when head raised. Dark-grey to tan overall, sometimes dust-coloured.
Habitat Short, open grassland near water with some trees and mud wallows.
Behaviour Active day and night, alternating between grazing and resting. Temporary groups may gather in shady areas or ridges during hot weather. Drinks daily when water available. Female follows calf when fleeing. Males create dung middens.
Breeding One calf born after 16-month gestation; grazes at 2 months, driven away at 2–3 years.
Feeding Grazes well-drained, well-trampled short grass almost exclusively, including regrowth after dry season fires.
Voice Usually silent, although males squeal, grunt and snort when challenging and courting.
Swahili Kifaru ya majani

Hotspots
Lake Nakuru NP, Solio Ranch, Lewa Downs WC

BLACK RHINOCEROS

Squinting over the brink of extinction

Long before the invention of firearms, black rhinos were highly successful plains mammals: long-lived, highly mobile and able to reach a broad variety of vegetation with their relatively long neck (for rhinos). Weak eyesight was no handicap for such a massive animal, and compensated for by keen hearing and sense of smell. Their horns are made of solid keratin – the same substance that makes up toenails and horses' hooves. Normally there are two, the larger at the front, but occasionally a rhino will have rudimentary third or even fourth horns, harking back to extinct ancestors that had several (a poacher's bonanza).

Although dark from afar, black rhinos appear black only after rain or bathing, and can be as pale and grey as a white rhino if they have been rolling in sand or ash during the dry season. Where several animals coexist, scuff marks and rubbings on trees or termite mounds are good signs of their presence; otherwise you'll be lucky to find them, although if the accounts of famous hunters are anything to go by black rhinos were not rare 100 years ago. In fact, there were still 40,000 black rhinos in Kenya during the 1970s, but despite the warnings of conservationists, Kenya's black rhino population plummeted to an estimated 400 animals by the millennium. The reason: its horns are worth more than gold to the men of Yemen as carved handles for their *jambiyya* daggers.

A controversial method of discouraging poachers has been the removal of the horns from living rhinos. But horns regrow and rhinos must be dehorned again every couple of years – tranquillised rhinos have a high casualty rate. Whether dehorned rhinos can survive for long in the wild is another question: far from being merely decorative, horns can be used as effective and lethal weapons (known to kill lions) in defending calves, and are used by males in courtship battles. And anyway, in the dense cover favoured by black rhinos, a poacher may not be able to tell whether it has been dehorned or not. ■

Recognition Huge (males weigh up to 1400kg) with thick hide, short legs and massive horned head. Upper lip is pointed and muscular – almost beaklike.

Habitat Mainly savanna with thickets and abundant shrubs; also semiarid thorn scrub to montane forest.

Behaviour Mainly diurnal. Breaks branches and loosens soil with horns. Females with young sometimes associate with others in home range. Males mark territories with dung middens and urine sprays. Calves reputed to run behind mother

Breeding One calf born, usually during rains, after a 15–16 month gestation; tended by mother 2–3 years until she next gives birth.

Feeding Browses on leaves, twigs and branches taken low down or broken off with horns. Seeks daily access to water.

Voice Usually silent; grunts, snorts and screams when alarmed or fighting.

Swahili Kifaru

Hotspots
Solio Ranch, Lewa Downs WC, Serengeti NP, Ngorongoro CA; extinct in Uganda

ROCK HYRAX

The elephant's tiny cousin

Recognition Rabbit-sized with short, rounded ears and no tail. Brownish coat of short, coarse fur with yellowish oval patch in middle of the back.

Habitat Widespread in savanna and semiarid country wherever kopjes, cliffs and rocky outcrops provide shelter.

Behaviour Mainly diurnal. Colonies number 10-30 animals, comprised of different families of related females each with a territorial male. Grooms regularly with claw-like inner toe on hind foot. Males usually call in the early morning and evening.

Breeding Young (1-4) are born furred with open eyes after 7½ months gestation. Most births in rainy season.

Feeding Grazes quickly with large mouthfuls; can climb trees to browse. Young graze almost at birth, although are not weaned for 1-5 months.

Voice Males utter far-carrying territorial yaps. Alarm call is a high pitched scream.

Swahili Pimbi

Groups of what look like football-sized guinea pigs sitting around on kopjes and cliffs are in fact hyraxes, a uniquely African group of herbivores. The rock hyrax is the most commonly encountered species and can readily be seen on rocky outcrops, which it often shares with bush hyraxes; and three species of hyraxes live almost exclusively in trees. Hyraxes share an ancient ancestry with aardvarks and elephants, but to make sense of this assertion it's probably best to imagine them as herbivores that were pushed off prehistoric savannas by the highly successful antelope family into other niches. Unlikely as it sounds, hyraxes have some elephantlike features, such as teats between their forelegs and a long gestation period. More obvious features to look for include blunt feet with rounded, nailed 'toes'; and upper incisors modified into tusks (sometimes seen when they yawn), which can deliver lethal damage during aggressive territorial encounters.

Rock hyraxes live in colonies on kopjes and cliffs; bush hyraxes are browsers that shelter in colonies side by side with rock hyraxes (their associations are in fact among the closest in the mammalian world). Both are savoured by leopards, genets and rock pythons; and Verreaux's eagles eat virtually nothing else. But hyraxes are a successful and widespread group: sweat on their rubbery footpads creates a sticky surface that allows them to scale near-vertical rocks and trunks, and thus rely on permanent shelter with accessible food.

Rock hyraxes are social and gregarious, sleeping together for safety and warmth – look for them sunning in huddles on ledges in the early morning (white stains on boulders, caused by urine, indicate active colonies). Colonies are dominated by an aggressive, breeding male (submissive hyraxes flatten their body and present their rump) – hyraxes typically enter holes, groups and conflicts backside-first to avoid those tusks. For such small animals they make some mighty noises, including high-pitched warning shrieks. Territorial male rock hyraxes may call on moonlit nights and tree hyraxes utter penetrating screams shortly after dark. ■

Hotspots
Lake Nakuru NP, Serengeti NP, Kilimanjaro NP

AARDVARK

A living fossorial

Seeing an aardvark twice presages a long life, according to one African belief. But although they are relatively common, they are entirely nocturnal and notoriously difficult to see, so you'd probably have to live a long time to see two anyway. In any case, any aardvarks seen are usually eaten (chances at longevity notwithstanding). And aardvarks aren't too popular among farmers because they dig holes large enough to endanger vehicles, stock and earthen dams. These pig-sized animals (the name in fact comes from the Afrikaans word for 'earth-pig') are referred to in some books as 'ant-bears' (although entirely unrelated to bears – which don't occur in Africa). In fact, the aardvark's lineage can be traced back 50 million years to *Phenacodus*, an ancestor it probably shared with elephants and hyraxes.

Savanna earth-movers

During the day aardvarks shelter in burrows, emerging a couple of hours after dark to hunt termites and other insects. When their huge ears pick up movements above and below the soil they dig furiously with stout forelimbs and powerful claws to uncover termite or ant nests, then quickly lap the insects up with a long, sticky tongue (which can protrude 30cm), swallowing with little chewing. As diggers, aardvarks are second to none in Africa: to escape predators, such as pythons, an aardvark bolts into a hole – of which there may be several in its territory – and at a pinch it can completely bury itself in 10 minutes. In the morning fresh diggings are often in evidence, and show how common these animals can be. Extensive, deep warrens with as many as eight entrances may be shared by several breeding females. More commonly, though, they dig a fresh 'camping' hole most nights only a few metres long and plug it with earth. Aardvark burrows are important refuges for other animals, such as bats, mongooses and warthogs, and their disappearance from an area can have a flow-on effect on many other creatures. ■

Recognition Compact and vaguely piglike with long tail. Long tubular snout and huge ears. Thick limbs with powerful front claws. Grey, seminaked appearance. Length 1.5m.
Habitat Widespread in grasslands and savanna. Adapts to many habitats, but absent from rainforests.
Behaviour Mainly solitary and strictly nocturnal. Active from 1 or 2 hours after dusk. Digs and shelters in extensive burrows (may be used by several animals) or overnight 'camps'.
Breeding Naked young (1–2) born after a 7-month gestation; follow mother after 2 weeks; independent at 6 months.
Feeding Termites, ants, beetle larvae and pupae are excavated and swept up with their long, sticky tongue.
Voice Usually silent; grunts very occasionally.
Swahili Muhanga or Kukukifuku

Hotspots
Lake Elementeita, Masai Mara NR, Serengeti NP

WARTHOG

Recognition An almost naked, grey pig with long, lank mane, massive facial growths, upward-curving tusks, and thin, tufted tail held high when running.
Habitat Common and widespread in savanna, open woodland and grassland, especially where aardvark burrows provide shelter.
Behaviour Diurnal. Sounders usually consist of sow and current brood. Bask in sun and huddle for warmth. 'Walk' on callused knees when rootling. Wallow daily in hot, dry weather. Males disperse after 4 years. Mature boars solitary.
Breeding Female gives birth to 2–5 piglets in a burrow after a 160–170 day gestation; weaned in 6 months.
Feeding Grazes a variety of grasses during rains, rootling for bulbs and tubers in dry seasons; occasionally eats fruit and carrion, and soil for minerals.
Voice Piglike grunts in alarm and squeals in distress.
Swahili Ngiri

Red-hot porkers

The sight of a line of young warthogs trotting behind mother with heads high, manes flowing and skinny tails held erect probably inspired their popular name 'Kenya Express'. But then again, it may have been the sight of a salivating boar chasing a sow in oestrus while muttering a guttural *chug-chug-chug*. Imagine it – the sow beds down for the night in an abandoned aardvark burrow, which she has comfortably lined with grass, while outside boars are still sniffing about after dark to see if she's in heat; if she fits the bill at least one suitor will waylay her when she emerges in the morning. With such enthusiasm it's not surprising that warthogs are prolific breeders, but it's perhaps just as well because lions are smart enough to wait outside an occupied burrow too – and if they're really hungry they'll even dig the warthog out.

Warts, tusks and all

Burrows are the key to warthog survival – they are most abundant where many burrows offer protection from inclement weather and predators, and provide secure birthing dens. Sounders (groups of females and their current broods) use up to 10 burrows in their home range and knowing where the nearest one lies can be a matter of life and death – all except large boars are popular prey for lions, cheetahs and hyenas, and infant mortality is particularly high. When pursued they bolt to the nearest hole, where an adult will turn at the last second to face the predator, backing down the hole and lashing out with those big tusks. Tusks (actually greatly enlarged lower canine teeth) also explain the gross facial 'warts': in trials of strength for mating rights boars push face to face then break off suddenly to swipe sideways with their tusks; the huge fatty growths protect the face from serious damage. Tusks are also useful digging tools when, on bended knees, warthogs rootle in soil with their hard, flexible snout disc. ■

Hotspots
Amboseli NP, Arusha NP, Queen Elizabeth NP

GIANT FOREST HOG

Precursor of the modern barnyard

Despite its large size and startling appearance, the giant forest hog was one of the last large animals to be discovered in Africa. Its singular appearance give clues to its ecology: the shaggy coat shows a tolerance for cold (giant forest hogs live as high as the upper slopes of Mts Kenya and Kilimanjaro); the wide mouth is designed for grazing (unlike other pigs, giant hogs rarely root for tubers and then only in soft ground); and the boars' massive facial growths indicate a propensity for fighting – this usually involves charging and ramming, and if two meet head-on, air compressed between the concave areas of their facial pads goes off like a gunshot.

Whereas warthogs are the dominant savanna pig and bushpigs inhabit dense forest, the giant hog occupies a niche between the two. Thus, although they rely on dense vegetation for shelter, they graze in adjoining glades and sward – often in the company of buffaloes (a precursor of the modern barnyard). Sounders are usually composed of a boar and sow with offspring from previous litters that live in overlapping home ranges. Very young piglets are straw-coloured and lie flat when mother sounds the alarm; nonetheless, predators take up to 50% of piglets each year. ■

Recognition Large. Covered with coarse black hair.
Habitat Dense forest and savanna mosaic.
Behaviour Uses shallow scrapes under logs as beds. Huddles in cold, basks after rain and fog. Wallows.
Breeding 2–11 piglets.
Feeding Grass and herbage.
Voice Grunts and barks.
Swahili Nguruwe nyeusi

> **Hotspots**
> **Queen Elizabeth NP,**
> **Aberdare NP**

BUSHPIG

Popular with predators but not farmers

Bushpigs are a favoured prey of leopards and spotted hyenas, chimpanzees will eagerly tear one up for food if they can catch it, and piglets are vulnerable to eagles and pythons. But in favourable conditions a bushpig population can increase quickly: sows mature at 18 months and give birth after only a four-month gestation. Piglets are farrowed in a den among vegetation or piles of boulders and branches. Dark brown with rows of light spots at birth, piglets remain hidden for up to two months – freezing to avoid detection when danger approaches – and stay with the sounder for about a year.

Even adult bushpigs are generally retiring, staying in cover during the day, resting in mounds of leaf litter during hot spells and usually venturing from cover only after dark. But it's usually easy to see where they've been by the trail of soil tossed with their tusks and upturned with their strong nasal disc (guineafowl sometimes forage among rootling pigs). These opportunists will also scavenge carrion and eat small animals. Bushpigs also make a mess of crops and, ironically, the persecution of predators has allowed them to become a serious agricultural pest in certain areas. But bushpigs are also widely hunted by people for food and domestication has been proposed as a way of alleviating hunting pressure. ■

Recognition Grey, brown or reddish; paler head, spinal crest, ear tufts and 'beard'.
Habitat Woodland, forest and adjoining cultivation.
Behaviour Holds tail down when running.
Breeding 3–7 piglets.
Feeding Sniffs for roots, bulbs, fruit, fungi.
Voice Soft grunts.
Swahili Nguruwe

> **Hotspots**
> **Ngorongoro CA, Lake**
> **Mburo NP**

HIPPOPOTAMUS

Recognition Huge and bloated with short legs, massive head and broad snout. Shiny grey with pink 'highlights'. Males weigh up to 3200kg.
Habitat Widespread; lakes and slow rivers with pools, shallow banks and adjoining grassland.
Behaviour Gregarious in groups of 10–15 females with young, led by dominant male. Males enlarge puddles to make temporary water-holes in rains. Large numbers congregate in dry seasons.
Breeding Single calf born underwater, mostly during rains, after 8-month gestation; suckles for 8 months.
Feeding Grazes up to 45kg of grass a night with wide, muscular mouth. Doesn't feed on aquatic vegetation.
Voice Noisy in water giving loud, distinctive wheeze-honks. Bellows and roars when fighting.
Swahili Kiboko

Front-end loader

A hippo out of water resembles a huge, naked bladder, although it can step pretty daintily if it's in a hurry (it's a good idea to keep out of its way). Hippos' skin is very thin and devoid of sweat glands – which means hippos can rapidly dehydrate and overheat – so most of their day is spent underwater with only eyes, ears and nostrils showing. Listen along a likely stretch of water for sighs as they surface and exhale; hippos can stay submerged for up to five minutes and remain virtually hidden among water weeds, suddenly emerging in a flurry of jaws and tusks. Evening and early morning are good times to see them on the move (especially if it's overcast), when they follow well-worn trails to and from nocturnal grazing areas. Lazing about in water burns very little energy and keeps hippos safe from predators (although crocs may take calves); however, it can lead to overcrowding and violent territorial disputes.

Occasional carnivores?

'Yawning' is a challenge to all comers – those jaws can open to 150-degrees and chop a croc in half. Territorial males back up and shower each other with urine and faeces as a sign of respect, but also fight often, and their sharp, 50cm tusks leave deep scars and sometimes fatal wounds. Sounds also play an important role in hippos' social lives: males, spaced apart in territories, advertise their dominance with loud and repeated honking. Previously believed to be exclusively vegetarian, researchers recently observed hippos devouring a dead impala in a waterhole, and even behaving aggressively towards crocodiles and hunting dogs at a carcass. You don't want to get too close to their back end either: hippos mark territories and grazing trails by spraying dung and waving their paddle-shaped tail at the same time, spreading it all over the place (including safari tents). But that's no deterrent to an enterprising parasite: clinging to the skin of these amphibious animals would be a precarious existence, so large freshwater leeches feed and breed while attached to the inside of hippos' rectums! ∎

Hotspots
Lake Baringo, Masai Mara NR, Murchison Falls NP (Victoria Nile)

GIRAFFE

Slow motion demolition balls

That neck is the longest in the animal kingdom, but still has only seven bones – the same as you and every other mammal. The biggest plus of such a towering reach is that it puts giraffes above all competition for browse (except elephants). The downside is getting a drink, which to achieve a giraffe must splay its front legs and bend down – a position that makes it vulnerable, but must be risked at least once a week. (To prevent fainting the arteries have special valves that stop blood rushing down to the head – and back when it stands up again.) Massive shoulders are needed to hold their neck up, and young bulls also use these to jostle, intertwining necks and delivering blows with their heads to assert dominance. 'Necking' thus establishes social hierarchies from an early age and adult males rarely contest seriously at mating time. It looks like slow-mo, but a swing from a bull's head can break his opponent's neck or jaw.

Despite their great size, giraffes blend in well with the surroundings, and aren't always easy to see with just head and neck showing behind a tree. In dry seasons they are more likely to be seen feeding along drainage lines on evergreen foliage, dispersing across the plains during the rains. Their coat markings follow several basic arrangements, but the pattern of each animal is unique, remains constant throughout life and tends to get darker with age. The three distinct races in East Africa, distinguished by their coats, are reticulated (inset), Masai (below) and Rothschild's giraffes (restricted to a few parks).

Giraffes never seem to be in a hurry, browsing placidly on even the thorniest acacias with agile lips and an amazing 45cm-long tongue. Even when walking they look relaxed, with both left legs then both right legs moving alternately – it's deceptive, for in full flight they can outrun any predator. ∎

Recognition Immensely tall (up to 5.2m) with long neck, legs and tail. Variable orange to dark-brown blotches on white to corn-gold background. Tapered head with short horns.

Habitat Widespread and common in savanna, open woodland and plains with thickets.

Behaviour Diurnal and partly nocturnal. Nonterritorial and loosely gregarious, spending most of the day chewing cud. Herds can be mixed or single-sex, but large bulls monopolise matings. Cows calve in the same area year after year.

Breeding Year-round. Calf born 1.8m high, after 2 weeks joins others in crèche for 3–4 months; weaned at 12 months.

Feeding Exclusively browsers, mainly on acacia leaves, buds, shoots and fruits, gathered high in trees and thickets.

Voice Normally silent, but utter snorts and grunts; musical notes occasionally reported.

Swahili Twiga

Hotspots

Meru NP, Samburu NR (reticulated giraffe), **Masai Mara NR, Serengeti NP** (Masai giraffe), **Lake Nakuru NP** (Rothschild's giraffe)

AFRICAN BUFFALO

Recognition Stocky and cattle-like. Black or dark brown with thick, upcurved horns on central boss. Reddish 'forest buffalo' are smaller with back-swept horns.

Habitat Mosaics of grassland, woodland and savanna within 15km of water; also swamps, floodplains and forest edge.

Behaviour Highly gregarious. Presence of herd often given away by cattle egrets. Drinks daily and licks termite mounds for salt. Bulls wallow to cool off and remove parasites.

Breeding One calf born (mostly in early rains) after an 11½-month gestation; weaned at approximately 10 months.

Feeding Grazes a wide variety of grasses, including coarse grass left by other species; browses herbs and foliage when grass is scarce.

Voice Usually silent; explosive snorts in alarm; calves bleat and cows grunt to call calves.

Swahili Nyati or Mbogo

Hotspots
Masai Mara NR, Ngorongoro CA, Serengeti NP; Semliki Valley WR (forest buffalo)

Fun with bovids

Perhaps no other large animal has the African buffalo's reputation: a big bull stands 1.7m at the shoulder – one is even reputed to have tossed a Land Rover. Lone bulls can be extremely dangerous animals, and even blind or injured buffaloes can survive for years because of their size and bellicosity. If you do have the misfortune to be chased – you'll know it when the bushes explode and 850kg of beef comes hurtling out at 55km/h – by the time your brain catches up with your legs it should direct you to climb a tree (on the side away from the buffalo or you'll be propelled into it). But otherwise, African buffaloes are basically cattle and like their domestic counterparts generally live in docile, grazing herds.

Ironically, unless you see bulls fighting or fending off lions, African buffaloes are pretty inactive. Most of a buffalo's day is spent grazing or chewing the cud. Highly social, buffaloes form large nonterritorial herds which can number as many as 1500 members, although herds of several hundred are more common. The activity and movement of the herd is tightly coordinated by a variety of signals including lowing calls (similar to those of domestic cattle) and smells (presumably for recognising individuals and predators).

If you approach a herd, several individuals strut forward with their head up to test the wind – a challenging pose that seems to presage a charge. Meanwhile, the remaining adults form a line with young sheltered in between before they turn and run with heads tossing. However, they will charge a predator en masse and rally to protect a stricken animal.

Herds reach their greatest size during the rains, when hundreds of animals may gather; dry seasons see them break into smaller 'clans' of 12 or so cows and their offspring, accompanied by adult bulls. Cows in oestrus attract bulls who posture for dominance, circling, pawing, thrashing bushes and sometimes charging head-on in violent clashes. Bulls past their fighting prime join bachelor herds – this is when they're dangerous, but also most vulnerable to lions. ■

INTRODUCTION TO ANTELOPES

Amazing graze

Where there's greenery there's usually an antelope to eat it. Some may lack charisma, but each is a piece of the ecological jigsaw and East Africa's 40-odd species range from duikers barely 35cm high to oxen-sized eland (inset). Think of them as deadly predators of plant life – not all of which is defenceless (many antelopes browse selectively because plants can send a toxic surge into leaves being attacked). Antelopes promote the cycle of growth by adding manure to the soil and themselves provide a perpetual larder for all those glamorous meat eaters.

*Like most tragelaphine antelopes, female **greater kudus** do not have horns.*

Antelopes chew the cud; nearly all young hide for a few weeks after birth before joining the herd; and females remain with a herd from birth, dominated by males whose competitiveness forces bucks to disperse as they mature. Antelopes' horns are permanent, although frequently damaged in fights, and never branched like the antlers of deer. All bucks have them (and females of some species) – ridged (annulated), twisted, straight or backswept – but they are mainly for competition, rather than defence (by the time a predator gets that close it's usually too late): it's mainly the males who strive for rank (and always for mating rights).

__Waterbucks__ show the typical reduncine antelopes' ridged (also called annulated) horns.

Making scents of it all

Male antelopes are usually called bucks and females does. Bucks of course are mainly interested in does when they're in oestrus, in which case they're ready to rut – the end result of which is usually the birth of a single fawn. All antelopes have glands,eg, interdigital glands between their hooves, for scent-marking territories with details of the owner's sex, age, and social and re-productive status (other territorial behaviour includes piling dung in middens). Some species leave black, tar-like secretions ('black pearls') by inserting twigs into the pit-like preorbital glands in front of their eyes. After a period of lying-out in the grass, many fawns join a crèche with others; playful young antelope leap into the air, known as stotting (or pronking), which when performed by adults is thought to discourage would-be predators by demonstrating the antelopes' fitness. ■

__Gerenuks__ are the most spe-cialised of the three species of gazelle in East Africa.

Hotspots

Masai Mara NR and **Serengeti NP** Variety (up to 17 species – several often feeding together) and numbers reach a crescendo during the wildebeest migration. **Samburu/Buffalo Springs NRs** Dry country species such as oryxes, gerenuks, kudus and dik-diks thrive in semiarid scrub. **Queen Elizabeth NP** Extensive wetlands are suitable for Uganda kobs, waterbucks and sitatungas.

__Topis__ and other alcelaphine antelopes live on grasslands, and rely on speed to flee predators.

Bushbucks are medium-sized forest antelopes that are rarely seen away from cover.

*Female **bushbucks** lack horns and are solitary except when accompanied by a calf.*

*At up to 1.3m at the shoulder, the mainly nocturnal **bongo** is the largest forest antelope.*

Sitatungas are restricted to permanent marshes and swamps.

SPIRAL-HORNED ANTELOPES

Magnificent seven

Forest or dense bush offered some tempting benefits for evolving antelopes, such as cover to hide in and a year-round food supply, but it came with some inherent problems – cover can be used just as effectively by predators, for example. A group of seven antelopes, collectively known as tragelaphines (spiral-horned antelopes is easier to say), has evolved various strategies that both overcome and exploit such habitats. Among them are the largest of all, the elands; some of the most distinctive, such as greater kudus; and the unique, semiaquatic sitatunga. All are browsers of young, nutritious vegetation, and immediately stand out from the crowd with flanks strongly marked in blotches and vertical stripes, and more blazes on head, chest and legs.

Females of most species are hornless and show a generic resemblance, but males carry distinctive, smooth, keeled horns that spiral or twist to some degree (most dramatically in greater kudus – inset). Stripes and blotches can make excellent camouflage, for example on the flanks of bongos and bushbucks they almost perfectly mimic sunlight dappled through the canopy, making these antelopes very difficult to detect until they break cover. But an unfortunate corollary of superb camouflage is losing sight of your family, so these highly visual animals communicate with subtle signals from an early age: females approaching their hidden young bob their heads, throat flashes showing vividly in the gloomy light; and when raised in panic their bushy tails show a white flag.

Shadow boxers

Spiral-horned antelopes are closely related to buffaloes and, like them, are built for neither speed nor endurance. All have a non-territorial herd structure, although only elands, which live in more open country, have a highly developed herd instinct. The rule with tragelaphines is low aggression in open, flexible societies where males dominate without confrontation, instead of

The swamp antelope

One of the most remarkable of all antelopes is the sitatunga, a long-legged tragelaphine adapted to exploit the abundant food resources in swamps: its shaggy coat is oily and water repellent; it is a good, if slow, swimmer; and extraordinarily elongated and splayed hooves allow it to walk on submerged vegetation. So specialised are its feet that a sitatunga can outrun predators through swamps, but on dry ground it walks rather clumsily with a spread-eagled stance. Sitatungas move slowly and deliberately to avoid detection, typically entering the water, gently sinking, then feeding with most of the body submerged. To more effectively conceal themselves from predators they can submerge until just their snout and part of their head show above the surface. Watching and waiting are the tricks to seeing sitatungas: they are most active between 6 pm and 10 am – watch along the paths and tunnels they form through reeds and rushes.

Blotches and stripes break up the outline of a female **lesser kudu** in dappled light.

Male **greater kudus** have the longest horns of any antelope, averaging 1.2m.

staking out a territory. Large males do most of the mating, their dominance enforced by side-on displays which enhance their markings; further refinements include a spinal crest, which can be erected in threat or courtship, and horning vegetation and soil as a mark of status.

Horns of the well-armed males are occasionally used in defensive wrestling (inset), but bucks of most species are generally solitary and experience surges of testosterone that lead to aggressive phases, known in Swahili as *ukali*. Ukali may be a cyclical phenomenon, which encourages other males to disperse for their own safety (lethal clashes sometimes occur when two bucks are ukali). Life in the open compels elands to seek security in large, mobile herds where females also establish a hierarchy and calves are vulnerable to male aggression. As a consequence, both male and female elands have horns. Doing their best to remain hidden doesn't help an antelope buff to find them of course, but at least all tragelaphines signal with barking calls. There seems to be a neat inverse correlation between the vibrancy of markings and their vocal aptitude; for example, sitatungas are weakly marked but call often from the safety of their swamps. Living in dense bush, distinctively-marked kudu bulls are more vulnerable to ambush and posture more or less silently. ■

The hoarse bark of the **greater kudu** (this is a female) is one of the loudest antelope calls.

Hotspots

Lake Mburo NP For bushbucks (found wherever there are thickets), elands and sitatungas. **Saiwa Swamp NP** Was proclaimed largely to protect sitatungas. **Meru, Tsavo** and **Ruaha NPs** Semiarid scrub is a favourite haunt of lesser kudus. **Lake Bogoria NR**, **Ruaha NP** and **Rungwa-Kizigo GR** Greater kudus are elusive in Kenya – these places offer the best chance of seeing one.

The nomadic **common eland** is the largest and slowest species of antelope in East Africa.

TOPI & HARTEBEESTS

Topis stand atop termite mounds to scan for danger or to advertise territorial status.

Topis usually calve at the end of the dry season and may mingle with herds of hartebeests.

Jackson's hartebeest is a sub-species of hartebeest found in Uganda and north-western Kenya.

Also known as kongoni, Coke's hartebeest is easily identified by its white rump.

Built for speed

The group of large antelope known scientifically as alcelaphines includes the topi, hartebeests and wildebeest. All are grazers whose most outstanding features are elongated jaws (their eyes always seem to be set higher up than you expect – see the topi inset), sloping hindquarters and powerful shoulders (wildebeest look like no other antelope – see the highlight page opposite). All live on the open plains in large herds, and rely on speed and stamina to escape predators. Life in the open demands long, strong legs for sustained, fast flight and a herding instinct for safety, and the evolution of a long face enabled these antelope to graze without the encumbrance of a long neck. Dense herds tend to create intense competition among males, and the short, muscular neck also cushions the blows when males drop to their knees for head-butting jousts.

Both topi and hartebeests are often seen standing watch on top of abandoned termite mounds. If conditions are stable enough small herds live in a permanent home range, but when grasslands dry out mixed herds aggregate and move on. At these times males display on the run with stylised gaits and postures, and dispense scent with vigorous kicks, capering and stamping – hence the eccentric cavorting of wildebeests.

The buck stops here

The hartebeest shows much variation in colour and horn shape over its wide distribution – the variations are so marked that several populations go under different names, eg, Coke's (also known as the kongoni) and Jackson's hartebeests. The fossil record shows that hartebeests have evolved only over the last million years or so; as their distribution becomes fragmented by agriculture the different races will most probably evolve into new species within the next million years – should they last that long. The hirola, formerly known as Hunter's hartebeest, now has the dubious distinction of being the world's rarest antelope. Numbers plummeted from 10,000 or so in the 1970s to under 1000, and possibly as few as 600, by the millennium. Hirolas appear to have suffered with the massive increase in cattle, with which they compete directly for food. ■

> **Hotspots**
> **Masai Mara NR** and **Serengeti NP** Large numbers of topis and kongonis. **Tsavo East NP** Last chance to see hirolas – many have been transferred here and appear to be holding their own. **Murchison Falls NP** Jackson's hartebeest is common north of the Victoria Nile.

WILDEBEEST

The rut well travelled

Probably no other antelopes spark as much excitement as wildebeests on their famous year-long cycle of grazing, rutting and calving known as 'the migration'. Up to 500,000 of them (along with some 250,000 plains zebras) cross the Serengeti grasslands to the fertile volcanic plains of the Masai Mara in a vast, constantly moving herd. The catalyst is the short grasses on which wildebeests depend – their wide mouth is perfectly suited to select nutritious leaf growing close to the ground, but they can't survive for long on anything else and must keep circulating as pasture becomes exhausted.

Gregariousness is a great asset for an animal permanently exposed on the sward and thousands of hooves probably confuse predators. But, unique among antelopes, wildebeests make even the arrival of the next generation a crowd spectacle. Females in the Serengeti synchronise the dropping of some 750,000 calves to within a few weeks of each other to coincide with the flush of grass in the rains. As conditions dry out, herds congregate in a massive, continuously moving stream that stimulates hormonal changes in both sexes. Females come into oestrus, and males respond by staking tiny territories that usually last only a few days and are defined by little more than a bull's behaviour – the head-shaking, cavorting and leaps that earned wildebeests their common name.

Bulls mate with as many cows as they can before the herd moves on, mothers travelling with calves towards the centre, 'single' females further out, dominant bulls on the edge and males trying to establish harems on the outside or trailing behind (it's all much clearer from the air). The migration is a time of plenty for lions and crocodiles waiting in ambush, and hundreds of wildebeests drown where noisy, thrashing bottlenecks form at river crossings. A few weeks pass and the cycle begins again – the plains can be bereft of wildebeests for up to eight months at a time before predators and safari operators alike hear that unmistakable bleating on the breeze and start licking their lips. ∎

Recognition Unique. Large with thick neck, shaggy horse-like mane and tail. Elongated head has white 'beard', black muzzle and cowlike horns. Grey to tan overall with darker brindling.
Habitat Short grass plains within about 20km of water.
Behaviour Diurnal and nocturnal. Cows congregate with young among territorial bulls during rains. Calving occurs between late January and mid-March. Females come into oestrus as they lead herds in annual migration. Old and sick animals are left behind.
Breeding Young born synchronously during wet season after 8-month gestation; can walk and run within minutes.
Feeding Grazes nutritious short grasses until exhausted; cannot survive long on coarse grass.
Voice Bulls give loud, froglike belching grunts when displaying.
Swahili Nyumbu

Hotspots
Nairobi NP, **Masai Mara NR** (July to October), **Serengeti NP** (November to June)

IMPALA

Recognition Grant's gazelle-sized. Fawn or tan above, paler on flanks (which lack stripes); white belly. Black stripes on haunches. Males have backward-sweeping ridged horns.

Habitat Open woodland near short to medium grassland on well-drained soils; avoids steep slopes.

Behaviour Active by day, feeding mostly at dawn and dusk, resting in shade to ruminate in between. Lies down in overcast weather. Bachelor males mix with females in dry seasons. Often associates with baboons. Can go without drinking.

Breeding One fawn is born in a sheltered spot after a 200-day gestation.

Feeding Consumes almost 100% grass during rains, switching to browse (70%) such as shrubs (especially *Acacia* and *Combretum*), seedpods and herbage in dry seasons.

Voice Loud snorts in alarm.

Swahili Swala pala

High-kicking 'gazelle'

You may see an impala and think 'gazelle', but in fact the impala is thought to be most closely related to topis, hartebeests and wildebeests. It's an understandable mistake, for the impala is about the size of a Grant's gazelle, and among the most agile and graceful of all antelopes. When a predator approaches (and lions, cheetahs and hunting dogs often do), a herd of impalas explodes in all directions. Well known for their leaping ability, impalas can clear 3m in height and 11m at a bound. Part of the bucks' strategy for dispersing scent is to high-kick, which releases pheromones from unique glands on their rear fetlocks (easily seen as black hair tufts). Such behaviour is reminiscent of wildebeests, but male impalas also show unique tongue-flashing behaviour when courting or competing with other males for dominance. Like gazelles, you can expect to see impalas in groups, but you won't necessarily see them out on the plains – impalas seek woody areas on the savanna edge, where they browse when the grass gets too dry.

Stuck in a rut

An abundance of provender encourages gregarious behaviour and does form 'clans' numbering 30 to 120 in overlapping home ranges. Males are also gregarious and often drift to different clans (something does hardly ever do). Such large herds of females promote keen competition among bucks: these testosterone-driven pawns spend up to 25% of their time shepherding does into their territories and fighting off bachelor wannabes. In East Africa the impala rut is virtually continuous; rutting bucks are very vocal – you'll probably hear their predatorlike roars in suitable habitat and even see bucks with injuries from stronger rivals. This is a good time to get close, as impala bucks are often preoccupied. The rut is so strenuous that most males are exhausted after about three months, by which time a dominant male from the ever-ready bachelor herd is able to oust him from his territory. Vanquished bucks return to the bachelor herd where they regain condition and status, upon which they usually set out to reclaim their territory! ∎

Hotspots
Masai Mara NR, Lake Manyara NP, Lake Mburo NP

HORSE-ANTELOPES

Warrior horses

Three species of large, gregarious antelope are among the most striking of large mammals, with long, pointed or back-swept horns, boldly patterned coats, and black-and-white 'war paint' on their face and muzzle (inset: oryx). Tall stature, long tail, large hooves (and in sable and roan antelopes, an upright mane) give them a rather horse-like look, and their collective name, hippotragines, stems from Latin meaning 'horse-goat'. These antelopes are adapted to hard country with unpredictable rainfall – country with few large competitors, but marginal enough that large home ranges must be defended.

*Both sexes of **roan** antelope have similar coloration that contrasts with their striking masks.*

Unusually for antelopes, the females' horns are well developed (although thinner than bucks') and are an effective deterrent to other mares competing for food. Adults are rarely taken as prey, relying on speed and agility to outmanoeuvre

predators, although hyenas, hunting dogs and lions take a toll of their young. But as a last resort, the horns can double as formidable weapons – especially the spearlike, 75cm-long horns of oryxes, which have been known to impale lions and kill people.

*Only mature male **sables** are black – any other black male on one's turf is challenged.*

These rare exceptions aside, horns are mainly used in ritual combat or when striving for rank in a herd, and all three species have evolved various means of lessening fatal clashes. Roan bucks fight on their knees to lessen the chance of serious injuries, but fights between sable males sometimes lead to fatal gorings. This is where the sable's bold, easily seen markings come into play: young male sables resemble females and only the dominant male is black – another black animal on his turf would present an immediate challenge. Adapted to follow infrequent rains in search of green growth, a territorial life is not usually possible for oryxes; instead, a breeding bull dominates a nomadic herd and tolerates the presence of other males. Should he show aggression to calves, females are well equipped to discourage him.

*Female and young male **sables** are russet, the bucks reaching adult coloration after five years.*

Young of all three species spend much time playing – staging mock duels and generally charging about, especially in the early morning before feeding starts in earnest. Oryxes in particular put on some showy high-stepping at dawn and during showers. ■

Hotspots

Samburu and **Buffalo Springs NRs** These semiarid reserves make ideal country for beisa oryxes. **Tsavo NP** The fringe-eared race of oryx can be seen south of the Tana River. **Ruaha NP** Roans and sables favour woodlands. **Ruma NP** Although virtually extinct in Kenya, roans can still be seen here. **Shimba Hills NR** Sables (also practically extinct in Kenya) are resident.

*The **beisa oryx** is a race of oryx found in eastern Kenya as far south as the Tana River.*

Black flank stripes and a swishing tail are the hallmarks of **Thomson's gazelle**.

'**Tommie**' fawns lie-up in long grass for a few days after birth, although mother is usually close.

The white rump patch above the tail is a ready identification feature of **Grant's gazelle**.

Seen side-on, **Grant's gazelles** lack a black flank stripe, although some can appear dark.

GAZELLES

At home on the range

The very name 'gazelle' conjures up images of grace and speed, and all three East African species have these attributes in spades. The two common medium-sized gazelles of the plains, Thomson's and Grant's, are grazers and browsers; the third species, the gerenuk, is common in semiarid country.

Life on open plains allows (and for safety's sake obliges) a herbivore to congregate in larger numbers than would otherwise be possible: herds of Grant's and Tommies often gather in hundreds – sometimes even with each other or other herbivores, such as zebras, topis, impalas and wildebeests. A great percentage of the 400,000 Tommies on the Serengeti Plains are migratory, mingling with zebras and wildebeests – a sight that could evoke thoughts of the former abundance of plains mammals.

All of the large predators will take gazelles when the opportunity arises: Tommies are a favourite of cheetahs and wild dogs; male olive baboons will tear a young gazelle apart for a bit of extra protein; and martial eagles take fawns. Survival in the open requires all antelopes to be constantly alert and able to flee with only split-second warning. Even topping 80km/h in flight, and dodging and jumping with great agility, gazelles are not

quite a match for cheetahs (inset), and run the risk of overheating when being pursued by wild dogs or hyenas.

Herd members communicate with signals to warn of predators: Tommies flicker that bold, black flank stripe by twitching their torso just as they are about to run for it; and Grant's have a flashy white rump that stands out like a beacon in flight. All gazelles have a dark stripe through the eye and pale eyebrows, and other signal patches are visible when they flag their heads, wag their tails or leap about.

Gazelles live in flexible societies with little ranking, herds of does grazing and ruminating in large, shared home ranges, walking to water and lying up together, and migrating in sometimes huge aggregations. Bucks fight in defence of territories where females graze and even maintain their territories after the females have moved on. Young are hidden for a few weeks after birth, female Tommies remaining nearby or joining 'maternity herds', which ably fend off marauding jackals. ∎

Hotspots
Masai Mara NR and **Serengeti NP** Great herds of Tommies and Grant's, often mixed with other herbivores. **Tsavo East NP** Peters' gazelle – a distinctive race of Grant's – is common in semiarid bush.

GERENUK

Striving for new heights

Gerenuks (from the Somali for 'giraffe-neck') are gazelles adapted to life in semiarid bush; such habitat favours only small herds and consequently more than 12 gerenuks are rarely seen together. Long, slender legs and an extraordinarily elongated neck enable gerenuks to browse on the small, nutritious leaflets of acacias high up in the foliage; and a narrow snout, tiny mouth and long, pointed tongue help them pluck flowers and seed pods from between the longest spines. But gerenuks further outstrip the competition by standing on their hind legs to feed – thus attaining a height of 2m from the ground, where only very young giraffe might compete. Gerenuks can be active at any time of day, although to avoid detection they freeze blending in with the thorny scrub.

Only male gerenuks have the distinctive forward-tipped horns – which grow up to 44cm. Young males associate with each other and with females but become increasingly intolerant of other males as they reach maturity. Like Thomson's gazelles, adult males mark their territories with black pearls of scent from their preorbital glands – a behaviour not seen among male Grant's gazelles. Females breed year-round; for the first six weeks, fawns conceal themselves by hiding motionless in vegetation to avoid marauding predators, such as hunting dogs, cheetahs, jackals and leopards. ■

Recognition A gazelle with very long limbs and neck. Red-brown saddle with buff body and white underparts. Large rounded ears, wedge-shaped head and long tail with black tuft.

Habitat Semiarid to arid bush, especially open, flat thornbush.

Behaviour Able to feed standing on its hind legs. During courtship male scent-marks the female with his preorbital glands.

Breeding Year-round. Single fawn born after 6½–7 months. Fawns can stand bipedally after 1 month.

Feeding Browses small-leaved, thorny trees and shrubs.

Voice Generally silent. Snorts to signal alarm. Males 'hum' during courtship.

Swahili Swala twiga

Hotspots
Samburu NR, Buffalo Springs NR, Meru NP, Tsavo East and West NPs

Bohor reedbucks can often be detected by their loud whistling, even when invisible in reed beds.

*Largest of the reedbucks, the **southern reedbuck** reaches its northern limit in Tanzania.*

*Large size and shaggy fur distinguish waterbucks – a white rump makes it a **defassa waterbuck**.*

*An elliptical rump patch distinguishes the **common waterbuck** from the defassa.*

REDUNCINE ANTELOPES

Easy-going waterside dwellers

If there is any antelope you are virtually guaranteed to see on safari it is the waterbuck, and despite a shaggy coat and sometimes pungent smell, this large, often approachable animal somehow maintains a stately bearing even when grazing up to its belly in water. Two subspecies are commonly seen: the defassa waterbuck, which has an all-white rump (used by mothers signalling their calf to follow), and the common waterbuck, in which the rump patch is so reduced it looks like the animal has just sat on a freshly painted toilet seat (it has the same signalling function, but looks more like a bull's-eye). Waterbucks belong to a group of antelopes called the reduncines, which lumps them with the Uganda kob and three reedbucks (southern, bohor and the less frequently seen mountain reedbuck – the East African race is called Chanler's mountain reedbuck). Reedbucks are mostly nocturnal, although bohor reedbucks often give themselves away at night with whistles.

Only male waterbucks and reedbucks have horns, albeit strongly ridged (annulated) ones, which point forward at the tips, but both sexes have many skin glands that make their coat greasy – possibly as an insulation from temperature extremes – and pungent (it is sometimes stated that the wa-

terbuck's strong scent deters predators, but plenty get eaten by lions and hyenas). As their name suggests, waterbucks are never found far from water and all reduncines are more or less attached to it (although mountain reedbucks seek a living on valley sides); bohor reedbucks, and waterbucks in particular, rely on waterside vegetation for cover when pursued. The attraction is a year-round supply of food on waterside grasslands; the price is a habitat that swings dramatically between floods and dry season fires. As a consequence, most reduncines have broad ecological tolerances (eg, bohor reedbucks stray as far as 25km away during drought) and a flexible herd structure to accommodate crowding during difficult times. All males are territorial (inset: defassa waterbuck), but in waterbucks at least, females appear to have no hierarchy. But a buck will tolerate several bachelors on his turf – as long as they show correct appeasement behaviour when he expects it! ∎

Hotspots

Hell's Gate NP Rocky slopes make a likely stakeout for Chanler's mountain reedbucks. **Sekenani Valley** Chanler's also live here just outside Masai Mara NR. **Lake Nakuru NP** Woodlands fringing wetlands are ideal for the defassa race of waterbuck; bohor reedbucks are also abundant. **Samburu** and **Buffalo Springs NRs** Common waterbucks resident.

UGANDA KOB

Sword fighters

Kob bucks have a distinctive look when they're trying to attract a doe's attention, strutting with head held high and horns pointing back horizontally. In fact, if it weren't for its mating habits the Uganda kob (a race of kob found in East Africa) would probably be a fairly unremarkable beast, looking superficially like impala and inhabiting floodplains like other reduncine antelope. They're recovering well after Uganda's civil war and are easy to see in some reserves (although they are not only found in Uganda), grazing on green belts near waterways during the dry season and moving to higher ground during the rains. Bucks usually hold territories some distance apart and females live in small herds with no apparent hierarchy, coming and going as they choose. But seasonal movements and the need to drink regularly force females into herds, sometimes totalling thousands of animals. Where these herds become resident, sheer weight of numbers keeps the grass short in recognisable 'kob fields'. But look closely at some of these fields and you'll see mainly males strutting about in that distinctive pose, like so many jocks in a gym.

This is where things start to get interesting: stimulated by the presence of female herds, the bucks (sometimes 40 per hectare) concentrate on 'leks' – areas of sward, often enclosed by longer grass – where they stake out territories radiating from one or more hubs of accumulated dung and urine-soaked soil. Here they fight all challengers for the privilege of mounting a doe, rarely retaining their court for more than a few days and often exhausting themselves within hours. Herds of bachelors wait nearby to fight, but it's not the bucks alone that attract the does – when researchers removed sections of turf and placed them outside the lek, does (and bucks) moved to the old turf in the new position. Turf soaked with oestrogen-charged urine attracts both sexes to the leks, and 90% of females enter an arena on their day of oestrus to mate with a few males that have won centrally placed courts. ∎

Recognition Like a stocky impala. Reddish or ochre with white markings on face and throat. Black on hocks. Females lack males' lyre-shaped horns.

Habitat River flats and short grasslands, especially those trampled by other grazers or created by fires.

Behaviour Diurnal and nocturnal. Gregarious, sometimes forming large herds within a short walk of water, but avoids flooded areas. Moving en masse when threatened confuses or intimidates predators; when pursued seeks refuge in water or reed beds.

Breeding Calf born year-round after 8-month gestation; remains hidden for 6 weeks then joins others in crèche.

Feeding Grazes short grasses cropped by other species, green flushes after fires, and 'kob fields'.

Voice Whistles and grunts to advertise territory.

Swahili Mraye

Hotspots
Queen Elizabeth NP, Murchison Falls NP

SMALL ANTELOPES

Common duikers are widespread in woodland, savanna and secondary growth.

*A rich network of veins in the nose of **Kirk's dik-dik** acts as an internal heat regulator.*

Steinbucks have a black nose stripe, large white lined ears and only a rudimentary tail.

*Black spots below their ears and a black tail help distinguish the **oribi** from the similar steinbuck.*

Miniature 'glandscape' painters

The ancestral antelope looked very similar to a number of rather solitary and small antelopes (some are miniature – blue duikers stand only 32.5cm at the shoulder) that exploit small niches from rainforests to cliff faces. Size apart, dik-diks, klipspringers, the savanna-dwelling steinbuck and oribi, and the nine species of forest-dwelling duiker bear the hallmarks of most larger antelopes, including white signal patches on the rump (a good way to detect duikers as they move through the forest gloom). All bucks have horns, albeit small and spiky ones, but ironically in territorial disputes they seem more inclined to use them and inflict more serious injuries than larger species.

Most species live in strongly bonded pairs and defend a home range marked extensively with their preorbital glands (inset: klipspringer) – modified in duikers as 'smear glands' along the muzzle – that keep others of the same species posted with details of the marker's age, sex and breeding condition. Although small antelopes feature regularly on the menu of many predators, they make size work in their favour by heavily scenting their territories and using the resulting invisible map to bolt to safety through dense undergrowth. Females and males

keep each other interested with pervasive physical and airborne scents strong enough for one species, the suni, to be known as the musk antelope. All except duikers also mark territorial boundaries with dung middens.

Although rather common in places, small antelopes typically escape detection by freezing until danger passes – the bold markings of many duikers break up their outline in dappled forest light. Nimble enough to climb sloping trunks and tangles of vegetation, duikers have a subtle but intimate awareness of their environment, relying for sustenance on fruit, flowers and leaves dropped or dislodged from the forest canopy by monkeys, birds and fruit-bats. Listen for foot stamping as a warning and, if your vocal skills are up to it, an imitation of their bleat can attract duiker bucks. Snorts or whistles in alarm are other giveaways for small antelopes – oribis in particular are vocal whistlers, and easily recognisable when they flee by stotting (modified in a distinctive 'rocking horse' movement). ∎

Hotspots

Lake Mburo NP A mosaic of thickets and grasslands make this an ideal location for oribis. **Arabuko-Sokoke NP** Supports four duiker species, including the rare Aders' duiker. **Hell's Gate NP** Steinbucks thrive among thickets and rocky ground.

KLIPSPRINGER

A head for heights

Even if you thought to look for an antelope high up on a cliff face, you could easily overlook a klipspringer because of its small size and nondescript coloration. Living as high as 4000m on Mt Kilimanjaro, their dense fur is made up of hollow hairs that retain heat and enable klipspringers to withstand extreme cold. But they still like to take in the morning sun, and this is when they are best seen, standing motionless and alert on rock ledges. When alarmed, klip-springers (from the Afrikaans 'cliff-springer') lightly bound away across boulders, landing on all fours on the tips of their modified hooves.

Typically in pairs, when they feel safe again they perform a whistling duet, the female calling straight after the male; klipspringers are very faithful to their territories, and whistling probably also advertises to other pairs nearby. Inaccessible rock faces and agility are their main protection against predators, although danger can still come from above in the shape of eagles, and the male invariably acts as sentry while the doe feeds or suckles their single kid. Klipspringers typically spend their entire adult lives on one territory, but should disaster strike their 'patch', they can survive in adjoining habitat such as valley floors for a time. ■

Recognition Compact, goat-like. Grizzled grey-brown.
Habitat Cliffs, rocky slopes.
Behaviour Rests during heat of day. Marks territories.
Breeding Single kid born after 6-month gestation.
Feeding Browses on herbs and foliage.
Voice Pairs whistle.
Swahili Mbuzi mawe

Hotspots
Aberdare NP, Arusha NP, Lake Mburo NP

KIRK'S DIK-DIK

Little antelope that nose best

Antelopes don't come much smaller than Kirk's dik-dik – despite its long, slender legs, the largest adult stands only 45cm high. Kirk's dik-diks always live in monogamous pairs, the buck whistling persistently when danger approaches while the doe and fawn hide – reunions that follow an escape include much nuzzling and scent-marking. They are commonly seen in the early morning and evening, quivering stock-still near a bush before bolting through the undergrowth.

It is remarkable that a browser so small can be so successful, but the secret to a dik-dik's survival is a thorough knowledge of its turf, enabling it to escape through low tangles of vegetation. Territories are actively marked with black pearls of scent on twigs and stems, and middens of their tiny dung pellets mark boundaries – where a midden overlaps two territories, both families add to it on their respective sides. Any strange new droppings in their territories are detected by that flexible nose and are added to (including those of elephants!). The inside of their nose is lined with blood vessels and also acts as a heat regulator: Kirk's dik-dik can increase its breathing rate from one to eight breaths a second, sending cooled blood back to the heart. ■

Recognition Tawny upperparts with grizzled back.
Habitat Bushy savanna edge.
Behaviour In pairs or with single offspring. May stand on hind legs when feeding.
Breeding Single fawn born after 6-month gestation.
Feeding Browses on shoots and foliage.
Voice A high *zik zik*.
Swahili Dikidiki

Hotspots
Samburu NR, Meru NP, Arusha NP

Hedgehogs *consume one-third of their weight every day in invertebrates, roots and fruit.*

Elephant shrews *sniff out small invertebrates in leaf litter with their prehensile snout.*

Found in grasslands, the solitary and nocturnal **Cape hare** *actually benefits from overgrazing.*

The **unstriped ground squirrel** *is a burrowing specialist of arid and semiarid country.*

SMALL ARMY OF THE BUSH

Rodents, insectivores and hares

A vast assemblage – both in species and individuals – of small mammals plays an important role in nearly every ecosystem, eg, as food for predatory mammals, birds and reptiles; and as predators of insects and other invertebrates. Among them are the familiar (though hardly glamorous) rodents, a large group – numbering 150 species in East Africa alone – which includes rats, mice and interesting variations such as squirrels, the springhare, porcupines and anomalures ('flying mice'). Other, unrelated small mammals that may be encountered on safari include several families of small carnivorous mammals loosely termed insectivores: the shrews, elephant shrews and hedgehogs; and the vegetarian hares, known scientifically as lagomorphs.

Beavering away in the treetops

All rodents have a dental arrangement that features prominent incisors (gnawing teeth). Squirrels are essentially arboreal rodents (although one or two are primarily ground-dwelling) and most are active during the day; they reach their greatest diversity in rainforests, where some species are attractively coloured. Anomalures are extraordinary rodents adapted to life almost exclusively in the treetops. A loose flap of skin stretching between the front and hind legs can be extended to become a gliding membrane, which enables anomalures to leap and sail between tree trunks, thus obviating the need to visit the ground. Like the more famous beaver (not found in Africa), anomalures shape their environment to suit their lifestyle. But instead of felling trees like beavers, flying mice prune the forest canopy to create flyways, and prune young trees near their food trees to eliminate competition. Apart from their outrageous behaviour, two common species also have outrageous names: the widespread Lord Derby's anomalure; and the fabulous-sounding Zenker's flying mouse, restricted to the Semliki Forest.

Porcupines are the largest rodents (the crested porcupine can weigh 25kg), and are armed with long, loose quills that act as a spiny deterrent to would-be predators. Life for a small rodent has many perils, so various families, such as blesmols, root-rats and mole-rats, attack plants from below and live almost permanently underground. But most extraordinary of the 'underground rodents' is the naked mole-rat (also called 'sand-puppy' – inset),

Get hopping

Hopping is a fast, economical mode of travel utilised by two groups of burrowing rodents: the desert-dwelling jerboas and the springhare, a rodent large enough to resemble a hare – if it weren't for its even more striking resemblance to the kangaroos of Australia. Like the kangaroo, the springhare is a prodigious jumper, clearing up to 4m in a bound while their long tail acts as a counterbalance. They also have in common large ears and huge feet, on which most weight is carried by the enlarged third toe. Like most kangaroos, springhares are nocturnal and hop semierect with the forelegs held up. However, unlike springhares, kangaroos are marsupials (carrying their young in a pouch) and their similarities have evolved through similar environmental constraints – a phenomenon called convergent evolution.

Ochre bush squirrels vary greatly, from a pale desert coloration to a darker mountain-dwelling form.

Berries and seeds form most of the red-bellied coast squirrel's diet in coastal East Africa.

an almost hairless burrower that lives in underground colonies of up to 75 individuals in semiarid areas. Sand-puppies, like bees and termites, have a distinct social order that includes a large, dominant female, 'drones' and workers. Drones attend the 'queen'; she produces pheromones that suppress the sexual development of her offspring, who then become workers that dig tunnels, forage and carry food. Small mounds of earth on tracks reveal the presence of colonies, and if you approach quietly you may see workers digging near the surface in the early morning, throwing up puffs of earth like miniature volcanoes.

A great sense of humus

The insectivores are a loose grouping of insect-eaters that includes hedgehogs and many species of shrew, the smallest of all mammals. Shrews look superficially similar to rodents but feed voraciously by ploughing through leaf litter and chewing up large numbers of insects, which they detect with a sensitive snout. Variations on the shrew theme include the aquatic otter shrews and the amazing hero shrew, whose backbone can support a man's weight. African hedgehogs look much the same as their European counterparts and roll up into a protective ball when threatened.

Elephant shrews aren't actually shrews or even insectivores. They belong to their own seprate (and uniquely African) group – some are almost as big as a rabbit. Hares live in open, scrubby country where they eat coarse grasses and herbage. They are common, but usually seen only when they break from cover. ■

Crested porcupines are nocturnal and solitary, retreating to a communal burrow by day.

Hotspots

Meru NP and **Samburu NR** These sandy, semiarid parks are ideal for naked mole-rats. **Kibale Forest NP** Offers nightly spot lighting walks where Lord Derby's anomalure is regularly seen. **Masai Mara NR** Springhares can be seen by spotlighting just outside the reserve.

East Africa's many species of mouse are important prey items for birds, reptiles and mammals.

BIRDS

The sky isn't the limit

Birds are among the most widespread and abundant of vertebrates. One or more species is found in every habitat on earth, but above all they are the supreme masters of an environment that few other animal groups have exploited: earth's vast atmosphere. This invisible medium fills every space, from still glades in dense forests to raging storm fronts; birds in their many forms – and there are well over 1200 species in East Africa alone – use air as a hunting ground, a courtship arena or an observation post.

Success of unprecedented scales

A few salient characteristics instantly distinguish birds from all other life forms. The key to their ecological success is feathers, a unique adaptation shared by all birds but by no other creatures. Birds evolved from reptiles and feathers from scales; like reptilian scales, feathers overlap to serve as waterproof insulation, but unlike scales they keep birds warm enough to maintain a high level of activity, and have further diversified to provide, for example, waterproofing, insulation against extreme heat or cold, and showy courtship plumes. But as organs of flight feathers are unsurpassed: they adjust subtly to the lightest breeze and compensate instantly for wind strength, direction and lift. Each group has differently-shaped wings to exploit their preferred habitat, and the independence afforded by aerial manoeuvrability has allowed the evolution of diverse hind legs, with feet adapted, for example, to swimming, grasping or running.

The more wings change ...

Despite the bewildering differences in colour and shape, all birds are structurally similar – indeed, more so than any other class of land vertebrates. All birds are warm-blooded and although lightweight bones riddled with air sacs help them remain airborne for long periods, even the most peripatetic must return to land to lay eggs. Mouthparts always feature a toothless bill that varies according to food preferences, eg, hooked for tearing flesh. Behaviour is also broadly similar across the world's 9000 or so species, and usually includes courtship rituals between sexes; nest-building and intensive parental care while raising young; and the defence of feeding or breeding territories by physical or vocal displays. Many species regularly undertake long migrations to escape inclement seasonal changes at their breeding or foraging grounds.

The pace, grace and taste race

East Africa's largest and heaviest bird (up to 136kg!), the ostrich, is also the world's biggest and takes a bundle of other accolades; in contrast, the mouse-coloured penduline tit measures only 65mm. Among the high flyers are the lammergeier and various swifts, which soar at 5000m over Africa's highest peaks. Opinions vary on the fastest, but it's usually cited as the peregrine falcon. However, the red-billed quelea is almost certainly the most abundant and flocks numbering millions can be the bane of farmers. Which makes the largest nest? For its size, the hamerkop takes the laurels with a massive domed structure weighing up to 40kg. And the most colourful? Take your pick. ■

OSTRICH

Recognition Huge bird with long, featherless neck and muscular legs. Loose plumage is black and white in male, grey-brown in female.
Habitat Dry, open savanna, desert and semidesert; not dependent on water.
Behaviour Alone or in groups. Runs from danger; males aggressive to people and predators. Young follow parents for 12 months. Sexually mature at 3–4 years; may live 30–40 years.
Breeding Nest a shallow scrape; about 20 eggs incubated 6 weeks. Chicks run well and form crèches.
Feeding Seeds, fruits, leaves, insects, lizards and small tortoises. Sand, stones and even coins and nails are swallowed to help digestion.
Voice Usually silent. Snaps bill and hisses. Breeding males utter a deep, descending boom.
Swahili Mbuni

Winning the ratite race

Ostriches don't bury their head in the sand, although they sometimes sit on their nests with neck outstretched on the ground to protect their eggs or chicks. Being the world's tallest living bird (up to 2.75m) with the largest eyes of any land animal (50mm in diameter – check out the lashes), they normally detect danger from afar. That includes you, but these huge birds can usually be spotted some way off in open country. They generally seek safety in flocks (watch for chicks trotting at the heels of adults); look among herds of antelopes or zebras, where they often mingle to lessen the chance of being surprised by a big cat. If threatened they're off, clocking up sprints at 70km/h in 3.5m strides, and outpacing any predator at 50km/h for up to 30 minutes. In a tight spot an ostrich can kill a lion by kicking with its massive feet – the inner claw is modified into a 10cm spike.

The ostrich is a ratite, part of an ancient group of flightless birds distributed across the southern hemisphere. Two distinct races inhabit East Africa: the 'common' and 'Somali' ostriches; males of the latter have a blue-grey neck and legs that contrast with their pink bill. During courtship displays, males crouch while rotating outstretched wings and sway their neck from side to side; the neck and legs glow bright orange-pink (common) or a deep blue (Somali). Several females – normally two to five, but up to 18 – lay eggs (the world's biggest, weighing 1.5kg) in the same nest, although only the male and major hen (she who lays first) incubate, he by night and she by day.

An incredible total of 78 eggs was recorded in one nest, but only 20 can be incubated at a time so the major hen rolls away those that aren't hers (perhaps recognising her own by the size, structure and shape of pores in the shell); other eggs are scavenged by hyenas and jackals. Chicks leave the nest within three days and follow the parents; when two families meet a dispute usually ensues and the winning pair adopts the other crèche – groups of 100 to 300 young can thus aggregate. ■

Hotspots
Samburu NR (Somali ostrich); **Masai Mara NR, Nairobi NP, Serengeti NP** (common ostrich)

GREAT WHITE PELICAN

Cooperative fishing armadas

Pelicans are readily distinguished by their pouch: an elastic flap of skin slung under the massive bill which in the breeding season glows with colour (as does the bird's bare facial skin). Great white pelicans love a crowd, and are often seen 'loafing' on banks with cormorants and the smaller pink-backed pelican (which looks silver-grey – the pink traces aren't always visible). For most of the day they sit or stand around looking elegant, preening or pulsating their pouch to cool off. But cooperative feeding by both species is a fascinating sight: up to 40 pelicans form a horseshoe and simultaneously dip their bills in the water to drive fish into the shallows; in a river they form parallel rows and move towards each other with a similar effect. With the prey effectively 'corralled', each pelican scoops fish and up to 13L of water into the pouch, the water is then forced out through the closed bill and the fish are swallowed. These heavy birds require a great effort to leave the water, taking a long run-up along the surface with laboured flapping, and stalling in a long skid when it comes to landing (not surprisingly pelicans are most abundant on large bodies of water). But if ungainly on land they are graceful in flight, soaring high on thermals in V-shaped flocks where each bird flaps its wings in turn. ∎

Recognition Huge (3m wingspan). White with black flight feathers, yellow bill, pouch and facial patch.
Habitat Lakes and rivers.
Behaviour Breeds in colonies. Young gather into crèches.
Breeding Lays 2 eggs.
Feeding 'Corrals' fish.
Voice Grunts and moos.

Hotspots
Lake Elementeita, Lake Natron, Lake Manyara, Lake Nakuru NP, Queen Elizabeth NP

AFRICAN DARTER

The solitary snakebird

Check branches overhanging freshwater lakes and slow rivers for an all-dark bird sitting with wings draped open. When wet, the African darter's poorly oiled feathers become waterlogged, which decreases buoyancy while it swims under-water. The feathers must be conditioned by long spells of drying in sunshine, hence the characteristic pose; the closely related cormorants also hang their wings out to dry. Like cormorants, the darter hunts fish, its powerful, fully webbed feet acting as oars underwater. But rather than pursue their prey, darters swim slowly underwater with wings partly outstretched, inviting fishes to take shelter beneath them then spearing them with a dagger-shaped bill. Unfortunately, people don't usually witness the hunt and small prey is swallowed underwater, but larger fish are impaled through the side and, when the darter surfaces, are shaken free and juggled in the bill until they can be swallowed headfirst. The darter usually feeds and swims alone with only its head and slender neck showing, earning it the alternative name 'snakebird'. Darters perch for long periods, usually chasing other birds from their immediate vicinity, although they nest in colonies in association with cormorants and herons. Darters' bulky nests are built in trees and nestlings are white (cormorant nestlings are black). ∎

Recognition Sinuous neck, long, stiff tail and pointed yellow bill. Rufous throat and white eyestripe. Length 75cm.
Habitat Wetlands.
Behaviour Usually solitary. Fishes in quiet waterways.
Breeding Lays 2–6 eggs.
Feeding Spears fish.
Voice Harsh croaks at nest.

Hotspots
Marsabit NP, Tana River Primate NR, Murchison Falls NP

HERONS, EGRETS & BITTERNS

All niches great and small

Watch for the amazing cloak-and-dagger fishing technique of the **black heron** at Lake Jipe.

Green-backed herons tend to skulk under overhanging vegetation at the water's edge.

The widespread **great white egret** is the largest of East Africa's six white egret species.

Superficially similar to the purple heron, the **goliath heron** stands out because of its large size.

Most of the 19 species of heron, egret and bittern in East Africa are common and easily recognised, but different enough to make watching them worthwhile. All have long legs, toes and necks, and dagger-shaped bills; differences are chiefly in coloration and size, although the all-white egrets can be difficult to tell apart: bill and leg colour are clues. At times the picture of still grace, at others angular and brittle-looking, all are deadly hunters of fish, frogs, rodents and other small animals. The long neck can be folded in a tight S-shape (and is invariably held thus in flight) and the bill harpoons prey with speed and accuracy.

Most species feed at water margins and at least one is usually present at every waterway, including mudflats and mangroves; several species can feed side by side without competing directly and their techniques are interesting to watch. All hunt by posing stock-still for long periods before striking, some even from a perch; other techniques include running, stirring mud with their feet or flapping their wings to startle prey. The 1.5m-tall goliath heron, the world's largest, spears fish farthest from shore; the 30cm-long green-backed heron snaps up tadpoles and insects. The

black heron has an amazing 'cloak-and-dagger' technique of spreading its wings in a canopy over the water then spearing fish that shelter under it. Night-herons are nocturnal; and bitterns are solitary, well-camouflaged inhabitants of dense reed beds. Several species attend locust plagues to feed on the insects: a flock of 40,000 egrets was once recorded at a swarm in Tanzania. Cattle egrets (inset) snap up insects disturbed by buffaloes and elephants – behaviour that has been shown to be much more effective than hunting alone.

During courtship several species of heron, egret and bittern grow long, fine plumes, and patches of bare facial skin change to intense colour. Watch for preening behaviour: herons comb their plumage with a special serrated claw on the middle toe. Usually silent, herons often make harsh territorial calls at the nest; most species nest communally and heronries can be noisy places. Most species also roost communally, flying sometimes great distances in V-shaped flocks at dusk. ∎

Hotspots
Lake Baringo and **Lake Nakuru NP** These Rift Valley lakes are especially good for seeing a wide variety of species. **Queen Elizabeth** and **Murchison Falls NPs** River cruises are recommended for great views of several species.

SHOEBILL

Plunging headfirst

Also known as the whale-headed stork, the shoebill's most striking feature – its bulbous, cloglike bill – measures some 19cm in length and is almost as wide. Although unique, the shoebill shares with herons the habit of flying with neck retracted; it has a small crest at the back of its head like a pelican; and shows storklike behaviour such as emptying bills full of water on the nest to cool its young. And while it may look like a large, silver-grey stork, pelicans may be its closest relatives. This solitary and stately bird is avidly sought by bird-watchers, even though most of the time it stands stock-still and stiff-legged on floating vegetation or at the water's edge, waiting for prey. Lungfish are its favourite meal and it's worth watching its technique, for when a likely victim surfaces all hell breaks loose: the massive bill is jerked forward, causing the bird to overbalance, collapse and submerge its entire head. Using its wings and bill it then levers itself upright, manipulates vegetation out of its mouth and swallows the victim – usually decapitated by the bill's sharp edges. Accuracy is everything, for its bill cannot usually be manoeuvred for a second strike. Incredibly, this unconventional and all-or-nothing fishing method is also practiced in flight on occasion – the bird collapsing bodily into the water. ∎

Recognition Large (1.2m-high), storklike and blue-grey with a massive bill.
Habitat Papyrus swamps and marshy lakes.
Behaviour Solitary. Walks on floating vegetation.
Breeding Lays 1–3 blue-white eggs in long rains.
Feeding Grabs mainly fish.
Voice Bill-clapping at nest.

Hotspots
Murchison Falls NP, Semliki Valley WR, PN de l'Akagera

HAMERKOP

Supernatural shape-changer

Related to the herons and storks, and commonly seen in their company, the hamerkop's distinctive profile earned it an Afrikaans name meaning 'hammerhead'. During courtship, and often at other times, hamerkops engage in unique 'false-coupling' behaviour where one bird sits on the back of another (male or female) – mating doesn't always occur and birds may even face in opposite directions. Feeding is more conventional: prey is snatched from shallow water; and fish may be scooped from the surface while flying into a head-wind. For unknown reasons hamerkops make a massive nest of twigs, sticks and even bones, usually in the fork of a tree, in which is secreted a brood chamber accessible only through a narrow tunnel. These huge constructions can weigh 40kg and be 1.5m deep; not content with one, some pairs build and abandon several nests in close proximity – various owl species readily take over their vacant nests. But perhaps the hamerkop has got it all sorted out: with so many nests to choose from, a would-be predator probably stands more chance of facing a genet, spitting cobra, monitor lizard or bee swarm (all of which use abandoned nests) than the bird itself. With such tenants in hamerkop nests it's no wonder Africans imbued hamerkops with supernatural powers. ∎

Recognition Bronze-brown. Crest offset by heavy bill. Length 50–56cm.
Habitat Lakes and rivers.
Behaviour Usually solitary, roosting in groups. Associates with large mammals.
Breeding Lays 3–6 white eggs year-round.
Feeding Frogs and fish.
Voice Strident yelping *yip-pur, yip-yip-pur-pur-yip*.

Hotspots
Nairobi NP (Athi River), **Amboseli NP**

*Flocks of migratory **Abdim's** storks descend on East African grasslands from October to April.*

*Uncommon but unmistakable, the **saddle-billed stork** usually hunts alone or in pairs.*

***Marabou storks** often join vultures at a kill, but are efficient predators in their own right.*

***Yellow-billed storks** are widespread and common at the edges of open waterways.*

STORKS

Stately sentinels

Stately and often colourfully marked, storks are generally found near wetlands, although some species are far less dependent on water for food resources than other waterbirds. Superficially similar to herons, they share with them long legs, toes and neck, although the latter is generally thicker and overall body shape is bulkier. All storks fly strongly with necks outstretched; they can often be seen soaring high in thermals, where their distinctive bill shapes make identification fairly easy. Marabou and saddle-billed storks are among the largest of flying birds, the latter with a 2.7m wingspan.

All eight species found in East Africa are predominantly white, black or black-and-white, and all have large bills adapted to a carnivorous diet consisting of small animals such as frogs, fish and rodents. The more generalised feeders, such as white and Abdim's storks, snatch insects, small rodents and reptiles with dagger-shaped bills; saddle-billed storks jab at fish in the shallows; and yellow-billed storks find aquatic prey in muddy water by the touch of their long, sensitive bill (inset). Marabou storks, the most predatory, have a massive 35cm bill used to pick over carrion and slay other animals, including birds as large as

flamingos. Marabous readily adapt to a scavenging life in cities and are often seen close to rubbish dumps in Nairobi or Kampala. Most specialised of all is the African open-billed stork: this all-black species has a distinctive tweezer-shaped bill, which it uses to remove snails from their shells.

White storks are famous in Europe for arriving en masse in spring and nesting on rooftops; large flocks return to East Africa between November and April. The arrival of another migrant, Abdim's stork, is usually associated with rains. Of the resident species, only woolly-necked and saddle-billed storks are solitary nesters; all others nest in colonies, sometimes in association with herons or cormorants. All species construct large, untidy platforms of sticks in trees, often near or over water; adults empty bills full of water over their chicks to keep them cool. Marabous have a strange habit of defecating on their legs to cool off – a habit they share with vultures. ∎

Hotspots

Masai Mara NR and **Ngorongoro CA** Flocks of white and Abdim's storks arrive between October and April. **Lake Turkana** and **Queen Elizabeth NP** Supports African open-billed storks. **Lake Baringo**, **Lake Naivasha** and **Queen Elizabeth NP** Yellow-billed and saddle-billed storks are widespread along these and other Rift Valley lakes.

IBISES & SPOONBILLS

Sacred waterbirds

Essentially waterbirds, ibises and spoonbills are biologically akin to herons and storks by dint of their long legs, toes and necks; the differences lie mainly in the shape of their sensitive bills. The most obvious feature of spoonbills – a flattened, spoonlike bill – is swept from side to side as they feed on microscopic water creatures, filtered through fine sieve-like lamellae (fine bony filters). The bills of ibises are not flattened and curve strongly downwards – designed for probing the mud for prey. Despite their different bills (and the fact that spoonbills are more tied to wetlands), the two groups are close relatives: occasionally ibises are seen sweeping their bills from side to side and spoonbills poking in soft mud.

The African spoonbill is common in shallow, slow-moving waterways in the company of other waterbirds, although

Eurasian spoonbills also occasionally stray to East Africa (especially at Lake Turkana in northern Kenya – it can be told apart by its black bill). Spoonbills and most ibises nest colonially in trees (often in association with herons, storks and cormorants) where they build untidy stick nests.

Ibises use their long, bowed bills to probe for crustaceans, snails and tadpoles. The most widespread species commonly forages on lawns and grasslands, and adapts readily to agriculture: on occasion it has averted devastation to crops by consuming plague locusts. In fact, this common, black-and-white bird was worshipped by ancient Egyptians, who associated its migration with the arrival of the fertile floodwaters of the Nile River every year. Mummified specimens have been found in ancient tombs, it is accurately depicted on wall friezes and to this day it is known as the sacred ibis (inset).

While sacred ibises are gregarious waterbirds, nesting in colonies and flying to communal roosts in V-shaped flocks at dusk, pairs of hadada ibises nest alone and often feed well away from water. The hadada's brash *ha-haha* call is one of the most distinctive sounds of the savanna, especially at dusk and dawn, and can be heard even in the parks and suburbs of cities. The closely related African green ibis is an inhabitant of mountain forests and is even less dependent on water, foraging in clearings, nesting in trees and even running along large branches. ∎

*Small groups of **sacred ibises** can be seen feeding in wetlands, cultivation and even gardens.*

***Hadada ibises** are another adaptable species, and often feed in urban parks and gardens.*

*The superficially similar **glossy ibis** is also widespread, but rarely seen far from water.*

*More dependent on water for feeding, **African spoonbills** breed in Rift Valley lakes.*

Hotspots
Lake Baringo, Lake Nakuru NP and **Lake George** These Rift Valley lakes are regular haunts of all bar the green ibis. **Mt Kenya** and **Kilimanjaro NPs** The high slopes of these mountains are the best places to seek green ibises.

GREATER & LESSER FLAMINGOS

Flocking pink

Masses of pink birds shimmering through the heat haze – audible but inaccessible across fields of treacherous mud – make a tantalising sight, and early Christians considered the flamingo to be the Phoenix, the legendary red bird that rises from the ashes of its own funeral pyre. Flamingos are instantly recognisable by their combination of pink coloration, and long, slender neck and legs. Where the two are found together, the pale pink greater flamingos (below) tower above the deep rose-pink lessers (left).

Few large birds are as gregarious as flamingos: great numbers concentrate in shallow lakes too alkaline or saline to support fishes (which otherwise compete for the tiny water animals or algae sought by flamingos); and food resources occur in such quantities that competition between individual birds is limited. Flamingos may spend hours standing or floating motionless, but their feeding method is unique among birds: while walking through shallow water with head upside-down and submerged, they sweep their angular bill from side to side. Food is caught in lamellae (fine bony filters) and excess water and mud are forced out by the tongue acting as a piston. Flamingos at Lake Bogoria NR have been estimated to consume 60 tonnes of blue-green algae a day.

Courtship rituals are conducted en masse: hundreds or thousands of birds stretch their necks and twist their heads in unison, stretch wings and legs, and strut through shallow water before abruptly changing direction. These displays synchronise hormone production and ensure a colony takes simultaneous advantage of optimum conditions to raise their young. However, breeding sometimes fails catastrophically and rising water levels can wipe out an entire season's efforts.

Adults flamingos have few predators, although their tongues were considered a delicacy in ancient Rome; marabou storks take a toll of eggs and chicks; and African fish eagles sweep over a flock to induce a panicked stampede then pick off injured birds. ■

Recognition Greater: Tall (1.5m) white or pale pink with long pale pink legs and S-shaped neck. Lesser: Shorter (90cm); deeper pink with darker bill and red legs.
Habitat Salt lakes, estuaries and coastal lagoons.
Behaviour Highly nomadic and gregarious. Flock-synchronised courtship. Flies with neck and legs fully extended.
Breeding Sporadic. A single egg is normally laid on a semiconical nest of mud surrounded by water in inaccessible mudflats.
Feeding Greater: aquatic insects, crustaceans and molluscs. Lesser: algae. Both filter food by sweeping the beak from side to side underwater.
Voice Goose-like honking; constant low murmuring while feeding in flocks.
Swahili Heroe

Hotspots
Lake Bogoria NR, Lake Nakuru NP, Lake Elementeita, Lake Natron, Lake Turkana, Lake George

DUCKS & GEESE

Dabbling and diving, grazers and dippers

Thanks to their long history of domestication, few birds are as universally recognisable as ducks and geese (collectively known as waterfowl); indeed few groups are so similar, with a broad, flattened bill at one end and strongly webbed feet at the other. Several of the 14 resident or nomadic species grace nearly all lakes, swamps and rivers, and migrants from Eurasia swell local numbers from November to March. All waterfowl are adapted to an aquatic life with insulating down beneath waterproof feathers; and most are strong flyers, taking off explosively and quickly attaining fast, level flight (among the fastest of flying birds) with neck outstretched. Food is typically vegetation and small invertebrates; each species of waterfowl occupies a slightly distinct feeding and breeding niche, and thus several can coexist without competing directly.

*The **white-faced whistling-duck** is the commoner of East Africa's two whistling-duck species.*

The most common species are easily identified by their bill colours, but look out for their different feeding behaviour. The so-called dabbling ducks (including red-billed teal and yellow-billed duck) upend in shallow water, paddling like mad to stay under and grazing weed from the bottom. In deeper water, Maccoa and white-backed ducks dive for a living, propelled by legs set well back, and swim with bodies low in the water. Egyptian geese (inset) are primarily grazers, pulling grass sometimes far from water. The African black duck inhabits forest streams and rivers, and even alpine tarns, where it dips its head to take prey from under submerged stones. East Africa's smallest duck, the African pygmy-goose, is at home diving among floating lilies.

*The male **knob-billed (or comb) duck's** fleshy comb swells during the breeding season.*

Many waterfowl are nomadic, often covering vast distances to reach new waterholes as an old one dries out. Breeding is usually prolific to take advantage of favourable conditions and numbers can build up quickly. Most are solitary breeders, laying in nests the female often lines with down. Young hatch covered in cryptically marked, waterproof down, and can walk and swim almost immediately, following their parents around and catching their own food. The other great distinction of these birds is of course their vocal repertoire: the familiar barnyard quacking is *de rigueur* for typical ducks, but the two species of whistling-duck are aptly-named for their sibilant whistling. ■

*The **African pygmy-goose** favours clear, quiet waters with floating vegetation.*

Hotspots
Lakes Elementeita, Naivasha and **George, Lake Nakuru NP** and **Lake Baringo** All common species and northern migrants can be seen on these Rift Valley lakes. **Masai Mara NR** Spur-winged geese frequently visit temporary wetlands.

*Like many African ducks, **red-billed teals** wander according to seasonal conditions.*

*The **black-shouldered kite** is commonly seen hunting rats and mice over grasslands.*

*Opportunistic **black kites** scavenge both from predators' kills and from rubbish dumps.*

*Few raptors are as striking or as graceful in flight as the widespread **bateleur**.*

*The **Gabar goshawk** is a swift bird hunter of dry woodland that occasionally takes reptiles.*

BIRDS OF PREY

Raptor round up

East Africa has around 80 species of birds of prey (or raptor) from three distinct families: the falcons; the eagles, hawks, harriers and vultures; and the secretary bird. In open savanna at least, it is not unusual to see several species in the sky at once, or perched on the same tree. They reach their greatest diversity in forests, although several species are found in every habitat. With a few notable exceptions – such as the brightly coloured bateleur – all are rather plain in coloration, although some are adorned with showy crests.

Raptor-watchers should look for huddled, dark shapes on topmost boughs (large species take longer to get going in the morning, and finish hunting earlier in the day, because they depend on thermals to gain altitude and soar). Note large, bulky nests in which an incubating bird may be sitting low with its mate perched nearby; listen for small birds (such as drongos) mobbing; and watch for large hawks drying their outstretched wings on exposed perches after a storm. Other giveaways include antelope legs wedged into branches (eagles' handiwork), piles of feathers where a bird has been plucked, and 'whitewash' below nests on cliffs. Rubbing styrene foam on glass to imitate a distressed rodent can have spectacular results; and watch for hawks seizing fleeing animals from grass fires.

Let us prey

Varying in size from pigeon-sized sparrowhawks to mighty eagles with a 2.5m wingspan, nearly all raptors are exclusively carnivorous, with talons to grasp or snatch prey, and a hooked beak for tearing flesh. Raptors have incredible eyesight, spotting a grasshopper at 100m and a hare at 1000m. Forest hawks are usually on the move with the dawn and insect-eating raptors start out once the sun makes their prey more active. Sparrowhawks and goshawks feed primarily on birds caught in mad dashes through foliage. Snake-eagles sit and wait for hours on a perch then drop onto snakes, which they kill and then swallow whole.

Masters of the air

Falcons are voracious predators that kill mainly birds on the wing, although there are exceptions: kestrels (a greater kestrel is shown) hover and pounce on mice and lizards, and pygmy falcons subsist on insects. Like other raptors, falcons have a strongly hooked bill and powerful talons superbly adapted for seizing prey. But in flight they show their true mastery, their long, narrow wings scything through the air in quick beats, picking up speed as prey is approached and building to a deadly crescendo in dives known

as stoops. Falcons are among the swiftest of birds (although such statistics are rarely measured accurately and doubtless have been exaggerated). The 19 species certainly have few enemies, save larger falcons, and none normally builds a nest, using instead cliff ledges and nests abandoned by other birds – the 20cm-long pygmy falcon is smaller than the buffalo-weavers whose old nests it uses!

The African harrier-hawk (or gymnogene – inset) has long legs with which it reaches into nests, cavities and under bark for prey, even hanging upside down from weavers' nests to extract chicks and eggs. Harriers methodically quarter grasslands, gliding on long, slender wings and dropping onto mammals and birds – their facial feathers are arranged in a disc, which heightens their hearing (like owls). And there are many other hunting strategies: bat hawks swallow bats whole in midair; Verreaux's eagles haunt cliffs and kopjes for hyraxes; African crowned eagles snatch monkeys from the forest canopy; and the martial eagle can bring down a small antelope and carry it to a perch.

Instead of elaborate plumage, raptors rely on dramatic aerial displays during courtship – such as free falling while grappling talons, and passing prey to one another while one bird flies upside down. Hawks often display late in the morning – watching for this behaviour is a good way to detect forest hawks. Each species has a different proportion of wing length to breadth, which in turn determines aerobatic manoeuvrability and speed. Thus, the broad wings of forest hawks help them manoeuvre through branches and foliage; and the great eagles have long, broad wings on which they can glide to great heights and distances. Most aerobatic is the bateleur (from the French for acrobat), a consummate glider that in courtship displays performs fast rocking motions on the wing. ∎

Hotspots

Masai Mara, **Samburu** and **Buffalo Springs NRs**, **Tsavo East** and **West**, and **Serengeti NPs** All excellent for raptor-watching; dozens of species from sparrowhawks to eagles. **Hell's Gate NP** Cliffs are home to augur buzzards and several species of falcon. **Mt Kenya** and **Kilimanjaro NPs** Hunting grounds for mountain buzzards and Verreaux's eagles.

Dark chanting goshawks typically scan for lizards and snakes from a prominent perch.

*Most **augur buzzards** occur in this colour form, but about one in ten has black underparts.*

*The solitary **tawny eagle** is one of the most widespread resident birds of prey in East Africa.*

*The mighty **martial eagle** is powerful enough to take storks and small antelopes.*

*Northern Tanzania marks the southern limit of the **Egyptian vulture's** distribution.*

***Hooded vultures** are widespread in reserves and outside human settlements.*

*Even when perched the **African white-backed vulture's** diagnostic feature can be difficult to see.*

***Rüppell's griffon vulture** is common in most reserves but most widespread in Kenya.*

VULTURES

Scavenging angels

Think of the great plains and the nightly carnage left by lions and hyenas, and you'll also probably get an image of squabbling flocks of gore-encrusted vultures eating the stuff few animals will touch. And fair enough, too, because with few exceptions that's basically what they do. Should they need an introduction, vultures are birds of prey adapted to eat carrion, their chief difference to other raptors being a usually bald head and neck (it's easier to feed and keep clean that way), and feet better suited to walking than grasping. It may not be an appealing way of life to us, but it's an extremely profitable niche to exploit.

Look for these great, bulky birds sitting at the top of acacia trees and on large, exposed branches – larger species are usually solitary. Although ungainly on the ground, all have long, broad wings superbly adapted for long spells of soaring and by midmorning these large birds are usually circling high on thermals. Vultures have a poor sense of smell, instead using their keen eyesight to follow other vultures and eagles, or scavenging mammals on the ground, that might lead them to a kill. If vultures are circling in the air over a carcass it's usually a sign that predators are still chewing away at it: if you're on foot, beware.

Carrion carry-on

Early morning is not usually a vulture's best time. After a cold night on the plains they take a while to get airborne owing to a lack of thermals, especially on an overcast day. Hunched up, most of the seven plains species are difficult to identify as anything other than vultures, but in flight their various features are more apparent. Larger species usually take precedence at a carcass although smaller vultures may gang up and chase them away; and

Bone crusher

Despite its name, which means 'lamb vulture', and great size (with a 2.8m wingspan this is one of the largest vultures) the

lammergeier probably doesn't kill lambs. In fact, it rarely kills anything in the rugged gorges and alpine areas it frequents. Like all vultures, it is a scavenger, but rather than tearing at flesh (something it could easily do with its hooked bill and curved talons), it eats whole bones and scoops out the marrow with its tongue. It particularly favours large leg bones, and any too large to be swallowed are dropped from a height of about 20 to 80m onto a well-used, flattish area of rock called an ossuary, until they smash or splinter. Ravens in alpine areas have also been seen trying this trick, although can't seem to manage it as well as their mentor. Also known as the bearded vulture because of its black, bristly 'beard' of feathers around the beak, the lammergeier is Africa's rarest vulture.

The **lappet-faced** (or **Nubian**) **vulture** *is particularly common during the wildebeest migration.*

White-headed vultures *are abroad early in the day and are often first at a carcass.*

each species is specialised to feed differently and thus has different headgear. The largest, the lappet-faced and white-headed vultures, tear open a carcass, eating the skin, as well as bones and sinews. They pave the way for vultures with a long, bare neck – Rüppell's griffon and African white-backed (inset) – to reach right into the guts to eat soft parts without getting their feathers caked in blood; they will even climb inside a rib cage. The comparatively small hooded and Egyptian vultures can't compete with larger species, instead grabbing scraps from the frenzy; crows and marabou storks also loiter for morsels.

Vultures may fast a week between kills, but it's not all gore and blood lust. Hooded vultures pick over human refuse; Egyptian vultures steal birds' eggs and smash them on the ground, and have learned to break open ostrich eggs with a rock. The boldly-marked palm-nut vulture is superficially similar to the African fish eagle (and may in fact be closely related), and like it feeds on fish and crabs. But, despite its hooked bill, this extraordinary vulture feeds mainly on the protein-rich nuts of palms, such as *Phoenix* and *Raphia* palms, a food source sought by many birds and mammals. All vultures are attentive parents: adults range up to 160km in a day as they follow the wildebeest migration across the Serengeti Plains before returning to the nest with food. ∎

The **palm-nut vulture** *is often seen in the vicinity of palms, especially near major rivers.*

Hotspots

Serengeti NP, **Ngorongoro CA** and **Masai Mara NR** Top spots for vultures because of high concentrations of predators and prey. **Samburu NR**, and **Mikumi** and **Meru NPs** Palm-nut vultures common. **Hell's Gate NP** Ruppell's griffons and Egyptian vultures nest here. **Mts Kenya** and **Elgon**, and **Kilimanjaro NPs** Best spots to look for lammergeiers.

White underwing coverts separate **African white-backed vultures** *from other species in flight.*

SECRETARY BIRD

Recognition Uniform grey with black 'thighs', flight feathers and loose crest. Bare orange facial patch and deep pink legs and feet. Long central tail feathers and outstretched legs obvious in flight.
Habitat Short grasslands with scattered thorn trees; common in agricultural land. Avoids hilly or rocky country.
Behaviour Usually solitary or in pairs, but groups may gather at locust plagues or bushfires. Nests and roosts on flat-topped acacias. Soars high on thermals. Kicks at tufts of grass or dung for prey. Regurgitates large pellets near roosts and nests.
Breeding Lays 1–3 eggs, usually in wet season; only one chick survives and fledges after 2–3 months.
Feeding Mainly large insects and spiders, but also reptiles, birds up to small hornbill size, small mammals (such as rodents, hares, mongooses and small cats) and carrion.
Voice Generally silent; a deep guttural croaking in displays, fights, at nest and in flight.

A voracious pedestrian

Stalking across grasslands with jerky precision and standing 1.2m high – tall enough to be seen from hundreds of metres away – this high-stepping bird of prey is unique to Africa. Its body and head resemble those of a large eagle, but despite its hooked bill it differs from other raptors in a number of ways. For example, its legs are three times as long as those of a 'conventional' raptor and jack it up to an ideal vantage point from which to look for a meal.

The secretary bird is known to stride up to 20km a day in search of prey, which it kills with a rain of swift kicks from its thick, powerful feet. When a snake is encountered – and dangerous vipers and cobras are attacked with relish – it is stamped to death in a lethal flamenco audible from some distance away. Speed and agility are the keys to handling venomous prey, and secretary birds' legs are heavily scaled for further protection. Small prey is swallowed whole – that includes snakes, but also eggs, chicks, entire wasps' nests and golf balls (by mistake); larger items are torn apart or cached under a bush for future reference.

The secretary bird's long, black crest flaps in the breeze and is said to resemble the quill pens worn behind the ears of 19th century scribes; another theory attributes the name to 'saqur-et-air', French-Arabic for 'hunting bird'. Despite the obvious eagle-like features, there is behavioural evidence for other possible origins. The long legs suggest a common ancestry with storks, and other storklike traits include extending its neck in flight, and head-bowing and bill-clapping displays between pairs at the nest. But courtship flights are very raptorlike, and include 'pendulum displays' where one bird drops in a graceful swoop from a great height with wings folded then pulls out of the dive to climb slowly and repeat the show. Pairs also tumble in mid-air with feet outstretched towards each other. ■

Hotspots
Masai Mara NR, Serengeti NP, Murchison Falls NP

AFRICAN FISH EAGLE

The voice of Africa

Whether perched at the top of a *Euphorbia*, head and breast glowing white, or sweeping low on a dive, few birds beg superlatives like this magnificent wetland predator. African fish eagles are common and in places live in comparatively high densities: an estimated 100 pairs live along the Kazinga Channel in Queen Elizabeth NP, and numbers have soared at Rubondo Island NP at Lake Victoria following the introduction of Nile perch into the lake. At some sites, such as Lakes Baringo and Naivasha, fish eagles have learned to take fish thrown into the air by boatmen. At first light their loud, ringing calls echo across lakes and river valleys – a sound so distinctive and recognisable that the fish eagle is known as 'the voice of Africa'. Pairs sometimes duet from perches, throwing their heads back until they are bent almost double.

Turbot-charged pirate

Closely related to the bald eagle of North America, fish eagles look regal wherever they perch, but these voracious raptors are so effective at fishing they can (and often do) spend as much as 90% of the day resting or preening. A hungry fish eagle stares intently at the water and, when a likely fish is spotted, makes a fast, sweeping dive, at the last second throwing its legs and huge talons forward to seize its slippery catch. Most prey consists of surface-feeding fish taken within 15cm of the surface, although if necessary it will plunge in bodily to a depth of 50cm. The largest catch recorded is 3kg, but anything over 2.5kg can't be lifted and must be dragged or 'rowed' with one foot through the water to shore. Any fish it can carry are consumed at leisure at a favourite perch. Fish eagles also rob other birds (and each other) of their catch: victims of their piracy can be as large as pelicans, herons and storks, or as small as pied kingfishers. Where there are no fish, eg, at Lake Bogoria, they prey on waterbirds – killing flamingos, and even wiping out entire colonies of herons, spoonbills and cormorants. ■

Recognition Pure white head, breast, back and tail contrast with rich chestnut belly and 'trousers', and black wings. Bill black with yellow base. Length 75cm.
Habitat Widespread near lakes, rivers and estuaries (occasionally forest); immature birds may wander far from water.
Behaviour Adults pairs sedentary and intensely territorial when breeding; may reuse the same nest for 10 years. Groups gather at fish strandings. Immatures may form loose non-breeding populations. Will cross large arid areas to reach isolated waterways.
Breeding Usually lays 2 eggs in large nest of sticks and papyrus near water. Chicks fledge at 65–75 days.
Feeding A large variety of fish and waterbirds (especially young birds); also scavenges dead fish and carrion (immatures may be seen at predators' kills).
Voice A loud and far-carrying *wee-ah*, *kyo-kyo-kyo-kyo* from a perch or in flight.

Hotspots
Lake Naivasha, Lake Baringo, Queen Elizabeth NP, Murchison Falls NP

*The noisy **coqui francolin** (it's call sounds like its name) is a secretive grassland species.*

__Shelley's francolins__ inhabit upland grasslands, where they crouch in grass to avoid danger.

*The **crested francolin** is commonly seen along park roads throughout the region.*

*Most active at dawn and dusk, **red-necked spurfowl** seek dense cover and roost in trees.*

FRANCOLINS

Chickens crossing the road

Francolins belong to the great order loosely known as 'game birds' – the pheasants, quails, partridges and jungle fowl (precursors of the domestic chicken) that have been the butt of hunters' activities for centuries. And it's not just humans – small cats and other predators readily stalk francolins – but these ground-dwelling birds are great survivors: they are abundant and come in many varieties. Francolins nest on the ground (although the retiring habits of some species mean that their nests are as yet unknown), and the downy, precocial chicks are well camouflaged and can run within hours. Walking (and running) are strong francolin traits – all species have stout legs and feet, and run fast to evade predators – only when push comes to shove will they take to the wing, flying low for a short distance before dropping to the ground again.

The basic francolin design is like a large, upright quail, with heavily streaked upperparts in greys, browns and black for camouflage, although some, eg, the red- and yellow-necked spurfowl, sport naked flesh on the face and neck which enhances their territorial displays. All have a strong, hooked bill useful for snatching small animals, picking up seeds and fruit, and digging for

bulbs. Like domestic hens, many rake the soil and leaf litter with their strong feet, and cocks of most species sport spurs on their legs.

Although a few species occur across Asia, Africa is the francolin stronghold and the 18 species found in East Africa range in size from 20 to 35cm. Many are common and a day's birding in any reserve is bound to encounter at least one species. Francolins often feed along roadsides in the early morning and late afternoon, or dart across the road in single file. Two of the most abundant – red-necked and yellow-necked spurfowl (inset) – are decidedly chickenlike, and are commonly seen standing atop termite mounds or roadside banks. Savannas and grasslands with thornbush in particular are francolin strongholds, although a few (such as Jackson's francolin) inhabit alpine meadows up to 4000m and others (eg Nahan's francolin) are specialised to life in dense forests. ∎

Hotspots

Masai Mara NR Red-necked spurfowl cross the road here. **Lake Nakuru NP** Coqui francolin on lakeside grasslands. **Serengeti NP** A reliable location for the grey-breasted spurfowl, a Tanzanian endemic. **Budongo FR** Nahan's and other rainforest francolin species can be found here (with patient searching).

GUINEAFOWL

Quintessential ground birds

With bare skinny neck and head, and stout, slightly hooked bill, the three guineafowl species could be cartoon caricatures of birds (in profile the vulturine guineafowl does look like Mr Burns from *The Simpsons*). Despite their reluctance to fly – preferring instead to run at full pelt away from danger, the helmeted guineafowl doing so with wings half open – guineafowl roost in trees at night. All species are immediately recognisable by their boxlike shape and black plumage punctuated by tiny white spots; and bizarre headgear is the order of the day: the crested guineafowl sporting a dishevelled mop of black feathers, and the helmeted guineafowl (inset) a bony knob like a top hat, which probably protects it during headlong plunges into the undergrowth.

Crested guineafowl venture from cover after rain, or cross roads at dusk and dawn.

Guineafowl are opportunists that consume a wide variety of small animals such as insects and small vertebrates; plant matter

such as seeds, fruit, berries and bulbs; and also raid crops. They also swallow grit to aid digestion. Helmeted guineafowl gather in flocks to drink (something all except vulturine guineafowl must do regularly) and also associate with mammals, such as rhinos, lions and mongooses, whose presence presumably discourages potential predators. Their relationship with baboons is less benevolent, for each tries to steal food from the other, but watch for the forest-dwelling crested guineafowl picking up scraps dropped by monkey troops moving through the canopy.

*The **vulturine guineafowl** is most adapted to arid and semiarid country.*

All species indulge in dust-bathing (loosening soil by pecking then tossing it over their feathers and shuffling to get an even coat); this behaviour is thought to condition their feathers and help to get rid of parasites. Startled birds that have been dust-bathing seem to explode in a cloud of dust before hightailing it. Many predators, ranging from large and small cats to chimpanzees, prey on guineafowl and, as they are as large as a farmyard chicken, the effort involved in chasing one down is usually rewarded with a good meal.

Vulturine guineafowl live in small groups and spend most of the day on the ground.

All guineafowl lay prodigious numbers of eggs (probably because of their high mortality rate) from which the chicks hatch more or less simultaneously and are led away from the nest almost immediately. As with most game birds, guineafowl chicks develop quickly and can fly within about two weeks. ∎

Hotspots

Masai Mara NR, Serengeti and **Lake Mburo NPs** Helmeted guineafowl are common. **Samburu** and **Buffalo Springs NRs** and **Meru NP** Support vulturine guineafowl. **Kibale Forest NP** and **Arabuko-Sokoke FR** Crested guineafowl are found here.

Helmeted guineafowl live in large flocks in grasslands and walk in single file to drink.

RED-KNOBBED COOT

A familiar wetland sight and sound

Coots belong to a widespread family that includes crakes, rails and moorhens; unlike most of their relatives, coots spend most of their lives swimming – their long toes are heavily lobed for paddling and their feathers waterproof for diving (something they do frequently to feed on aquatic vegetation). Their characteristic nasal piping is one of the most evocative of wetland sounds, and flotillas of red-knobbed coots, sometimes numbering thousands, drift among ducks and other waterbirds on freshwater lakes.

During the breeding season the two small, fleshy knobs at the top of their white headgear (which stands out at quite a distance) become swollen and brightly coloured – hence the name. Otherwise, the red-knobbed coot is very similar to its counterparts in other parts of the world (a familiar sight on many ornamental lakes) – even the 'pumping' motion of the head as it swims is common to coots everywhere.

Although they spend little time on land, they can run well and when taking flight coots patter across the water's surface for some distance. The common moorhen, which often lives side by side with red-knobbed coots, is superficially similar, but at a glance can be told apart by its red head 'shield' and yellow-tipped bill. ■

Recognition Velvety black; white bill and head 'shield' surmounted by two small red knobs. Length 45cm.
Habitat Lakes and swamps.
Behaviour Gregarious. Builds floating nest platforms and 'false nests' for resting.
Breeding Lays 5–7 eggs.
Feeding Aquatic vegetation.
Voice Hoots *hoo-hoo* and a metallic, nasal *kiik*.

Hotspots
Lake Baringo, Lake Naivasha, Marsabit NP

BLACK CRAKE

Waterside opportunist

Crakes and rails almost exclusively exploit the cover and feeding opportunities provided by dense stands of reeds or rushes fringing slow waterways. The downside is that they have a reputation for being difficult to see among the forest of stems (often calling near an observer but remaining invisible). However, the black crake is an exception and this common bird is readily seen on virtually any East African wetland. Black crakes have a similar shape and size to most other crakes and rails, with a rather slender body (hence the expression 'thin as a rail'), strong legs and feet, and a short bill. Using reeds as cover, crakes typically feed on mud exposed at water's edge, darting back to cover should danger threaten (the best way to see most species is to wait patiently for one to make its nervous feeding forays onto the mud). Black crakes often feed in the open for extended periods, and will readily use hippos' backs as stepping stones (although they can fly and swim well). Like most of the family they feed on a variety of small animals, ranging from worms and snails to insects, tadpoles and frogs; but black crakes also scavenge from carcasses; perch on warthogs' backs to pick off parasites; and climb waterside trees to steal birds' eggs and chicks. ■

Recognition Slaty black; pale green bill, red legs, feet and eyes. Length 20cm.
Habitat Vegetation beside freshwater lakes and swamps.
Behaviour Often walks on floating vegetation.
Breeding 3 eggs laid in bulky nest in waterside vegetation.
Feeding Small animals.
Voice Harsh 'krrok-krraaa'.

Hotspots
Lake Baringo, Lake Naivasha, Murchison Falls NP

GREY CROWNED CRANE

Regal trumpeters

No need for superlatives – suffice to say this is one of the most elegant birds in all of Africa, and Uganda's national bird for good reason. Other cultures around the world associate cranes with longevity and fidelity, and pairs of grey crowned cranes stay together until one dies: they preen each other's golden crest, perform loud duets and dance in spontaneous displays of head-bobbing, bowing, stick-tossing, and high leaps with wings outstretched. One pair's exuberance will stimulate others in a flock to leap into the air, and up to 60 birds have been seen dancing together for a few minutes before settling down again to feed.

Grey crowned cranes (the very similar black crowned crane sometimes visits East Africa – there are records from Lake Turkana and Murchison Falls NP) fly with neck and legs outstretched, often making loud, trumpeting calls as they head to roost at dusk. They are the only cranes able to perch, and consequently roost and, on rare occasions, even nest, in trees. Normally though they nest in wetlands and forage in grasslands, sometimes walking between the two and grazing en route or stamping the ground to scare up insects. Look for grey crowned cranes feeding in groups, and among baboon troops and herds of impalas or zebras. ■

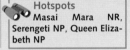

Recognition Slate grey with black, white and chestnut on wings. Red throat wattles. Strawlike crest. 1.1m tall.
Habitat Marshes, grasslands.
Behaviour Gregarious outside breeding season.
Breeding Lays 2–3 eggs.
Feeding Opportunist: eats grain, tubers and insects.
Voice Trumpeting *oo-waang*.

Hotspots
Masai Mara NR, Serengeti NP, Queen Elizabeth NP

KORI BUSTARD

Strutting their stuff

Although all bustards can fly strongly should the need arise, they are consummate walkers – some would say strutters, because their habit of pointing their bill upwards as they walk away from an intruder gives them a dignified, even aloof air. Two or three species are commonly seen in suitable habitat, typically decked out in greys and browns that camouflage them among the muted tones of the grasslands. The kori is the biggest East African bustard (up to 1.2 m tall) and Africa's heaviest flying bird, weighing up to 18kg (despite having long legs its rather small feet render it incapable of perching in trees); look for it peering over the top of the grass. Eggs are laid on the ground and the chicks are also superbly camouflaged – the nest and eggs of Hartlaub's bustard have never been found. Koris are especially fond of toasted insects and small animals, and are readily seen gathered at grassfires where pickings are good. But the best time to watch bustards is during courtship: the male kori bustard puffs out his white throat feathers in a huge bulging ruff, flips up his startling white undertail feathers and booms loudly (this performance can last several days). The male black-bellied bustard stands atop a termite mound, launches himself into the air then falls bodily back to earth. ■

Recognition Heavily built. Back brown, mantle black, head white. Black cap.
Habitat Grasslands and cultivation.
Behaviour Usually solitary.
Breeding Lays 2 eggs.
Feeding Fruit, seeds and small animals.
Voice Deep *voom-voom-voom* by displaying males.

Hotspots
Masai Mara NR, Amboseli NP, Serengeti NP (January to March)

WADERS

The **greater painted-snipe** is a colourful wader that typically skulker at the edge of swamps.

Black-and-white plumage and an upturned bill make **pied avocets** unmistakable.

Their doglike yapping make **black-winged stilts** stand out on shallow wetlands.

The nocturnal **violet-tipped** (or **bronze-winged**) **courser** can often be seen on tracks at night.

International commuters

Every autumn thousands of small to medium-sized shorebirds (commonly known as waders) arrive in East Africa to spend the equatorial 'winter' on coastal mudflats, and the margins of freshwater swamps and lakes. Among them are some long-distance champions – stints, sandpipers, redshanks, Eurasian curlews, common greenshanks and ruffs (inset) – which breed as far away as the Arctic Circle and make a trip of several thousand kilometres twice annually. Here all but one (the African snipe is resident in East African grasslands) sit out the northern winter, taking advantage of the mild climate to regain condition after the rigours of breeding and migration. In their winter outfits most of these migratory waders are rather drab (and consequently a magnet for serious birders, who spend hours trying to work out which is which), but each has a specialised bill shape and size for probing mud, which offer clues to their identification.

The loose term wader also covers several closely related families, not all of which make these long trips; many of these are attractively marked and common. The black-winged stilt and pied avocet are black-and-white, the stilt's coral-pink legs matched only by those of flamingos for length in proportion to body size. The avocet's distinct upturned bill is used to scythe through shallow water for aquatic insects and crustaceans. Other closely related families include the jacanas and thick-knees (dikkops).

But East Africa has so many surprises in store for a birdwatcher that you may even rethink preconceptions about waders. For example, the large crab-plover smashes open crab shells with its chisel-like bill, and is unique among waders for digging and laying eggs in burrows. The ploverlike coursers and pratincoles frequent dry land and are often seen far from water – coursers running after prey and the long-winged pratincoles hawking insects (particularly locusts). Several coursers are nocturnal but readily seen by spotlighting, and two or three species of coursers and pratincoles can coexist in the same habitat by feeding at different times of day. Temminck's courser picks over burnt ground for insects, and is so specialised to this habitat that its eggs are almost black to match the charred earth. ∎

Hotspots

Arabuko-Sokoke FR Nearby Mida Creek adjoins the park and is the most important wader haunt in Kenya. **Lake Nakuru NP** Marshy ground at the lake's corners attracts migratory waders November to April. **Murchison Falls NP** Stilts along the Victoria Nile, rock pratincoles at and above the Falls.

PLOVERS

Grassland sentinels

Plovers are members of the large group of shorebirds often known as 'waders', although many species are found far from water in grasslands and cultivated fields. Several large species are often seen on savanna game drives. In fact, they are often heard well before they are seen because they protest loudly at the approach of any intruder – animal or human – and act as sentinels of the grasslands. Their raucous calls may also be heard at night and are one of the most distinctive bird calls – the blacksmith plover sounds like metal banging on metal.

All plovers have a compact body, large head and short, blunt bill. The larger savanna-dwelling species tower above most others on comparatively long legs, while the smaller species – which tend to stay near the muddy edges of waterways – look decidedly 'dumpy' but run quickly. The savanna species tend to

be boldly marked with white wing-flashes visible in flight; some have coloured facial wattles (most developed on the African wattled plover) and the black-headed plover has a wispy crest.

The savanna specialists eat mainly large insects, but the long-toed plover forages on floating vegetation. Typical plover feeding behaviour involves standing still, running a short distance, pausing to look for food, then running to the prey and dipping their beaks to snatch it up. Smaller plovers can be well camouflaged and are first noticed when they run, sometimes virtually at your feet. With another technique (called foot-trembling) plovers stir up prey by vibrating their toes through short grass or on dirt. Several smaller plovers feed on shorelines and mudflats among other waders; they include some long-distance migrants from Eurasia, such as golden and grey plovers, which 'winter' in East Africa from October to April.

All plovers nest on the ground, although the nest is hardly more than a scrape (even in the middle of a track); savanna species aggressively protect their young, but smaller species like Kittlitz's and three-banded plovers (inset) rely more on camouflage. The eggs and young of all plovers are cryptically marked, and chicks can run and hide soon after hatching. In sandy soil parents may bury their eggs when away from the nest. ∎

Hotspots
Lake Nakuru NP Kittlitz's, chestnut-banded and migratory plovers feed on the shores of the lake. **Masai Mara NR** and **Serengeti NP** Savanna species (African wattled, blacksmith and crowned plovers) are resident. **Murchison Falls NP** Long-toed plovers are common on floating vegetation.

Blacksmith plovers are normally seen in pairs or small flocks near water.

The *spur-winged plover* is most common near waterways in northern Kenya.

Look for *black-headed plovers* in dry bush, sometimes far from water, near tracks and airstrips.

Wattled plovers are large, colourful birds often seen in pairs in moist, short grasslands.

AFRICAN JACANA

Walking on water

Competition for resources is keen at the water's edge, but few birds have adapted to life 'on top' of the water and none as successfully as the jacanas (although the long-toed plover is another notable example). Jacanas (the lesser jacana also lives in East Africa) live virtually their entire life afloat: hugely elongated toes spread their weight so they can run across water lilies, Nile cabbage and other floating masses as well as soft mud; when walking on submerged vegetation they can appear to walk on water; alternatively, the back of a hippo makes a good vantage point. At a pinch they can dive, and fly (clumsily) with legs dangling – often giving their harsh call in flight.

Most bodies of still water with lily pads or other floating vegetation will have a few jacanas (although they can be hard to see if a dropping water level has caused the shadows of drooping lilies to break up the view); watch for the blue headgear, wing stretches and jacanas in flight. The sexes look alike, but any aggression is likely to be from a female defending her territory – all parental care is by the male. He incubates the eggs by holding two under each wing; chicks can walk soon after hatching, but the male carries them under his wings for protection and even moves the eggs in this manner should rising water cause the destruction of the nest. ■

Recognition Chestnut body, white face and breast. Blue bill and 'shield'. 30cm.
Habitat Swamps and lakes.
Behaviour Gregarious outside breeding season.
Breeding Lays 2–5 eggs on floating vegetation.
Feeding Insects and small water animals.
Voice A harsh rattle.

Hotspots
Lake Baringo, Lake Naivasha, Lake Manyara NP, Queen Elizabeth NP

SPOTTED THICK-KNEE

Wader that walks by night

Among the many offshoots from the large shorebirds group is a small family of mainly nocturnal waders known as thick-knees (although their 'knees' are barely thicker than those of other birds), dikkops or stone curlews. Large for waders, long-legged and equipped with very large eyes, thick-knees hunt insects and other small animals at dusk and after dark with ploverlike 'walk-pause-peck' behaviour. Spotted thick-knees are commonly encountered on tracks at night, but during the day rest in dry areas under bushes; when accidentally flushed from cover their large size and sudden appearance can be startling. Normally when danger approaches they crouch down, lying flat on the ground with neck extended; another tactic is simply to walk away and blend in with the countryside. Males and females are thought to mate for life and both care for the young; their nest is a shallow scrape on the ground sometimes lined with vegetation, stones or animal droppings. As with most waders, spotted thick-knee chicks can walk soon after hatching, their down blending superbly with rocky soil when they lie flat to avoid detection (the water thick-knee is commonly seen near water during the day and is reputed to lays its eggs near basking crocodiles as a deterrent to predators). ■

Recognition Fawn upperparts spotted brown. Yellow legs, bill and eyes. 43cm.
Habitat Grasslands, open woodland and rocky country.
Behaviour Usually solitary.
Breeding Lays 2 eggs.
Feeding Eats small animals.
Voice Musical *pe-pe-pe-peou-PEOU-PEOU-PEOU-pee-pi-pe-pe-pe*.

Hotspots
Masai Mara NR, Serengeti NP, Kidepo Valley NP

AFRICAN SKIMMER

Cuts like a knife

Of the three species of skimmer found worldwide, only one is found in Africa. Usually seen sitting on sand bars with heads pointing into the wind in the company of gulls and terns (their close relatives), on close inspection skimmers reveal an extraordinary feature: the lower half of their bill extends 1 to 3cm beyond the tip of the upper one. While it may look deformed, it is actually a superb design for a unique fishing technique: flying in a straight line some 5cm above the surface, the skimmer's lower mandible slices through the water at a 45-degree angle while the mouth is held open, snapping shut the instant it comes in contact with a fish (an action that whips the head round under the body).

In cross section the skimmer's bill is extremely narrow and so streamlined – to reduce drag in the water – that it can skim while gliding. The lower jaw grows faster than the upper one, and is worn away by abrasion with sand and objects underwater – young birds learning to skim sometimes practice on sand by mistake. Because this is a tactile and not a visual technique, skimmers can fish at dusk and even on the darkest nights (they're best seen heading out to feed around dusk). To compensate for bright reflections a skimmer's pupils narrow to a slit like cats' eyes, unlike those of any other birds. ■

Recognition Black upperparts, pure white below. Large scarlet bill tipped yellow. Length 40cm.
Habitat Broad waterways.
Behaviour Breeds in colonies. Some populations migrate.
Breeding Lays 2–3 spotted eggs in sand scrape.
Feeding Skims for fish.
Voice A repeated, sharp *kip*.

Hotspots
Lake Turkana (Allia Bay), **Queen Elizabeth NP** (December to May)

SANDGROUSE

Painted water carriers

Unrelated to grouse, although they do look superficially like stocky, painted pigeons, sandgrouse are primarily birds of semiarid country. The five species are essentially ground birds, eating mainly seeds picked up while walking in pairs or small flocks. Subtle patterns of buff, tan and black disrupt their outline, and the well-camouflaged eggs are also laid on the ground. Strong, pointed wings enable them to fly away from danger and to survive in even the most arid country (if food is available) by transporting them long distances – they will travel up to 20km daily to reach water. The best way to see sandgrouse is to wait by a waterhole at dawn or dusk, when flocks drift in to drink. Wave after noisy wave lines up at the water's edge, each bird dipping its bill for a few seconds before taking off again. And watch for males bathing – what they're actually doing is soaking up water in modified belly feathers, which they then take back to the nest and allow the chicks to suckle. ■

The black-faced sandgrouse is often seen in pairs (this is a male) along tracks far from water.

Hotspots
Samburu and **Buffalo Springs NRs** Black-faced sandgrouse common. **Meru** and **Tsavo West NPs** Chestnut-bellied sandgrouse resident. **Lake Turkana** Lichtenstein's and four-banded sandgrouse found nearby. **Masai Mara NR** and **Serengeti NP** Good for yellow-throated sandgrouse.

*Male **yellow-throated sandgrouse** – usually seen feeding alone or in pairs, but drinking in flocks.*

PIGEONS & DOVES

The **Namaqua dove's** long tail makes it unique among African pigeons. This is a male.

Small flocks of **speckled pigeons** are a common sight near cliffs and buildings.

Ring-necked doves are probably the most common and wide-spread of all East Africa's pigeons.

Expect to see **laughing doves** both in city gardens and along tracks in national parks.

Secrets of success

It would be hard to credit the lives of such ostensibly gentle birds with any sort of drama, but when it comes to feeding, courting and mating (all of which most pigeons and doves do a lot of) they are as competitive as any other birds. This successful family is represented by 24 species in East Africa, although many of the ubiquitous doves and turtle doves look very similar and pose some tricky identification problems for birders. Several of these mainly ground-feeding birds, including ring-necked, red-eyed and laughing doves, will commonly be seen walking along tracks at the edge of grasslands. More colourful species, such as the African green and olive pigeons, are also common but usually feed on fruit in trees. Waterholes are always good places to look for pigeons and doves (inset: ring-necked dove), since most species must drink daily.

All pigeons and doves fly well – the doves and turtle doves often breaking from just under your front wheels. Explosive take-offs are one of the secrets of their survival, along with good camouflage and loose-fitting feathers, which often leave a would-be predator empty-handed. They also have a rapid reproductive turnover: most species are prolific breeders (in fact it's all

some of them seem to do, and you'll probably see a few bowing and cooing as a preliminary to mating). Their nests are usually just a formality – a loose, untidy platform of twigs, although some nest on rock ledges – but the parents have a legendary propensity to sit tight on the nest, deserting a clutch to a predator only at the last second. And the young grow faster than just about any other birds, developing for the first few days of life on a highly nutritious solution ('pigeon's milk') of digested seeds from the crop of the parent – a trait pigeons and doves share with parrots.

Like those of waterfowl and a few other domesticated birds, the calls of pigeons and doves are famous, and many are variations on the familiar cooing. Although similar, once recognised the calls are a useful aid to identification. Forest-dwelling species can be much harder to pin down among dense foliage, but look for them at dawn winging across the canopy or sitting high on exposed snags, something they may do for long spells. ∎

Hotspots

Masai Mara NR Plenty of doves in the savanna plus African green pigeons along the Mara River. **Kilimanjaro NP** Forest and montane species; doves where forest abuts savanna edge. **Kibale Forest NP** Rainforest attracts fruit-eating pigeons.

PARROTS & LOVEBIRDS

Loud colours of the forest

The popular conception of colourful parrots screeching across the African sky is a bit misleading: they certainly screech, but only eight species live in East Africa. Virtually every aspect of parrot biology relates to life in the trees. Strong feet and claws – two toes pointing back and two forward – grasp food and clamber through foliage. Their distinctive, hooked bills crush nuts and tear bark, and act as a 'third leg' when climbing; food held in the feet is manipulated with a strong, thick tongue. Their bright colours, so obvious in flight, disrupt their outline among greenery and blossom. And nests are usually in tree hollows where the eggs are safe from all but monkeys, snakes and tree-living mammals. Parrots often alight on exposed perches to take the early sun and are often noisy when feeding – when a threat appears the birds fall silent only to explode in all directions from the foliage in a burst of colour (behaviour that is thought to confuse predators). Lovebirds are small enough to be overlooked; some species sleep upside down, hanging on with their claws. ■

*In East Africa, the **grey parrot** is now common only in Uganda's rainforests.*

> **Hotspots**
> **Kibale Forest NP** The rare African grey parrot may still be seen here. **Mt Kenya NP** Red-fronted parrots in tall forest above 2000m. **Serengeti NP** Fischer's lovebirds common in acacia woodland.

*The **brown parrot** (also known as Meyer's parrot) is usually seen in pairs in savanna.*

CUCKOOS & COUCALS

Parasitic parents

The trait of laying eggs in another bird's nest is not unique to cuckoos, but few other birds are as adept at shirking the burden of parenthood. And with around 17 species in East Africa alone, their diversity reflects the success of 'nest parasitism'. Although most are common some aspects of their behaviour are still a mystery. During courtship males typically call for hours on end and even at night (a colonial official once requested the removal of cuckoos for disturbing his sleep). Females lay their eggs in the nest of the 'host' species. Upon hatching, the cuckoo chick evicts the rightful eggs or chicks and is raised by the unsuspecting parents: such are the joys of parenting that the adult hosts (often tiny warblers – watch for parties of small birds mobbing cuckoos) don't seem to realise that their pride and joy is many times their own size. Exceptions to the parasitic rule are the five species of coucal, large, mainly ground-dwelling cuckoos that build their own nests and incubate their own eggs. ■

*The **diederik cuckoo's** most common call sounds like dee-dee-dee-DEEderik.*

> **Hotspots**
> **Masai Mara NR, Serengeti NP** and **Lake Mburo NP** Widespread savanna species such as red-chested and diederik cuckoos, and white-browed coucals are commonly seen. **Bwindi Impenetrable NP** Excellent for larger rainforest cuckoos.

*The **white-browed coucal** is a skulker, but is the most widespread coucal in the region.*

Ross' turaco is a large, striking species of forest edges in western Kenya and Uganda.

*Look for **Schalow's turaco** in forests along the Mara River or in Tanzania's Crater Highlands.*

Hartlaub's turaco is common in upland forests of Kenya and Tanzania as high as 3000m.

*The **white-bellied go-away bird** often perches on top of acacias with its crest raised.*

TURACOS

Tree turkeys

The crimson wing-flashes of a large green bird gliding across the trail are often your first view of a forest turaco, for although large birds (most measure about 40 to 43cm) and rather poor flyers, they move about branches and foliage with great agility and can be tricky to spot. Unique to Africa, turacos are often brilliantly coloured and are one of the highlights of a safari (visually, although not ecologically, they replace parrots as one of the most attractive groups). At least one species is found in most habitats, and several may occur in close proximity – especially in the rainforests of Uganda and western Kenya, where turacos reach their greatest diversity and size.

The 75cm-long great blue turaco is the largest species and common in the canopy of undisturbed rainforest. Its former epithet 'tree turkey' is a gross misnomer: although it can run fast on the ground, it's hard to imagine a turkey running along branches with the great blue's agility. Despite its size it can reach fruits and berries at the end of slender branches, even hanging upside down to do so. Turacos are among the most vocal of forest birds, one call sometimes setting off a chain of responses throughout the canopy. Calls are one of the tricks to locating turacos and

once recognised, they will be found to be quite common.

Many colourful turacos also inhabit savanna and semiarid country; on safari you'll probably encounter the mainly grey plantain-eaters and go-away-birds. Plantain-eaters don't eat plantain or bananas, but the go-away-birds are noisy turacos, their calls sounding like a nasal *g'way, g'way*; the eastern grey plantain-eater makes a chimplike hooting that featured in the soundtrack to *Tarzan* movies. Savanna species are not so agile as their forest-dwelling relatives, clambering about in acacias and keeping a lookout from the treetops. The bare-faced (inset) and white-bellied go-away birds are often seen around safari lodges, bare-faced in the west and white-bellied in the east.

All turacos are almost exclusively vegetarian, eating fruits, leaves, flowers and buds – great blue turacos feed leaves to their young. Most leave the trees to drink or bathe; parties of go-away-birds can be seen drinking at pools and great blue turacos eat moss near streams. ∎

> ### Hotspots
> **Kampala** Eastern grey plantain-eaters live in city parks. **Entebbe Botanic Gardens** Shelters rainforest turacos such as great blues. **Mt Kenya NP** Hartlaub's turaco is common. **Masai Mara NR** and **Serengeti NP** Go-away-birds are easily seen.

OWLS & NIGHTJARS

Creatures of the night

Most owls are essentially nocturnal and no group of birds is more successful at hunting at night. Armed with grasping talons, hooked bill, and soft plumage for silent flight, a disclike arrangement of facial feathers funnels sounds to their hypersensitive ears. All are carnivorous; specialists include the white-faced scops owl (inset), which takes a high percentage of scorpions in its diet; and Pel's fishing owl, which hunts fish along rainforest rivers – even wading to do so. Admirable though their nocturnal lifestyle is, it usually makes seeing owls considerably more difficult than hearing them. Fortunately, several of East Africa's 18 species are comparatively common. Savanna-dwelling eagle-owls, such as the pink-lidded Verreaux's eagle-owl, can sometimes be located during the day by the mobbing behaviour of smaller birds. Not surprisingly, most are best seen by spotlighting: by driving slowly

African scops owls occur in two colour varieties; their call is a common savanna night sound.

the eyeshine of one or two species can usually be picked out. Spotted eagle-owls are often on the move at dusk, their bulky silhouettes standing out against the sky; and African wood owls commonly hunt around lodges. The African scops owl is the smallest and possibly commonest species, but during the day its camouflage can render it almost invisible against bark.

The large **Verreaux's eagle-owl** often perches in an exposed position during the day.

On a night drive you will probably see one or several nightjars taking off from the track before you, their eyes reflecting in headlights. Also nocturnal, nightjars share owls' soft plumage and silent flight, but are essentially aerial hunters that snap up insects in flight with their wide gape. Nightjars have weak feet and a small body but long, usually slender wings; most roost and all nest on the ground, a trait for which they are superbly camouflaged in intricate patterns of brown, buff and black. Nightjars cannot hunt effectively in dense forest: watch for them hawking in clearings and over fields or grasslands. The problem with nightjars is getting one of the 18 species to sit still long enough to look at; even then, the identification of most is extremely difficult and more reliably made by their distinctive calls (notable exceptions grow extraordinary wing feathers when courting, eg, pennant-winged and standard-winged nightjars). ■

African barred owlets are best seen in coastal woodland, and are often active in twilight.

Hotspots

Lake Baringo Verreaux's eagle-owls and white-faced scops owls hunt here. **Rukinga Ranch** Spotted eagle-owls are common. **Murchison Falls NP** The place for Pel's fishing owls as well as pennant-winged nightjars (March to September) and standard-winged nightjars (November to February). **Mt Kenya NP** Montane nightjars are resident around the Met Station.

This **Gabon nightjar** shows a typical nightjar's pose and cryptic coloration.

SPECKLED MOUSEBIRD

Recognition Short, stout body with very long, stiff tail. Nondescript grey-brown overall; short, sometimes whitish crest. Thick, finchlike bill and deep pink legs.
Habitat Open areas with trees, such as savanna, gardens and agricultural land.
Behaviour Gregarious and sedentary. Roosts, dustbathes and basks in groups. Clusters can gather several times a day, but especially in cold weather. Males (mainly) preen each other. Mobs coucals and small predators such as shrikes and kingfishers.
Breeding Nest is a cup in a bush or tree; has smallest eggs of any nonparasitic bird.
Feeding Largely vegetarian: fruit, buds, leaves, entire flowers, nectar and even dead bark. Can eat some plants poisonous to other species. Eats earth.
Voice Whistles and chatters throughout the day. Usual contact call a soft *siu-siu*.

Hanging garden birds

Mousebirds are endemic to the African continent (there are four species in East Africa), and have an engaging and comical habit of hanging from branches and wires. A mechanism on their toes locks the feet in position and the articulation of their legs means the feet are held at 'shoulder' height when hanging. Mousebirds are largely vegetarian, and it is thought that by hanging the sun warms their belly and helps them digest food. But during sleep (something speckled mousebirds do for up to 12 hours) their metabolic rate can fall by 90% and they also like to warm up in the early morning – pairs even warm each other by hanging breast to breast.

Speckled mousebirds are highly sociable, living in family groups that fly with apparent discipline in single file from one bush only to crash-land in the next. Flight – whirring wing beats alternating with direct glides – looks fast but actually isn't, but strongly hooked claws help them to clamber about in trees. Large groups may visit one fruiting tree, a trait that doesn't endear them to gardeners. But garden pests or not, their resemblance to mice is owed to the texture of their soft, hairlike feathers; and to their habit of running fast along branches, up tree trunks and along the ground, long tail trailing behind. When threatened, mousebirds hang in dense vegetation, dropping to the ground to hide if necessary, then climbing back up when danger passes.

Group members cluster together at times during the day and even nesting is a social affair: chicks are fed by the parents and by youngsters from previous broods that act as helpers. And adding to so many unique features is the absorbing behaviour of the chicks: when about 10 days old they start toying with nest material; once they leave the nest they play games with other young birds (such as running, wrestling and chasing), and also engage in head-shaking, sudden leaps, mutual feeding, building nests and playing with twigs and leaves. ∎

Hotspots
Masai Mara NR, Serengeti NP, Queen Elizabeth NP

KINGFISHERS

The hole story

Common in most habitats, East Africa's 15 species of king-fisher include the world's largest and smallest species, but the basic form doesn't vary: all have a large head with long, pointed bill, compact body and very short legs. During the breeding season pairs make vocal displays to each other and to defend their nest – woodland kingfishers are particularly aggressive, chasing away other hole-nesting birds, small hawks and even people. But at other times, and despite their bright coloration, most savanna and forest species are easily overlooked because of their habit of perching motionless for long spells – until a large insect or small lizard walks by, in which case it will be suddenly dived upon, taken back to the perch and bashed repeatedly to remove legs, wings or pincers before being swallowed whole.

Kingfishers also use the diving approach when bathing and hunting, by crash-landing in water. Pied, malachite, giant and a few other kingfishers are usually easier to see because they dive from exposed perches near water, such as overhanging branches, jetties and boats.

The abundant pied kingfisher can also be seen hovering over water (inset) up to 3km from land. To catch fish, am-phibians and crustaceans, kingfishers have eyes that adjust instantly from daylight to underwater vision, but they must also learn to judge depth, refraction and the likely escape route of their quarry: watch for kingfishers bobbing their head to take aim before diving.

The pied kingfisher is the only species that roosts and nests communally – sometimes alongside colonies of bee-eaters – and one in three pairs has helpers that assist with feeding young and defending the nest. All kingfishers nest in holes and their short legs are ideal for scuttling along narrow tunnels. Usually they dig a tunnel in a sand bank (a record 8.5m-long tunnel was dug by a pair of giant kingfishers), but smaller species may nest in the sides of aardvark burrows; tree-nesting species always enlarge an existing hole; and rainforest-dwelling kingfishers excavate arboreal termite mounds. All the action takes place indoors, but after the chicks fledge adults may be seen feeding them outside the nest for a few days. ■

Hotspots
Lake Nakuru, **Queen Elizabeth** and **Murchison Falls NPs**, and **Lake Baringo** Pied and malachite kingfishers are common. **Meru** and **Serengeti NPs** Good spots to look for grey-headed and striped kingfishers.

The **grey-headed kingfisher** perches conspicuously in savanna and woodland.

Woodland kingfishers are most common in woodland west of Kenya's Rift Valley..

Although no more than 12cm in length, the **malachite kingfisher** stands out even from a distance.

Giant kingfishers can be seen at Kenya's Lake Baringo and on Lake Victoria near Entebbe.

*Flocks of the migratory **Eurasian bee-eater** visit East Africa between September and April.*

*The gregarious **carmine bee-eater**, East Africa's largest species, is attracted to grassfires.*

*Long tail feathers make the **white-throated bee-eater** stand out in semiarid country.*

*Look for **white-fronted bee-eaters** hawking insects along Rift Valley watercourses.*

BEE-EATERS & ROLLERS

A visual feast with aerobatic feats

Closely related to kingfishers, the equally or even more colourful bee-eaters and rollers are bird highlights of any safari. For travellers from higher northern latitudes, where bright colours among birds are comparatively rare, their glowing range of colours are a delight to the eye and a relief from the greens and browns of the savanna; there are also several unusual variations found in rainforests.

African bees have a fearsome reputation, but being such an abundant food resource it was inevitable that at least one group of birds should tackle them. Bee-eaters appear to do so with relish, and nowhere have they reached the diversity they boast in East Africa (16 species) although some are seasonal migrants and a few have ranges that only just reach the region. All are very similar in size (mostly 20 to 25cm in length) and shape: streamlined with pointed, down-curved bills and long, swallowlike wings. But their habit of perching on exposed branches to watch for likely prey makes them easily seen and identified, and because all are brightly coloured their antics are a pleasure to watch.

Many species hunt from perches (along which they may huddle in rows at night or in cold weather), chasing the bees that make up a substantial percentage of their diet, but also tackling dragonflies, cicadas, and potentially dangerous wasps and hornets. After a sometimes animated chase which can include corkscrew turns, they return to their perch and bash the insect against a branch – taking care to rub off the stings of bees and wasps – before swallowing it whole. These thrashings can often be heard from several metres away. Larger species, such as the Eurasian and carmine bee-eaters, spend much time hawking insects on the wing, although the latter follow tractors and bushfires, and readily perch on mobile sites, such as ostriches, bustards, zebras and antelopes – subduing prey against the bird's back or antelope's horns! Bee-eaters are so specialised at catching insects on the wing that they ignore insects crawling along the ground.

Rocking rollers

The seven species of roller are also colourful and several, such as the lilac-breasted and Abyssinian, sport long tail feathers. The lilac-breasted roller (inset) is in places very common, easily seen and photographed, and probably elicits more admiration from visitors than any other bird in East Africa. Like most of their relatives, rollers are not known for their song – typical calls are cackling or croaks – but a male displays by 'rolling' (an aeronautical term): flying slowly upwards with languorous flaps, he coasts down

again, rocking from side to side to show off his prominent pale wing patches (pictured) and usually cackling as he goes. Rollers also catch prey from a conspicuous perch: savanna species pouncing on ground-dwelling invertebrates and forest species hawking flying insects in the canopy. Lilac-breasted rollers also sometimes follow and catch prey disturbed by dwarf mongooses. You might also be the target of attention from one of these flashy birds – male rollers defend a territory and become pugnacious towards other birds, mammals and even people.

Adultery, robbery and other nesting habits

Like their kingfisher cousins, all bee-eaters nest in holes: forest species in trees, others in tunnels excavated in riverbanks (inset: carmine bee-eaters) or road cuttings. Larger, more aerial feeders often live colonially in cooperative (and competitive) units of related birds. Helpers, usually blood relatives such as the previous year's offspring, assist with incubation and feeding, and in turn gain an apprenticeship in parenthood. But helpers sometimes also lay an egg or two in the nest at which they are helping. In fact, studies of colonies have revealed complicated and shifting alliances: adultery is rife among mated pairs, females lay in the nests of other females (a practice known as 'egg dumping'), and some birds habitually attempt to rob others of food. Pairs will also nest separately, which is the usual practice among smaller species, such as the little and Somali bee-eaters.

Although hardly musical, bee-eaters have pleasant calls (at least when compared to the kingfishers), which are transcribed as a liquid, trilling *krreep-krreep*. All species sound more or less the same, and once the basic pattern is learnt, calls are easily recognised and a good way to detect bee-eaters in the canopy or flying overhead. ■

Hotspots

Lake Baringo Hosts Madagascar (May to September), blue-cheeked (October to May) and carmine bee-eaters (September to March). **Murchison Falls NP** Red-throated bee-eaters breed January to March; also carmine, little and swallow-tailed bee-eaters, and Abyssinian rollers. **Samburu NR** Dry country species – white-throated (September to April), little and Somali bee-eaters, plus abundant lilac-breasted rollers.

Usually seen in pairs, the **little bee-eater** is one of the most widespread species .

The **swallow-tailed bee-eater** is best sought in northern Uganda and southern Tanzania.

Eurasian rollers overwinter in East Africa, arriving in October and departing in April.

The **lilac-breasted roller** quickly becomes a familiar sight on safari across East Africa.

HOOPOE

Outsized pied butterfly

The hoopoe is so unlike any other bird that its image is un-mistakable on ancient Egyptian tombs (among several other common African birds, such as the sacred ibis). Its name comes from its call – even its scientific name *Upupa epops* evokes the soft *hoo-poo-poo* which can be heard from several hundred metres away and is sometimes repeated for hours on end. Hoopoes are not rare and at times (during migration) are common in East Africa – their appearance often evokes comment from people on safari. Their most unusual feature – a large, floppy crest that is usually held flat along the crown – is held erect like an untidy fan when the bird is alarmed. But they are rather unobtrusive birds that feed on the ground and are often first noticed in flight – an undulating, butterflylike flap-and-glide which shows off the boldly contrasting black-and-white pattern of their broad wings and banded rump. Courtship displays are even more striking, with pairs flying slowly round their territory one behind the other.

Disappearing act

When feeding, hoopoes walk jerkily along the ground on rather short legs (one feature which betrays an ancestry shared with kingfishers), jabbing left and right at loose soil with their bill, or digging vigorously enough to make sods fly. Large prey items may be snatched and beaten against a hard surface (another kingfisher trait). When a predator passes overhead, the hoopoe flattens itself against the ground with wings spread, tips almost touching, tail fanned and bill pointing straight up; the effect of the disruptive pattern on its wings and back makes it almost invisible, especially against rocky ground. Groups of hoopoes sometimes roost one to a tree in copses, using the same perches for weeks on end.

Hoopoes are strong migrants: birds that breed in Europe arrive south of the Sahara in October; and birds that breed in Africa (including East Africa) migrate seasonally across the African continent. The two subspecies have subtle plumage differences (although apparently no behavioural differences) and you will sometimes see reference to 'African' and 'Eurasian' hoopoes because some taxonomists regard the two as separate species. ∎

Recognition Pink-rufous or cinnamon with black-and-white wing bars and black tail; folding crest with black tips. Slender, down-curving black bill. Length 28cm.
Habitat Flat or undulating wooded savanna with sparse ground cover; also cultivation, orchards and lawns.
Behaviour Usually seen singly or in pairs, flying into a tree when approached; loose flocks form on migration. Pairs territorial and may use same nest hole in successive years. Males usually call from elevated perch.
Breeding Lays 4–6 eggs in a hole in a bank, tree, wall or termite mound.
Feeding Probes ground for large insects, their larvae and pupae; also takes worms, spiders, molluscs, small reptiles and (rarely) eggs.
Voice Low, soft but far-carrying *hoo-poo-poo* repeated every few seconds during breeding season.

Hotspots
Buffalo Springs NR, Serengeti NP, Kidepo Valley NP

GREEN WOOD-HOOPOE

Iridescent chatterboxes

Noisy, gregarious and conspicuous, the presence of these agile insect-hunters is typically announced by loud chattering before they break cover and fly between trees in single file. Wood-hoopoes are unique to Africa and are related both to true hoopoes and hornbills (scimitarbills differ from wood-hoopoes in name only, although they tend to be less vocal and gregarious than wood-hoopoes). All wood-hoopoes and scimitarbills are characterised by long, slender bodies with a long tail and a long, down-curved bill. Adult plumage in all species is dark but iridescent: appearing black in some lights, close-to it changes from shimmering green to blue or violet that contrasts with the vegetation. Green wood-hoopoes, the most widespread species, feed on a wide variety of insects and other small animals. Small, animated parties of these engaging birds scamper along branches and up trunks, probe crevices and lever up bark as they search for prey, or hang upside down using their tail as a brace to peer into holes.

Green wood-hoopoes (they can look very blue in dull light) display noisily to each other while foraging, chuckling, bowing and rocking with tail spread and wings partly open, and sometimes pass bits of bark or lichen between each other using their bills, before moving on. And listen for them hammering like woodpeckers, bashing prey against the bark or pecking at a beetle they've wedged in a crevice. Groups sometimes roost together in tree cavities (a scarce resource for which they must compete with other animals – including bee swarms), where they are sometimes caught by nocturnal predators such as genets and safari ants. Hollows play an important role in breeding as well: unable to excavate their own nest holes, wood-hoopoes rely on naturally occurring holes or those abandoned by barbets and woodpeckers. ∎

Recognition White wing and tail spots stand out from all-dark iridescent plumage in flight. Bright red bill and feet.

Habitat Common in savanna, woodland, riverine forest and gardens below 2800m.

Behaviour Gregarious, groups usually following the male as he forages. Prises off flaking bark by inserting and opening bill. Flock members jointly investigate potential breeding holes. Secretes musky odour from rump glands.

Breeding Nests in existing cavity in tree or post, usually after long rains. Up to 10 nonbreeding helpers may assist with rearing young.

Feeding Takes a wide variety of insects, especially caterpillars, beetles and larvae; also fruit, centipedes, small lizards and birds' eggs.

Voice Noisy: a weird chuckling chorus starts slowly then accelerates.

Hotspots
Masai Mara NR, Mt Kenya NP, Serengeti NP

HORNBILLS

*Large size makes **southern ground hornbills** stand out from a distance in grasslands.*

*The distribution of the **Abyssinian ground hornbill** is restricted to the semiarid zone.*

__Red-billed hornbills__ feed largely on the ground, often in mixed flocks with other species.

__Von der Decken's hornbill__ - one of three species that associate with dwarf mongooses.

Eyelashes to die for

Chameleons are a favourite food of many of East Africa's 20 hornbill species, as are other lizards, insects and fruit; and larger species eat virtually any animal they can swallow, including eggs, birds and fruit-bats. Whatever their preferences, hornbills are among the most conspicuous, noisy and engaging of large birds to be seen in savanna and forest. All hornbills have long eyelashes, but those of the ground hornbills are very long and thick, and can be seen easily. And all have a large, sometimes colourful bill, which in some, such as the trumpeter hornbill (inset) is adorned with a casque – a hollow protuberance thought to resonate when the birds call. Noise plays a big role in a hornbill's life: they call for many reasons (for example, to contact each other or establish territories) – their nasal honkings are a good way of locating them; and a unique feather arrangement makes their wing beats audible from some distance away.

Several species live side by side in most areas and up to eight may coexist in forest communities, where different species may even nest in the same tree. Early morning is the time to watch for their complex interactions: calls signal communal roosts waking up; flocks fly across the canopy to fruiting trees with a loud whoosh of wings; black dwarf hornbills hawk insects and catch prey displaced by columns of safari ants; red-billed dwarf hornbills join feeding parties of squirrels and other birds; and white-crested hornbills alert monkeys to danger in their mutual territories. Interaction with other animals is not unusual: watch for chanting goshawks taking quail flushed by ground hornbills, and ground hornbills themselves can give away the location of lions or a leopard.

Self-sealing prisoners

All hornbills nest in cavities, usually in a tree, and pairs spend much time inspecting holes. After mating, females of most species seal

themselves into a suitable nest by plastering up the entrance with mud, sticky fruit and droppings, until only a slit remains – an effective barricade against predators. There she raises the chicks, cramped with long tail bent vertically over her back, while the male passes food through the entrance. The exceptions to the rule are the ground hornbills: they also nest in hollows only the females don't get bricked in; southern ground hornbills (pictured) are one of the few species known to breed cooperatively – up to six immature and adult helpers assist at the nest.

Of mongooses and hornbills

Dwarf mongooses roam in packs, searching out small animals such as insects and lizards, and retreating to their dens in abandoned termite mounds at night or during the heat of the day. Their diet is exactly the same as that of three species of hornbill (Von der Decken's, eastern yellow-billed and red-billed) and a remarkable and possibly unique feeding strategy has evolved: the hornbills walk along with foraging mongooses, snapping up food disturbed or flushed by their companions. Although there is some competition, high-leaping grasshoppers are usually too fast for the mongooses, and cryptic prey are missed by the hornbills, which hunt by sight. Both also take rodents if the opportunity arises, but the hornbills never eat the rat-sized baby mongooses.

This relationship is no accident; the hornbills wait until the mongooses start foraging in the morning, chivying them along by walking among them until they get moving. And if the mongooses take more than an hour to wake up, one or two birds peer down the mound's ventilator shafts and honk repeatedly until the mammals emerge, yawning and bleary-eyed. Both mongooses and hornbills are eaten by a variety of large hawks, and if this arrangement seems one-sided, it has been shown that the birds provide early warning of the marauders – giving mongoose 'guards', that watch from termite mounds or trees, extra eyes and more time to forage for themselves. Mongooses get decidedly agitated when their hornbills don't show, trotting up and down the mound and making half-hearted forays into the grass. ∎

*The **African grey hornbill** is one of several small species common on savannas.*

*Watch for **trumpeter hornbills** flying in large, noisy flocks in search of fruiting trees.*

*Like most species, female **red-billed hornbills** are sealed into their nest and fed by the male.*

Hotspots

Tsavo NP Studies on mongooses and hornbills were conducted here and the three hornbills species in question are easily seen. **Masai Mara NR** and **Serengeti NP** Southern ground hornbills wander the grasslands. **Murchison Falls NP** Good for Abyssinian ground hornbills. **Semliki NP** The hotspot for rainforest hornbills, with nine species recorded.

*Lake Manyara and Tarangire NPs are good places to seek the **crested barbet**.*

*Pairs of **red-and-yellow barbets** are commonly seen duetting from termite mounds.*

BARBETS

Colourful tree dwellers

Like their relatives the woodpeckers, barbets and tinkerbirds are usually found in trees (although a few barbets spend much time on the ground). But unlike woodpeckers these stocky, generally short-tailed birds come in many colours and patterns. Least colourful are the tinkerbirds (although the yellow-rumped tinkerbird's pervasive *tonk-tonk-tonk-tonk* call is one of the most common bush sounds). Some barbets are clad in subdued shades, but others range from black-and-white to bright blue, red and yellow. All barbets and tinkerbirds nest in holes, which they excavate in branches or tree trunks with their strong, pointed bill (which in many is surrounded with prominent bristles). Most species eat mainly fruit, although all include some insects in their diet. Tinkerbirds are the most arboreal and forage with other birds in the canopy; many barbets perch for long periods in tall, dead trees. Fruiting fig trees are ideal places to stake out, and several species of barbet and tinkerbird may gather at one tree, feeding among starlings, pigeons and other birds. ■

Hotspots
Serengeti NP For common savanna species. **Kakamega FR** Good rainforest pickings, including grey-throated and yellow-billed barbets. **Saiwa Swamp NP** Nesting double-toothed barbets.

WOODPECKERS

Important woodland drummers

Wood is the key to woodpecker ecology – they even drink from small puddles in tree forks – but although some species hammer vigorously to dig out grubs, others pry off flaking bark, glean insects from foliage or extract ants from crevices with a long, barbed tongue. Other physical adaptations that help them exploit the forests' rich insect resources include strongly clawed feet on short legs; stiff, pointed tail feathers that prop them up as they cling vertically to tree trunks; and a strong, chisel-like bill for excavating holes in trees (muscles at the base of the bill act as shock absorbers and nostrils covered by feathers exclude flying woodchips). The 20 woodpecker species in East Africa exploit many subtle forest niches (eg, Tullberg's woodpecker often forages among trees that have been killed by fire); and several species can often be found in close proximity. The birds themselves play a pivotal role in wooded ecosystems: woodpeckers are among the only animals that actually create cavities in living wood, and their hole construction benefits many species of bird, mammal, reptile and even insect. ■

*The widespread **golden-tailed woodpecker** forages low in trees in savanna and woodland.*

*Similar in size, the shy **bearded woodpecker** often feeds high in trees and flies far if disturbed.*

Hotspots
Masai Mara NR and **Serengeti NP** Cardinal and bearded woodpeckers are widespread in savanna. **Bwindi Impenetrable NP** Rainforest-dwelling Elliot's and buff-spotted woodpeckers.

GREATER HONEYGUIDE

Prince of thieves

It's not much to look at (and this is the gem among the 14 species), but the greater honeyguide is an amazing bird. Firstly, although its standard fare is insects it also eats beeswax, which it digests with special stomach bacteria. Secondly, it lays its eggs in other birds' nests – typically those of woodpeckers and barbets. When laying, the female greater honeyguide sometimes punctures or removes the eggs of the host; if she doesn't, her chick has a hooked bill with which it kills its foster siblings (or pushes them out of the nest) so it is raised alone – it is fed on the hosts' diet until it fledges 30 days later. And thirdly, greater honeyguides lead people to beehives so they will break them open – the only honeyguide thought to do so. It is often stated that honeyguides lead ratels (and possibly mongooses, genets and baboons) to hives, but there's little hard evidence for this. Conspicuous when 'guiding', the bird moves from tree to tree with a fluttering flight and a loud, continuous chattering, flicking its white outer tail feathers and stopping to watch the progress of its follower. After the hive is opened it feeds on the wax, larvae and eggs – any bee stings are resisted by its thick skin. Greater honeyguides also obtain beeswax at abandoned hives without a helper if the hive has already been broken. ∎

Recognition Grey-brown with white ear patch, whitish underparts and black throat. Stubby pink bill. 19cm.
Habitat Open woodlands.
Behaviour Solitary. Perches for hours. Harasses drongos.
Breeding Lays 1 white egg.
Feeding Insects, beeswax, bee larvae and eggs.
Voice Continuous *bur-witt*.

Hotspots
Masai Mara NR, Serengeti NP, Lake Mburo NP

LARKS

Cryptic grassland songbirds

Like many other grassland birds, most of East Africa's 25 species of lark are cryptically coloured, their muted shades of brown, tawny and buff often echoing the soil colour where they dwell. Many superficially resemble pipits, and larks are also essentially ground-dwellers: they are often encountered along vehicle tracks in savannas and grasslands; and their nests are always well hidden in tussocks. Larks have strong legs and feet (some species have long hind claws that facilitates walking over tussocks) and readily run to escape danger, although all can fly well. Their strong, hard bill is adapted to a diet containing a high percentage of seeds. Larks and pipits were once believed to be closely related, but larks are possibly distant relatives of the sparrows – sparrow-larks show obvious similarities. And larks advertise their territories with long display flights which often involve complicated – and beautiful – song sequences. The famous skylark does not occur in East Africa, but one of the most evocative sounds on the rustling grasslands of the Serengeti Plains is the plaintive whistling of the rufous-naped lark. ∎

*The **rufous-naped lark** shows the shape, coloration and vocal prowess of a 'typical' lark.*

*Bold markings break up the outline of **Fischer's sparrow-lark** among stony ground.*

Hotspots
Masai Mara NR and **Serengeti NP** Grassland species such as rufous-naped and flappet larks. **Lake Turkana** Arid-zone specialists: crested larks and chestnut-headed sparrow-larks.

Common near human habitation, **red-rumped swallows** *gather mud to make their nests.*

Lesser striped swallows *often form large flocks and perch with other species on wires and twigs.*

SWALLOWS & MARTINS

Living the high life

Swallows and martins are small, active birds, familiar to most people as harbingers of seasonal change and because several species nest in or near human dwellings. Their supremely aerial lifestyle has led to a streamlined body with long, narrow wings for powerful, sustained flight; and many species sport distinctive forked tails with long streamers (that have also given their names to a family of large butterflies – the swallowtails). All feed exclusively in flight by scooping up insects with their wide mouth, and tend to be gregarious in flight; several species are often seen together – look for them hawking above marshes and swamps at any time of day. Many flash with iridescence and have contrasting pale underparts or reddish markings on their head and throat. The familiar and cosmopolitan barn swallow is just one of 23 resident and migratory species, including various martins and rough-wings, that occur in East Africa. Swallows and martins sometimes nest in colonies, most building a cup-shaped nest of mud pellets gathered waterside or at drying puddles. ■

Hotspots
Murchison Falls NP Swallows and martins feed between the high banks of the Victoria Nile. **Lake Turkana** Rock martins inhabit local gorges.

Recognition Grey-brown upperparts and breast; darker on head; white belly with yellow vent. 20cm.
Habitat Virtually anywhere with trees or shrubs.
Behaviour Normally in pairs, congregating at fruit trees.
Breeding Lays 2–3 eggs.
Feeding Fruit and insects.
Voice Melodious chortlings.

Hotspots
Common in hotel grounds, towns and gardens

COMMON BULBUL

Tuneful early riser

If any bird can be called ubiquitous in East Africa it is the common bulbul (also known as yellow-vented or dark-capped bulbul). It is neither showy nor colourful and its behaviour is unobtrusive, except for its melodious calls, but it readily adapts to human settlement and is common in city parks and gardens. Indeed, although common bulbuls generally avoid dense forest, they spread along roads and railways, and will fly over the canopy to reach jungle plantations and camps. They can become a nuisance stealing scraps from safari lodges and are easily caught when intoxicated from eating fermented fruit.

Common bulbuls are quick to spot a predator, such as a snake or owl, which they scold noisily. But it is for their calls that they are best known: their chortlings start well before dawn and can continue for two hours after sunrise; they sometimes congregate at dusk and are often the last birds to sing, bedding down well after sunset with much fussing and twittering. The common bulbul is part of a complex family that includes many similar species of greenbul and brownbul (whose identification birdwatchers can scratch their heads over); the common bulbul makes a useful reference point when trying to identify unfamiliar species in a new habitat. ■

WAGTAILS, PIPITS & LONGCLAWS

Tail-pumpers of gardens and grassland

Whether running along safari lodge rooftops, flitting along streams or snapping up flies from under the hooves of large animals, East Africa's six wagtail species are distinctive and common. The African pied wagtail is one of the most easily recognised and is readily seen foraging in flower beds and on lawns, snatching insects (inset) off the ground or after a chase. All wagtails pump their tail up and down when standing still (something they don't do very often) and walk, rather than hop, with an exaggerated back and forth head movement.

African pied wagtails are highly adaptable, and can live in cities, cultivation or forest edges.

At first sight pipits bear little resemblance to wagtails, but they are closely related: they too forage on the ground and snap up insects, and typically pump their tail when they stand still. But while many wagtails are boldly marked, most pipits are

grassland dwellers and coloured accordingly in subdued shades of brown and buff. The widespread grassland pipit is commonly seen running down tracks ahead of a vehicle, pausing often before scooting off again. Several pipits are migratory and sometimes associate with wagtails outside the breeding season at communal roosts, gathering at dusk in tall trees and reed beds. Many

The migratory yellow wagtail can be seen at the edge of waterways from September to April.

pipits and larks look superficially similar, but they belong to different families and are generally not regarded as close relatives. The glorious exception among the drably coloured pipits is the golden pipit, which in flight resembles a great yellow butterfly.

The six species of longclaw – so-called because their hind claw is extremely long, enabling them to walk over tussocks – tend to stand more upright than pipits and have longer legs; they also have colourful underparts and don't pump their tails. Longclaws are usually not difficult to spot, and often indulge in melodious territorial songs in flight or from an exposed tussock. Both pipits and longclaws build a grass nest on the ground during and after the rains, when growing grass affords more concealment for nests and young. In a remarkable example of convergent evolution, the yellow-throated longclaw is almost identical in appearance, nesting and habits to the unrelated meadowlarks, the familiar songbirds of North America. ∎

Yellow-throated longclaws are common grassland birds seen on the ground or perched in a bush.

Hotspots

Masai Mara NR and **Serengeti NP** Several species of pipit and longclaw in grasslands. **Tsavo East NP** Golden pipit and Pangani longclaw country. **Aberdare NP** Yellow wagtails are common around buffalo herds, African pied around lodges. **Kilimanjaro NP** Mountain and grey wagtails beside highland streams.

The rosy-breasted longclaw's coloration is brightest during the breeding season.

*Parties of **arrow-marked babblers** forage for insects and other small animals in bushy savanna.*

***Brown babblers** replace arrow-marked babblers in western Kenya and northern Uganda.*

*The **zitting cisticola** is a typical representative of these vocal but plain grassland warblers.*

***Willow warblers** are common migrants to East Africa between September and April.*

BABBLERS

A family affair

Throughout their range in Africa and Asia, the large and varied babbler group are renowned skulkers of forest undergrowth. Fortunately in East Africa a few species are quite easy to see, and can even become semitame around lodges. Most are thrush-sized birds (20 to 23cm in length) with strong legs and feet, and typically forage for insects and other small animals on the ground. East African species are not brightly coloured, although most are highly gregarious – feeding, resting and roosting in small flocks, and lining up on branches to indulge in mutual preening. And these animated parties also draw attention to themselves with frequent vocalisations – sometimes in duets or choruses. Babblers are rather sombrely marked in greys and browns, but eye colour can be an important clue to identification and differs for all East Africa's babblers. As their name suggests, parties of chatterers are very vocal, but the six species of illadopses are forest skulkers that pose a challenge to ardent birdwatchers. ■

> ### Hotspots
> **Samburu NR** Rufous chatterers common in semiarid thornbush country. **Budongo FR** Uganda's illadopsis headquarters features four species. **Usambara Mountains** Several localised species in montane forest, such as spot-throat, dappled mountain-robin and pale-breasted illadopsis.

WARBLERS

Little brown jobs

To the uninitiated, a birdwatcher's obsession with small, nondescript birds is inexplicable when there are so many colourful and large birds to look at. But among birds, beauty does not equate rarity and to hard-core birders the identification of every bird is important – especially the 'little brown jobs' (LBJs). Enter the warblers: small (usually up to 15cm), insect-eaters that typically live in dense vegetation. Many, such as camaropteras, crombecs and eremomelas, are attractive little birds, but the harder the challenge the greater the sport, and there are few greater challenges than the 32 species of grassland warbler known as cisticolas. Resplendent in buff, grey, white and brown, they all look almost identical and are best told apart by their calls when they're breeding: apart from the singing, whistling and trilling cisticolas, there's the thoroughly modern rock-loving cisticola, and the less melodious winding, rattling, wailing and croaking cisticolas. Several commemorate ornithologists of the British Empire, such as Hunter and Carruthers; then there's the wing-snapping cisticola; and, for the prurient, the foxy and red-faced cisticolas. ■

> ### Hotspots
> **Masai Mara NR** and **Serengeti NP** Several species of cisticola can easily be seen in grasslands. **Bwindi Impenetrable NP** For black-faced rufous warbler and Grauer's rush warbler.

THRUSHES, CHATS & RELATIVES

A multitude of singers

Apart from the thrushes – famous as songbirds around the world – this large and varied family includes the boldly marked wheatears, which in East Africa include both resident and migratory species; a few specialists of cliffs and rocky country (such as the colourful cliff chats and the migratory common rock thrush); and the rainforest-dwelling alethes, akalats and ant thrushes, which forage among leaf litter for insects flushed by columns of driver ants. If the diversity weren't enough, confusion can arise because widely distributed species can go by different names in different countries.

At least one species is found in nearly every habitat and several may live in close proximity, for example, in tropical rainforest at Budongo FR. It's hard to generalise about the 73 East African members of this enormous family, but all are usually solitary, small- to medium-sized birds with comparatively long legs and a shortish bill; other features, such as body shape, tail length and coloration vary considerably. But among the many variables one feature stands out in a few species at least: their vocal ability. Tuneful examples include the nightingale (this legendary singer is a migrant to East Africa); the white-browed robin-chat – a common garden bird with a fine repertoire of musical whistling; and the spotted morning thrush, which often greets the dawn around safari camps.

The olive thrush will probably be the first member of the family you encounter because, like its European and American cousins, it has adapted well to human habitation and forages while hopping across lawns. Peak-baggers will almost certainly encounter the alpine chat – a confiding bird at mountain picnic sites as high as 5200m. The sooty chat (inset) is a conspicuous species of open country, where it digs nest tunnels in termite mounds (on which it frequently perches) and abandoned aardvark burrows. Wheatears also inhabit open country, where they perch in an upright stance; migrant species can be abundant en route to and from their northern breeding grounds, and the resident capped wheatear may be seen feeding on emerging termites. ■

> ### Hotspots
> **Lake Nakuru NP** Migratory wheatears in season. **Masai Mara NR** White-browed robin-chats and spotted morning thrushes around lodges. **Lake Baringo** White-shouldered cliff chat and brown-tailed rock chat resident at cliff faces. **Udzungwa NP** Relict forest has a high diversity of thrushes.

The **white-browed robin-chat** (or **Heuglin's robin**) is a familiar songbird of gardens and forests.

The **collared palm thrush** (or **collared morning-thrush**) is often found near palm trees.

White-shouldered (or **mocking**) **cliff chats** are vocal birds easily seen on Rift Valley cliffs.

The **olive thrush** is the common thrush of forests and gardens in upland East Africa.

*Their eye rings distinguish **white-eyed slaty flycatchers** from other grey flycatchers.*

*The **African grey flycatcher** is the most widespread of the 'typical' flycatchers in savannas.*

*Although its colour can vary, the **African paradise flycatcher's** tail makes it unmistakable.*

FLYCATCHERS

Restless wing and bill snappers

Three families of birds (the 'true' flycatchers, monarch flycatchers, and a family of 'African flycatchers' that includes the batises and wattle-eyes) are broadly lumped as flycatchers largely as a result of similarities in their foraging behaviour: all are small, sometimes hyperactive birds that catch insects in a variety of ways. Gleaning insects from foliage is a feeding technique common to most, but aerial pursuits launched from a perch are more characteristic of some groups. These insect-catching sallies are also used by other birds, such as drongos and some kingfishers, and are known as 'flycatching' (appropriately enough) regardless of the species. Flycatching is entertaining to watch, and can involve sudden turns and corkscrew movements during which the bill is sometimes heard snapping shut.

One or more flycatchers can be seen in most habitats, and they can be quite tolerant of people. Wattle-eyes are small flycatchers of rainforest undergrowth, usually replaced in drier habitat by batises – small, shrikelike birds boldly marked in grey, black and white – which hunt in pairs or small family groups. Wattle-eyes and batises both 'snap' their wings in flight but are readily distin-

guished: only wattle-eyes have a coloured fleshy wattle surrounding the eye. The so-called monarch flycatchers are larger and pugnacious, and some are colourful; the 'true' flycatchers are rather nondescript grey and brown birds of forest edges, some of which are Eurasian migrants.

Monarch flycatchers are renowned for their crests and long tails, but without a doubt the most spectacular species is the common, easily recognisable African paradise flycatcher. The male's long tail streamers can measure more than twice his body length and are shown off to perfection in flight. Many colour variations exist for this species: rufous is the most common form, but it can also be grey or white, and all three shades can occur on the one bird. The African blue flycatcher is another restless forest monarch with a showy tail, which it fans open and shut, perhaps to startle insects. Like many flycatchers, monarchs build a neat, cup-shaped nest decorated with lichen and moss and bound with spiders' webs (inset: African paradise flycatcher). ■

Hotspots
Ssese Islands Numerous colour varieties of African paradise flycatchers living side by side. **Kakamega Forest NR** Good for rainforest wattle-eyes. **Murchison Falls NP** Silverbirds are common in thorny bush and savanna.

WAXBILLS

Jewels in the undergrowth

'Finch' is a term that covers a multitude of forms, from sparrows to brilliant seed-crackers, and these mainly seed-eating birds are the most diverse bird group in East Africa (other finches include the weavers, whydahs and canaries). There's a lot of grass out on the savanna, and a host of finches has evolved ready to pounce on heads of ripe seeds or slide down stalks to pick them off the ground. Many species have a red, waxy-looking bill, and the term 'waxbill' is commonly used to cover some 50 small, mainly colourful species with names such as twinspots, firefinches, silverbills, crimsonwings, grenadiers and cordon-bleus. Many are also popular caged birds and known by other names in captivity.

Peters' (or *red-throated*) *twinspots* are birds of coastal forest undergrowth.

Look for waxbills on roadsides and the edge of savanna and fields, and in flocks mixed with other species, especially where grass is seeding. Many are common and some are confiding

(such as red-billed firefinches and cut-throat finches – inset), often nesting near human habitation. A number of brilliant species, including seed-crackers and crimsonwings, inhabit undergrowth of the rainforest edge; and the all-dark negrofinches are forest species, which eat largely insects and berries (watch for them higher up in the canopy than other species, and often in association with sunbirds). However, despite their bright colours, waxbills can easily be overlooked; for example, when flushed, quail-finches fly a short distance then drop vertically to the ground and run like quail. And waxbill calls are often just high-pitched, sibilant whispers that can be mistaken for those of insects; indeed, the locust-finch measures only 9cm in length and looks like a large grasshopper flitting between seed heads.

*The **African firefinch** feeds on fallen grass seeds at the edge of forests and cultivation.*

Most waxbills build untidy domed nests of grass; some simply add material to the gaps under hamerkop or secretary bird nests; others, such as silverbills and some mannikins, use old weaver nests; and blue-capped cordon-bleus and bronze mannikins sometimes build near hornet nests. Bright spots, usually hardened callosities, on the gape and inside the mouth of chicks invoke an irresistible feeding response in parents in the darkness of the nest chamber – a feature mimicked by whydah chicks that parasitise waxbill nests. ■

Southern cordon-bleus (or blue waxbills) are most common in southern Tanzania.

Hotspots

Kakamega Forest NR Rainforest and undergrowth favoured by negrofinches and seed-crackers. **Mt Kenya NP** Forest edge, grassland and streamside tangles for waxbills and crimsonwings. **Kidepo Valley NP** Rolling grasslands and acacia savanna where 26 species have been recorded.

*Look for **purple grenadiers** along tracks in grasslands, savanna and thickets.*

*Small, active groups of **white helmet-shrikes** are common in savanna and semiarid country.*

*The **white-crowned shrike** is a familiar site perched on bushes or posts nearly everywhere.*

*Search the Serengeti, Lake Manyara and Tarangire NPs for the long-tailed **magpie shrike**.*

*A grey mantle and lack of white wing patches separate **long-tailed fiscals** from common fiscals.*

SHRIKES, BUSH-SHRIKES & HELMET-SHRIKES

Living larders

With such an abundance and selection of thorns across the savanna, it's not surprising that something has found a use for them (albeit one that may appear gruesome to humans). Thus lizards, beetles, crickets, small birds and rodents may sometimes be seen impaled on the long, pointed spines of acacias. European settlement has also been adapted to the job and barbed wire does nicely too. This is the work of shrikes, perching birds boldly marked in black, white, greys and browns, often with a black 'mask' across the face.

The so-called 'true' shrikes, some of which are migratory, are birds of open country that typically hunt by waiting on a likely perch and dropping onto their victim. Slender and upright, they have short legs, strong feet and hooked claws; at the business end, their large head supports a heavy, thick bill with an obvious hook at the tip. Several species are resident and common; when migrants pass through they can be abundant one week and gone the next.

Glamorous it ain't, but their hunting is effective: small vertebrates are pinned down and killed by repeated strikes to the back of the head – at least they're dead when they get impaled. Spikes keep prey steady while it's being eaten, but catering aside, storing food also has the advantage of providing insects on a cool day when fewer are about – impaled beetles can take hours to die, so they could even be fresh. It is also believed that these larders attract females, who are presumably impressed by a male's hunting skills. But other birds steal such food stores, and anything spiked on a whistling thorn bush is asking to be carried away by the ants that live in them.

Shrikes colourful and unusual

In complete contrast, the many species of bush-shrike – a family whose members go under names such as brubru, boubous, tchagras and gonoleks, for example – run the whole gamut of

A hangman by any other name ...

Common fiscals (pictured) are certainly common and often seen perched on wires and posts, where their neat black-and-white plumage stands out from a distance.

A fiscal was a senior judicial officer that dressed in black and white during Cape Colony days; the shrike's other common name 'Jackie Hangman' is perhaps less obscure. In fact, anywhere shrikes are known in folklore they have a reputation for cruelty and attract less than complimentary local names. For example, the scientific name *Lanius*, used for 'true' shrikes, means butcher; *pies-grieche* is a French handle meaning 'sadistic magpie'; and the German *neuntoter* ('nine dead') refers to the red-backed shrike's supposed penchant for murdering nine victims before resting. Cheery stuff, but happily other shrike names have origins in their calls, such as boubou or gonolek; and the name 'gorgeous (or four-coloured) bush-shrike' says it all, really.

The *black-crowned tchagra*, like most tchagras, often hunt in undergrowth.

The *grey-headed bush-shrike* is a large woodland species that often hunts in the canopy.

colours from subdued browns and greys, to radiant gold and scarlet contrasting with black. Some, such as the papyrus and black-headed gonoleks, are among the most beautiful of East African birds. However, although they're worth the effort, bush-shrikes are not nearly so easy to see, and many are skulking inhabitants of dense foliage and thickets (although many respond well to a playback of their calls). Bush-shrikes also have stout, hooked bills and several species are boldly marked in black-and-white, but they don't impale food on spikes and rather than sitting and waiting, they are active hunters through foliage.

Helmet shrikes are yet another family of shrikes that takes advantage of the abundant insect prey (although some ornithologists don't regard 'true' shrikes, bush-shrikes and helmet-shrikes to be closely related). Helmet-shrikes are highly sociable birds with typical shrike features, such as a powerful bill. In all but one species the head is adorned with a ruff of stiff, forward-pointing feathers, and some also have coloured wattles surrounding their eyes. Helmet-shrikes travelling in parties of up to 20 birds search trunks, branches and leaves for insects, on which they feed almost exclusively. They may roost communally, but only one pair in the group normally breeds at a time, and in some species other group members help with nest-building and feeding the chicks. ∎

The *rosy-patched bush-shrike* looks like no other shrike and often perches conspicuously.

Hotspots

Masai Mara NR, Serengeti and **Murchison Falls NPs** Several species of 'true' shrike live side by side on the savanna plains, their numbers augmented by migrating shrikes in season; bush-shrikes also resident. **Kibale Forest NP** (Bigodi Wetland) Supports papyrus gonoleks.

Tropical boubous are common skulkers of gardens, woodland and savanna.

ORIOLES

African golden orioles migrate from southern Africa and can be seen between April and August.

Golden songbirds

Usually heard before they are seen, orioles are medium-sized, rather starlinglike birds that live virtually their whole lives in the canopy of woodland and forest. All of East Africa's seven species are golden yellow, suffused with olive or with contrasting black on their wings and tail. If you can locate the source of their liquid, fluting calls – they sound a bit like their common name – you'll also see a strongly pointed, bright red bill and bold, red eyes. Common in woodland and gardens, orioles rarely descend to the ground and fly with deep undulations, sweeping up to a perch like a woodpecker. Watch for them plunge-bathing by dropping from a perch into a puddle or pool and, during showers, tipping forward on a branch with wings outspread. Generally solitary outside the breeding season, orioles sometimes join mixed feeding flocks and congregate at fruiting trees. Their main food, large insects, is vigorously flogged against a branch before swallowing – hairy caterpillars are flayed by this method. ■

Eurasian golden orioles head south from October to December and return in March and April.

Hotspots
Nairobi NP Good for the widespread black-headed oriole and migrants in season. **Bwindi Impenetrable NP** Pristine rainforest supports montane, forest and migratory species. **Arabuko-Sokoke FR** The northernmost location for green-headed orioles.

COMMON DRONGO

Recognition Black with metallic blue sheen and 'fishtail'. Red eye. Length 25cm.
Habitat Open grassy areas and forest edges.
Behaviour Solitary or in pairs. Catches small animals fleeing grassfires.
Breeding Usually 3 eggs in a shallow, woven nest.
Feeding Chiefly insects.
Voice Metallic 'twanging'.

Hotspots
Nairobi NP, Serengeti NP, Queen Elizabeth NP

Feisty opportunist

Another contender for ubiquity is an all-black, slightly iridescent bird that can also be quite fearless of people – the common drongo (the similar velvet-mantled and square-tailed drongos also live in East Africa). Although they may sit still for long spells, common drongos (the name predates the pejorative definition familiar to Australians) are usually conspicuous on a horizontal branch or exposed limb. They fearlessly pursue flying predators, such as hawks and crows, sometimes in pairs, and press home their attacks with pecks or buffeting. But for all their jauntiness drongos are rather voracious predators themselves. They take mainly insects, but sometimes rob other birds of their catch and are not averse to taking nestlings. Nonetheless other small birds readily nest in the same tree as drongos, perhaps comforted by their pugnaciousness towards other predators. Drongos typically chase likely prey from a perch, snatching it in flight or pursuing it to the ground, where it is dispatched or dismembered while being held down with the feet. Common drongos also follow bands of dwarf mongooses and seize prey disturbed by the mongooses' progress. Rather tuneless but at times enthusiastic singers, their loud, metallic notes can continue through the hottest part of the day and into the night. ■

PIED CROW

Murder most fowl

Because of their large size, mainly black coloration and often haunting calls, crows and ravens are well known around the world. Several species commonly associate with humans and their apparent liking for battlefields has instilled a crow mythology in many cultures. Crows eat mainly small animals, but also carrion when available (a group of crows is called a 'murder') and they often arrive at a carcass even before vultures and kites assemble.

The pied crow is a consummate opportunist and readily takes food scraps discarded by people; it is now the common scavenger in many settlements, where flocks of hundreds may gather at rubbish dumps. This trait is common to many crow species, and pied crows scavenge side by side with brown-necked ravens where the two overlap. But the house crow – introduced from the Indian subcontinent and now a common pest in coastal cities – demonstrates more than any other species this family's adaptability. Opportunistic and bold, it takes the eggs and young of other birds; kills small birds and harasses large ones; rides the backs of livestock and pecks at their sores; thrives near rubbish dumps; and in places has ousted the native pied crow – a house crow control program has been initiated in Kenya. ■

Recognition Glossy black; white saddle and belly. 46cm.
Habitat Grassland, cultivation, savanna and towns.
Behaviour In pairs and small flocks; roosts communally.
Breeding Lays 4–5 eggs in bulky nest during rains.
Feeding Carrion, small animals, fruit and grain.
Voice Harsh *aaahnk*; croaks.

Hotspots
Nairobi, Kampala, Dar es Salaam and virtually any town or village

OXPECKERS

Lust for lice

The two species of oxpecker are members of the starling family specialised to eat parasites such as ticks and lice clinging to the skin of large animals. Flocks of one or both species can usually be seen on or near herds of antelopes, and many other herbivores large and small – including livestock. At first glance the relationship seems rosy – the oxpeckers hopping over their hosts and exploring their crevices in their quest to remove parasites – but elephants are particularly intolerant of these birds and pastoralists regard them as a nuisance. Both species certainly eat a significant quantity of parasites (100 adult ticks per day, according to one estimate), plucking them out bodily or gleaning them with a scissoring motion of their bill. But they also keep wounds open to feed on blood, pus and any parasites attracted to the gore – injured animals are particularly susceptible and often lack the strength to chase the birds off. Oxpeckers also rip mouthfuls of hair from mammals to line their nests – a comical sight but not one necessarily enjoyed by the victims. ■

*The **yellow-billed oxpecker** is now rare outside reserves; its pale rump stands out in flight.*

Hotspots
Masai Mara NR, Serengeti NP and **Ngorongoro CA** A few oxpeckers can usually be seen wherever there are concentrations of large animals.

*Expect to see **red-billed oxpeckers** around buffalo herds and on virtually any large animal.*

*Look no further than city streets for **red-winged starlings**, which nest on cliffs and buildings.*

*Common in savannas and gardens, the **greater blue-eared starling** looks its best in sunlight.*

Rüppell's long-tailed starling is East Africa's only all-blue iridescent starling with a long tail.

*Adult **superb starlings** are stunning but common birds that can be a pest at picnic tables.*

STARLINGS

East Africa's birds of paradise

The oily gloss of the common starling so familiar in Europe (and where it has been introduced in North America and Australia) offers only a glimmer of the magnificence to which its cousins in Africa attain. Starlings were described by one ornithologist as Africa's birds of paradise and nowhere else on earth can show off such a colourful range of this garrulous, sociable family (of which oxpeckers also form a part – see separate section). Many of the 30 species in the region are brilliantly iridescent, the various glossy starlings flashing blue, violet, indigo and bronze, and others sport bold patterns or other features.

Starlings reach their greatest diversity in savanna, but at least one species can be seen in most habitats, from high mountain grasslands and rainforest canopies to semidesert; look for the red-winged starling in cities, where it clings to the vertical faces of tall buildings like artificial cliffs. Most African starlings are omnivorous opportunists, eating insects and spiders, or vegetable matter such as fruit and grain; the superb starling can become quite fearless of people, even raiding picnic tables.

Starlings inhabiting forests generally have shorter legs and a larger proportion of fruit in their diet, and longer-legged savanna species spend more time on the ground where they take live food. Wattled starlings (inset) are respected for delivering farmers from locust plagues; and some species feed in association with others, eg, savanna starlings with weavers and forest starlings in bird waves. The harsh alarm calls of each species are similar and can be recognised by different starling species – even monkeys and oxpeckers' hosts (such as buffaloes and antelopes) are known to respond to them.

Moots and choirs

Most starlings nest in loose colonies or at least in clusters of nests. A nest is usually in some sort of cavity, most commonly

The goss on gloss

Nearly all of East Africa's starling species show some degree of glossiness in their plumage, but these fast-flying birds don't

always allow lingering views in which to nut out their identification subtleties. Four species are entirely glossy-black with chestnut wing patches; and the eight glossy starlings (*Lamprotornis*) look, well, glossy blue. The trick with the black *Onychognathus* starlings is to make a quick assessment of tail length: short tail means Waller's starling and long tail means bristle-crowned, but slender-billed and red-winged starlings are so similar that habitat and elevation are the best ways to separate them in the field – the former lives in montane forests as high as 4500m and the latter is more a lowland species common in cities and gorges. The so-called glossy starlings are very tricky to identify and at first you'll just have to accept the word of an experienced guide. Only Rüppell's long-tailed starling has a long tail, but distribution is a clue: the greater blue-eared starling (pictured) is the most widespread and the black-bellied starling more coastal; the greatest zone of overlap occurs in Uganda – good luck!

*Probably the pick of the bunch, **golden-breasted starlings** are restricted to semiarid areas.*

*Migratory **purple starlings** are most commonly seen between March and September.*

a hole in a tree, cliff, river bank or building, but for forest dwelling species it can be a tangle of vines or epiphytes; nest holes of barbets or woodpeckers are readily appropriated and magpie starlings are unique for nesting in termite mounds. A few never use holes, building instead bulky nests of grass, twigs and leaves with a side entrance; red-winged starlings make cup-shaped nests strengthened with mud on rock faces and large buildings; and for extra protection slender-billed starlings nest behind waterfalls. A few glossy starlings place shed snake's skin in a nest, and many species decorate with fresh green leaves and even flowers.

Usually sociable, most species show sporadic movements related to the availability of food; regular migrations are undertaken by magpie and Hildebrandt's starlings according to rainfall. At the end of the breeding season family groups link with other groups while foraging to number 100 or more individuals and even more at roosts, where thousands may congregate (known as moots). Many species gather in trees during the middle of the day and sing in 'choirs' for long spells; the purpose of such behaviour is unknown. ■

***Fischer's starlings** are birds of drier country that often feed with other species on the ground.*

Hotspots

Tsavo East NP Savanna species such as golden-breasted, Fischer's and migratory Hildebrandt's starlings. **Mt Kenya NP** Kenrick's and Abbott's starlings inhabit montane forests as high as 2500m; slender-billed starling in alpine moorland up to 4500m. **Murchison Falls NP** Six species of glossy starling have been recorded.

***Magpie starlings** breed in May to June, and wander widely at other times through savanna.*

Collared sunbirds inhabit forests and gardens; females (above) lack the males' violet gorget.

*The widespread **scarlet-chested sunbird** of gardens and woodland has an iridescent green throat.*

*The similar **Hunter's sunbird** frequents drier country and has iridescent violet 'shoulders'.*

*The **white-bellied sunbird** is a southern African species, but occurs in southern Tanzania.*

SUNBIRDS

Iridescent jewels

If not the biggest then sunbirds are certainly among the most colourful of East Africa's birds. At least one of the 53 species can be seen wherever there is an abundance of nectar-producing flowers, from the semiarid zone to rainforests and even near the top of the highest peaks where few other birds survive. Sunbirds reach their greatest variety in rainforests, but many are restricted in range to specific habitats, such as coastal woodlands (eg, the Amani sunbird – a relict species restricted to Kenya's Arabuko–Sokoke Forest and isolated Tanzanian mountains such as the Usambaras and Udzungwas) or alpine moorlands (eg, scarlet-chested malachite sunbird). In fact, sunbirds nicely demonstrate the amazing variety of birdlife in East Africa: closely-related species that occur in adjoining areas indicate that a common ancestor evolved into two or more species under changing environmental conditions. Thus, 'pairs' of similar species occur throughout the region, eg, Hunter's and scarlet-chested sunbirds, and malachite and scarlet-tufted malachite sunbirds.

Home in the dome

The basic sunbird body plan is small (as small as 8cm, but ranging up to 15cm in some species whose tail streamers are almost as long again) with a sharp, downcurved bill showing much variation in size and curvature. Males of nearly all species have patches of iridescence that can cover most of the body or be restricted to patches on the throat, rump or head. The combinations are dazzling, from the large malachite, bronze and tacazze sunbirds in shimmering green or bronze with long tail streamers; to dozens of smaller species sporting splashes of violet, gold and amethyst. Several are also augmented with red, yellow or orange 'normal', ie, non-iridescent feathers that may be exposed only during displays or preening. Many species look

The 'hummingbirds' of Africa

Sunbirds are sometimes compared to the hummingbirds, a group not found in Africa, but the similarity is only superficial and they

are not closely related. However, sunbirds occupy a similar ecological niche and only hummingbirds surpass them in their most remarkable feature – iridescence. Unlike 'normal' feathers, in which colour is caused by pigmentation, iridescence is caused by a modified feather structure which creates a reflective surface. Iridescent feathers have a weak structure and therefore flight feathers are not iridescent – iridescence typically appears as a throat patch (gorget), but in males of several species, such as the beautiful sunbird, covers almost the entire body. Iridescent feathers change colour according to the angle of the viewer; for the wearer, this may have a role in bluff or territorial display: when a male that appears black or dull side-on suddenly turns to face a rival, the rival is suddenly confronted by an intimidating burst of colour.

*Variable (or **yellow-bellied**) sunbirds are widespread in savanna and common in gardens.*

Golden-winged sunbirds visit gardens at forest edges between 1800 and 3000m.

very similar and provide enticing identification problems so valued by birdwatchers: females and immature males of many otherwise brilliant species have drab plumage with little iridescence. And to complicate matters, several species, such as the mouse-coloured sunbird, lack iridescent patches.

Still, identification isn't everything and sunbirds are active little birds worth watching at any time. They flit about restlessly and males pugnaciously defend territories against other sunbirds. Although all sunbirds eat at least some insects, caught in flight or while perched, the main food source for most is nectar sipped with a specialised tongue while beak deep in a flower, or after the base of the bloom has been pierced with the sharp bill. They lean into flowers while perched next to them (see the southern double-collared sunbird pictured inset) or feed while hanging upside-down. Usually solitary or in pairs, larger groups may congregate during seasonal flowerings of favoured plants, such as aloes, lion's-paw mints (*Leonotis*), flame-trees and mistletoe.

Nesting in all species conforms to a pattern: a domed nest of woven grass and fibres of vegetation, usually suspended by several tendrils or fibres from a branch or twig. Some variations include a 'porch' over the entrance. Most species lay only one or two eggs, which are incubated by the female although the male also helps with raising the young. ■

*The **malachite sunbird** is a bird of montane vegetation and lives as high as 3000m.*

Hotspots

Mt Kenya and **Kilimanjaro NPs** Montane specialists, such as tacazze sunbirds, and scarlet-tufted malachite sunbirds feeding at giant herbs. **Lake Baringo** Several dry-country species, such as beautiful sunbird, are resident. **Bwindi Impenetrable NP** A host of rainforest species can be seen.

White-browed sparrow-weavers often visit feeding tables at safari lodges.

*Endemic to northern Tanzania, **rufous-tailed weavers** can be seen in NCA and the Serengeti.*

*The nest of the **golden palm weaver** is often suspended under palm fronds.*

*The **lesser masked weaver** is one of East Africa's most widespread and gregarious species.*

SPARROWS, WEAVERS, BISHOPS & WIDOWS

Industrious nest spinners

A few finches native to East Africa are recognisable as sparrows, even chirping and habitually living near people like their kin across much of the world. But their close relatives have evolved into an extraordinary variety of weavers, brightly coloured bishops, and widows with elaborate tail plumes. The diversity of these groups is staggering – 81 species – and one, the red-billed quelea, is one of the most abundant birds on the planet: at times it is so numerous that flocks number in the millions and break branches with their weight when they land.

Weavers are mainly decked out in yellow with black, rufous, orange or brown highlights – exceptions to the colour rule are the malimbes, in which yellow is replaced by red. Confusing enough when nesting, their identification is a birdwatcher's nightmare outside of the breeding season, when many of the colourful males moult into a drab, sparrowlike plumage and form mixed flocks with females and other species. Still, they are energetic builders of intricate and distinctive woven nests; the majority nest socially and weaver colonies can become virtual cities of grass apartments smothering entire trees – they can be seen in virtually any town or village, as well as in the wilds, where palms and spreading acacias might be draped with hundreds of nests (inset).

Each weaver species has its own trademark architecture and many nests can be identified by shape alone. Some nests hang from intertwined stems like a pendulum; others are onion-shaped or have a long, narrow entrance like an upside-down flask; some are neat balls holding two papyrus stems together; and buffalo-weavers build large, untidy accumulations of grass with multiple entrances in which several pairs live and roost. Weaver colonies are noisy and constantly busy: birds coming and going with nest material; males courting females, and rivals stealing nest material. Unlike their savanna counterparts, some

Cuckoos up the spout

For weavers (and indeed all birds), success depends on building a nest secure enough to raise a brood and withstand the attentions of predators. And so successful are many at building such nests that other birds, such as waxbills and pygmy falcons, find abandoned weavers' nests attractive enough to shelter or even nest in themselves. Pygmy falcons are mainly insect hunters and don't bother the weavers, but there's nothing much the weavers can do about a gymnogene (also called African harrierhawk) robbing a nest. These specialised raptors hang upside down from the nest and insert a long, double-jointed leg to extract an egg or chick. Diederik cuckoos commonly parasitise lesser masked weavers (pictured), but the weavers are fighting back: certain populations build entrance spouts so tight that the cuckoos can't get into the nest and have even been found wedged in so tightly they have died in the spout.

Pale eyes help distinguish **Speke's weaver** from several similar species.

Male **southern red bishops** get their brilliant plumage only in the breeding season.

forest weavers are solitary or feed in pairs, and don't build colonial nests; they frequently associate with 'bird waves' moving through the forest. Malimbes are agile canopy feeders and another outstanding species is the parasitic weaver, which lays its eggs in the nests of warblers such as prinias and cisticolas.

Red bishops and black widows

Outside the breeding season, male bishops and widowbirds are streaked and drab like many other weavers, and sometimes form large, nomadic flocks. But when courting is in full swing they are eye-catching and colourful birds, moulting into black plumage with flashes of orange, yellow or red; male widowbirds also grow elaborate plumes – those of the long-tailed widowbird can be three times as long as its body.

Males of most species of bishop and weaver are polygamous, mating with several females if their courtship performances are suitably impressive, and building a nest for each. Male bishops stand out perched high on stems across swathes of rank grasslands and perform display flights with feathers fluffed out, some becoming almost spherical in the process. Male widows stake out territories where they display, the most spectacular being Jackson's widowbird, which tramples an arena in long grass where it jumps up and down with wings and long tail spread – several sometimes performing in a small area. ■

In courtship finery the male **long-tailed widowbird** grows a tail nearly 50cm long.

Hotspots
Masai Mara NR Savanna, marsh and grassland are varied habitats for nearly 30 species. **Samburu NR** Semiarid acacia country heaving with buffalo-weavers, social weavers and others. **Bwindi Impenetrable NP** Several rainforest-dwelling weavers can be seen among bird feeding parties.

*Look for **paradise whydahs** in drier country near water, often accompanying other species.*

WHYDAHS

Flamboyant nest parasites

It is perhaps not surprising that several of the 160-odd East African species of finches should adopt parasitism as a breeding strategy: the eight species of seed-eating whydahs (the name comes from a town in Benin) and indigobirds do just that. However, on hatching the young don't evict or kill their foster siblings (unlike cuckoos, for example). Instead, they are raised alongside them, and even associate with their foster family for some time after leaving the nest. Like their foster siblings, whydah and indigobird chicks have colourful callosities inside their mouths which stimulate their foster parents to feed them. Adults look nothing like their unwitting hosts, and feed and drink alongside them. Females, juveniles and non-breeding males all have typical, nondescript 'finch plumage'. But when males develop courtship colours, indigobirds are entirely cloaked in deep, satiny blue and whydahs, in true East African fashion, develop long, showy tail plumes. ■

> **Hotspots**
> **Tsavo West NP** Straw-tailed and paradise whydahs are common in low scrubby bush. **Nairobi NP** Good chance of seeing the widespread village indigobird. **Kidepo Valley NP** Semiarid savanna is ideal for four species of whydah.

CANARIES

Robust ancestors of caged pets

If you've ever wondered where those caged songsters come from, East Africa has 15 species, some of which go under the name of seedeaters and one, the oriole-finch, looks like a miniature oriole, complete with black head and red bill. Canaries are yet another part of the great assembly of finches, closely related to goldfinches, and quite common in most bush habitats. The streaky seedeater is common near settlements and a few other species share its reputation as something of a pest – those stubby, almost conical bills are adept at cracking open seeds. Look for canaries and seedeaters at the edge of crops and gardens, associating in small groups, with other canary species and with other finches. Wild canaries bear little resemblance to their rather pallid captive relatives, although a few are also prodigious songsters – male yellow-fronted canaries gather to sing in treetops and are also caught for the pet trade. Other canary species build cup-shaped nests of grass in trees and bushes, sometimes in loose colonies. ■

*The **streaky-headed seedeater** is typical of some of the drabber canary species.*

Yellow-fronted canaries feed in small flocks and sound rather like a caged canary.

> **Hotspots**
> **Nairobi NP** Brimstone canary is common in bush and the edge of cultivation. **Mt Kenya NP** Forest edge is ideal for several species along the Naro Moru Trail. **Kibale NP** Papyrus choking the Bigodi Wetlands support papyrus canary.

PIN-TAILED WHYDAH

A conspicuous roadside flirt

When travelling between parks you'll often see birds perched along roadsides: common fiscals are among the more obvious, and male pin-tailed whydahs perched on wires, fence posts and prominent branches – their long tail feathers drifting in the breeze – quickly become a familiar sight. These gregarious birds normally travel in small flocks numbering 20-30 birds; males are polygamous (ie, typically mating with more than one female), and during the breeding season flocks are typically composed of one breeding male for every five or six females and nonbreeding males. Breeding males are pugnacious and have been know to chase birds of other species from feeding stations. And even outside the breeding season pin-tailed whydahs are conspicuous while feeding: they jump backwards along the ground, scattering soil to expose fallen seeds (when breeding males do this their long tail flaps with each hop).

The male's coloration is attained at the start of the long rains; afterwards he moults through motley stages to finally resemble the females and nonbreeding males (see photo top right) In nonbreeding plumage the various species of whydah can be very difficult to tell apart – birders should try to visit East Africa when birds start breeding. While he's in the mood the male pin-tailed whydah is a sight worth seeing: he sings as he flies around a perched female with gentle undulations, his tail bouncing up and down; she responds by shivering her wings. Once the formalities are over, females also work hard at reproducing: whydahs are nest parasites, ie, they lay their eggs in the nests of other birds (usually waxbills), which then invest all the energy necessary to raise the whydahs' young. Each female removes one egg of the host for each egg she lays, typically laying only one or two per nest, but occasionally laying in more than one nest. After laying, the parents have nothing more to do with the raising of their offspring: the unwitting hosts feed and raise the aliens alongside their own chicks. ∎

Recognition Breeding males black and white with long (20cm) tail streamers and bright red bill. Females similar to nonbreeding males.
Habitat Forest edge, savanna and cultivation as high as 2500m; also in suburban gardens.
Habits Males sing while perched on a bush, post or stalk. In East Africa parasitises common, black-rumped and fawn-breasted waxbills. Nonbreeding flocks may number 100 birds. Coloured callosities in mouth of nestlings resemble those of hosts' chicks.
Breeding Eggs white. Nestlings fledge after 17-21 days. Fledglings associate with foster parents before becoming independent.
Feeding Finds seeds by jumping backwards while raking the ground with claws; sometimes hawks insects in flight.
Voice A high-pitched tseet tseet tsuweet, frequently repeated.

Hotspots
Masai Mara NR, Serengeti NP, Murchison Falls NP

MORE CREATURES
GREAT AND SMALL

The hidden multitude at your feet

With so many large, highly visible and world-famous mammals and birds to see, it's not surprising that East Africa's small, reclusive and cryptic creatures often get overlooked. In fact, the majority of Africa's reptiles, amphibians and invertebrates have never been systematically studied – even though these groups are undoubtedly more diverse than mammals and birds. So while viewing large mammals and colourful birds is still the priority on most safaris, keeping an eye open for the less-obvious creatures offers an alternative but equally unique experience for the keen wildlife watcher.

Let the scales fall from your eyes

Reptiles are abundant and diverse in East Africa, from giant carnivores such as the Nile monitor and bank-basking Nile crocodile, to the smaller but brightly coloured agama lizards and slow-moving, swivel-eyed chameleons. Snakes are less conspicuous and include some superbly camouflaged and patterned species. The largest, the 4m-long African rock python, can suffocate and swallow a small antelope; others like puff adders, mambas, cobras and vipers are famously venomous, but your chances of coming to face to face with one are rare. Amphibians are abundant in rainforests, where their breeding choruses can be deafening, but Kenya's Arabuko–Sokoke Forest is a seasonally dry environment which supports an extraordinary diversity of frogs. Rainforests are also hotspots for butterflies – of which East Africa boasts hundreds of showy species.

Reasons to be cheerful

Most people would rather not know about some of the small-est animals of the African bush, particularly those that might bite. But forewarned is forearmed and unpleasant though some are, everything from lions to safari ants plays a role in the ecosystem. A point in case is dung beetles, whose sole reason for living is to seek out animal droppings which they bury next to their eggs. You'll probably see several dung beetles rolling perfectly spherical balls of dung much larger than themselves along paths. Upon hatching, the beetle grubs eat their way through their nursery larder before turning into pupae and hatching into adult beetles. Be grateful: the average elephant consumes 100 tonnes of herbage annually, and if it wasn't for these animated poop-scoops you'd need more than a 4WD to get through it.

Another group of insects which has an even greater impact on wildlife and ecosystems is termites. There's an awful lot of vegetation growing out there, more than the large herbivores can consume, and behind the scenes millions of termites are also chewing away at it, turning cellulose into protein.

Less benevolent are the blood-sucking tsetse flies, but in a sense you can thank them for much of the wildlife you see on the savanna today. Tsetse flies are found only in certain habi-tats (bushy savanna and miombo woodland are favourites), and here they hunt large animals (including humans). Because some transmit the deadly sleeping sickness, areas which harboured tsetse flies were shunned by pastoralists and large mammals proliferated (the Masai Mara is probably the most famous of these areas). Sleeping sickness is all but eradicated, but tsetse flies are still attracted to blue clothing. ■

NILE CROCODILE

Recognition Powerful jaws and tail. Olive or dull grey.
Habitat Freshwater.
Behaviour Basks. Female guards nest and hatchlings.
Breeding Lays 30–40 eggs which hatch after 90 days.
Feeding Strictly carnivorous.
Voice Young yelp when hatching.
Swahili Mamba

Hotspots
Lake Turkana, Masai Mara NR, Murchison Falls NP

Aquatic killing machine

The Nile crocodile is Africa's biggest reptile by far, an unrivalled aquatic killing machine reaching a length of up to 6m. Smaller crocs eat mainly fishes underwater or snatch swimming birds from the surface, but for a large one virtually any animal is fair game, including antelopes, livestock and even big cats. Adult crocs take many migrating wildebeests and zebras crossing rivers, such as the Mara and Talek rivers; and are responsible for hundreds of human deaths every year. A crocodile can stay submerged with only its eyes and nostrils above the surface, waiting to ambush prey – shine a torch over a swamp at night and the reflected eyeshine will show just how abundant they can be.

When an animal gets too close the croc lunges with incredible power and speed, propelled by its massive tail, drags its victim underwater and drowns it. Several crocs may gather at one floating carcass, clamping teeth onto the flesh and spinning to rip off chunks. Adult crocodiles have no predators, although territorial disputes between males can cause serious injuries; and hippos will nudge them off a sandbank and even bite one in two if it threatens a calf. But for a young croc to reach maturity it must first dodge birds, fish and larger crocodiles. ■

NILE MONITOR

Recognition Grey-brown to olive-green with bands of yellowish spots. Up to 2m.
Habitat Savanna, waterways.
Behaviour Solitary. Males fight for territory.
Breeding Lays 20–60 eggs.
Feeding Insects, crabs, small vertebrates and carrion.
Voice Hisses.
Swahili Buru kenge

Hotspots
Masai Mara NR, Serengeti NP, Murchison Falls NP

The lizard king

East Africa's largest lizard, the Nile monitor, is a solitary reptile typically seen ambling through the savanna or lounging on a branch overhanging water. Watch early in the day for it catching some rays on an exposed rock, sandbank or tree stump. Basking warms them up for the hunt but, like most reptiles, monitors have low energy requirements and can go for long spells without eating. Normal locomotion is a slow, meandering gait (a large one sometimes dragging its belly along the ground), but Nile monitors are proficient swimmers that readily take to water if threatened – young ones don't venture in too deep in case a crocodile is waiting.

Any nook or crevice is investigated for a morsel; prey includes a large variety of small animals, from insects and birds to small mammals as large as a mongoose. Eggs are a favourite, and monitors readily dig up unguarded crocodile eggs and climb trees to rob birds' nests. That long forked tongue constantly flicking in and out is completely harmless; in fact, it helps detect prey by transferring scent to an organ in the roof of the mouth (called a Jacobson's organ). However, monitors can inflict a serious bite. Adult monitors have few predators, although they are sometimes taken by pythons, crocodiles and large raptors such as martial eagles. ■

LIZARDS

Running colours and horned warriors

Like other reptiles, lizards have scales and rely on the sun to warm their bodies (despite this many geckoes are nocturnal, and actively hunt insects and other small prey). Most conspicuous are the brightly coloured agamids that run over large rocks such as kopjes. The bright orange head of the male common agama stands out from a distance to attract potential mates – look carefully nearby and you'll probably see a cluster of females watching him, although they are camouflaged perfectly against the rock. Other species are not so easy to see, but by turning over loose rocks and logs (be sure to replace them, and watch for snakes and scorpions) you may uncover a gecko – rainforest geckos are best sought by picking out their eyeshine at night with a torch.

Look near brightly-coloured male **common agamas** *for groups of well-camouflaged females.*

Folklore has it that chameleons dive for cover when they hear

hornbills honking. However, this would be hard to prove because they are usually well camouflaged and you'd have to find one first (locating chameleons is chancy, but they're often seen crossing roads). If hornbills strike terror into chameleons, these utterly harmless lizards scare the bejesus out of most Africans, who believe children will be born hideously deformed if a

Other colourful species of **agamid** *exploit the many small niches in the savanna.*

pregnant woman sees one. And they do look like they were designed in a boardroom, although they are in fact ideally suited to an arboreal lifestyle, with eyes that swivel independently on scaly cones; a sticky, muscular tongue that can shoot out the length of its body to grab an insect; paired toes for clinging to thin branches; and a prehensile tail coiled like a watch spring.

Chameleons' heads are large and domed, and in some species are adorned with neck shields, horns and other weaponlike growths (inset) used by males in territorial disputes. Chameleons are probably most famous for their ability to change colour and it has been speculated that one would explode if placed on a tartan rug. In truth their colour-changing abilities are often exaggerated, being generally restricted to shades of green, grey and brown, and take several minutes to perform. However, some males flush with bright colour when trying to attract a mate or ward off another male straying into his territory. When males lock horns the trees don't exactly shake with chameleon warfare, it's more a determined pushing until one gives way. ■

Dwarf chameleons measure only 11cm long and can change colour quickly.

Chameleons' superb camouflage make them difficult to see in the trees, but they often cross roads.

Hotspots
Lake Nakuru NP The Baboon Cliffs are a good place to get close to agama lizards, although they inhabit kopjes in many reserves.

The superbly camouflaged
Gaboon viper *is armed with 5cm fangs – the largest of any snake.*

Puff adders *are common savanna snakes that are often seen crossing roads after rain.*

Look for **tree frogs** *clinging to vertical surfaces or the underside of leaves in wet areas.*

Rocket frogs of the genus Ptychadena *might be seen at Kenya's Arabuko–Sokoke Forest.*

SNAKES

Giving reptiles a good rep

Although many animals feed on snakes, including secretary birds, snake-eagles and mongooses, seeing a snake is usually a matter of chance and whatever their reputation the majority are harmless to people. Many are nocturnal, so if you particularly want to see them you could improve your chances by spotlighting at night. The biggest East African species, the African rock python, occasionally reaches 6.1m (although 4 to 4.5m is more common) and is often abroad late in the day where rock outcrops, such as kopjes, provide cover. Rock pythons asphyxiate prey as large as a small antelope by wrapping it in muscular coils. Some snakes inject venom into their prey through hollow teeth (the well-known fangs) and names like vipers, adders, mambas and cobras will be familiar to many people. From the safety of a vehicle you can watch them hunt and appreciate their subtle, often beautiful coloration. Normally sit-and-wait predators that strike with split-second speed, puff adders are often on the move after rain. Cobras are famous for their 'hood' that spreads as they rear up to strike; spitting cobras have modified fangs that accurately spray venom several metres. ■

Hotspots
Tsavo and **Lake Nakuru NPs**, **Kakamega Forest**

FROGS & TOADS

The best of both worlds

Collectively known as amphibians, frogs and toads are instantly recognisable by their large eyes, webbed feet and (usually) moist skin. All are more or less dependent on freshwater to raise their young, although there are many ingenious variations on the theme. Eggs usually hatch into tadpoles with gills that eventually develop legs and breathe air. Adults are carnivorous, snatching insects and other small animals (an African bullfrog was recorded eating young puff adders!) with their broad, sticky tongue. Arabuko–Sokoke Forest is the number one place for frogs in Kenya, with at least 25 species known; activity peaks at the start of the long rains when their loud calls make a deafening chorus in suitable breeding areas. During the day many shelter under logs and rocks, but amphibians are best detected at night with a torch – look among vegetation in shallow water, and in dense foliage for tree frogs. Calls are distinct for every species and one of the best ways to locate frogs and toads. ■

Hotspots
Lake Mburo NP Low-lying grasslands that flood during the rains sometimes have huge concentrations of frogs. **Kakamega Forest** and **Semliki NP** These rainforests can be productive 'frogging' habitat.

THE SMALL FIVE

Consider the small things in life

The chase for the so-called 'big five' (elephant, buffalo, lion, leopard and rhino – reputed by hunters to be the most dangerous game) is a high priority on many safaris. Nothing wrong with that of course, but once the pressure's off, spare a moment for some of the smaller, less glamorous animals that are usually overlooked on safari.

Elephant shrew

Elephant shrew Mammals don't come any smaller than shrews and although the smallest weighs only 2g, each has every sense and organ of an elephant 2.85 million times its weight. Elephant shrews are giants among midgets – weighing-in at a leaf-trembling 440g – and even have a long, prehensile snout with which they sniff out prey in leaf litter. Some are boldly patterned and can measure 23cm from chequered rump to the end of their quivering 'trunk'. The best places to see elephant shrews are at Arabuko–Sokoke FR (golden-rumped elephant shrew) and Budongo FR (chequered elephant shrew).

White-headed buffalo-weaver

Buffalo-weaver So-called because of their habit of perching on the back of buffaloes and other large animals. These large (20cm) mainly black, white or black-and-white members of the weaver family build huge, untidy domed nests in which several pairs nest. Buffalo-weavers are common in savannas, sometimes in large flocks: Samburu NR has abundant white-headed buffalo-weavers.

Ant-lion

Ant-lion Small, conical pits in sandy soil indicate the presence of these voracious (though tiny) insect predators. Ants blundering along the rim of the pit lose their footing and tumble into the open jaws of the ant-lion waiting buried in the sand below – few escape. Despite their fearsome demeanour, ant lions are actually the larvae of lacewings – harmless flying insects with transparent wings. Look for ant-lions' pits in sheltered, sandy soil.

Leopard tortoise

Leopard tortoise Only grass and flowers quake at the approach of this slow-moving antithesis of the sleek, predatory cat. Its dense, bony shell protects it from most predators, although some birds (such as ostriches) swallow young ones whole or drop adults from a height to crack them open. Sex looks hilarious and males grunt audibly with the effort. A leopard tortoise could be encountered in virtually any savanna country; Serengeti NP, and Masai Mara and Lake Bogoria NRs are good places to try.

Rhinoceros beetle True rhinoceros beetles are insects of the rainforest (males have large, hornlike projections on their head). But on safari you're more likely to see dung beetles (pictured) rolling balls of dung along tracks. An army of dung beetles of many species buries a massive tonnage of dung with their eggs – the larvae recycle the waste material and themselves become food for insect-eating animals. ■

Dung beetle

RESOURCE GUIDE

The following information isn't meant to be comprehensive; we've put together some key references and contacts as a starting point.

RECOMMENDED READING

Field guides

Mammals The most comprehensive field guide, *The Kingdon Field Guide to African Mammals* by J Kingdon, covers all mammals of continental Africa with colour illustrations and is packed with background information. The alternatives, *A Field Guide to the Larger Mammals of Africa* by J Dorst & P Dandelot, and *A Field Guide to the Mammals of Africa including Madagascar* by T Haltenorth & H Dillerare, are bit out of date but also worthwhile.

Birds First stop is *Field Guide to Birds of Kenya and Northern Tanzania* by D Zimmerman, D Turner & D Pearson; it is written by experts and simply the best for the region. The only guide to cover the rest of Tanzania plus Uganda is *Birds of Eastern Africa* by B van Perlo. Birders visiting Uganda should also buy *Where to Watch Birds in Uganda* by J Rossouw & M Sacchi, which gives site-by-site information on all the national parks plus a comprehensive bird list.

Reptiles and amphibians There is comparatively little reference material on East African herpetology. *Reptiles & Amphibians of East Africa* by N Hedges gives a basic introduction; otherwise there's *Poisonous Snakes of East Africa* by A & J MacKay; and *The Dangerous Snakes of Africa* by S Spawls & B Branch.

Invertebrates *The Butterflies of Kenya & their Natural History* by N Torben & B Larsen covers every species in colour. *African Spiders an ID Manual* by A Dippenaar-Schoeman & R Jocque is pitched at those more technically minded.

Marine life *The Guide to the Seashores of Eastern Africa and the Western Indian Ocean Islands* edited by M Richmond, covers many groups of marine animals and plants, as well as the better-known shells, fish, crustaceans and birds. *Reef Fishes of the Indian Ocean* by G Allen & R Steene, shows a good range in field guide format.

Checklists

The East Africa Natural History Society publishes authoritative, up-to-date checklists on mammals and birds, including the *Check-list of the Mammals of East Africa* (which covers all species known from Uganda, Tanzania and Kenya) and the *Check-list of the Birds of Kenya* (which is updated periodically). A comprehensive and up-to-date checklist of Ugandan birds is included in *Where to Watch Birds in Uganda* by J Rossouw & M Sacchi. *Bird and Mammal Checklists for Ten National Parks in Uganda* is available at the Uganda Wildlife Authority office (☎ 041-34 62 87) in Kampala and is also useful.

Background reading

The Safari Companion by R Estes is the classic guide to further understanding of the behaviour of African mammals, and Estes' *Behaviour Guide to Mammals of East Africa* goes into even more detail. *Portraits in the Wild – Animal Behaviour in East Africa* by C Moss describes the life histories of a number of large mammals.

To identify spoor and scats you can't go past C & T Stuart's *Field Guide to Tracks & Signs of Southern and East African Wildlife*; and *The Art of Tracking – The Origin of Science* by L Liebenberg gives fascinating background theory to the subject.

Those who want to know more about our closest relatives should read *Demonic Males* by R Wrangham & D Peterson. *Chimpanzee Cultures* edited by R Wrangham, W McGrew & De Waal is also recommended. Pioneering chimp researcher Jane Goodall's *In the Shadow of Man* and *Patterns of Behaviour – Chimpanzees at Gombe* are bibles on the topic. C Uhlenbroek's television series *Chimp Diary* and *Cousins* are also available in book form. The bestselling *Gorillas in the Mist* by D Fossey is still a good read; and the intimate lives of baboons come under the spotlight in *Almost Human: A Journey into the World of Baboons*, by S Strum.

Island Africa by J Kingdon is a readable and thought-provoking book on evolution across the continent. Kingdon's encyclopaedic *East African Mammals: An Atlas of Evolution* is a fund of information in language accessible to nonexperts. More extensive reading can be enjoyed in the monographs by J Scott, illustrated with his excellent photos, such as *The Great Migration*, *The Leopard's Tale*, *The Marsh Lions* (with B Jackman), *Painted Wolves* and *Kingdom of Lions*. There is also a book of the popular *Big Cat Diary* television series Scott presented with S King.

Budding ornithologists should dip into the multi-volume *Birds of Africa* series by L Brown, E Urban & K Newman or the 12 volume *Handbook of Birds of the World* edited by J del Hoyo, A Elliot & J Sargatal – both profusely illustrated and covering all the birds of Africa in detail.

Stories of heroic and sometimes bitter fights to save East Africa's big game are told lucidly and emotionally by those in the front line. Recommended are: *The End of the Game* by P Beard, and *Battle for the Elephants* by I & O Douglas-Hamilton. *Horn of Darkness – Rhinos on the Edge* by C Cunningham & J Berger looks closely at south-west African rhinos, but is still relevant to poaching everywhere.

Periodicals

Swara magazine, published by the East African Wildlife Society, features photos and articles on conservation, reserves and wildlife. *Kenya Birds* is published by the Department of Ornithology at Nairobi Museum; those with a more scientific interest in birds should take a look at their *Scopus*. The East African Natural History Society publishes *NatureKenya* and *NatureUganda*; both cover a broad range of topics. For the conservation-minded, *Oryx* published by the Flora & Fauna Preservation Society (c/o Zoological Society of London) has a strong African focus.

Bookshops

International Before your trip it's worth checking out the comprehensive range available from mail-order natural history bookshops; several have a web catalogue and online ordering service.

- **American Birding Association** (USA & Canada ☎ 800-634 7736, fax 590 2473; international ☎ 719-578 0607, fax 578 9705; 🖳 www.americanbirding.org/abasales), PO Box 6599, Colorado Springs, Colorado 80934, USA.
- **Andrew Isles Natural History Books** (☎ 03-9510 5750, fax 9529 1256, [e] books@AndrewIsles.com, 🖳 www.AndrewIsles.com), 115 Greville St, Prahran, Victoria 3181, Australia.
- **Natural History Book Service** (☎ 1803-865 913, fax 865 280, [e] nhbs@nhbs.co.uk, 🖳 www.nhbs.com), 2–3 Wills Rd, Totnes, Devon TQ9 5XN, England.

- **Subbuteo** (☎ 870-0109 700, fax 699, e info@wildlifebooks.com, 💻 www.wildlifebooks.com), The Rea, Upton Magna, Shrewsbury SY4 4UR, England.

Kenya Bookshops in Nairobi generally stock a good range of field guides, 'coffee table' books and maps; apart from those listed below there's a bookshop at the Nairobi Museum and in foyers of the major hotels. Shop around because prices vary. Some key booksellers are:

- **The Book Villa** (☎ 02-22 33 79, fax 21 58 37), IPS Building, Standard St (PO Box 40453), Nairobi.
- **Book Corner** (☎ 02-24 02 59, fax 21 55 90), Mama Ngina St (PO Box 14757), Nairobi.
- **Prestige Booksellers & Stationers** (☎ 02-22 35 15, fax 24 67 96), Prudential Assurance Bldg, Mama Ngina St (PO Box 45425), Nairobi.
- **Text Book Centre** (☎ 02-74 74 05, fax 22 57 79, e info@tbc.co.ke), Ground Floor, Sarit Centre, Westlands, Nairobi.

Tanzania Dar es Salaam has a variety of bookshops offering a range of publications on parks and wildlife; a smaller selection is available in Zanzibar and Arusha.

Uganda Some field guides are available in the Uganda Tourist Board office (☎ 041-34 21 96), Backpackers Hostel & Campsite (☎ 041-27 20 12) and in bookshops at major hotels. Otherwise, there's:

- **Aristoc Booklex Ltd** (☎ 041-34 43 81, fax 25 49 68), Diamond Trust Building, corner of Colville St and Kampala Rd (PO Box 5130), Kampala.

TOUR OPERATORS

Although safari and tour operators abound throughout Africa, the industry is haphazardly regulated and not all tours are safe, informative or environmentally sound. The following operators we feel know their stuff and will offer safe, informative and interesting wildlife-watching experiences.

International

International wildlife conservation organisations such as the World Wildlife Fund (www.worldwildlife.org/travel) run natural history tours to East Africa. It's also worthwhile checking listings of international wildlife tour operators in well-regarded wildlife magazines (like *BBC Wildlife*). Several specialist wildlife, nature and bird tour companies that use only professional guides schedule regular trips to East Africa:

Birdquest (☎ 1254-826 317, fax 826 780, e birders@birdquest .co.uk), Two Jays, Kemple End, Stonyhurst, Lancashire BB7 9QY, England.
Falcon Tours (☎ 08-9336 3882, fax 9336 3930, e falcon@highway1 .com.au), Unit 11, 342 South Terrace, South Fremantle, WA 6162, Australia.
Field Guides Inc (☎ 512-327 4953, fax 327 9231, e fgileader@ aol.com, 💻 www.fieldguides.com), PO Box 160723, Austin, Texas 78716, USA.
Naturetrek (☎ 1962-733 051, fax 736 426, e inquiries@naturetrek .demon.co.uk), Chautara, Bighton nr. Alresford, Hampshire SO24 9RB, England.
Ornitholidays (☎ 1243-821 230, fax 829 574), 1–3 Victoria Drive, Bognor Regis, West Sussex PO21 2PW, England.

Sunbird (☎ 1767-682 969, fax 692 481, e sunbird@demon.co.uk, 🖳 www.osme.org/sunbird/index.html), PO Box 76, Sandy, Bedfordshire SG19 1DF, England.
VENT (Victor Emanuel Nature Tours) (☎ 512-328 5221, fax 328 2919, e VENTBIRD@aol.com, 🖳 www.VENTBIRD.com), PO Box 33008, Austin, Texas 78764, USA.
WCS (Wildlife Conservation Society) (☎ 212-439 6507, e travel@wcs.org, 🖳 www.wcs.org), Central Park Zoo, 830 Fifth Avenue, New York, New York 10021, USA.
Wings (☎ 520-320 9868, fax 320 9373, e wings@wingbirds.com, 🖳 www.widdl.com/wings), 1643 N. Alvernon Way, Suite 105, Tucson, Arizona 85712, USA.

Kenya

Kenya has a guide accreditation system (see the 'Guide and tours' section of the Wildlife-Watching chapter) – inquire whether your safari operator uses accredited guides (although some reputable companies use good guides that aren't accredited).

Abercrombie & Kent (A&K) (☎ 02-33 49 55, fax 21 57 52, e ASKA&K@abercrombiekent.com, 🖳 www.abercrombiekent.com), Bruce House, Standard St, Nairobi.
Bike Treks (☎ 02-44 63 71, fax 44 24 39, e biktreks@form-net.com, 🖳 www.angelfire.com/sk/biketreks), PO Box 14237, Nairobi.
Cheli & Peacock (☎ 02-74 83 07, fax 75 02 25, e chelipeacock@attmail.com, 🖳 www.chelipeacock.com), PO Box 39806, Nairobi.
EAOS (East African Ornithological Safaris) (☎ 02-33 11 91/33 16 84, fax 21 65 28, e eaos@africaonline.co.ke, 🖳 www.savannah camps.com), 11th floor, Fedha Towers, Standard St (Box 48019), Nairobi.
Gametrackers (☎ 02-33 89 27, fax 33 09 03, e game@africaonline .co.ke, 🖳 www.gametrackers com), 1st Floor, Kenya Cinema Plaza, Moi Ave (PO Box 62042), Nairobi.
Let's Go Travel (☎ 02-34 03 31/21 30 33, fax 33 68 90/21 47 13, e info@letsgosafari.com, 🖳 www.letsgosafari.com or www.kenya-direct.com/letsgo), Caxton House, Standard St (PO Box 60342), Nairobi.
Sirikwa Safaris (☎ 0325-20061 c/o Soy Trading), PO Box 332, Kitale.
UTC (United Touring Company) (☎ 02-33 19 60, fax 33 14 22, e utcn @africaonline.co.ke), PO Box 42196, Nairobi.

Tanzania

The country (especially in Arusha) is overflowing with tour operators; some are good, others are more interested in your cash than showing you wildlife. Keep in mind that most reliable companies are accredited – see the Ecotours listing in the sidebar of each reserve in the Tanzania section of the Parks and Places chapter.

Uganda

There is no wildlife guide accreditation scheme in Uganda, but members of the Association of Uganda Tour Operators (AUTO) must adhere to a strict code of ethics. All companies listed here are full members of AUTO with their own vehicles and can provide a tour with a wildlife focus.

Abercrombie & Kent (☎ 041-26 67 00, fax 26 67 01, e akug10@calva.com), PO Box 7799, Kampala.
Afritours & Travel (☎ 041-23 35 96, fax 34 48 55, e afritour@swiftuganda.com), PO Box 5187, Kampala.
African Pearl Safaris (☎ 041-23 35 66, fax 23 57 70, e apsafari@swiftuganda.com), PO Box 4262, Kampala.

Delmira (☎ 041-23 54 94, fax 23 19 27, |e| delmira@imul.com), PO Box 9098, Kampala.
Eden Travel (☎/fax 041-26 67 94, |e| hn10@calva.com), PO Box 5937, Kampala.
G&C Tours (☎/fax 041-32 14 79, |e| gctours@imul.com), PO Box 619, Entebbe.
Green Wilderness Group/Semliki Safaris (☎/fax 041-25 97 00, |e| gwg @swiftuganda.com), PO Box 23825, Kampala.
Mantana African Safaris (☎/fax 041-32 01 52, |e| mantana @infocom.co.ug), PO Box 11060, Entebbe.
Phoenix Tours and Travel (☎ 041-23 60 96, fax 23 60 97, |e| phoenix@starcom.co.ug), PO Box 3127, Kampala.
Volcanoes (☎ 041-34 64 64, fax 34 17 18, |e| volcanoes@infocom.co.ug), PO Box 22818, Kampala.

Rwanda and Democratic Republic of the Congo (DRC)

At the time of writing gorilla tourism had just restarted in Rwanda, but no tour companies were operating in the country – operators in Uganda can probably help. Be sure to make full inquiries about security when planning a trip to these worthwhile but potentially dangerous areas.

PARKS & CONSERVATION AUTHORITIES

Kenya Kenya Wildlife Service (KWS) (☎ 02-50 06 22, fax 50 17 52, |e| kws@users.africaonline.co.ke), Langata Rd (PO Box 40241), Nairobi.
Tanzania National parks: Tanzania National Parks Authority (TANAPA) (☎ 057-2371/4082, fax 8216), PO Box 3134, Arusha. Game reserves: Wildlife Division, Ministry of Natural Resources and Tourism (☎ 051-86 63 76, 86 60 64), Ivory Room, Pugu Rd at Changombe Rd (PO Box 25295), Dar es Salaam. Marine parks and reserves: Fisheries Division, Ministry of Natural Resources and Tourism (☎ 051-11 61 62, fax 11 03 52, |e| fisheries@twiga.com), PO Box 2462, Dar es Salaam.
Uganda Uganda Wildlife Authority (UWA) (☎ 041-34 62 87, fax 34 62 91, |e| director@uwahq.uu.imul.com, 🖳 www.visituganda.com), Plot 3, Kintu Rd (PO Box 3530), Kampala.
Rwanda Office Rwandais du Tourisme et des Parcs Nationaux (ORTPN), (☎/fax 070-76512/4), BP 905, Kigali.
DRC Institut Congolais pour la Conservation de la Nature (ICCN – formerly IZCN) (☎ 12-33250), BP 868, Kinshasa 1.

NATURALISTS' ASSOCIATIONS

The following local and international organisations run projects and activities in East Africa. Inquire about volunteer work.

African Bird Club c/o BirdLife International, Wellbrook Court, Girton Rd, Cambridge CB3 0NA, England.
African Wildlife Foundation Kenya: PO Box 48177, Nairobi. USA: 1717 Massachusetts Ave, NW, Washington, DC 20036, USA.
BirdLife International Wellbrook Court, Girton Rd, Cambridge CB3 0NA, England.
Born Free Foundation (☎ 01403-240 170, fax 327 838, |e| wildlife@bornfree.org.uk), 3 Grove House, Foundry Lane, Horsham, West Sussex, England RH13 5PL.

Dian Fossey Gorilla Fund International (☎ 800-851 0203/404-624 5881, fax 404-624 5999, e 2help@gorillafund.org, 🖳 www.gorilla fund.org), 800 Cherokee Ave, SE, Atlanta, Georgia 30315-1440, USA.

East African Natural History Society (EANHS) Kenya (☎ 02-74 99 57/90, fax 74 10 49, e eanhs@africaonline.co.ke): PO Box 44486, Nairobi. Uganda (☎ 041-54 07 19, fax 53 35 28, e eanhs@imul.com): c/o Dept of Zoology, Makerere University, PO Box 7062, Kampala.

East African Wildlife Society (☎ 02-57 41 45, fax 57 03 35, e eawls@form-net.com), (PO Box 20110, Nairobi) Riara Rd, Kilimani, Kenya.

Eden Wildlife Trust (☎ 02-58 27 70), Kitisuru Rd (PO Box 14157), Nairobi, Kenya.

Flora & Fauna Preservation Society (FFPS) c/o Zoological Society of London, Regents Park, London NW1 4R4, England.

Frankfurt Zoological Society (☎ 69-943 4460, fax 943 9348), Alfred-Brehm-Platz 16, 60316 Frankfurt am Main, Germany.

Friends of Conservation PO Box 74901, Nairobi, Kenya.

Jane Goodall Institute Tanzania (e mwangazo@hotmail.com): PO Box 727, Dar es Salaam. Uganda (fax 041-23 37 88, e orothen@imul.com): PO Box 4187, Kampala. JGI also has branches in the USA, UK, Canada, Holland, Germany, South Africa, Taiwan and Congo.

Tanzania Wildlife Protection Fund (☎ 051-86 63 77, fax 86 34 96, e selousgamereserve@cats-net.com), PO Box 1994, Dar es Salaam, Tanzania.

Wildlife Conservation Society (☎ 718-220 5111, fax 364 4275, e feedback@wcs.org, 🖳 www.wcs.org), 2300 Southern Blvd, Bronx, NY 10460, USA.

Wildlife Conservation Society of Tanzania (☎ 051-11 25 18, fax 12 45 72, e wcst@costech.gn.apc.org or wcst@africaonline.co.tz), Garden St, Dar es Salaam, Tanzania.

Worldwide Fund for Nature Kenya (☎ 02-33 29 63): 3rd Floor, Embassy House, Harambee Ave (PO Box 62440), Nairobi. UK (☎ 1483-426 444): Panda House, Weyside Park, Godalming, Surrey GU7 1XR, UK. USA (World Wildlife Fund) (☎ 202-293 4800, fax 293 9211, 🖳 www.worldwildlife.org): 1250 24th St, NW, Washington, DC 20037-1175, USA.

WEB SITES

The following web sites offer useful background information on wildlife and wildlife research.

www.africanbirdclub.org How to find and identify problematic birds in the region.

www.cheetah.demon.nl/eawls.html The East African Wildlife Society's home page, with links to projects such as hirola, roan antelope and hunting dog.

www.CITES.org Background information on the Convention on the International Trade in Endangered Species.

www.earthwatch.org Describes research projects (some in East Africa) coordinated by Earthwatch in which paying customers can participate.

www.janegoodall.org Overview of news, projects and activities of the long-running chimpanzee study and conservation organisation.

www.kilimanjaro.com Background on the mountain plus information on East African reserves and a book list.

www.museums.org.ke Web site of Kenya's national museum in Nairobi.

GLOSSARY

adaptation – physical or behavioural trait that helps an organism survive or exploit an environmental factor.

algae – primitive water plants.

alpha male or female – dominant animal in a hierarchy, eg, primate troop (a sometimes tenuous position).

amphibian – animal that lives part of its life cycle in water and part on land, eg, frog.

annulated horns – ridged horns of some antelope species, eg, oryxes, impalas.

aquatic – living in freshwater (*compare with* marine).

arboreal – tree-dwelling.

arthropod – invertebrate characterised by a segmented body and jointed legs, eg, insects.

artiodactyl – an even-toed ungulate, ie, hippos, pigs, giraffes and antelopes.

asynchronous – not occurring simultaneously, eg, the hatching of eggs.

avian – characteristic of birds, eg, avian behaviour.

bachelor group or herd – aggregation of non-breeding adult and subadult males, eg, antelopes.

big cat – the largest cat species, ie, lions, leopards and cheetahs (in Africa).

big five – The five large animals (ie, rhinos, buffaloes, elephants, lions and leopards) regarded as the most dangerous to hunt (and therefore the most prized) by colonial hunters.

binocular vision – vision with overlapping field of view to give a three-dimensional perception of space; best developed in cats and primates.

biodiversity – faunal and floral richness characterising an area.

biomass – total weight of living organisms in an ecosystem.

bipedal – standing or walking on two legs, eg, humans.

bird wave – a feeding party of birds, especially in rainforest, containing various species.

birder – a keen birdwatcher.

blind – *see* hide.

bluff – behaviour to convince a predator or rival that the bluffer is stronger.

bolus – ball of food or dung.

boss – head covering that supports horns, eg, on buffalo.

bovid – a member of the antelope family (Bovidae).

bovine – cattle-like in appearance or behaviour.

brood – group of young animals produced in one litter or clutch.

browse – to eat leaves and other parts of shrubs and trees (*hence* browser).

bull – male buffalo, elephant, giraffe etc.

callosity – hardened area of skin, eg, on face of warthog (*also called* callus).

camouflage – coloration or patterning that helps an animal blend into its surroundings.

canid – any dog, fox, jackal etc (ie, a member of the family Canidae).

canine – doglike; also relating to or belonging to the family Canidae (dogs, jackals etc).

canines – the four large, front teeth at the front of the jaws; well developed for killing in carnivores and fighting in baboons.

carnassials – shearing teeth near the back of carnivore's jaws.

carnivore – a meat-eating animal.

carrion – dead or decaying flesh.

casque – prominent bony growth surmounting the bill of some hornbills and head of guineafowl.

cellulose – component that strengthens the cell walls of plants, supporting them and forming stems.

cheek pouch – extension of cheeks for the temporary storage of food, eg, in monkeys.

class – a major division of animal classification, eg, mammals, birds, reptiles etc.

climax forest – mature forest.

cold-blooded – animals that regulate body temperature by using an external heat source, eg, reptiles and amphibians (*also known as* ectothermic).

colony – aggregation of animals, eg, birds, that live, roost or breed together (*hence* colonial).

commensalism – close but independent association between two unrelated animal species.

contiguous – adjoining, eg, woodland spanning two adjacent reserves.

coursing – to run down prey along the ground mainly by sight, eg, hunting dog.

courtship – behaviour (often ritualised) associated with attracting a mate.

crèche – young birds or mammals gathered for safety.

crepuscular – active at twilight, ie, evening or before dawn.

crustacean – arthropod with gills, which can breathe underwater or survive in damp conditions.

cryptic – behaviour, appearance or lifestyle that helps conceal an organism from predators.

cud – partly digested plant material regurgitated and chewed by resting ruminants.

decurved – downward-curving.

dewlap – loose skin (eg, in eland) or feathers under the chin.

digit – finger or toe.

dimorphism – having two forms of colour or size, eg, spotted and black leopard (*see* sexual dimorphism, polymorphism).

dispersal – the movement of animals (eg, after breeding or rains) or plants (eg, seeds) across a geographic area (*compare with* migration).

displacement activity – behaviour performed out of normal context, eg, grooming when an animal is stressed.

display – behaviour transmitting information from the sender to another, often associated with threat, defence of territory, courtship etc.

diurnal – active during daylight hours (*opposite of* nocturnal).

diversity – variety of species or forms in an area.

dorsal – upper (top) surface, ie, the back on most animals (*opposite of* ventral).

down – loose, fluffy feathers that cover young birds and insulate plumage of adults.

drey – nest of squirrel.

dung – excrement (faeces).

dung midden – accumulation of dung as a territory marker, often accompanied by scent-marking (*see* latrine).

ear-tuft – wispy hairs extending beyond ear-tips (eg, caracal) or erectile feathers near ears (eg, some owls).

ecology – study of relationships between organisms, their environment and each other.

ecosystem – a community of living organisms and their physical environment.

edge – transition zone between two habitats, eg, savanna and forest – hence edge species (*also called* ecotone).

endangered – in danger of imminent extinction if trends causing its demise continue.

endemic – found only in a certain area, eg, turacos are endemic to Africa.

environment – physical factors that influence the development and behaviour of organisms.

epiphyte – plant growing on another for support, eg, orchids on a tree.

equatorial – living on or near the equator.

erectile – can be erected, eg, hair or feathers erected in defense or courtship displays.

estrus – *see* oestrus.

evolve – to change physical and/or behavioural traits over time to exploit or survive changing environmental constraints.

faeces – excrement.

family – scientific grouping of related genera, eg, Felidae (the cat family).

farrow – litter of pigs (*also verb*).

feline – catlike; also related to or belonging to the Felidae (cat family).

feral – running wild, eg, escaped domestic stock.

fledgling – young bird able to leave the nest, ie, to fledge.

flight distance – distance at which an animal will flee from a predator or observer.

flight feathers – large wing feathers.

flock – group of birds, sheep or other herbivores (*also verb*).

foliage – leafy vegetation, eg, on trees.

folivore – a leaf-eating animal.

fossorial – adapted for digging.

frugivore – a fruit-eating animal.

gallery forest – forest growing along watercourses, which thus may extend into an adjoining habitat.

game – wild animals, especially mammals and birds, hunted by humans for food and sport.

genera – plural of genus.

genus – taxonomic grouping of related species.

geophagy – eating rock or soil, eg, elephants at Mt Elgon.

gestation – period young mammals develop in the womb before birth.

glaciations – periods during ice ages when glaciers covered large areas of the earth's surface.

gland – *see* scent gland, and inguinal, interdigital and preorbital glands.

glean – to feed by gathering, eg, along branches or among foliage.

granivore – a grain-eating animal.

gravid – pregnant or bearing eggs.

graze – to eat grass (*hence* grazer).

great ape – any of the large, tailless primates, ie, gorilla, chimpanzee and human beings.

gregarious – forming or moving in groups, eg, herds or flocks.

guano – phosphate-rich excrement deposited by seabirds and bats, usually accumulated over generations.

habitat – natural living area of an animal; usually characterised by a distinct plant community.

hackles – long, loose feathers or hairs on nape or throat, often erectile.

harem – group of females that mate with one male; the male defends his harem against other males.

hawk – to fly actively in search of prey, eg, insects, usually caught in the open mouth.

helper – animal, usually from a previous brood, which helps parents raise subsequent brood or broods.

herbivore – a vegetarian animal.

herd – social group of mammals.

hide – artificial construction, usually of wood, for the observation of animals while keeping the observer hidden (*also called* blind).

hierarchy – order of dominance among social animals, usually with a dominant individual or caste and one or more tiers of power or function, eg, termites, primates.

hive – home of bees or wasps.

holt – otters' den.

home range – the area over which an individual or group ranges over time (*compare with* territory).

host – organism on (or in) which a parasite lives; bird which raises young of parasitic species.

immature – stage in a young bird's development between juvenile and adult.

incisor – front (ie, cutting) teeth.

incubate – to hatch eggs using warmth.

inguinal gland – scent gland in groin area.

insectivore – an insect-eating animal.

interdigital gland – scent gland between hooves, eg, on antelopes.

invertebrate – an animal without a spinal column or backbone, eg, insects, worms.

iridescence – metallic sheen on many insects and birds, eg, sunbirds.

jinking – moving jerkily or with quick turns to escape a predator.

juvenile – animal between infancy and adulthood (mammals) or with first feathers after natal down (bird).

kali – Swahili for fierce or angry.

kopje – outcrop of rock on savanna plains.

lamellae – comblike plates in the bill of some birds (eg, flamingos) that filter food from water.

latrine – site where mammals habitually deposit dung or urine (*compare with* dung midden).

leap – the collective term for leopards.

lek – communal arena for mating and territorial sparring (antelopes) or courtship displays and mating (birds).

loaf – to laze about, especially used in describing bird behaviour.

localised – found only in a small or distinct area.

lying-out – remaining motionless with head flat on the ground to avoid danger (eg, antelopes).

mammal – 'warm-blooded', furry or hairy animal that gives birth to and suckles live young.

mandible – lower part of beak or jaw.

mantle – shoulder or upper back area on birds or mammals.

marine – living in the sea.

matriarchal – female dominated.

matrilineal – relating to kinship or descent down the female line.

melanism – naturally occurring excess of dark brown pigment that produces black forms of some animals, eg, leopards and servals.

midden – see dung midden.

migration – regular movement, often en masse, from one location to another, eg, wildebeests, shorebirds (hence migratory, migrant).

miombo – fire-resistant deciduous woodland, especially that dominated by Brachystegia.

mob – to harass a predatory animal, eg, small birds mobbing an owl; often in response to a distress call.

monogamy – having one reproductive partner for life, eg, bat-eared fox.

montane – living or situated on mountains.

moult – to shed and replace all or selected feathers, skin or fur, usually prompted by seasonal or behavioural changes, eg, courtship.

musth – a frenzied state of sexual readiness in certain large male mammals, eg, elephants (also spelled must).

mutualism – behavioural cooperation between two species where both benefit (also called symbiosis).

natal – pertaining to birth.

nestling – young bird until it leaves the nest (see fledgling).

nest parasitism – laying eggs in the nest of another bird species and taking no further part in rearing the offspring (also called brood parasitism).

niche – specialised ecological role played by an organism.

nictitating membrane – semi-transparent membrane that draws across eyes of birds and some reptiles.

nocturnal – active at night.

nomadic – wandering in search of resources, eg, food or water.

oestrus – period when female mammal is ovulating and therefore sexually receptive (also spelt estrus).

omnivore – an animal that eats both plant and animal matter.

opportunist – animal that finds prey virtually anywhere while expending as little energy as possible.

order – grouping of one or more animal families, eg, cats and dogs into Carnivora/carnivores.

pair bond – social ties that keep mates together, reinforced with grooming, calls etc.

parasite – plant or animal that obtains nourishment during all or part of its life from another life form, usually to the detriment of the host.

pelagic – living at sea, ie, in or above open water.

perissodactyl – an odd-toed ungulate, ie, rhino, horse.

photosynthesis – process whereby plants convert sunlight, water and carbon dioxide into organic compounds.

pioneer – the first species of to colonise an area.

piscivorous – fish-eating.

plantain – large, tropical plant (similar to banana plant).

plantigrade – walking with the whole foot on the ground, eg, elephant, humans.

plumage – birds' feathers, often used to describe total appearance, eg, drab plumage.

polyandry – female having access to more than one reproductive male.

polygamy – having access to more than one reproductive mate.

polygyny – male having access to more than one reproductive female.

polymorphism – having more than one adult form, size or colour.

precocial – being able to walk or run (eg, wildebeest), forage (eg, ostrich) or swim shortly after birth (hatching).

primitive – resembling or representing an early stage in the evolution of a particular group of animals.

predator – animal that kills and eats others.

prehensile – flexible and grasping, eg, tail, fingers.

preorbital gland – scent gland in front of the eyes, (in antelopes), used to mark territory.

present – to show genital region as appeasement (eg, apes) or to indicate readiness to mate.

prey – animal food of a predator.

pride – collective term for lions.

primate – a monkey, prosimian or ape.

pronk – see stot.

prosimian – 'primitive' primate, eg, bushbaby.

prusten – loud sniff made by female leopard to call cubs.

pug – footprint or other imprint left on the ground by an animal.

quadruped – four-legged animal.

quarter – to systematically range over an area in search of prey, eg, jackals, birds of prey.

race – see subspecies.

raptor – bird of prey, hawk, falcon, vulture, owl.

recurved – upward-curving, eg, bill of avocet.

regurgitate – to bring up partly digested food from crop or stomach, particularly when feeding young.

relict – remnant of formerly widespread species, community or habitat, now surrounded by different communities.

reptile – a scaly, 'cold-blooded' vertebrate, ie, turtles, crocodiles, snakes and lizards.

resident – an animal that remains in an area for its entire life cycle.

rinderpest – disease of cattle that can affect related animals, eg, antelopes.

riverine – living near or in rivers or streams.

rodent – any of the many species of rat, mouse, squirrel, etc.

roost – area where mammals (eg, bats) or birds gather to sleep, sometimes in large numbers (*also verb*).

ruminant – ungulate with four-chambered stomach (rumen) that chews the cud (*hence* ruminate).

rump – upper backside of mammal or bird, often distinctively marked, eg, antelopes.

rut – (antelopes) the mating season (*also verb*).

saddle – mid- to lower-back area on mammals and birds.

sagittal – pertaining to upper seam of skull, eg, sagittal crest on male mountain gorilla.

savanna – vegetation zone characterised by contrasting wet and dry seasons where grassy understorey grows with scattered trees and shrubs.

scavenger – animal that feeds on carrion or scraps left by others.

scent gland – concentration of special skin cells that secrete chemicals conveying information about the owner's status, identity, reproductive state etc.

sedentary – animal remaining in one area for all or part of its life cycle (*see* resident).

selection – process whereby traits that don't further an organism's reproductive success are weeded out by environmental or behavioural pressures.

sexual dimorphism – differences between males and females of the same species in colour, size or form; spectacular examples occur in many birds.

sibling – related offspring with the same parents (*hence* foster-sibling in brood parasites).

signal – movement or trait that conveys information from one animal to another, eg, danger.

skein – collective term for geese.

slough – to shed skin when growing, eg, reptiles.

sounder – group of pigs.

sow – female pig.

spawn – eggs of fish and amphibians, usually laid in water (*also verb*).

speciation – process whereby species are formed.

species – organisms capable of breeding with each other to produce fertile offspring; distinct and usually recognisable from other species, with which the majority don't interbreed.

spoor – animal track or tracks.

spraint – otter urine, used as territorial marking.

spur – horny growth on some birds, eg, on forewing (lapwings) or 'heel' (francolins).

spy-hop – to jump above vegetation, eg, grass to check bearings, threats etc.

stage – level in development of an organism.

stalk – to pursue prey by stealth.

stoop – the powerful dive of a bird of prey.

stot – stylised high leap while bounding, especially by young antelopes in play and adults when fleeing (*also called* pronk); thought to display fitness to would-be predators.

streamer – long tail feather, eg, of swallows.

subadult – last stage of juvenile development, usually characterised by near-adult coloration, size or plumage.

subdesert – semiarid area with more rainfall, vegetation and biodiversity than true desert.

subordinate – individual ranked below another in a hierarchy.

subspecies – population of a species isolated from another population (eg, by landforms) that has developed distinct physical traits (*also called* race).

succulent – fleshy, moisture-filled plant, eg, euphorbias.

sward – a stretch of grass.

symbiosis – see mutualism.

talon – hooked claw on a raptor.

taxonomy – scientific classification of organisms according to their physical relationships (*also called* systematics).

tectonic – pertaining to changes in the earth's crust caused by movement below its surface.

temporal gland – facial glands between the eyes and ears of elephants that secrete temporin.

termitary – earthen mound constructed by a termite colony (*also called* termitarium).

terrestrial – living on the ground.

territory – feeding or breeding area defended against others of the same species (*compare with* home range).

thermal – rising air column; used by large birds to gain height.

troop – group of monkeys or baboons.

tropical – found within the tropics, ie, between Tropics of Cancer and Capricorn.

tsetse fly – blood-sucking fly.

tusker – large elephant or boar.

tusks – greatly enlarged canine teeth, used as tools, or in defense and ritual combat.

ungulate – a hoofed animal.

ventral – lower (under) side of an animal (*opposite of* dorsal).

vertebrate – an animal having a backbone, ie, fish, amphibians, reptiles, birds and mammals.

vestigial – small, nonfunctional remnant of a feature formerly present, eg, vestigial horns.

vocalisation – sound made orally by an animal as a signal.

volplane – steep, controlled dive on outstretched wings, eg, by vultures to a kill.

waders – shorebirds and related families, eg, plovers.

warm-blooded – maintaining a constant body temperature by internal regulation, eg, birds and mammals (*also known as* endothermic).

warren – network of holes used as shelter and nursery.

wattle – fleshy (and sometimes brightly coloured) growth often prominent in courtship, eg, on birds.

yearling – a mammal in its second year of growth.

PHOTO CREDITS

Luke Hunter **5** column 1, **6** column 3, **15**, **209**, **220** column 3, **224** top & bottom, **226** column 4, **233** top, **245** column 1, **266** column 2, **279** bottom, **312** column 1 Richard I'Anson **50** top, **222** column 3, **242** top, **270** inset, **274** top, **284** column 3, **318** bottom Dennis Johnson **138**, **172**, **250** bottom Dennis Jones **66** top, **136**, **146**, **159**, **221** bottom, **227** top, **229** bottom, **234** bottom, **240** top, **242** bottom, **246** column 4, **247** column 2 & inset, **249** top & bottom, **254** column 2, **258** column 2, **266** column 3, **270** column 4, **272** column 2, **273** column 1, **277** inset, **287** column 4, **291** column 2 & inset, **304** column 3, **312** column 2 Dave Lewis **40** bottom, **48** top & bottom, **49**, **123** Leanne Logan **44** top T Longton/BirdLife International **104** Tim Low **42** bottom, **62** bottom, **63** inset, **64**, **65**, **319** column 3 Andrew MacColl **6** column 4, **271** inset, **287** inset, **296** column 3 D Mason/WINDRUSH PHOTOS **229** top, **305** column 3 Mike McKavett/WINDRUSH PHOTOS **309** column 1 J L McKay **105** bottom, **194**, **320** column 4 Richard Mills **42** top, **282** bottom, **296** column 1, **298** column 3, **300** column 4, **305** inset, **307** column 1, **313** column 1 & 3, inset Dietmar Nill/BBC Natural History Unit **306** column 2 Arthur Morris/WINDRUSH PHOTOS **309** column 4, **310** column 3 Nick Ray **319** column 2 Mitch Reardon **58** bottom, **71** main & inset, **72**, **94** top , **97**, **100** top & bottom, **114**, **139**, **140**, **148**, **150**, **162**, **164**, **214** top, **216** top & bottom, **220** column 1, **221** top, **223** top, **226** inset, **231** top, **236** top, **237** top & bottom, **240** bottom, **241** top, **244** bottom, **245** column 2, **252** column 2, **253** bottom, **256** column 1–3, **258** column 3, **259** column 1, **264** inset, **266** insert, **275** top, **276** column 2, **293** bottom, **295** inset, **304** inset, **317**, **319** column 1 Susan Rhind **151** top, **168** Jonathan Rossouw **62** top, **166**, **175**, **177**, **197** Mike Scott **232** top, **258** column 1 Edward AM Snijders **54**, **56**, **133** bottom, **152** Deanna Swaney **290** inset David Tipling **78** top, **267** column 2, **269** column 3 & inset, **273** column 2 & 4, **280** column 2, **281** column 2 & 3, **292** top, **302** column 1, **304** column 4 Ray Tipper **263** top, **270** column 2, **271** column 4, **275** bottom, **284** column 4, **290** column 1, **291** column 3, **298** column 1, **299** column 2, **300** column 3 Nigel Tucker/BBC Natural History Unit **305** column 2 Dr CR Tyler/ WINDRUSH PHOTOS **286** inset, **306** column 1 Andrew van Smeerdijk **6** column 1, **74** top, **166** bottom, **187** bottom, **195**, **212** **220** column 4 & inset, **225** top, **228** top & bottom, **243** top, **246** inset, **251** column 4, **254** column 4, **267** column 3, **268** top, **285** column 4, **289** column 1 Ariadne van Zandbergen **5** column 3 & 4, **7** column 2, **53**, **70** bottom, **77**, **87**, **92**, **98**, **107**, **122**, **124**, **128**, **132**, **141**, **142**, **145**, **147**, **154**, **156**, **158**, **160**, **170** left & right, **176**, **184** top & bottom, **185**, **192**, **198**, **205**, **207**, **212** column 2 & 3, **213** column 1, 3 & 4, **217** top & bottom, **238** bottom, **246** column 1 & 2, **247** column 3, **248** column 1 & 3, **251** column 3, **252** column 3 & 4, inset, **253** top, **255** top, **256** column 4, **259** column 2, **269** column 1, **277** column 1, **280** column 1 & 4, **281** column 4, **286** column 2, **290** column 2, **297** column 2, **298** column 2, **301** column 3 & inset, **308** column 1 & 4, **312** column 3 & 4, **318** top, **321** column 1 David Wall **5** column 6, **6** column 2, **41** bottom, **44** bottom, **74** bottom, **75** main, **82**, **83** inset, **95**, **96**, **137** top, **182** top, **186** top, **187**, **212** inset, **215** top, **218** top, **235** top & bottom, **245** column 3 & 4, **248** column 2 & 4, **254** column 3 & inset, **256** inset, **261**, **265** top, **267** inset, **272** column 1 & 4, **273** column 3, **274** bottom, **276** column 3 & inset, **277** column 2, **279** top, **290** column 3, **312** inset Mark Webster **79** main Tony Wheeler **250** top, **290** column 4 Miranda Wills **51**, **234** top, **243** bottom E Woods/ WINDRUSH PHOTOS **294** column 4 Leonard Douglas Zell **47**

INDEX

LONELY PLANET

You already know that Lonely Planet produces more than this one wildlife guide, but you might not be aware of the other products we have on this region. Here is a selection of titles that you may want to check out as well:

East Africa
ISBN 0 86442 676 3
US$24.99 • UK£14.99

Kenya
ISBN 0 86442 695 X
US$19.95 • UK£12.99

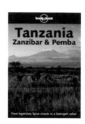

Tanzania, Zanzibar & Pemba
ISBN 0 86442 726 3
US$17.95 • UK£11.99

Africa on a shoestring
ISBN 0 86442 663 1
US$29.99 • UK£17.99

Read This First: Africa
ISBN 1 86450 066 2
US$14.95 • UK£8.99

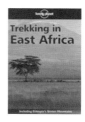

Trekking in East Africa
ISBN 0 86442 541 4
US$17.95 • UK£11.99

Healthy Travel Africa
ISBN 1 86450 050 6
US$5.95 • UK£3.99

Swahili phrasebook
ISBN 0 86442 509 0
US$5.95 • UK£3.99

Available wherever books are sold

RESEARCH

Both authors visited as many of the national parks and other reserves as possible during the research for this book. In cases where access was not possible (eg, for reasons of safety), material was drawn from sources such as scientific papers and authoritative publications, and corroborated by experts.

In their research the authors have drawn on their experience, their contacts and their personal observations. They have not necessarily been able to see everything in the parks they visited, and they have not gone on every available ecotour. Instead, they have used their expertise to judge what to bring together in as accurate a picture of a place as possible.

Common names for many wide ranging African mammals and birds vary across the continent; and no two references agree completely on names (scientific or common). Mammal names used in this book follow the *Check-list of the Mammals of East Africa*, published by the East Africa Natural History Society. For birds we followed *Birds of Kenya & Northern Tanzania* by Zimmerman, Turner and Pearson; and *Birds of Eastern Africa*, by van Perlo.

We welcome feedback to help us improve new editions. All information is passed on to the authors for verification on the road. The best snippets are rewarded with a Lonely Panet guidebook.

Send all correspondence to the Lonely Planet office closest to you:

Australia Locked Bag 1, Footscray, Victoria 3011
USA 150 Linden St, Oakland, CA 94607
UK 10A Spring Place, London NW5 3BH
France 1 rue du Dahomey, 75011 Paris

Map Legend

HYDROGRAPHY

	Reef
	Coastline
	River, Creek
	Lake
	Intermittent Lake
	Salt Lake
	Spring, Rapids
	Waterfalls
	Swamp

ROUTES & TRANSPORT

	Freeway
	Highway
	Major Road
	Minor Road
	Vehicle Track
	Walking Track
	Ferry Route
	Train Route & Station
A10	Route Number

BOUNDARIES

	International
	Regional

MAP SYMBOLS

◎	**CAPITAL**	National Capital
●	**CAPITAL**	Regional Capital
◉	**CITY**	City
○	Town	Town
◎	Village	Village
●		Point of Interest
●		Geographic Feature
●		Hydrographic Feature
●		Reserve/Wildlife Park
		Airfield
		Camping
		Cave
		Cliff or Escarpment
		Forest
		Garden
		Gate
		Hotel
		Lodge or Hut
		Lookout
▲		Mountain or Hill
)(		Pass
		Ruins
❶		Tourist Information

AREA FEATURES

	Beach
	Park
	Urban

ABBREVIATIONS

CA	Conservation Area
CP	Conservation Park
CR	Conservation Reserve
FR	Forest Reserve
GR	Game Reserve
MP	Marine Park
MNP	Marine National Park
MNR	Marine National Reserve
NP	National Park
NR	National Reserve
NrP	Nature Park
PN	Parc National
RR	Regional Reserve
SF	State Forest
SP	State Park
SR	State Reserve
WPA	Wilderness Protection Area

Note: not all symbols displayed above appear in this book

ABOUT LONELY PLANET GUIDEBOOKS

Lonely Planet published its first book in 1973 in response to the numerous 'How did you do it?' questions Maureen and Tony Wheeler were asked after driving, busing, hitching, sailing and railing their way from England to Australia.

Written at a kitchen table and hand collated, trimmed and stapled, *Across Asia on the Cheap* became an instant local bestseller, inspiring thoughts of another book.

Eighteen months in South-East Asia resulted in their second guide, South-East Asia on a shoestring, which they put together in a backstreet Chinese hotel in Singapore in 1975. The 'yellow bible', as it quickly became known to backpackers around the world, soon became the guide to the region. It has sold well over half a million copies and is now in its 10th edition.

Today an international company with offices in Melbourne (Australia), Oakland (USA), London (UK) and Paris (France), Lonely Planet has an ever-growing list of books and other products, including: travel guides, walking guides, city maps, travel atlases, phrasebooks, diving guides, cycling guides, healthy travel guides, restaurant guides, world food guides, first time travel guides, condensed guides, travel literature, pictorial books and, of course, wildlife guides. Many of these are also published in French and various other languages.

In addition to the books, there are also videos and Lonely Planet's award winning Web site.

Some things haven't changed. The main aim is still to help make it possible for adventurous travellers to get out there – to explore and better understand the world.

At Lonely Planet we believe travellers can make a positive contribution to the countries they visit – if they respect their host communities and spend their money wisely. Since 1986 a percentage of the income from each book has been donated to aid projects and human rights campaigns.

> Lonely Planet gathers information for everyone who's curious about the planet – and especially for those who explore it first-hand. Through guidebooks, phrasebooks, activity guides, maps, literature, newsletters, image library, TV series and Web site we act as an information exchange for a worldwide community of travellers.

LONELY PLANET OFFICES

Australia
Locked Bag 1, Footscray, Victoria 3011
☎ 03 8379 8000 fax 03 8379 8111
e talk2us@lonelyplanet.com.au

USA
150 Linden St, Oakland, CA 94607
☎ 510 893 8555 or ☎ 800 275 8555 (toll free)
fax 510 893 8572
e info@lonelyplanet.com

UK
10a Spring Place, London NW5 3BH
☎ 020 7428 4800 fax 020 7428 4828
e go@lonelyplanet.co.uk

France
1 rue du Dahomey, 75011 Paris
☎ 01 55 25 33 00 fax 01 55 25 33 01
e bip@lonelyplanet.fr
🖳 www.lonelyplanet.fr

World Wide Web: 🖳 www.lonelyplanet.com *or* AOL keyword: lp
Lonely Planet Images: e lpi@lonelyplanet.com.au